HULL 2017

2,017 FACTS ABOUT HULL
AND PEOPLE ASSOCIATED WITH THE CITY

JAMES L. ORWIN

First published by Dancing Sisters (Hull) in 2017

Amended and reprinted in August and November 2017

This compilation © 2016 James L. Orwin

dancingsisters.co.uk

ISBN 978-0-9932330-8-1

ISBN 978-0-9932330-9-8 (ebook)

ACKNOWLEDGEMENTS:

First and always foremost I would like to thank my wife Julie for her love and patience over 40 years.

Also, love to Neve, Grace, Chloe, Archie, Millie, Maisie and Jack.

Particular thanks are due to those forthright friends whose frankness and honesty has helped to reshape this work into what it has become.

All remaining errors and deficiencies are my own.

Those who have provided encouragement, assistance and information, or who responded to my queries, include: Pat Albeck, Natalie Baker, Bill Benson, Geoff Brear, Andy Fletcher, David Fletcher, Harry Fletcher, Matthew Fletcher, Jean Hartley (RIP), Anne James, Wendy Loncaster, Mary McCollum, Marjorie Raines (RIP), Frank Newsum, the Orwin family, John Osborne, Bob and Rose Sandham, Neil Sinyard, Andrew H. Spicer, Norman Staveley, Sam Sterrett and family, Martin Taylor, Dean Wilson, Bruce Woodcock, the staff at the Hull History Centre, the staff at the Hull Register Office and the Census Customer Service team at the Office of National Statistics.

The digitized publications at archive.org have been invaluable in the creation of this compilation.

I should also like to acknowledge the contributors to the Wikipedia page on the 'Port of Hull', which shows the online encyclopedia at its best. The referencing and linking to external original sources is exemplary.

The writing and publication of this book is in no way connected with the official Hull City of Culture 2017 team or its associated projects.

AND NOBODY APPLIED FOR ARTS FUNDING

Introduction

On 1 January 2017, in the one hundred and twentieth anniversary year of being granted the status of *City* (22 June 1897, on the occasion of Queen Victoria's Diamond Jubilee), Hull begins its 12 month tenure as UK City of Culture 2017.

This collection of facts is intended for everyone who has any kind of connection with Hull; but I hope it will be of most interest to those who were born here, live here, or have ancestors who were born or lived here.

It is not intended as a narrative—although it is primarily structured chronologically—or a 'History' of the city; nor to deal with any specific aspect of Hull, or its inhabitants, other than to highlight its many contributions to global culture and society in general. There are numerous comprehensive books available—many of which have furnished the facts collected here—that deal with the general history of Hull; and seemingly countless volumes that cover a single Hull-related personality or topic, from individual biographies to the origin of street names; from the founding and development of companies such as Reckitt & Sons Ltd., or W. Boyes & Co. (or institutions such as the Charterhouse or Trinity House), to histories of the city's three major sporting teams.

I expect I have omitted facts that some might consider essential for inclusion, and included facts that others might feel are redundant or trivial. My intention has been to cover as wide a range of topics as possible, whilst at the same time providing enough facts about individual subjects to ignite the curiosity of readers to want to discover more. The number of facts related to any particular topic should not be assumed to be an indication of hierarchy, or a personal order of importance or significance regarding the subjects included; other compilers, no doubt, would have selected a widely different array of facts; or, given the same title, would have produced a completely different book.

When it was announced that Hull was to be UK City of Culture 2017, many must have wondered, as I did, how that would be managed: would the organisers highlight the variety of contemporary activities taking place within the city, *alongside* the historical figures and events associated with Hull; or would they see it as an opportunity to draw the best in contemporary culture *to* the city, for the local population to experience and enjoy. There are clearly merits to both approaches; and a generally satisfactory mix will be a real achievement.

In January 2012, I was more than a little disappointed when BBC Radio 1 came to Hull to showcase its 'continued commitment to new music' and featured very little of the new music being created here, but brought bands, musicians and singer-songwriters to the city from some fairly distant places. Fears of a similar situation for 2017 were voiced in 2013, not long after the UK City of Culture 2017 decision had been announced. All we can hope is that a suitably accommodating balance can be achieved—in terms of both the sums of funding awarded, and the people whose projects are supported with that funding. By the time this book is available, we will already know.

As far as 'outside' culture being brought into our city is concerned, I have noted here occasions when a range of world-famous celebrities have visited Hull, including The Beatles, Jimi Hendrix, Harry Houdini, Laurel and Hardy, and Pink Floyd; or were thought to have visited Hull, namely Rembrandt.

There is a rich history of Hull-born people going on to become world-improving individuals; and many have come here from elsewhere to make their name (and leave their mark) by contributing to the fabric of our city. In the first case, people such as Ebenezer Cobb Morley, Geoffrey Dummer, John Ellerman, Edward Arthur Milne, J. Arthur Rank, John Venn and William Wilberforce; in the second, J.H. Fenner, T.R. Ferens, Isaac Reckitt, and T.J. Smith.

Of those who were born here and stayed a lifetime, I should particularly like to mention Jean Hartley—whom I was fortunate enough to know as a friend—who (with her husband George) as a working-class twenty-year-old, with none of the advantages of position, family or wealth, set up a publishing concern that would launch (from a small house in Hessle) the literary career of one of the greatest poets of the twentieth century.

When I was a boy it was possible to look at the players of the city's three main sporting teams and see many first-team players who were local: from the same school, street, road or club as we aspiring young fans. It didn't seem so extraordinary an idea that we might one day play for Hull FC, Hull KR or Hull City (and therefore, by extension, Manchester United, Spurs, Liverpool—or even our national team). People from the same schools we or our parents attended went on to become notably successful businessmen; or, in some cases, internationally respected career actors or musicians. All things seemed possible.

Hull FC continue to provide that kind of inspiration today, fielding four Hull-born players (with three more on the bench) in their Challenge Cup winning side at Wembley in August 2016. Contributions by two natives of Hull were instrumental in the Challenge Cup victory: Jamie Shaul's 75th minute try and Danny Houghton's last minute tackle which prevented Warrington's Ben Currie stealing the glory.

It would be difficult to overstate the importance of the Hull Dock Company or, more generally, the Port of Hull in the commercial and economic growth of the city, and its geographic spread; or the emotional impact and hope-quenching finality of 'Lost with all hands' on its inhabitants. Because of the overwhelming centrality of the fishing industry in relation to Hull, I have attempted to list—using Brian Langley's *Lost Trawlermen of Hull* as my main source of reference—as many as possible of the vessels posted as 'Lost with all hands': from the Andrew Marvel in March 1883 to the FV Gaul in February 1974. The frequency with which such incidents occurred is sobering in the extreme, even without taking into account the additional losses when not *all* hands were lost.

If the humanity of any group—from a nuclear family to an intercontinental tribe—can be measured by how it distributes the benefits of its successes and achievements; and how the individuals within it confront disaster, unite and comfort one another when tragedy strikes; then, historically, Hull is equal to any and ahead of most. From the fatal rebellious courage of Sir John Hotham, through the dogged determination of William Wilberforce, to the charitable philanthropic activities of Thomas Robinson Ferens, James Reckitt, and John Alderson; from the fierce loyal advocacy of Lillian Bilocca and the 'Headscarf Revolutionaries' of Hessle Road, through the empathetic dedication of Sir Brian Rix, to the unstinting energies of Hull Bee-Woman, Jean Bishop, the people of Hull have always been ready to stand up and be counted.

It is my sincere hope that some of the names, deeds and achievements included here will inspire the young people of Hull, and serve as an example: that it is possible to be a native of this city and to go on to change the world. They only have to grasp the baton and run.

FACTS?

Until fairly recently (within the past twenty years?), Hull City Association Football Club promoted the 'fact' that the club's first home kit featured white shirts. The evidence presented for this was a photograph purportedly taken before Hull City's first ever home game, against Notts County at The Boulevard in 1904. The photograph shows two teams: one sporting white shirts, the other wearing the familiar black and white stripes of Notts County. Somewhat incongruously, in the middle of the two teams surrounded by dignitaries, is a seated female holding a floral tribute. Research by Nicholas Turner, published on the Hull City fan website, ambernectar.org, systematically and emphatically destroys this 'white shirt' myth by identifying the said photograph with a completely separate game—held to raise funds for a charitable cause—which was played eighteen months after City's inaugural game against Notts County.

In a different arena: in December 2011 Professor Brian Cox commented in *The Sun* on the scientists at the Large Hadron Collider at CERN revealing 'that they may have glimpsed the Higgs boson "God particle"—the key to unlocking the universe's mysteries':

> In science we need evidence, and that means actually seeing one of these elusive and desperately strange Higgs particles.

And then, with no discernible hint of irony:

> ... there is a chance that particle collisions will produce pictures in the cameras that look just like Higgs particles when, in fact, they are not.

Admittedly, Cox qualifies this latter statement (with a seemingly nonsensical):

> The way to be sure is to collect more pictures.

Further: following the release of his 2015 film *Steve Jobs*, director Danny Boyle was interviewed on BBC's *Newsnight* programme by Evan Davis, who posed the following query:

> One of the things the film has attracted is a bit of an argument about how far a movie about a real guy can bend facts and take dramatic licence in order to create a great narrative.

Boyle's response:

> I think it comes partly out of a despair at how unreliable facts are. And so what you end up developing, if you're dealing with real life, is you end up developing a sense ... it's the bullshit sense—it's the bullshit detector that goes: "I don't believe that."

I hope what I'm driving at is clear: the concept of Fact means different things to different people.

The 'facts' listed here have been compiled from a wide variety of sources, including the works of historians and chroniclers (present and past) of Hull's development into the city it is today; amongst whom are Charles Frost, Thomas Gent, Paul Gibson, Alec Gill, Edward Gillett & Kenneth McMahon, Brian Langley, Robb Robinson, James Joseph Sheahan, Thomas Sheppard, and James Smith.

My main objective in compiling this collection is to bring together, in one volume, 'facts' about disparate subjects relating to Hull: history, sport, industry (including the frequently tragic trawling industry), buildings, institutions, cinemas, theatres, music, entertainment, the docks, worthies, personalities, and more; in the hope that the vast majority of readers will find it of interest on various levels.

I should point out that in researching the 'facts' for inclusion I have found a range of inconsistencies and contradictory information, from which I have often had to deduce a 'best guess'. For example: Ronald Bergen's obituary of the Hull-born film director Ralph Thomas, published in *The Guardian* of 20 March 2001 and the entry on Thomas at the Internet Movie Database (IMDb) website record his date of birth as 10 August 1915; while the *Oxford Dictionary of National Biography* article, by Andrew H. Spicer, gives it as 11 August 1915—the actual date recorded on Ralph Thomas's birth certificate.

Furthermore, several sources (including the websites of the *Hull Daily Mail* and the Fleet Air Arm Officers Association) record the R38 Airship disaster as having occurred on 23 August 1921, whereas others, such as the BBC News website, and Grace's Guide (quoting from the *Air Ministry R38 Court of Inquiry Terms of Reference*) record the date as 24 August 1921.

The blue heritage plaque erected on the old Rose, Downs and Thompson building in Caroline Street makes the following somewhat woolly claim for the company's ferro-concrete workshop:

> Constructed in 1900, this ferro-concrete workshop was
> the first using the Hennebique system

It does not specify whether it was the first ever, the first in Britain, or the first in England. Patricia Cusack in her 'Agents of Change: Hennebique, Mouchel and ferro-concrete in Britain, 1897–1908', published in *Construction History, Vol 3*, 1987, points out that while the Hennebique system had been used in Switzerland, and in Cairo in 1895, the 'first documented case of the use of Hennebique's reinforced-concrete system in the UK was Weaver's Mill, Swansea [which one could surely also class as a workshop] in 1897', the year François Hennebique took out his main British patent. Cusack goes on to document the fact that Hennebique's UK agent was Louis-Gustave Mouchel, who licensed the process to Rose, Downs & Thompson 'who wished to build their own factory extension (1900) and subsequently built a public bridge in Hull'; built over the former Foredyke Stream, New Cleveland Street in 1902.

The first edition of Basil Reckitt's *History of Reckitt & Sons Ltd.* places in 1894 the purchase of Swanland Manor by James Reckitt; *A New History of Swanland: the 18th & 19th Century* (2002), published by the Swanland Village History Group, records the date as 1884.

Alec Gill, in his *Lost Trawlers of Hull* (1989), records the name of the Hull trawler H615 as Ann Sins, whereas the hulltrawler.net website mainly records it as Ann Sims, and Brian Langley's list of Hull's lost trawlermen records the H615 as Ann Sins in four instances and Ann Sims in one instance (I have assumed Alec Gill to be correct).

Brian Langley's *Lost Trawlermen of Hull* names Raymond Wilson (33) of 57 St. Nicholas Avenue, Hessle as a sparehand on the Kingston Peridot (H591), whilst various other sources, such as the *Yorkshire Post*, *Hull Daily Mail* and the hulltrawler.net website, name him as Skipper of the vessel.

The annals of Yorkshire from the earliest period to the present time has the Union steam-packet disaster occurring on 14 June 1837; whereas *The Spectator* reported the incident in its 10 June edition, and refers to it happening on the *previous* Wednesday [7 June].

And perhaps most notably: on the website of the Hull History Centre the page titled 'History of Hull Docks' informs us that The Dock, Hull's first enclosed dock, 'was purchased by Hull Corporation for £100,000'; yet the section about Queen's Gardens on their page titled 'Parks and Gardens' tells us: 'Hull Corporation purchased Queen's Dock [formerly The Dock] from the North Eastern Railway Company in 1930 for the sum of £117,000'.

Also, the Hull History Centre website's page titled 'Hull Hospitals' credits the foundation of the Hull Lunatic Asylum (later De la Pole Hospital) to 'Dr John *Anderson*' [it should read *Alderson*] and a surgeon named Ellis.

The Hull History Centre (along with the riverhumber.com website) gives the date of the opening of the William Wright Dock as 24 May 1873; whereas various other sources, including the *Hull Daily Mail*, report that it was not opened until 1880; and *The Engineer* of 28 April 1876 reported the ceremony for the laying of the foundation stone by Sir William Wright as having taken place on the previous Wednesday [26 April 1876]—a full three years after the date the History Centre gives for the *opening* of the dock.

Finally, the Humber Dock. Wright (1875), a former Chairman of the Hull Dock Company, who has the aforementioned dock named in his honour, gives the date of the laying of the first stone of the dock as 13 April 1807:

> The first stone was laid on the 13th of April 1807, by
> Mr. Henry Maister, the then Chairman of the Company

(he neglects to give a date for the commencement of construction, though he does record that it 'opened in the year 1809'); whereas Timperley (1842), former resident engineer for the same company, states that work was begun on the dock early in 1803. While these two statements are not mutually exclusive or blatantly contradictory, if both are correct, then there was *either* a four year period between the commencement of construction and the laying of the first stone, *or* following the laying of the first stone the rest of Humber Dock was completed within 14 months. Baldwin (1973) states: 'The work began in earnest in 1803...The dock was first flooded in December 1808 and the formal ceremony was performed in the following June. It had taken at least eighteen months longer than Rennie had anticipated...' This last statement seems to cast suspicion on Wright's account of the timescale. Sheahan, writing within living memory of the dock opening, agrees with Timperley; the Hull History Centre page on the 'History of Hull Docks' concurs with Wright: 'Construction started in 1807 and it opened to shipping in 1809' [maximum 3 years]. Simpson (2009) takes both dates to be correct. The British History Online website states: 'Humber Dock, covering 6½ acres, was begun in 1803 and finished in 1809'. Everyone seems to agree that the dock was officially opened in 1809; but apart from that we're faced with a bowl of 'fact' muesli.

(Another confusion for me is how Hull Museums can give the title of a 1945 painting by Fred Elwell as 'The Visit of Sir Winston Churchill (the Tarran Luncheon)' when Churchill didn't actually become 'Sir Winston' until 24 April 1953.)

Whilst not being able to provide the kind of assurances offered by Sheahan: 'for the delay has afforded time to verify the correctness of almost every statement'; or Frost: 'spared no expense of time or labour to render the work complete', I hope not to be found too often guilty of recycling the mistakes of others at the expense of original research.

In her *Etiquette in Society, in Business, in Politics, and at Home* (1922), American author Emily Post offers some suggestions for the appropriate ending to a 'formal note':

> "I remain, dear madam," is no longer in use, but "Believe me" is still correct when formality is to be expressed in the close of a note.
>
> Believe me
>
> Very sincerely yours,
>
> or
>
> Believe me, my dear Mrs. Worldly,

When reading Fowler's *Life and Letters of the Rev. John Bacchus Dykes* (1897), I was struck by how many of the letters—with Dykes both as writer and recipient—closed with 'Believe me'.

My message to readers of this compilation of facts is: Don't (necessarily) believe me. Be suspicious of all 'facts', not just those presented here.

THE FACTS:

1: The extensive peat marshlands of the River Hull Valley, formed by decayed vegetation in the valley's waterlogged and flooded areas, were known locally as 'carrs', and the name survives in several present day street names and areas across the city: 'Carr Lane', 'East Carr Lane', 'West Carr Lane', 'Woldcarr Road', etc. The lower River Hull Valley consisted of silt marshland (saltmarsh), with deposits carried by tidal flooding from the river Humber; the middle and upper River Hull Valley consisted of fresh-water marshland and swamp, with water inundating the north and west of the valley from the powerful natural springs of the Yorkshire Wolds and streams carrying rainwater from the Holderness levels.

2: There is no mention of Hull in the Domesday Book of 1086, though nearby Willerby, Hessle and Ferriby all are mentioned. Also mentioned is Myton, a hamlet (belonging to the Manor of Ferriby) situated at the conflux of the rivers Hull and Humber.

3: The Cistercian Meaux Abbey was founded in 1150 by William le Gros, 1st Earl of Albermarle, who appointed Adam (a monk of Fountains Abbey, with which Meaux was affiliated) as the first Abbot. In 1160 Adam (who had retired, having brought the monastery 'to the brink of ruin') was succeeded by Philip (formerly abbot of Hovedøya in Norway, and prior at Kirkstead, Lincolnshire).

4: There has been some speculation and disagreement between the various historians of Hull about the location of the vills of Wyke and Myton. This difference of opinion centres around the use of the word 'Wyk' in Maud Camin's original grant of covenant to the monks of Meaux Abbey (Melsa). John Roberts Boyle appears to agree with Charles Frost—based on the assumption that 'Wyk' is used not as a common noun, but as a place name—that they were two separate places, both situated in the broader manor of Myton; whereas J. Travis Cook (1890) appears to interpret 'Wyk' as a common noun, suggesting that Wyk and Myton were interchangeable names for the identical same place.

5: Wyke, a small settlement developing alongside Myton, is first recorded in a grant of land dated 1160. The town of Wyke (also variously known as Wyke-upon-Hull, or simply Hull) rapidly became an established settlement.

6: The first recorded mention of Hull as a port was in 1193 when the wool contributed by various monasteries for the ransom of Richard I was collected at 'the port of Hull'. A few years later (1198) Gervase de Aldermanbury, as Chamberlain of London, accounted for 225 Marks as money received in fines 'taken at Hull' (for 45 sacks of wool).

7: By the end of the 12th century the Cistercian Meaux Abbey, near Beverley, had acquired all of the land that made up the hamlet of Myton, including Wyke, (10 bovates, equivalent to approximately 150 acres) and converted the hamlet to a monastic farming estate, or grange.

8: Boyle (1890) tells us that 'Myton possessed a chapel, affiliated to the mother church of Hessle' before the close of the 12th century; and restates Frost's contention that the importance (as a mercantile centre and port) of the location which King Edward I restyled 'Kyngeston-upon-Hull' in 1299 had been established well before that time.

13th century

9: The earliest notice providing evidence of a place of religious worship in Hull is from 1204, during the reign of King John, when the monks of Melsa were ordered to re-build a chapel in Myton, which they had destroyed. The monks paid 100 shillings as compensation to Richard Ducket, the then parson of the Church of Hessle (the mother church).

10: In approximately 1253 devastating floods changed the course of the river Hull penetrating as far inland as Cottingham, with a good portion of the Meaux-owned area of Myton collapsing into the Humber.

11: The first charter giving permission for a fair to be held in Hull was granted in 1278. Hull Fair opened for the first time that year, running for 15 days from 9 March.

12: Boyle (1890) suggests: 'The site of the chapel of Myton is very probably that occupied by Holy Trinity Church'; which was founded in 1285 by James Helward, firstly as a chapel of ease to the mother church at Hessle. In 1986 a blue heritage plaque was erected on the south side of Holy Trinity Church (opposite Vicar Lane) to mark the church's construction. The inscription reads:

> Construction began in 1285 on the site of an earlier church. HOLY TRINITY is England's largest parish church by area. The transepts include some of the earliest medieval brickwork in Britain

13: In 1289 Robert de Scardeburgh, Dean of York, assigned 'to the Carmelite Brethren or White Friars' a messuage [a house with surrounding land and out-buildings] in 'Wyk-upon-Hull'. It is believed that this messauge was the foundation of the White Friars monastery, from which the name Whitefriargate is derived.

14: In January 1293 a valuation of Wyke was carried out for King Edward I; and by March of that year the monks of Meaux Abbey had sold both Wyke and Myton to Edward

3

for the sum of £103 2s 8d (the previous year Wyke and Myton had been valued for taxation purposes at £126 15s).

15: The first recorded use of the town's new name is in a writ for an inquiry directed to the King's Bailiff of 'Kyngeston-super-Hull', dated 5 November 1294.

16: The Royal Charter of 1299 was granted upon the petition of the people of the town, presented to Edward I in person whilst he was a guest of Lord Wake at Baynard Castle, Cottingham, at Christmas 1298.

17: On 1 April 1299 King Edward I granted the townsmen of Hull a Charter, bestowing on them all the privileges commensurate with the inhabitants of a 'Free Borough'; such as the right to hold a market two days a week (Tuesday and Friday), and a fair for thirty days of the year, starting on 26 May. Along with the King's Charter came the new name of King's Town upon Hull. It would henceforth be self governing, with its own court, coroner and taxation.

18: In 1299, following the granting of the King's Charter, improvements were made to the town's harbour to make it more suitable (and more attractive an opportunity) for those engaged in maritime trade.

14th century

19: In 1300 a Royal Mint and an exchange were established in Kingston upon Hull.

20: The Royal Mint, established at Hull in 1300, had four furnaces, and the coins struck here have on them the legend: *Vill de Kyngeston*.

21: In May 1300, whilst touring the north, the King (Edward I) took a brief detour to inspect his acquisition and his newly created borough. Whilst in the town he bestowed the sum of 5s in alms on the Carmelite Brethren (*Fratribus de Monte Carmel 'de Hull*).

22: In the early 14th century the port of Hull was a principal supply port for Edward I in his war with the Scots.

23: In 1301, following a letter dated 18 March that year from Archbishop Thomas Corbridge to the Prior and Convent of Gisburne calling for the dedication of a cemetery 'to the Chapel of the Town of Kyngestone', a cemetery was consecrated at Hull's Holy Trinity Church.

24: In its early days Hull was governed by a 'royal keeper' (sometimes described as Bailiff), John de Husthwaite being the first to hold the office between 1293–6. Husthwaite was succeeded by Richard Oysel, described as 'Keeper' of the town. In 1301 during Oysel's term of office as royal keeper he employed Robert de Barton as the town's Bailiff.

25: The port of Hull was frequently called on to provide men, ships and supplies for both the Scottish and French wars. In 1301 this amounted to a single ship. However, so spectacular was Hull's growth that in 1359, just sixty years after the granting of the Royal Charter, it was called upon to provide Edward III with 11 ships and 466 men towards the campaigns.

26: Hull's Great Thornton Street was formerly known as Gallows Lane, gallows having first been erected there in 1302.

27: At the start of the 14th century, Hull and Beverley were the first places in England where a local brickmaking industry was established, and locally manufactured bricks were used in the building of the transepts of Holy Trinity Church.

28: In the early 14th century the newly named port of Kingston-upon-Hull attracted many merchants from neighbouring towns hoping to take advantage of fresh commercial opportunities. These included William de la Pole, a wealthy wool merchant and royal money lender, who not only established the de la Pole family dynasty, but also facilitated the foundation of the city's Charterhouse monastery.

29: According to both Sheahan and the History of Parliament website, Hull first sent representatives (two burgesses) to Parliament in 1305. The earliest known parliamentary representative was Michael de la Pole, who was returned in 1375. Avery (2008) records the date Hull first sent representatives to Parliament as 1304, and names the two as Robert de Barton and Richard de Gretford.

30: In 1316 (following a writ of inquiry initiated in the reign of his father Edward I) Edward II granted permission for a ferry to be established between Hull and Barton in Lincolnshire. In 1999 a blue heritage plaque was erected on the old ticket office on Nelson Street, opposite the Victoria Pier, to mark the location of the departure point of the Humber Ferry. The inscription reads:

> A ferry between Hull and Lincolnshire was first recorded in 1315. THE HUMBER FERRY operated between here and New Holland from 1825 until the completion of the Humber Bridge in 1981

31: In 1320, with the churchyard of Holy Trinity being considered too small for the burial requirements of the town, the inhabitants of Hull petitioned King Edward II to grant them a piece of land called Le Hailles, situated at the west end of the existing churchyard. The grant described the land as 'a waste piece of ground called Le Hailles, at the west end of the churchyard thereof, being thirteen perches and three feet in length, and ten perches and nine feet in breadth'.

32: The first recorded chamberlains of Hull were William and Richard de la Pole, who held office between 1321–4.

33: In 1322, in response to the Scots' incursion south into Yorkshire, the burgesses of Hull petitioned King Edward II for a Royal license to allow them to fortify the town with ditches and castellated walls, which the King duly granted. Prior to that date the town was unprotected by any fortifications.

34: More than 4.5m locally made bricks were used in the construction of the town walls, which were begun in 1322.

35: The fortification of the town walls provided improved security for the port, the new walls extending from the mouth of the river Hull along the bank of the Humber (reaching up to what is now Humber Street), and from the south-west corner of Humber Street to the north end of High Street.

36: Hull's first town defences consisted of brick-built walls, with four main gates (Hessle, Myton, North and Beverley), several posterngates, and as many as thirty towers.

37: St. Mary's Church, originally a chapel of ease to North Ferriby, was built in 1327, but there is no formal record of when the church's separation from the parish of North Ferriby took place.

38: In a Charter dated 6 May 1331 the office of Warden of Hull was abolished, and the governance of the borough was confided to a mayor and four bailiffs.

39: Hull's first mayor, appointed in 1332, was William de la Pole. In 1332 Edward III, accompanied by a party of nobles and attendants, came to Hull, and whilst here inspected the recently constructed fortifications, which far exceeded his expectations. Before his departure the King, after being so loyally welcomed by the townsfolk and lavishly entertained by the mayor, knighted William.

40: Besides William de la Pole, a number of other wealthy Hull merchants provided loans to help Edward III finance the French wars in the early 1340s: these included Robert de Upsale and Robert de Preston (£200), Alan Cok (£136), and Henry de Brisele (almost £600).

41: The foundation stone of the Carthusian priory of St. Michael (later the Charterhouse) was laid by Sir William de la Pole in around 1350.

42: While wool had been the main export since before the 1299 Charter, cloth became a significant commodity passing through the port from the mid-point of the 14th century, with Hull becoming third in importance amongst the provincial ports exporting it.

43: In 1369 Trinity House was founded when 49 men and women formed a Guild in honour of the Holy Trinity; pledging themselves (among other things) to help each other in poverty and sickness, to attend the funeral whenever a member died, and to say Mass and make offerings for the soul of the deceased. In 1986 a blue heritage plaque was erected at the corner of Posterngate and Trinity House Lane to mark the location of Trinity House (and the Carmelite Friary that formerly occupied the site). The inscription reads:

> Founded in 1369, the Guild of the Holy Trinity acquired important maritime and charitable functions. The site of TRINITY HOUSE was occupied prior to 1539 by a Carmelite Friary. Trinity House was granted a Royal Charter in 1541. This building was erected in 1753

44: As early as 1376 the mayor and burgesses of Hull complained to the King (Edward III) that the town had great difficulty in obtaining fresh water, and that any that could be transported by boat from Lincolnshire could only be obtained at great expense. They pointed out that the town would be ruined unless His Majesty would give his assistance in providing some means by which their lack of fresh water might be overcome. Michael de la Pole and others, under the umbrella of a Royal Commission, set about investigating the matter.

45: Hull's Charterhouse (the *Maison Dieu*: 'God's House' hospital) was established and endowed on 1 March 1384 by Sir Michael de la Pole. His father, Sir William de la Pole, had laid foundations on the site some time around 1350, but had died (in 1366) before work could be completed. Sir William's original intention had been to found a small hospital there. Sir Michael de la Pole completed the construction of the house, with the King's license being granted in 1377, and installed in it 13 Carthusian monks.

46: Some time around 1384, Michael de la Pole built a manor house at the corner of where today Lowgate and Alfred Gelder Street meet, almost opposite St. Mary's Church. It was later to become known as Suffolk Palace, and later still as The King's Manor. Some time after 1513 it came into the hands of Henry VIII, who stayed there when he visited Hull in 1541. In 1953 a white heritage plaque was erected on the former main Post Office building at that location to mark the site. The inscription reads:

> Site of the manor house of Sir William de la Pole (first mayor of Kingston upon Hull, 1331) and of the SUFFOLK PALACE erected by Sir Michael de la Pole, Earl of Suffolk. The palace was seized by the Crown (1504) and became known as "The King's Manor"

15th century

47: In May 1401, so that fresh water could be conveyed into the town, it was decided that a ditch should be dug running from Anlaby's Julian Spring to Hull.

48: In the 15th century several members of the de la Pole Family met violent deaths: Michael, 2nd Earl of Suffolk, fought with Henry V in France and, after contracting dysentery, died on 17 September 1415 during the siege of Harfleur; his son, also Michael, 3rd Earl of Suffolk, died at Agincourt on 25 October 1415. His younger brother William, 4th Earl of Suffolk and 1st Duke of Suffolk, was eventually beheaded (on 2 May 1450).

49: Michael de la Pole (3rd Earl of Suffolk) was one of only two English noblemen to die at Agincourt—the other was Edward of Norwich, 2nd Duke of York.

50: In 1430 William de la Pole, 1st Duke of Suffolk, married Alice Chaucer the granddaughter of the great medieval English poet Geoffrey Chaucer.

51: In a Royal Charter of 1440 Henry VI incorporated the town and constituted Hull a separate and distinct county, with its jurisdiction extended to cover Hessle, North Ferriby, Swanland, West Ella, Kirk Ella, Tranby, Willerby, Wolfreton, Anlaby, and the site of the Priory of Haltemprice. Hull could thenceforth hold annual elections to appoint a mayor, who would be selected from a body of 13 aldermen.

52: Regarding the significance of the three crowns on the city's coat of arms, the Hull History Centre suggests:

> The most likely explanation is that the three crowns represent the Holy Trinity. In the middle ages, the Holy Trinity—God the Father, Son and Holy Spirit—was a popular religious cult in Hull, and Holy Trinity Church and Trinity House commemorate this. Alternatively the

three crowns are to mark that Hull is the King's Town, as in Kingston upon Hull. It may be that the true explanation is a combination of the two, and that perhaps more importantly it's simply that they look good.

However, the earliest surviving example of the coat of arms (in the east window of St. Mary's church, Lowgate) dates from the mid 15th century, at which point Hull had been granted three major Royal Charters: 1299, 1331 and 1440; could it be that each of the three crowns represents one of the kings who granted Hull its three most significant Royal Charters: Edward I (1299), Edward III (1331) and Henry VI (1440)?

53: Hull's is the only municipal coat of arms in the country protected from misuse by a private Act of Parliament.

54: In 1447 Hull Corporation was empowered to elect an Admiral of the Humber, which title (by virtue of the office) falls to the mayor.

55: Following the extension of the County of Hull in the mid 15th century, Julian Well and Derringham Dyke were absorbed into the county, and in 1449 the Priory at North Ferriby gave permission for pipes to be laid on its land between Springhead and Hull. In 1613 three engineers—Richard Sharpleigh (London), William Maltby (London) and John Cater (Lincolnshire)—were invited to Hull with a view to their improving the town's water supply. They leased some land from the Corporation and built a water works 'from which the water was conducted by pipes to all parts of the town'.

56: According to wishes stated in his will, dated 27 January 1450, William de la Pole was interred in Hull's Carthusian Monastery.

57: In 15th century Hull a street by the name of Pole Street connected Lowgate to the Charterhouse, which was itself connected to the bank of the river Hull by a short street named North Pole Street.

58: In 1454 the Hull Corporation dismissed two minstrels from their service. As the minute detailing their dismissal refers to them as 'histriones', meaning actors, and one of them is specifically named (John Wardlaw), he is the first Hull actor whose name is recorded.

59: In August 1461, with Hull having extensive debts as a result of expenses incurred during the Wars of the Roses, a decision was made to take up and sell the town's lead water pipes in an effort to raise money towards settling those debts.

60: Hull Grammar School is Hull's oldest school, having been endowed by Bishop John Alcock in 1479, but with possible indications of it existing since the mid 14th century. In 1583, the building being 'in a ruinous state', Alderman William Gee opened a subscription to have it rebuilt. The rebuilding of the school was probably completed in 1585. In 1988 a blue heritage plaque was erected on the side of the Old Grammar School, in South Church Side, to mark the site of the school whose 'old boys' include Andrew Marvell and William Wilberforce. The inscription reads:

> The Old Grammar School was built in 1583 and remained a school until 1878. Famous Old Boys include Andrew Marvell & William Wilberforce. This fine building became a museum in 1988. 'HANDS ON HISTORY' open to the public 10.00am–5.00pm Sun 1.30–4.30

61: In the 15th century the river Humber was fresh enough to sustain vast numbers of salmon swimming up-river; and sturgeon of eleven stones or larger could reach as far as Tadcaster.

62: The total build cost of a house constructed (partly of brick, with 3,500 roof tiles) in Hull between 13 April and 24 June 1499 was £15 16s.

16th century

63: In 1522 Holy Trinity Church was put under a severe interdict (a punishment by the [Roman Catholic] Church forbidding certain sacraments, or rites, to its adherents); the doors and windows were closed up with thorns and briars, and its bells were silenced. No worship was performed in the building, and everyone venturing to enter it was declared to be accursed; and the dead were not permitted to be buried there.

64: The houses of both Blackfriars (Augustinian) and Whitefriars (Carmelite) were dissolved in 1539.

65: In 1540 Henry VIII 'pulled down the body of the Church and steeple' of St. Mary's church (leaving just the chancel standing) as it obstructed his view from Suffolk Palace. The materials were used in the fortifications of the town.

66: Henry VIII made brief visits to Hull in September and October 1541, and by February 1542 had decided that further fortification was necessary to protect the port, and a 'notable fortress' was required.

67: Henry VIII provided £18,000 for a fortress to further protect Hull, but by the time it was completed, at the end of 1543, more than £23,000 had been spent on it.

68: A Charter granted by Edward VI in 1552 extended the area of the town, without assigning to the Corporation any property, granting it lordship of the manor of Myton, and one-sixth of the manor of Sutton.

69: A gold chain presented to the Corporation in 1554 by Sir William Knowles was to be kept and worn by every mayor during his term of office: on Sundays, great holidays, and on all extraordinary occasions; a penalty of £40 was imposed for every such occasion it was not worn.

70: In 1554 the gold chain of office worn by the Mayor of Hull weighed around 4 ounces, but by 1571 its weight had almost tripled to 11.375 ounces.

71: In 1575, in anticipation of a Royal visit, it was ordered that all the houses in Hull were to be painted, with the gable ends to be either repaired or taken down.

72: In 1559 citizens of Hull could be fined heavily for keeping a pig within the town walls for more than 6 days; a similar penalty awaited anyone having a haystack inside the town.

73: Having been visited by the Plague in 1472, 1476 and 1478, Hull fell victim to the Black Death once again in 1576. This was mainly confined to Blackfriargate, which was so deeply infected that the avenues leading there were walled up, leaving just two openings where watchmen were placed to ensure that only provisions and medicine gained entry, and none of the infected escaped. These measures, imposed in an attempt to isolate the contagion, were generally effective and the epidemic soon subsided, with less than 100 citizens losing their lives.

74: By 1577, as a preventative measure against the spread of fire, thatched roofs on buildings in Hull had been banned.

75: In 1583, at the request of the city's mayor and aldermen, the Lord President of the North came to Hull to sit as judge to try suspected criminals, including 'three poor old women', who were tried for witchcraft. One of the women was sentenced to stand in the pillory on four separate market days, and to be imprisoned for a year.

76: The alderman and merchant William Gee, who held the office of Mayor on three occasions (1562, 1573, 1582), was a generous benefactor to the town. In 1583 he spent £300 on rebuilding the Grammar School, and in 1600 he founded Gee's Almshouse in Chapel Lane, with rooms for 'ten poor women having no children'.

77: In 1585, as a fire precaution, brewers and bakers in Hull were forbidden from lighting their fires before 2am; and the fires had to be extinguished by 10pm.

78: John Hotham (1589–1645), who in 1642 would refuse Charles I entry into Hull, was the eldest surviving son of John Hotham (d. 1609), High Sheriff of Yorkshire and a Member of Parliament for Scarborough (1584).

79: Luke Fox, a Younger Brother of Trinity House, who set out on his voyage on 7 May 1631, was born in Hull on 20 October 1586 (Sheahan refers to him as 'the earliest of the known Hull authors' and attributes to him 'the revival of an attempt to discover a north-west passage'). The vessel he commanded for his expedition was the pinnace Charles (80 tons burden).

17th century

80: John Hotham was still a minor when he first married (Katherine, daughter of Sir John Rhodes of Barlborough, Derbyshire) on 6 February 1607.

81: In 1613 Andrew Barker, an Elder Brother of Hull's Trinity House and the captain of the Heartsease, took aboard an Inuit in a kayak off Greenland. Sadly the Inuit died three days later, but the 12-foot long bone-framed, skin-covered kayak and its contents (the body of the

Inuit, his coat, bag, oars and mast), were brought home to Hull and are now on display in one of the rooms of Trinity House.

82: On 11 April 1617 John Hotham was knighted by King James I; and in May 1619 he acquired a 'passport' to travel abroad, serving as a volunteer alongside Ernst von Mansfeld defending Bohemia for the Elector Palatine.

83: The great 17th century metaphysical poet and politician Andrew Marvell was born in the rectory at Winestead on 31 March 1621. He was baptized in the church of St. Germain, Winestead on 5 April that year— by his father, who was rector at the church. Marvell was educated at Hull Grammar School; and in 1659 and 1660 was elected Member of Parliament for Kingston-upon-Hull.

84: On 4 January 1622 Sir John Hotham purchased a baronetcy and became 1st Baronet of Scorborough. He served as Member of Parliament for Beverley between 1625–1629, and was appointed Governor of Hull in 1635. (Between 1607 and 1635 he was married 5 times.)

85: Having earlier in the year published *North-West Fox...* (a record of his expedition) Luke Fox died in poverty in Whitby in July 1635.

86: Sir John Hotham was a leading supporter of Sir Thomas Wentworth; and when the Crown proposed, in 1639, replacing Hotham as Governor of Hull, Wentworth spoke up in Hotham's defence, but without success: in the spring of that year Hotham was replaced as Governor by Captain William Legge.

87: In 1640 Sir John Hotham (along with Sir Hugh Cholmley) drafted Yorkshire's petition of 28 July (which Sir Thomas Wentworth described as 'mutinous') insisting that mustering the county's militia without pay would be impossible. Two months later, the pair were instrumental in organizing a further petition, this time from the gentry of Yorkshire, requesting that Charles recall Parliament; they were warned by the King that if they persisted in their opposition to the Crown they would be hanged.

88: In 1640 Sir John Hotham was returned for Beverley to the Short Parliament called by Charles I to raise money to finance the military struggle with Scotland.

89: Sir John Hotham retained his seat for Beverley in the elections to the Long Parliament (established in November 1640) and quickly asserted himself as one of its most active and vocal members.

90: As a precursor to later events, on 11 January 1642 Charles I appointed the Earl of Newcastle as Governor of Hull; however, Parliament appointed Sir John Hotham.

91: In April 1642, during the English Civil War, Hull Corporation (supporting the Parliamentarians) denied King Charles I entry into the town. Sir John Hotham, who in 1639 had been deprived by Charles of his office of Governor of Hull, had taken command of the town and refused the King admission, thereby denying the Royalist cause access to a store of much needed armaments held within the town's walls. In 1953 a white heritage plaque was erected at the ruins of Beverley Gate to mark the location where King Charles I was denied entry into the town. The inscription reads:

> Site of the principal entrance of the ancient walled and fortified town c. 1321—c. 1780 BEVERLEY GATE here Sir John Hotham, the Governor, denied entry in 1642 to King Charles I—the first overt act of the Civil War

92: On 23 April 1642, while Sir John Hotham was refusing King Charles I entry into Hull, the Duke of York (later James II), the King's nephew (Prince Elector of

Palatine), the Earl of Newport, Lord Willoughby and Sir Thomas Glenham were all being entertained at the Trinity House.

93: In July 1642 Charles I began the First Siege of Hull: Sir John Hotham had been ordered by Parliament to seize the town to prevent Charles I gaining access to the local military stores and arms; and Hotham facilitated the removal of the arms to the Tower of London in support of the Parliamentarian cause. In a move to help defend the town from the Royalist forces, the banks of the rivers Humber and Hull were cut so as to allow the land surrounding the town to become inundated 'to a considerable depth with sea water'.

94: In response to the Parliamentarian forces inundating the land surrounding the town, and in an attempt to weaken the resolve of its citizens and defending forces, Charles I had the town's supply of fresh water diverted into the Humber; and, to take command of the Humber, ordered the building of forts at both Paull and Hessle Cliff. Before too long it was clear to Charles that the siege had been unsuccessful, so he disbanded his forces and withdrew to York.

95: Following the First Siege of Hull, Sir John Hotham became increasingly disaffected with the Parliamentarian cause, and when his son Captain John Hotham was imprisoned at Nottingham Castle by Cromwell on 22 June 1643, Sir John abandoned his former loyalty to Parliament. The Commons then instructed Sir Matthew Boynton to seize Hull, which he (with the support of the townspeople) successfully achieved on 29 June.

96: The Second Siege of Hull was prosecuted by the Earl of Newcastle on 2 September 1643, who once again cut off the supply of fresh water to the town, along with the supply of provisions 'from the surrounding country'. As with the first, this second siege also failed, following a 'most vigorous and determined sortie' made upon the Royalists on 11 October and the subsequent withdrawal of the Earl of Newcastle's forces to York—breaking up roads, cutting open canals and destroying bridges as they went, to hinder the Parliamentarian forces' pursuit of them in their retreat.

97: On 7 September 1643 Sir John Hotham was ejected from his parliamentary seat and sent to the Tower, some of his correspondence with the Earl of Newcastle providing compelling evidence of their conspiracy. In November and December 1644 he was tried by a court-martial, and on 7 December he was sentenced to death.

98: On 1 January 1645 Captain John Hotham (1610–1645) was beheaded on Tower Hill after (like his father) being court-martialed and found guilty of treason.

99: On 2 January 1645 Sir John Hotham, having been found guilty of 'traitorously betraying the trust imposed upon him by Parliament, and with perfidiously adhering to the enemy', suffered the same fate his son had met the previous day, and was executed by decapitation on Tower Hill.

100: Following his execution on the block at Tower Hill on 2 January 1645, Sir John Hotham was buried at All Hallows, Barking.

101: Upon the execution of both Sir John Hotham and his son, Captain John Hotham, the family estates passed to Sir John's 12-year-old grandson, also named John, who sat for Beverley almost continuously from 1660 to his death in 1689.

102: The Maister family was one of Hull's most prominent and wealthy merchant families. Living on the east side of High Street (backing on to the river Hull) the family originally came from Kent; but would eventually provide a number of representatives for the town: William Maister was Sheriff in 1645 and 1699, Mayor in 1655, and MP for Hull in 1701, 1705–06, 1710, and 1713–14; and Henry Maister was Sheriff in 1729, Mayor in 1677 and 1694, and MP for Hull in 1732 and 1734.

103: Between 1650–52 Andrew Marvell worked as a tutor to twelve-year-old Mary Fairfax, the daughter of Thomas Fairfax, the former Lord General of the Parliamentarian forces; and in 1653 he became tutor to Oliver Cromwell's ward, William Dutton.

104: On 2 September 1657 Andrew Marvell was appointed Latin secretary to John Thurloe, Secretary to the Council of State and head of the Government's Intelligence Service; and in January 1659 he was returned as one of two MPs for Hull. He was re-elected in 1661, and continued as parliamentary representative for the town until his death.

105: By the mid 17th century the river Hull was so overcrowded with vessels that ships were being damaged, and delays in handling and shipping were reaching critical levels, resulting in preliminary investigations being carried out into the expansion of facilities at Hull.

106: In the mid 17th century Hull was the only English port which had no 'Legal Quay' where Customs officials could inspect 'dutiable' goods; instead, cargoes had to be inspected aboard the berthed vessels at the private wharves of the merchants.

107: Holy Trinity Church (which was consecrated in 1425) officially became a Parish Church in its own right in 1661.

108: The Dutch-born painter Marcellus Laroon (the elder), who lived in Yorkshire for many years, told George Vertue that he had seen Rembrandt in Hull in

1661. Local Art Historian, and former Hull University Medical Officer, Robert Raines has pointed out that if this were true, Laroon would have been 'hardly a young man'. Laroon (1653-1702) would have been at most nine years old. [There are just two sentences in Sheahan's history of Hull relating to Rembrandt supposedly living in Hull: 'Van Rijn Rembrandt, the celebrated painter and etcher, practised his art at Hull for some time. He died in 1674, aged 68'.] (see fact 1,344 and fact 1,939)

109: Following the separation of Holy Trinity Church from the parish of Hessle in 1661, the Hull Corporation (with Royal assent) elected Mr Nicholas Anderson as the church's first vicar in May 1662, a position he held for 27 years.

110: The grandfather of the abolitionist William Wilberforce, also named William Wilberforce (1690-1776), built up the family fortune in the maritime Baltic Trade, and was Mayor of Hull in both 1722 and 1740.

111: Andrew Marvell died on 16 August 1678 at Great Russell Street, London, after contracting malaria following a visit to Hull in July of that year. He was buried in the south aisle of St Giles-in-the-Fields, London.

112: Andrew Marvell published just one poem under his own name during his lifetime: 'The First Anniversary of the Government under O.C.'

113: Following the pulling down by Henry VIII of the steeple of St. Mary's, Lowgate in 1540, the church remained without a steeple for over a century and a half, until foundations for a new tower were laid in 1696, it being completed the following year. The tower was heightened during restoration work carried out between 1861-3 by Sir George Gilbert Scott, with the present tower standing at 106 feet.

18th century

114: Hull poet William Mason was born at the vicarage of Holy Trinity on 12 February 1725. His great-grandfather, Robert (d. 1718), had been both Sheriff of Hull (1675) and twice Mayor of Hull (1681 and 1696). His father was Controller of the Customs at the port of Hull from 1696; his mother, Mary (*née* Wild) died in 1725, before William had reached his first birthday, and was buried at Holy Trinity on 26 December 1725. A street named in his honour (Mason Street) was built by Joseph Sykes at the beginning of the 19th century.

115: In 1733 the Hull Dock Company (officially: the 'Dock Company at Kingston-upon-Hull'), the first statutory dock company in Britain, was formed by the Hull Corporation, Hull Trinity House, and Hull merchants.

116: The equestrian statue of King William III (William of Orange), affectionately known locally as King Billy, was erected by subscription at a cost of £893.10s. Peter Scheemakers, the statue's sculptor, had lost out to fellow sculptor Michael Rysbrach in a competition to create an equestrian statue of King William III for Bristol, and subsequently received £50 compensation from that city; he then persuaded Hull to commission its own statue of King Billy, which was completed in 1734 and inaugurated on 4 December that year. It was re-gilded in 1821 and again in 1834.

117: Peter Scheemakers was an advocate of the classical idiom, and King Billy was not the first of his subjects to be depicted as a Roman warrior. A myth surrounding Scheemakers is that he took his own life after realizing he'd forgotten to include King Billy's stirrups. In reality, the stirrups were omitted deliberately, in keeping with the classical style of the statue; and Scheemakers lived to the age of ninety, a further 47 years after he'd created King Billy for the people of Hull.

118: Local legend has it that whenever the clock of Holy Trinity Church strikes midnight (some say when it strikes thirteen), King Billy will dismount the equestrian statue in Lowgate and pop across to the King William (King Billy) public house for a drink. Further, it has been said that a thistle, which was formerly under the foot of King Billy's horse, was stolen by the Jacobites.

119: On 24 November 1739 the *Hull Courant*, the first newspaper to be produced in Hull, was published for the first time, by local bookseller and stationer John Rawson. The *Courant* was a four-page folio with which was 'presented weekly to each purchaser a sheet of [Laurence Clarke's] *History of the Bible*'. Rawson had a shop in the Butchery, Queen Street, but moved to the Star, Lowgate, near the Market Place in January 1742. Following his death on 30 October 1787 he was succeeded by his son William.

120: Blaydes House at 6 High Street, Hull—the former home and business premises of the Blaydes family of ship-builders, ship-owners and merchants—was built around 1739-40. The Blaydes family owned two shipyards: one on the river Hull; the other at Hessle Cliff. The house was bought by Henry Hodge (a local oil seed merchant and oil mill owner) in the 1850s, and was acquired by the University of Hull in 1999 and was subsequently restored. The building is currently home to the Heritage Consortium's Postgraduate Certificate in Heritage Training programme. In 1986 a blue heritage plaque was erected on the building to mark it as the location of the Blaydes family home. The inscription reads:

The Blaydes Family, prominent merchants, shipbuilders and citizens lived here, close to their counting house, shipyard quays and warehouses, in the 17th and 18th centuries. BLAYDES HOUSE, partially rebuilt c.1760, was restored by the Georgian Society for East Yorkshire in 1982.

121: Early in the morning of 12 April 1743 the High Street home of the Maister family was discovered to be on fire. Henry Maister's wife Mary returned to the house in an attempt to rescue their youngest child, but they—along with two maidservants—were killed in the fire. In 1990 a blue heritage plaque was erected on the building to mark the location of the Maister family home. The inscription reads:

> The Maister family were prominent Hull merchants in the 17th and 18th centuries. MAISTER HOUSE was rebuilt after a fatal fire in 1743 with the advice of Lord Burlington. The staircase hall is open to the public during office hours

122: Following the fire of April 1743, Henry Maister began rebuilding Maister House in 1744; but this time installed a stone staircase and wrought iron balustrades. Unfortunately, he didn't live long enough to see the rebuilding completed. He died in December 1744.

123: William Mason greatly admired Andrew Marvell, and like Marvell began his formal education at Hull Grammar School. His first significant and widely praised poem: 'Musaeus: a Monody to the Memory of Mr Pope, in Imitation of Milton's Lycidas' was completed in 1747.

124: During his time at Cambridge University, William Mason struck up what would become a lifelong friendship with Thomas Gray (most famous as the author of 'Elegy Written in a Country Churchyard'), although Gray was nine years older than Mason.

125: William Mason's father, the Reverend William Mason (1694–1753), was vicar of Holy Trinity Church from 1722 until his death on 26 August 1753.

126: In 1756 the Hull Corporation commissioned surveys from Joseph Page and Charles Tate to seek out a suitable site for a new harbour; at the same time, the Customs were looking to end the situation where cargoes had to be inspected at the port's private wharfs, and to have the customs procedures incorporated into a new Legal Quay.

127: John Alderson MD, one of Hull's most influential benefactors and a keen promoter of art and culture in the town, was born in Lowestoft in 1757 and baptised on 4 June that year. He was just three years old when his father (Rev. James Alderson) died, and he grew up in Ravenstonedale, Westmorland, being educated at the free grammar school there.

128: William Wilberforce, best known for his association with the abolition of the slave trade, was born on 24 August 1759 at 23–25 High Street, Hull. His parents, Robert (a local merchant) and Elizabeth (*née* Bird) had three children, William was the youngest child, and the only son.

129: William Wilberforce was brought up with all the advantages that wealth and position can bring, although his father died when William was just nine years old.

130: On 25 September 1765 William Mason married Mary Sherman (the daughter of the local Garrison storekeeper) at St Mary's, Lowgate. Sadly, she died of consumption less than two years later, on 27 March 1767, at Bristol Hot Wells where she had been taken in the hope of being cured. She was buried at Bristol Cathedral.

131: At the age of seven William Wilberforce was sent to Hull Grammar School; and between 1771–76 he boarded at Pocklington School, before entering St. John's College, Cambridge in October 1776, where he graduated BA in 1781 and MA in 1788. At the age of twenty-one he was elected MP for Hull, and struck up what would become a lifelong friendship with William Pitt the younger—a former Cambridge University contemporary.

132: In 1767 reports for the Hull Corporation, by Robert Mylne and Joseph Robson, recommended a new harbour be constructed on the east side of the river Hull.

133: After his father's death, William Wilberforce was sent to live with his uncle (also William Wilberforce) and aunt at Wimbledon and St. James's Place, London.

134: In 1768 a 'new elegant Theatre' was opened in Hull, which (after the granting of a Royal patent in 1769) became the Theatre Royal in 1770.

135: The Theatre Royal was constructed on land known as Abisher's Yard in Finkle Street, and was bounded by Mytongate to the north and Blanket Row to the south; it was officially opened on 3 October.

136: The Theatre Royal became part of the Yorkshire Circuit of theatres owned and managed by Joseph Baker, who in 1765 took on Tate Wilkinson as a business partner. When Baker died in 1770, Wilkinson became the sole proprietor and manager of the York Circuit, including the Theatre Royal.

137: With medicine being a family profession, John Alderson trained as a surgeon in Norwich under his elder brother James; and, while still living in Norwich, served as a Lieutenant and Surgeon to the West Norfolk Militia, with whom he first came to Hull in 1770. He studied Medicine at Edinburgh for a year, after which he began practicing in Whitby, North Yorkshire. He was awarded his MD by Marischal College, Aberdeen in 1785.

138: In his will of 1770 Thomas Gray appointed William Mason his joint executor, along with James Browne, President of Pembroke Hall, Cambridge.

139: Benjamin Blaydes was three times Mayor of Hull, and was head of the firm of Blaydes, Loft, Gee & Co., ship-owners and general merchants, who were first to 'commence the Hull and Hamburg trade, which they carried on with sailing vessels'. Benjamin Blaydes died in 1771, at the age of 62.

140: In 1772 agriculturalists owning land for which efficient drainage of the river Hull was crucial, commissioned John Grundy the younger to assess the impact on drainage of a proposed new quay on the river. Grundy was tasked with investigating three possible options: widening the harbour; utilising the channel behind the Garrison; and utilising the moat around the town. However, he identified the further possibility of creating a relief channel in the ditches: the use of gates in the channel would offer the possibility of providing facilities for both a wet dock (at the east end) and a dry dock (at the south).

141: In 1782 a vessel named Bethia was launched at Hull. Built by the local Blaydes shipbuilding family, the Bethia (initially used in connection with the Baltic timber trade) was purchased by the Admiralty in 1787, taken to London, and modified at the Deptford Dockyard in preparation for an expedition to collect breadfruit in the South Seas. The ship was renamed Bounty, put under the command of William Bligh, and sailed on 23 December 1787 from Spithead, bound for Tahiti. In 1986 a blue heritage plaque was erected at 6 High Street to mark the location of the Blaydes shipyard. The inscription reads:

> Shipbuilding has been an important industry in Hull since the 18th century. From the mid 1600s BLAYDES

SHIPYARD built whalers, sailing ships, and warships, reputedly including in 1784 the 'Bethia' later renamed the 'Bounty' of mutiny fame

142: As a garden designer, William Mason designed several flower gardens for the houses and estates of friends, his most influential being the walled garden for Lord Harcourt at Nuneham Courtenay, Oxfordshire, created in 1772-3.

143: William Mason wrote subversive satires under the pseudonym of Malcolm MacGreggor, the most famous of these being 'An Heroic Epistle to Sir William Chambers' (1773).

144: By 1773 reports had been prepared by John Wooler (on the cost) and John Smeaton (on the effect on the river) of John Grundy's suggestions for the proposed new quay. The dock was costed at around £55,000–£60,000, and the Legal Quay at £11,000–£12,000. Smeaton concluded that the adverse effects on the river would be negligible.

145: Until 1773 maritime trade was conducted through the 'Haven' (or Old Harbour), a series of wharves on the west bank of the river Hull onto which backed the merchants' houses on High Street.

146: In April 1774 the recently established 'Dock Company at Kingston-upon-Hull' obtained its first Act of Parliament, by which the shareholders were incorporated, and empowered to construct 'a basin or dock to extend from the river Hull to a certain place in the town of Kingston-upon-Hull, called Beverley Gates ... for the admission of loaded ships'. The Act also allowed the construction of 'a quay or wharf, and other conveniencies and necessaries, and for the maintenance of the dock and quay', and the levying of charges 'to be paid to the Company by all ships frequenting the port'.

147: The construction of The Dock (later the Old Dock; and finally Queen's Dock) was begun in May 1774 following Royal Assent being given to the Act of Parliament, which included provisions to minimize the effects on the drainage of the land upstream and to allow the Dock Company to raise up to £100,000 through shares and loans.

148: A payment of £300 by Hull Corporation to John Grundy in November 1774 suggests that Grundy may have been the designer of Hull's first enclosed dock.

149: In 1774 Henry Berry, Liverpool's second dock engineer, was engaged as consultant to superintend the building of The Dock. As Berry's role was mainly conducted by letter, Luke Holt, a carpenter and resident engineer from Middlestown, West Yorkshire, was engaged as Berry's resident engineer when construction began in March 1775.

150: The Act of Parliament sanctioning the building of Hull's first dock allowed 7 years for its construction, but the work was completed in just four years.

151: The first stone of The Dock was laid on 19 October 1775 by the Mayor of Hull, Joseph Outram.

152: In 1776, even before its completion, the foundations of The Dock proved to be inadequate, and extra piles had to be driven in; it eventually cost £73,000 to complete, and was opened to water for the first time in August 1778. In 1953 a white heritage plaque was erected on the side of the fountain on Wilberforce Drive, opposite Hull College and the Wilberforce monument, to mark the site. The inscription reads:

> The site of these gardens was occupied until 1930 by the port's first enclosed dock known as QUEEN'S DOCK Authorised in 1774. The gardens with the town

docks delineate the walls and moat which once encompassed the old town

153: At seventeen William Wilberforce entered St. John's College, Cambridge where he first met William Pitt, who was to become Britain's youngest Prime Minister at just 24 years old.

154: William Mason's *The Poems of Mr Gray, to which are Prefixed Memoirs of his Life and Writings* (1775) was critical in establishing the reputation of Thomas Gray.

155: William Mason's successful lawsuit in 1777 against the Scottish bookseller John Murray for printing (without permission) fifty lines by Thomas Gray, had long-term implications for English copyright law, resulting in the extending of authors' rights. Mason had declined to settle out of court, instead pursuing the matter and creating a legal precedent.

156: On 19 August 1778 John Rogerson became the last criminal to be publicly executed in Hull, when he was hanged for 'coining' (counterfeiting coins).

157: When The Dock opened to shipping on 22 September 1778, the first ship to pass through the dock gates, carrying the board of the Dock Company, dignitaries and a musical band etc. was the Hull whaler Manchester; she was followed by a vessel called Favourite.

158: The brewery that would eventually become Hull Brewery was originally founded by an inn keeper called Thomas Ward, who at the time of his death owned two inns in Church Lane: the Portsmouth and the George and Dragon. Ward entered into a partnership with John Firbank in March 1782 and they bought a former oatmeal mill located at the corner of Posterngate and Dagger Lane, where they built a brewery.

159: John Alderson started his medical practice in Hull in 1780, aged twenty-three. He was elected Physician to Hull General Infirmary in 1792, at which time the infirmary was situated in Prospect Street, where the Prospect Centre now stands. Besides this post, Alderson also lectured in Physiology, and was Consulting Physician to the Hull lying-in charity.

160: Hull General Infirmary (opened towards the end of 1782) was originally a 20-bed hospital based in a house in George Street. In 1784 it moved to new premises—designed by George Pycock and built at an eventual cost of almost £4,700—on the old Beverley turnpike road (now Prospect Street). In 1884, following the laying by the Duke and Duchess of Edinburgh of a foundation stone for a new building, it was renamed the Hull Royal Infirmary.

161: On 12 May 1786—prompted by the burning after hanging of Phoebe Harris, when a reported 20,000 people had watched as her body was consumed by flames—William Wilberforce announced to the House of Commons his intention to move a Bill opposing the burning after hanging, of women convicted of treason (so that instead the bodies may be handed over to anatomists for dissection); but since the Bill also proposed the extension of dissection after execution beyond solely murderers—to include rapists, arsonists, burglars and robbers—the Lords rejected it.

162: In 1786 John Alderson married Sarah Scott of Beverley; they had eleven children, just five of whom survived beyond infancy. He first moved his family to Hull in 1787.

163: In May 1787, following a conversation under the subsequently named 'Wilberforce Oak' with William Pitt and William Grenville, William Wilberforce reached the conclusion that he should actively promote the movement for the abolition of slavery and become the campaign's voice in the House of Commons.

164: On 29 May 1787 the first issue of the *Hull Packet* was published, printed by George Prince of Scale Lane. In November 1827 the paper was enlarged and re-titled the *Hull Packet and Humber Mercury*, the printer and publisher being Mr T. Topping of Lowgate.

165: An entry, dated 28 October 1787, in William Wilberforce's journal records what he perceived as his two main challenges: 'God Almighty has set before me two great objects, the suppression of the slave trade and the reformation of manners'.

166: In 1787 Hull's Trinity House founded the Hull Trinity House Marine School, which opened on 2 February that year with just 36 pupils. The first Master was the Rev. T.O. Rogers, the then curate of Sculcoates Church.

167: The barque Alexander was a Hull-built transport ship with the First Fleet carrying British convicts for the colonisation of Australia in 1788. It arrived at Port Jackson, Sydney on 26 January 1788.

168: On 4 April 1789, five months after arriving at Tahiti, the time came for William Bligh and the Hull-built Bounty to move on to the West Indies. On 28 April, after just three weeks of their onward voyage, the crew of the Bounty, led by Fletcher Christian, staged a mutiny and ordered Bligh (along with his supporters) into the 'ship's boat' and out into the open sea. The story of the incident was told in *Mutiny on the Bounty*, the 1932 novel by Charles Nordhoff and James Norman Hall, before being dramatized in the 1935 film of the same name, starring Charles Laughton and Clark Gable.

169: On 12 May 1789 William Wilberforce set out his

convictions in relation to the abolition of the slave trade, when he delivered a three-and-a-half-hour speech to the Commons highlighting the inhumane conditions the victims were forced to suffer during transportation, condemning the slave trade more generally, and responding to the economic arguments for the continuation of the trade.

170: Thomas Wilson, the founder of the famous Hull-based Wilson Line shipping company, was born in Hull on 12 February 1792 and baptised at the Dagger Lane Chapel.

171: Isaac Reckitt was born on 27 December 1792, in Wainfleet, Lincolnshire. He was the youngest of 12 children born of Thomas and Katharine Reckitt (*née* Massey), a Quaker family (at least 5 of their children did not survive infancy).

172: The *Hull Advertiser* newspaper appeared for the first time on 5 July 1794, published by William Rawson of Lowgate.

173: In 1794, in a move to source a supply of fresh, clean water for its citizens, Hull Corporation bought Julian Springs for £150, and acquired further springs at Anlaby in 1825.

174: James Alderson, the fourth son of John Alderson MD, was born on 30 December 1794; he was baptised in the Presbyterian Church, Bowlalley Lane on 18 April 1795, and received his early education at the school of the Rev. George Lee, a Unitarian minister at Hull (later buried in the chancel of Holy Trinity Church).

175: In 1796, the first steam-packet constructed in England was built at Wincolmlee on the river Hull, under the direction of Messrs. Furness and Ashton, who later had a patent granted. Following successful experiments in the late 1780s in which a steam vessel constructed by Furness and Ashton 'plied on the river between Hull and Beverley', the pair built a much larger vessel and engine, and sent it to London to be completed and tested. The vessel was subsequently bought by the Prince Regent (later George IV), who had it fitted out as a pleasure yacht. The Prince showed his gratitude by granting Furness and Ashton a pension for life of £70 a year each.

176: In 1796 Thomas Ward (founder of the brewery that would become the Hull Brewery Co. Ltd.) died, his daughters Mary and Ann eventually inheriting the brewery. Mary married shipbuilder Robert Gleadow that same year and upon his death in 1826 their son Robert Ward Gleadow (with his wife) took over the brewing business. In 1846 they entered into a partnership with William Thomas Dibb to form Gleadow, Dibb & Co. (incorporated as a private limited company on 27 March 1885, with William Dibb being appointed as the company's first Chairman). In 1868 Gleadow, Dibb & Co. moved into newly built premises: the Anchor Brewery, in Sylvester Street.

177: On Friday 31 March 1797 William Mason fell and injured a leg as he stepped into his carriage. While he was able to officiate at Aston church on the Sunday, he died from the injury the following Wednesday, 7 April.

178: William Mason died at his rectory in Aston; he was buried at All Saints Church, Aston, on 11 April 1797.

179: Thought to have been celibate until his late-thirties, William Wilberforce married Barbara Ann Spooner on 30 May 1797, little more than a month after their first meeting. They had six children, four boys and two girls, all of whom survived into adulthood.

180: James Acland, the radical municipal reformer, printer and an early compiler of electoral statistics, was born in London on 21 March 1799. He moved to Bristol in 1827, founded *The Bristolian* newspaper and was imprisoned for publishing libellous comments in its pages, before moving to Hull in 1831 and setting up his *Hull Portfolio* newspaper 'for the exposure of corporate abuses', its first edition being published on 20 August 1831.

181: In 1799 William Mason was memorialised in Poets' Corner, Westminster Abbey. Situated in the east aisle on a wall near to the memorial to Thomas Gray (whose epitaph was composed by Mason), the monument is signed J. Bacon, 1799.

182: By the last decade of the 18th century, following the commercial success of Hull's first enclosed dock, it became clear that there was significant demand for a second dock. Whereas the entrance to the first dock was from the river Hull, an Act of Parliament was passed in 1802 for a new dock to be constructed with access from the river Humber.

19th century

183: The foundation stone of the Hull Subscription Library's new building in Parliament Street was laid by Dr. John Alderson on 21 June 1800, with the first general meeting of its subscribers taking place on 1 July 1801.

184: John Alderson published a range of treatises, from 'An Essay on the Improvement of poor Soils', suggesting how agriculture can benefit from a proper mixture of soils and a system of crop rotation using plants of dissimilar characteristics; to 'An Essay on Apparitions', describing how various forms of hallucinations can be explained as a consequence of a sufferer's physical ailments.

185: The National Census of 1801 reported the population of the township of Hull as 29,516.

186: Under the second Dock Act (1802) the Dock Company acquired possession of 'the land and buildings belonging to his Majesty's military works on the east side of the river Hull, except the Citadel itself and its foreshore'.

187: The original number of shares held in the Hull Dock Company was 120, but in 1802 Parliament empowered the company to increase that number to 180, the additional shares raising over £82,000, which was put towards the construction costs of a second dock.

188: George Myers, the builder and craftsman commonly known as 'Pugin's Master Builder', was born at 8 Ordovas Place, Chariot Street, Hull in 1803.

189: In 1803 Tate Wilkinson was succeeded as manager of the York Circuit of theatres by his son John; and in 1808 John Wilkinson considered enlarging and refurbishing the Theatre Royal on Finkle Street. Unable to realise his plans, he bought some land in Humber Street from the Corporation and built a new Theatre Royal there.

190: In 1805 John Alderson's wife Sarah and three of their daughters died within a few months of each other. Following his wife's death, Alderson moved house, to 4 Charlotte Street, Hull.

191: The original plans for Hull's second dock were produced by John Rennie and William Chapman, who jointly directed its construction.

192: The main roads from Hull to Anlaby, Beverley, Cottingham, Hessle and Holderness were originally formed in 1803 as a result of a petition to the King 'to make direct ways and causeways to the neighbouring towns'.

193: The work on Hull's second dock (later named Humber Dock) was begun in 1803 under resident engineer John Harrop, who had worked as a carpenter on the construction of Hull's first dock, and had subsequently become a salaried employee of the Hull Dock Company.

194: Sir William Wright tells us that the first stone of the Humber Dock was laid on 13 April 1807 by 'Mr. Henry Maister, the then Chairman of the Company'. In 1990 a blue heritage plaque was erected on the exterior of No. 9 Humber Dock Street to mark the location of the city's second enclosed dock. The inscription reads:

> Designed by John Rennie, this dock was completed in 1809 along the line of the medieval town walls. Excavated material from HUMBER DOCK was used to reclaim the area south of Humber Street. The dock was reopened as a Marina in 1983

195: The site on which the Humber Dock was constructed was formerly 'a play-ground near Hessle Gate, and was called "Butt Close"'.

196: The original engineers' estimate for the construction of the Humber Dock was £84,000, an extremely unrealistically low figure: the works being completed in 1809 at a cost of £233,000. The cost was shared between the Hull Dock Company (50%), Trinity House (25%) and Hull Corporation (25%).

197: Upon its completion the Humber Dock was 914 feet long and 342 feet wide, with a water area of approximately 7 acres, large enough to contain 'seventy square-rigged vessels, with ample room for moving them'. Water was let in to the dock for the first time on 3

December 1808; but it wasn't officially opened for business until 30 June 1809.

198: The final cost for the construction of Hull's Humber Dock was so much greater than the original estimate that a further Act of Parliament had to be passed in 1805 in order that additional finance could be raised.

199: The east bank of the river Hull boasted at least three dry docks: Crown Dry Dock, 104 feet by 21 feet; Union Graving Dock, 214 feet by 48.5 ft (constructed by William Gibson and opened on 24 of August, 1805), and a third dry dock slightly upstream of North Bridge.

200: William Wilberforce was elected to Parliament as representative for Yorkshire, unopposed, on five occasions: 1784, 1790, 1796, 1802, 1806.

201: John Ellerthorpe, who would become known as the 'Hero of the Humber', was born in 1806 at Rawcliffe near Snaith—but moved to Hessle some time around 1816 when his father became the ferry-man between Hessle and Barton. He started working for the Hull Dock Company in 1845, eventually becoming Foreman of the Humber Dock Gates. An exceptionally strong swimmer who regularly swam in the Humber for pleasure, in 1820 (aged 14) he prevented his father's death by drowning after he had fallen overboard from the ferry he operated. Over the next forty years, Ellerthorpe went on to save the lives of upwards of 30 others.

202: Henry Cooper was born at Lime Street, Hull on 4 May 1807. The son of a whaling merchant and, on his mother's side, a descendant of Joseph Priestley (the famous theologian and chemist credited with discovering oxygen), he first entered into a partnership with William Lunn, before being appointed Surgeon to Hull Infirmary. He was subsequently elected as Physician to the

Infirmary, succeeding Sir James Alderson. He became the first Chairman of the Hull School Board (a position he held for six years) and had the Sir Henry Cooper Schools in Bean Street named after him. He was President of the Literary and Philosophical Society between 1848–51, in 1856 and in 1857.

203: Following ten years of committed campaigning, and persistence in the Commons by William Wilberforce, the Abolition Act: *An Act for the Abolition of the Slave Trade* received its Royal assent on 25 March 1807.

204: Hull's Corporation Pier was built in 1809 and was initially a simple ferry pier running parallel to the mainland.

205: It wasn't until 1809 that the provision of a dredger for the Humber Dock was put out to tender. The dredger eventually used was supplied by John Rennie's London workshops and became operational about three years later.

206: Opened on 1 May 1810 with a production of James Thompson's *Tancred and Sigismunda*, along with the John O'Keeffe farce *Agreeable Surprise*, the second Theatre Royal (in Humber Street) was designed by Charles Mountain the younger. It had a 54 feet deep stage, a domed ceiling over the pit and orchestra, an elliptical ceiling over the proscenium, and could accommodate 1,700 people. The interior was decorated in pink, white, yellow and grey, and the boxes (in triple tiers) were lined in red fabric.

207: The proscenium of the Humber Street Theatre Royal consisted of marbled painted pillars, an arched top, and dark-red curtains edged in gold. Below the stage were dressing rooms for the male actors, while the dressing rooms for the female actors, along with the manager's office, were backstage.

208: The Humber Street Theatre Royal was 125 feet long and 60 feet wide. Built on the site of the former Gleadow's ship yard, its auditorium had a middle gallery (with boxes) that could seat 700 people, and an upper gallery running right round the theatre, the whole structure of the galleries being supported by cast iron columns.

209: Sculptor Thomas Earle was born at Osborne Street, Hull in June 1810, and baptised at Holy Trinity Church on 5 December that year. His father, John (d. 1863) was a stonemason, architect and sculptor. Thomas began working as a sculptor at the age of 12, working alongside his father, but also attended drawing classes at Hull's Mechanics' Institute.

210: The National Census of 1811 reported the population of the township of Hull as 26,729.

211: Hull's Botanic Gardens, covering a site of approximately six acres at the end of Linnaeus Street, opened for the first time on 3 June 1812. The group responsible for its construction included William Kirby (1759–1850), local botanists Peter William Watson (1761–1830), William Spence (1783–1860) and Adrian Hardy Haworth (1767–1833). The Gardens' curator, James Niven, had previously worked at Kew Gardens, and would go on to design the layout of Pearson Park.

212: John Alderson was one of the founders and President of the Botanic Gardens in Hull.

213: In 1813 John Alderson was made Freeman of the Town, in acknowledgement of his active involvement in facilitating the artistic and cultural development of the citizens of Hull.

214: In 1814 John Alderson—along with a surgeon named Ellis—founded the Hull Borough Lunatic Asylum for Paupers (later the Sculcoates Refuge for the Insane), in Boteler Street—now Gibson Street, off Cannon Street.

215: Charles Henry Bromby, born in Hull on 11 July 1814, was appointed Bishop of Tasmania in 1864. He was the son of John Healey Bromby, vicar of Holy Trinity Church.

216: The first steam boat ever to ply the river Humber was the Caledonian, which ran between Hull and Gainsborough for the first time on 12 October 1814.

217: By 1814 the entrance lock and basin for the Old Dock were in such a 'ruinous state' (Timperley) that they had to be completely rebuilt, with work commencing in May 1814 under the direction of John Rennie, with George Miller serving as the resident engineer. Following the rebuilding, the lock and basin were re-opened on 13 November 1815.

218: As a boy (c1817) George Myers was apprenticed to the Master Mason at Beverley Minster, William Comins, where he continued to work until 1829.

219: In 1819 Hull millwrights Norman and Smithson built the Maud Foster windmill (in Boston, Lincolnshire) for Thomas and Isaac Reckitt. The windmill cost around £1,827 to construct. As a consequence of successive poor harvests, the Reckitt brothers' milling business failed in 1833, and the partnership was dissolved.

220: In 1819 the Hull-built bomb vessel (a vessel primarily armed with mortars rather than cannons) HMS Hecla was an exploration ground-breaker with three journeys to the Arctic in search of the Northwest Passage.

221: Weddle and Brownlow were the first company to introduce steamers between Hull and Hamburg, with their steamer London being the first on that line.

222: Having worked in the Sheffield area as a travelling salesman in the iron industry, Thomas Wilson set up his own business in 1820, before going into partnership with John Beckington (Newcastle) to form Beckington, Wilson & Co. (iron merchants), whose office was at 14 Salthouse Lane, Hull.

223: In 1821 Hull millwrights Norman and Smithson built Skidby Windmill. The mill was classified a Grade II listed building on 6 May 1952, and is the last working windmill in East Yorkshire.

224: The first sea-going steamer to sail from Hull was the Kingston (owned by Brownlow & Co., Hull), which began trading between Hull and London in 1821. The Kingston was built at Thorne by R. Pearsons & Co., with engines by Overton of Hull; it was launched on 7 March 1821.

225: The Kingston-upon-Hull Gas Light Company, founded as an oil gas company, was established by an Act of Parliament on 19 April 1821. The company, whose works were on the former site of the Union School of Hope in Broadley Street, was authorized to supply the Old Town area, and the townships of Myton and Sculcoates.

226: Cuthbert Brodrick was born in Hull on 1 December 1821, the sixth son of John Brodrick, a local ship owner and merchant. Educated at Kingston College, at sixteen he was articled to the local architect Henry Francis Lockwood. After completing his articles Brodrick took a year out to tour buildings in Europe; and then set up on his own account as an architect in Hull.

227: The National Census of 1821 reported the population of the township of Hull as 31,425.

228: The Hull Literary and Philosophical Society was founded in 1822, with John Alderson becoming the Society's first President; and on Monday 30 October

1823, at the Society's first meeting for the reading of papers, Alderson presented a paper on 'a new theory of the earth'.

229: John Bacchus Dykes, who composed the music for, among others, the hymn 'Eternal Father, Strong to Save', which was sung in many a Hull school's morning assembly, was born in Hull on 10 March 1823.

230: John Bacchus Dykes' father, William Hey Dykes, was the manager of the Hull branch of the Yorkshire District Bank; his grandfather, the Rev. Thomas Dykes, founded and was the first incumbent of St. John's Church (completed in 1792), which was located where the Ferens Art Gallery now stands. From the age of ten, John occasionally deputised for his uncle on the organ at St. John's.

231: In 1825 John Alderson was one of the founders (and as its President, presented the inaugural address) of the Hull Mechanics' Institute.

232: A clause in the Humber Dock Act (1802) stipulated that the Dock Company was required to construct a third dock whenever a specified level of shipping tonnage was reached, providing grant was made available for them to do so; but the company decided upon the necessity of a third dock before the specified tonnage level was reached and they decided to construct it solely at their own expense.

233: In October 1826 construction work was begun on Hull's third dock, Junction Dock, under the direction of (and with a design by) James Walker; with Thomas Thornton, the company's resident engineer, acting as superintendent of the works. The following July, John Timperley succeeded Thornton's position as resident engineer.

234: The site on which Hull's Junction Dock was constructed was formerly the exercise ground of the old Yeomanry Corps and was known as the Old Artillery Ground.

235: Hull's Junction Dock was constructed at a cost to the Dock Company of £186,000.

236: In June 1827 Thomas James Smith (the founder of Smith & Nephew) was born in Whitfield, near Haydon Bridge, the first of four children born to Horatio Nelson Smith and his wife Jane. He later trained as a pharmacist and became apprenticed to a dispensing chemist at Grantham, Lincs.

237: In 1827 George Myers met A.W.N. Pugin (9 years junior to Myers) for the first time, when Pugin visited York Minster to sketch. It would be ten years before they met again.

238: In 1828—with commendable foresight on the part of the Hull Dock Company—when the Hull Oil Gas Company had been granted permission to lay a gas pipe under each of the locks of the Junction Dock, the company chose to 'lay two pipes in each place at their own expense, in order to prevent the possibility of a monopoly, and so at all times secure to the town and its environs a supply of gas at a reasonable rate'.

239: Upon its completion in 1829, Hull's Junction Dock was 645 feet long and 407 feet wide.

240: Junction Dock covered an area of six acres, large enough to contain 'sixty square-rigged vessels, with room for passing to and from the [two adjoining docks]'.

241: Officially opened on 1 June 1829, the construction of Junction Dock was completed in around 30 months.

242: Prior to the opening of Junction Dock, approximately 36,000 tons of material a year was dredged from the Humber Dock.

243: In April 1829 George Myers returned to Hull and subsequently started up in business with his friend Richard Wilson.

244: On 10 May 1829 George Myers married his first wife Isabella, daughter of William Patterson of Beverley, Yorkshire; they had two sons. Isabella died in 1834 giving birth to a third son, who died soon after.

245: John Alderson gave his services to Hull Infirmary free of charge, and also founded the Hull and East Riding School of Medicine and Anatomy. He held the belief that 'literature is indispensable to the happiness and prosperity of a commercial town'.

246: John Alderson laid the Foundation Stone of the Mechanics' Institute building in Charlotte Street shortly before his death in 1829.

247: John Alderson died on 16 September 1829 and was buried in the family vault at St. Mary's Church, Sculcoates.

248: Following the death of John Alderson, an estimated 12–15,000 people gathered to pay their final respects to a man who played such a significant role in the life and educational development of the people of Hull.

249: Upon the death of his father, James Alderson succeeded to a large and lucrative practice in Hull, the East Riding and North Lincolnshire; and, like his father before him, was elected Physician to the Hull Infirmary.

250: From 1830–39 James Alderson was joint proprietor (along with Richard Casson) of the Sculcoates Refuge for the Insane, which was founded by his father. Around 1838 this partnership established larger premises on a site at the top of what is now Argyle Street, Anlaby Road.

251: Isaac Reckitt's first two business enterprises: a Boston-based milling business (1830–34) in partnership with his older brother, Thomas; and his own Nottingham-based business as a corn factor (1834–40) both failed.

252: The partnership between George Myers & Richard Wilson enjoyed early success, which enabled them to take extensive builders' yards in Paragon Street and Carr Lane, and a wharf at the confluence of the rivers Hull and Humber.

253: The city of Vancouver in British Columbia, Canada, sprang up from Gastown ('Gassy's Town'), which was named after John 'Jack' Deighton (Gassy Jack), who was born in Hull in November 1830 the last born surviving child of Richard and Jane Deighton, who owned a silk, cotton & wool draper's shop in Brook Street (the area now dominated by the Prospect Centre). They also had a dyers business.

254: Ebenezer Cobb Morley (his mother's surname was Cobb; his father's, Morley), acknowledged as the founding father of the Football League, was born in Hull on 16 August 1831. He studied Law (setting out as a solicitor's articled clerk) eventually qualifying in 1854. A keen sportsman, particularly rowing, Cobb Morley lived in Barnes, Surrey from around 1858; and practised as a solicitor in London. He formed Barnes Football Club in 1862, and was instrumental in the formation—on 26 October 1863—of the Football Association of England, drafting the FA's first set of rules. He became Secretary of the FA (1863–6) and was the Association's second President (1867–74).

255: Opposing the monopoly and fares of the Royal Charter (the established ferry between Hull and Barton) James Acland chartered a steamer, which he named Public Opinion, whose first trip was made on 12 September 1831. Subsequently Public Opinion was seized by the Admiralty in relation to a damages collision claim. Acland lost the case and was ordered to pay damages of one farthing; plus £268 in costs. In order to avoid imprisonment Acland opened a subscription to help pay the costs.

256: On 1 November 1831 James Acland set up a stall on the north side of the equestrian statue of King Billy, upon which he affixed banners protesting 'Free Trade' and 'No Tolls', along with the inverted town arms; refusing to pay the market tolls, and persuading other traders to follow suit. He formed an anti-toll association, and the Hull and Sculcoates political union.

257: In 1831 James Alderson helped to found the Hull and East Riding School of Medicine, where he became the school's first Professor of Medicine.

258: In 1831 the Mechanics' Institute commissioned Thomas Earle to create a statue of John Alderson (Earle's first public work), which was paid for by subscription of the Institute's members. The statue was originally displayed in the Hall of the Mechanics' Institute, but is now on display in Hull City Hall.

259: In 1831 a marble memorial tablet to John Alderson was erected in the north transept of Hull's Holy Trinity Church.

260: John Alderson's four surviving sons Christopher, John, Ralph Carr, and James all followed the established Alderson career path by working in medicine.

261: The National Census of 1831 reported the population of the township of Hull as 36,293.

262: Following an outbreak of cholera in 1832, Hull Corporation reinvigorated its attempts to find a supply of clean water, and appointed a Waterworks Committee to investigate possible sources. The Committee's findings resulted in the construction of the Stoneferry Waterworks, which took its water supply from the river Hull. However, even after it had been filtered, consumers still felt the water was polluted; and the contaminated water was thought to be the cause of a second epidemic of cholera, which killed 1,860 people in Hull in 1849.

263: In 1832 James Acland opened a small shop at 23 Queen Street, Hull selling such goods as 'Anti-corporate tea', 'Public-opinion coffee' and 'Radical tobacco'.

264: Legendary virtuoso violinist Nicolo Paganini performed in Hull twice towards the end of his life, first on 13 February 1832 at the Theatre Royal, and finally at the same venue on 10 October 1833.

265: Charles Henry Wilson (son of Thomas Wilson) was born in Hull on 22 April 1833. Educated at Kingston College, Hull, he joined the family business, becoming a full partner and joint manager of the company in 1867.

266: With increasingly deteriorating health during 1824, William Wilberforce resigned his parliamentary seat early in 1825, and moved to Highwood Hill, Mill Hill, Middlesex in 1826. Following a severe bout of influenza in 1833, and having sought relief in the waters at Bath, he moved back to London in mid July. It was here on 26 July he welcomed the news that the Bill for the Abolition of Slavery had passed its third reading in the House of Commons. He died on 29 July 1833 at 44 Cadogan Place, Sloane Street, London. He was interred at Westminster Abbey on 3 August, close to his friend, the former Prime Minister, William Pitt.

267: On 12 August 1833, at a public meeting held at Hull's Guild Hall, consideration was given to the most appropriate way in which to commemorate William Wilberforce. Five resolutions were carried at the meeting, including:

> 4. That it is the opinion of this meeting that an obelisk or pillar will form the most striking and appropriate memorial.
>
> 5. That a subscription be entered into for the purpose of carrying the proposed object into effect.

268: On 16 September 1833 the unveiling took place of a statue, created by Richard Westmacott Jr. and funded by public subscription, commemorating John Alderson's service to Hull and its citizens. The statue, originally sited outside the old Royal Infirmary in Prospect Street, was relocated in front of the new Hull Royal Infirmary on Anlaby Road in 1972. The statue was recognised as a Grade II listed structure by English Heritage in 1994.

269: Robert Applegarth, trade unionist, abolitionist and radical reformer, was born in Hull on 26 January 1834. With no formal education, he started working at the age of 10 and eventually became a carpenter. Following his mother's death not long after their move to Sheffield in 1852, Applegarth married; and, due to her ill-health, left his wife Mary in England while he went to live for a period in America. Upon his return to Sheffield he joined the local carpenters' union, and in 1861 steered it into membership of the recently founded Amalgamated Society of Carpenters and Joiners, before becoming its General Secretary and, subsequently, a significant trade union leader.

270: On 1 August 1834 the foundation stone was laid for the Wilberforce monument (at its original location at the corner of St. John's Street, close to where the Beverley

Gate once stood, and adjacent to where the contemporary Princes Quay shopping centre now stands). The foundation stone was laid by Richard Bethell MP, of Rise, who was the Chairman of the Memorial Committee.

271: Mathematician, logician and philosopher John Venn—who in his 1881 book *Symbolic Logic* introduced pictorial illustrations of the relation between sets, that we now know as Venn diagrams—was born in Hull on 8 August 1834. His father was the Reverend Henry Venn, Rector of the parish of Drypool, and later Secretary to the Church Missionary Society. John was educated at Highgate and Islington, before progressing to Gonville and Caius College, Cambridge in 1853; he received his degree in Mathematics in 1857, and went on to produce ground-breaking work on the frequency theory of probability.

272: The Wilberforce monument, which now stands in front of the Hull College of Further Education, was built in 1834 by Hull's Messrs. Myers & Wilson.

273: The statue of Wilberforce which stands on top of the Doric column was 'an afterthought', and was finally put in place on 12 November 1835.

274: Following the municipal elections of December 1835, and the overthrow of the old Hull Corporation (none of the former aldermen was re-elected), the newly installed reformers set the Corporation on a course to divest itself of all the 'ostentatious frippery of the defunct Corporation'. The first Property Committee of the new Corporation valued the furniture, plate, linen, wine, etc. in the Mansion House, and the Corporation regalia, at £2,632. The Corporation's 'Cellar of fine old wines' was sold for £945 at auction (by Mr F. Stamp) on 16 March 1836.

275: Despite the new Hull Corporation of 1836 passing resolutions to dispense with the corporate regalia (the

Sword of State, mace, and cap of maintenance etc.) a Town Council meeting carried, by seventeen to four, a proposal that 'all the paraphernalia which belonged to the Corporation should remain in the Mansion House, in the custody of the mayor for the time being'. All the items that were then unsold, remained locked in a room in the Mansion House until 1851 when Alderman Bannister, at the start of his mayoralty, had them cleaned and restored to their former use.

276: In February 1836 Alderman Thomas Thompson published a design he had requested from James Oldham for a dock on the foreshore of the Humber, west of the entrance to the Humber Dock. In 1860 the West Dock Company was formed with the intention of constructing such a dock in the same location. The Hull Dock Company responded with their own proposal with a more comprehensive design for a dock 'and other works' on the same site, and it was their proposal that was approved by the Committee of the House of Commons, passing in to law in 1861.

277: Joseph Henry Fenner, the founder of the Fenner Group of companies, was born in 1836 (christened on 27 July that year) in Brixton, Surrey.

278: A modern police force was established in Hull by Andrew MacManus in 1836. Besides Mr MacManus as Chief Constable, the force consisted of 4 inspectors, 11 sergeants, and 125 constables. The police station was located in Parliament Street, off Whitefriargate, in part of what was the old Charity Hall workhouse.

279: On 7 June 1837, just over a year after its launch, the boiler of the steam packet Union exploded, destroying the vessel as it lay off the jetty in the Humber Dock basin, resulting in the death of 23 people including some who had congregated on the jetty for the vessel's departure.

280: Frederick Brent Grotrian was born in London in 1838, but by 1892 was operating as a local seed and grain merchant from 188 High Street, Hull. He became a J.P. and a Conservative Member of Parliament for Hull East Division; and in 1890—following the death of its first editor and publisher George Eastwood—became the sole proprietor of the *Hull Daily Mail*.

281: Thomas Tomlinson Cussons, the founder of Cussons & Son, was born in Hull in 1838. He established the Cussons brand initially as a brand of medicines, but eventually moved into the production of soap products. He was Chairman of Cussons & Son from 1889–1905, and following his death in 1927 his son Alex Cussons transformed the company into a global brand, among whose products was the famous *Cussons Imperial Leather* soap.

282: Johann Strauss (1804–1849) performed three concerts in Hull. The dates being 22 and 23 October, and 23 November 1838.

283: Before his partnership with John Beckington was dissolved in 1836, Thomas Wilson had already begun investing in ships; and in June 1840 he formed a new partnership by the name of Wilson, Hudson & Co. This firm was awarded a government contract to provide a weekly steam ship mail service from Hull to Christiansand and Gothenburg—commencing on 2 June 1840, using steamers chartered from the St. George Steam Packet Company.

284: The Hull and Selby Railway Company was formed on 11 August 1834; and Hull's first railway, the Hull and Selby line—one of the first constructed and almost 31 miles in length—was brought into use on 1 July 1840. The line's first station was in Kingston Street; and in its first week of operation the service carried 4,526 passengers.

285: On 7 August 1840 the clock of Holy Trinity Church, which until then had a single face, 'began to mark the lapse of time on four faces' (Sheahan). The clock itself was built in 1772 by Joseph Hindley of York. Sheahan tells us 'there are four mahogany dials, each upwards of 13 feet diameter; 4 pairs of copper hands, each pair including their balances, weighing 4st.; 16 wheels, plain and angular; 8 pinions, 5 iron frames, 106 feet of conveyance rod, and 8 universal shifting joints'.

286: On 11 December 1840 the great composer and piano virtuoso Franz Liszt performed in Hull (to somewhat indifferent reviews) at the Concert Rooms in Kingston Square.

287: Isaac Reckitt bought the established starch business of Charles Middleton on Dansom Lane—to set himself up in starch manufacturing—on 1 October 1840, with his first sales being recorded on 15 December 1840. In 1986 a blue heritage plaque was erected at the Dansom Lane works to mark the founding of the now global concern of RB (formerly Reckitt Benckiser). The inscription reads:

> Founded 1835 in Search House Lane and taken over by Isaac Reckitt in 1840 the former KINGSTON STARCH WORKS (the site of which is now within Reckitt and Colman's) formed the basis of a wide ranging household products industry

288: At forty-eight years old, Isaac Reckitt set up in starch manufacturing with £820 borrowed mainly from close relatives and in-laws. The single product the factory manufactured was starch, made from wheat flour.

289: Although the starch business bought by Isaac Reckitt belonged to Charles Middleton, he actually rented the factory from which it operated—from a man named Joseph Kember.

290: Dansom Lane was formerly known as Clow Lane; but, following the construction of several wind mills on the lane around the end of the 18th century, it became known as Mill Lane. It was renamed Dansom Lane after Bill Dansom, the owner of a farm on the lane.

291: In 1840 the Hull and Selby Railway owned a 4,000 square-yard wharf at Limekiln Creek (thought to have been the original outlet of the river Hull into the Humber before it was diverted to follow the line of Sayer Creek). Limekiln Creek was also the location of a railway goods station from which the Manchester, Sheffield and Lincolnshire Railway operated a lighter service.

292: In 1840 the then diagonal (NE/SW) eastern pier at the front of Hull's Humber Dock basin was reconfigured square to the dock to become L-shaped.

293: James Alderson was town councillor for East Sculcoates from 1840–43 and took a close interest in promoting education in Hull. He was a keen supporter of the Mechanics' Institute, founded by his father in 1825.

294: Robert Rix was born in March 1841 at Burnham Overy, Norfolk. After running away to sea at the age of twelve, he eventually settled in Stockton-on-Tees, marrying Margaret Dobson in 1862 (the couple had seven children). A sea captain and merchant adventurer, he set up a shipbuilding business in Stockton before he began trading out of the port of Hull in 1873. Rix and his family moved to Hull in 1883 and eventually invited his three sons to join him in the family business. This was the foundation of what would become J.R. Rix & Sons, the Hull-based, family-owned business whose Registered Office is at Witham House, 45 Spyvee Street, Hull. The company's operations centre primarily around petroleum and fuel distribution.

295: On 18 March 1841 George Myers married his second wife Judith, the daughter of David Ruddock of Horbury, Yorkshire. They had three sons and three daughters.

296: In 1841 John Bacchus Dykes moved with his family to Wakefield and attended the Proprietory School until 1843 before, in October, going up to St. Catharine's College, Cambridge. There he studied under Professor Thomas Attwood Walmisley and, in 1843, founded (with William Thomson and John Airey) the Cambridge University Musical Society. In January 1847 he graduated with a BA in Classics.

297: Historically, the Drypool area of Hull has been susceptible to flooding, and the Works of Isaac Reckitt's starch factory in Dansom Lane suffered this fate in 1841. Reckitt's fourteen year old son, Francis, returned home from his school in Pontefract to help 'man the pumps'.

298: The National Census of 1841 reported the population of the township of Hull as 41,629.

299: The marine artist Thomas Jacques Somerscales was born in Hull on 29 October 1842. By the age of 21 he'd taken up a career as a naval schoolmaster, but was discharged from the Royal Navy in 1869 at Valparaiso, Chile, after contracting a fever. He subsequently taught at the Artizan School, Valparaiso; and, in 1872, exhibited a series of landscapes in Santiago.

300: In 1842 the Mechanics' Institute Lecture Hall (or saloon), built in the grounds to the rear of the Mechanics' Institute at 2 George Street, was opened with a tea party, public meeting, concert and ball. The foundation stone of the saloon (which was connected to the main building of the Institute by a short covered pathway) had been laid by Dr. James Alderson.

301: George Myers moved with his family to 9 Laurie Terrace, St. George's Road, Southwark, London in 1842, and within three years had established workshops at Ordnance Wharf, Belvedere Road, Lambeth, just downstream from Westminster Bridge. The location of his workshops—in close proximity to both the Thames and Waterloo Station—ensured he was well placed to take advantage of the business opportunities during the building boom of the mid 19th century.

302: Hull's South-end Graving Dock was the first dry dock at the port of Hull. The first stone of the dock was laid by the Mayor of Hull, William Baldwin Carrick, on 28 March 1843. Once the largest graving dock in Hull, it was given Grade II listed building status on 28 July 1998.

303: In 1844 Hull's South-end Graving Dock was completed at a cost of £10,000. Built to a depth of 22 feet, its original dimensions were 220 feet long by 60 feet at its widest point.

304: Towards the end of 1843, in an effort to cut costs incurred by paying commissions to agents, Isaac Reckitt's son George (then 18 years old) persuaded his parents to allow him to embark on 'travelling' to promote the company's Patent Starch. George Reckitt did this with a good degree of success, but it was not until the company introduced Soluble Starch in 1844 that the business finally started to turn a profit.

305: On 29 April 1844 the foundation stone was laid for the Stoneferry Waterworks (which processed water from the river Hull); the first supply from there being issued on 24 August 1845.

306: On 21 May 1844 *The London Gazette* published a notice (dated 1 May 1844) informing readers that an application was being made 'to Parliament in the present session' by Hull's Dock Company to build a 'branch dock on the western side of the Humber Dock'.

307: On 15 June 1844 the partnership between George Myers and Richard Wilson was dissolved 'by mutual consent'.

308: On 20 November 1844 *The London Gazette* published a notice (dated 11 November 1844) informing readers that an application was being made 'to Parliament in the ensuing session' by Hull's Dock Company for 'enlargement' of the branch dock.

309: On 5 June 1845 the Helen McGregor (owned by Gee & Co.) was the first steamer to run between Hull and St. Petersburg.

310: In 1845 James Alderson left Hull and returned to London, where he settled in Berkeley Square. He came back to Hull in about 1846 and built a large house called Albion House, in Albion Street, but he occupied it only occasionally and in 1864 it was sold for £1,418 and converted into the Church Institute.

311: George Myers' work for Augustus Pugin included the building of cathedrals at Birmingham (St. Chad's, completed in 1841), Newcastle upon Tyne (St. Mary's, completed 21 August 1844), Nottingham (St. Barnabas, opened in 1844) and Southwark (St. George's, formally opened on 4 July 1848).

312: Victoria Dock, the first Hull dock east of the river Hull (and connected by basins with both the rivers Humber and Hull) was constructed between 1845 and 1850, and became the main dock for the timber trade. It was expanded in the subsequent two decades, including the construction of large timber ponds.

313: On 12 October 1846 the New Amphitheatre (built

and owned by Mr Stephen Kirkwood) was opened on Paragon Street. Within a few months it had been renamed the Royal Amphitheatre, and in September 1847, in what some saw as a move to tempt patrons away from the Theatre Royal on Humber Street, the then lessee and manager (Mr Egerton) renamed it the Queen's Theatre.

314: The first licensee for dramatic productions at the New Amphitheatre was William Cooke (lessees of the theatre were granted only temporary licences, with Cooke's running for just a 13-week season). Cooke's successor, whose tenancy was granted for 16 weeks from March 1847, was Monsieur Tourniaire of the renowned equestrian circus family, who had announced that he intended to open the amphitheatre 'with his highly-talented and unrivalled company of equestrian, antipodean, gymnastic and acrobatic professors'.

315: The first stone of Victoria Dock was laid on 5 November 1846 by John Beadle. Excavations had begun in September the previous year.

316: The proscenium of the Queen's Theatre consisted of a 40 feet arch supported by two pilasters; its stage was 90 feet deep, and the auditorium featured three rows of balconies.

317: The Hull Dock Company engineer on the Railway Dock was John Bernard Hartley, son of the engineer of Liverpool docks, Jesse Hartley.

318: The Railway Dock, smaller than the previously constructed docks with an area of under 3 acres, was constructed at a cost of £106,000. The site upon which it was constructed was formerly called Dock Green.

319: The Railway Dock was constructed to facilitate the transfer of goods between the Hull and Selby Railway and merchant ships, and was opened for shipping on Friday

18 June 1846. Its official opening took place on 3 December 1846. In 1997 a blue heritage plaque was erected on the north elevation of the Hull Marina Office building at Warehouse 13 on Railway Street, on the side of the Marina, to mark the location of the city's old Railway Dock. The inscription reads:

> The dock behind you was opened in 1846 and was the first in the port to have direct railway access. RAILWAY DOCK. The dock closed to commercial shipping in 1968 and was reopened as a marina in 1983

320: Pablo Fanque (born William Derby)—immortalised by John Lennon in 'Being for the Benefit of Mr. Kite!' on The Beatles' *Sgt. Pepper's Lonely Hearts Club Band* LP—appeared for an eight-night run at the Queen's Theatre on Paragon Street, from 22 November 1847. Fanque returned to Hull with his Royal Circus on the evening of Friday 7 January 1848, taking his benefit at the theatre on 10 January, and closing on 15 January, before moving on to Sheffield.

321: Thomas Robinson Ferens, after whom the Ferens Art Gallery and one of the city's main thoroughfares (Ferensway) are named, was a politician, philanthropist, and industrialist. Born on 4 May 1847 in East Thickley, County Durham, Ferens took a position in 1868 as a clerk for James Reckitt of Reckitt & Sons, eventually becoming Chairman of the company. He gave to the city over £1m (equating to over £45m today), funding a dedicated art gallery (The Ferens) and helping to establish University College Hull.

322: On 10 September 1847 the internationally renowned 'Swedish Nightingale', Jenny Lind, appeared at the Queen's Theatre in Paragon Street. The rival Theatre Royal had announced Lind as a forthcoming attraction three months earlier, but manager and lessee Mr Egerton somehow persuaded her to perform at the Queen's Theatre before she played the Theatre Royal, which she did on 18 September 1848. Lind's final appearance in Hull came after she had been persuaded by the Bishop of Norwich in 1849 to retire from the operatic stage and sing only 'for the glory of God'. She performed at the Music Hall in Jarratt Street on 7 April 1856.

323: In 1847, in direct competition with the patent Theatre Royal in Humber Street, Mr Egerton, the lessee of the Queen's Theatre altered the time of commencement of productions at the theatre, with doors now opening at 'Half-past Six' and the curtain rising 'precisely at Seven o'Clock'. In a further move to attract the patrons of the Theatre Royal, Egerton offered 'Half-price at a Quarter before nine' admission.

324: In 1847, seven years after its foundation, the trading profit of Isaac Reckitt's starch business reached £1,000 for the first time. The following year (1848) the trading profit reached £1,700; and by 1850 the figure had reached £2,500.

325: In 1847 Isaac Reckitt learned that the factory of the starch works, along with land he was renting in Dansom Lane, was to be put up for sale. He could not afford to buy them at that time, but during the following year business had improved to such an extent that by August 1848, and with a full order book, he had bought the Works outright for £1,125.

326: In 1847 Hull's Corporation Pier was extended to connect to the mainland by way of a platform, forming a T-shaped pier.

327: Following the promising signs of success in relation to his Soluble Starch product, Isaac Reckitt borrowed the sum of £300 from his nephew Alfred in order to develop sales in that area. By 1847, due primarily to the industrious 'travelling' efforts of George Reckitt, the company was showing a marked increase in revenue, and George was made a partner in January 1848.

328: When George Reckitt entered into partnership with his father Isaac the firm became known as Isaac Reckitt & Son. Second son Francis began 'travelling' in the North of England, leaving George to concentrate on generating sales in the Midlands and the South of England.

329: Hull's Paragon Station—the construction of which was begun in 1847 to a design by the prolific railway buildings architect G.T. Andrews—was opened on 8 May 1848 'without any particular éclat'; and was extended in 1904. In 1986 a blue heritage plaque was erected on the station concourse to mark the year the station opened, and the designer of its 1904 enlargement. The inscription reads:

> Opened in 1848 and substantially enlarged to a design by William Bell in 1904, PARAGON STATION was the principal Hull passenger station of the North Eastern Railway which, with its dock, cartage, hotel and shipping interests, was a major local employer

330: In 1848 Hull's Citadel ceased to be used by the War Department for regular military purposes, and was subsequently transferred to 'that of the Woods and Forests' [Commissioners of Woods, Forests, Land Revenues, Works and Buildings?].

331: At the end of the 1847 season the Queen's Theatre closed for three months—a period in which substantial upgrading refurbishments were carried out—re-opening in March 1848. However, in August 1848, due to the 'severe indisposition of Mr Egerton', Charles Dillon stepped in as manager of the theatre. The following year, in March 1849, the theatre opened under the management of a new lessee, John Caple.

332: On 20 July 1849 John Bacchus Dykes was elected Minor Canon at Durham Cathedral, before being made Precentor there on 19 November the same year—a position he held until 1862 (though he retained the minor canonry). The University of Durham awarded him an honorary DMus. in 1861.

333: Henry Cooper MD (1807–1891) became Lecturer on Materia Medica at the Hull School of Medicine and, in 1849, was appointed Superintendent of the Sculcoates District during the Hull cholera epidemic of that year. He was Mayor of Hull in 1854–55.

334: Henry Cooper read a paper titled 'Address in Medicine' at the British Medical Association Meeting in Hull in 1848; and, in response to the Hull cholera epidemic of 1849, he authored the pamphlet 'Medical Topography and Vital Statistics of Hull' (1849). In 1874, following retirement, he was elected Consulting Physician to Hull Infirmary, and became Chairman of the Board of Management.

335: Isaac Reckitt's first home in Hull was in St. Quintin's Place, Drypool, but he later (1849) moved to Williamson Street (Holderness Road), where he and his wife Ann would remain for the rest of their lives.

336: In 1849 James Reckitt joined his father in the family business; helping out in the office, copying orders, making out invoices and delivery notes, and dispatching orders.

337: In 1849, during the ravaging cholera outbreak in Hull, Isaac Reckitt was prosecuted for keeping pigs in the town. His defence against the charge was based on the fact that his pigs were well kept and clean, and was supported by statements he obtained from his neighbours, resulting in him winning the case.

338: Hull's Royal Station Hotel, originally consisting of only three storeys, was designed by G.T. Andrews and was completed in 1849.

339: The *Illustrated London News* of 9 February 1850, reported that a fire had destroyed the London premises of George Myers, consuming timber yards, offices, saw mills, workshops and their contents, including valuable stone carvings of work in progress.

340: Upon completion Victoria Dock, formally opened on 3 July 1850, covered an area of almost 13 acres and could hold '120 square-rigged ships'; the entrance into the dock from the river Humber was 60ft (18m) wide; the entrance from the river Hull was 45ft (14m) wide, but this entrance was 'closed and remodelled' in 1964. The construction costs of the dock amounted to upwards of £300,000.

341: At least 30,000 people attended the opening ceremony for Hull's Victoria Dock in July 1850: all the principal shops in the town closed; bells were rung in churches; flags were displayed on houses and musical bands paraded through the streets. At 10.30am the mayor and dignitaries from the Corporation, Trinity House, the Hull Dock Company and others, accompanied by the band of the 46th regiment, travelled in procession from the Dock Office to the ceremony.

342: At the opening ceremony for Victoria Dock, the gates of the basin were opened just after 11am to let water in, then Mr T. Firbank (Chairman of the Hull Dock Company) declared the dock open and its name to be Victoria Dock, in honour of Queen Victoria. The vicar of Holy Trinity then blessed the dock before the official opening of the dock was signalled by the firing of a salute from a battery in the Citadel. The mayor (T.W. Palmer) then congratulated the Dock Company on the completion and opening of the dock.

343: Covering a greater area than its rival the Theatre Royal, the Queen's Theatre was over 200 feet long on its Paragon Street frontage and 70 feet long on its South Street frontage. The stage was 90 feet long and ran the full width of the building. Reports record the capacity of the theatre as 'calculated to accommodate 3,000 people'.

344: Lessees of the Queen's Theatre included John Caple (1849) William Batty (1849), Messrs. Ringold and Munro (1850), Bastien Franconi (1852), and former manager of the Theatre Royal in Humber Street, Henry Beverley (also 1852). Early in 1853 the theatre was being advertised as the Royal Queen's Circus (still under Henry Beverley); and in December 1853, as the Monster American Circus, sole proprietor, Mr J. Macarte, late Queen's Theatre.

345: On 25 July 1850, at St. Michael's Church, Malton, John Bacchus Dykes married Susannah Thomlinson Kingston, the daughter of George Kingston. They had eight children.

346: In 1850 Thomas Wilson's son, David, became a partner in his father's shipping firm; with second son John subsequently becoming the firms agent in Gothenburg, and two of Wilson's other sons, Charles and Arthur becoming partners and joint managers of the firm in 1867. It was Charles and Arthur who built up the family business into a global concern, inaugurating routes to America and India.

347: By the mid 1850s Isaac Reckitt & Sons were offering over 20 product lines, though starch remained the company's key product.

348: After the dissolution of the Messrs. Myers & Wilson partnership in 1844, Richard Wilson struggled working in business alone, and by 17 May 1850 was bankrupt.

349: After working initially on British ships—as did his two older brothers—Jack Deighton worked on several American ships before joining the clipper Invincible in New York for a trip to San Francisco.

350: After landing in San Francisco, Jack Deighton, attracted by the Gold Rush, left Invincible and headed for California, in search of gold, but with little success; he then decided to try his luck with the Fraser River Gold Rush in 1858, but sadly he fared no better there.

351: In September 1851, 'to celebrate his marriage', William Jackson opened his first small grocery shop, in Scale Lane, Hull. Today, the William Jackson Food Group includes 'a portfolio of five food businesses and a pub in different but complimentary market areas'. The food businesses are: Aunt Bessie's, Jacksons, MyFresh, Abel & Cole, and The Food Doctor; the pub is the Ferguson Fawsitt Arms (Walkington).

352: Hull's Station Hotel was officially opened on 6 November 1851. It was renamed the Royal Station Hotel following a visit by Queen Victoria and her Royal party on 13 October 1853. The first floor of the hotel was given over as apartments to the Queen and her suite, with the Royal household occupying the second floor. An apartment at the south-east corner of the hotel was converted into a throne room, with three chairs: one each for Victoria, Prince Albert and the Prince of Wales.

353: George Myers and Augustus Pugin became both real friends and successful collaborators, with Myers completing approximately forty major contracts for Pugin, culminating with the Medieval Court at the Great Exhibition of 1851.

354: The established ferry service between Hull and Barton-upon-Humber faced stiff competition when a rival service was started between Hull and New Holland in 1826. Unable to continue, the Hull to Barton ferry closed in 1851.

355: The National Census of 1851 reported the population of the subdivision borough of Hull as 84,690.

356: In January 1852 Isaac Reckitt & Son first bought some ultramarine; the company's first sales of its *Laundry Blue* (which the ultramarine was used to manufacture) were made the following month.

357: In April 1852 Isaac Reckitt & Son's first sales of *Black Lead* were made. Initially, the *Black Lead* product was bought-in from De Beers (London), but in 1855 machinery was installed in the Reckitt Works to enable the company to manufacture it themselves. The initiative was a great success, and *Black Lead* outgrew the company's *Blue* product.

358: On 31 May 1852 George Myers entered into an agreement with David Burton, jnr. and Hull surveyor George Wilkinson for rebuilding St.Michael's Church, Cherry Burton. The architect was Jonathan Forman.

359: In November 1852 Cuthbert Brodrick was appointed architect for the Hull Royal Institution, the foundation stone of which was laid by the Earl of Carlisle and Lord Londesborough on 17 May 1853, the year Brodrick won an open competition to design Leeds Town Hall. He later went on to win the competition to design Hull Town Hall (1861); and also designed the Grand Hotel, Scarborough.

360: By 1852, having entered into partnership with his two eldest sons David and Joseph as 'Myers & Sons', George Myers owned brickyards in Ealing and quarries in Somerset, as well as his premises at Ordnance Wharf; and, in that year, he moved to a more spacious house, at 143 Clapham Road, Lambeth.

361: Augustus Pugin favoured working with George Myers because of Myers's ability and willingness to work 'without true architectural drawings'.

362: Hull-born George Myers was the favourite builder of the Rothschilds and, between 1852–54, he built Mentmore Towers, Buckinghamshire, for Baron Mayer de Rothschild.

363: In 1852 Francis Reckitt joined his father and his brother George, becoming a partner in the family business and the name of the company was appropriately changed from Isaac Reckitt & Son to Isaac Reckitt & Sons.

364: After the death of Augustus Pugin in September 1852 George Myers carved the full length effigy (designed by Pugin's son E.W. Pugin) on his tomb in St. Augustine's Church, Ramsgate.

365: On 1 June 1853 the York and North Midland Railway opened its Victoria Dock Branch Line to passengers, thereby connecting Victoria Dock with the rail network. It was closed to passengers on 1 June 1864.

366: By the end of 1853 John Caple, formerly manager and lessee of the Queen's Theatre in Paragon Street, had become the lessee of rival establishment the Theatre Royal in Humber Street.

367: Joseph Rank was born at Holderness Road, Hull on 28 March 1854, the oldest surviving son of miller James Rank and his wife Mary (*née* Parrott). Following the death of his father in 1874, Joseph set up his own business in 1875; and married Emily Voase on 15 June 1880. He built the engine-driven Alexandra Mill, incorporating the latest roller-milling technology, in 1885; followed by the Clarence Mills, before incorporating as a private limited company (Joseph Rank Ltd.) on 12 May 1899. Besides the Clarence Mills (which had expanded to produce 100 sacks of flour per hour by 1904) Rank built a mill and silo at the Victoria and Albert docks to service the London area. In 1994 a blue heritage plaque was erected at the former windmill on Holderness Road, Hull, to mark Joseph Rank's birthplace. The inscription reads:

> In a cottage near this his grandfathers [sic] mill was born JOSEPH RANK 1854–1943 founder of the milling firm of Joseph Rank Ltd

368: In September 1854 Joseph Wolfenden and Robert Melbourne became joint lessees of the Queen's Theatre, beginning what would become a much celebrated period in the history of the establishment. The division of labour between the pair saw Wolfenden taking on the responsibilities of General Manager whilst Melbourne assumed the role of Stage Manager. This successful partnership lasted until Wolfenden's early death in 1861, at the age of 34, after being thrown from his horse.

369: On Saturday 14 October 1854, during a royal visit, the Mayor of Hull, Henry Cooper, was knighted by Queen Victoria (to the delight of the gathered crowd) in a seemingly impromptu ceremony on the Corporation Pier.

370: On the 20 November 1854, Joseph Wolfenden and Robert Melbourne were presented with a purse of gold, subscribed for 'by a number of gentlemen' as 'a mark of respect'; and at the final performance of the Christmas pantomime (8 February 1856) H.E. Dearsley Esq. presented each of them with a silver tea service, subscribed 'by their tradesmen' in appreciation of their 'liberal and spirited management' of the theatre.

371: Between 1854–55, T.J. Smith studied at University College, London, where in June 1855 he passed the initial Pharmaceutical Society of Great Britain examination. The society, founded in April 1841, was then a recently established institution.

372: T.J. Smith studied at University College, London at the same time as the Quaker Joseph Lister, later Lord Lister and one of the pioneers of antiseptic surgery.

373: James Alderson was Treasurer of the Royal College of Physicians from 1854–67, and took great interest in its administration. He was especially proud of having unearthed the original charter granted by Henry VIII, which had long been lost.

374: Between 1854–59 Hull-born George Myers built the first military barracks at Aldershot.

375: Hull-born mathematician John Venn once built a machine for bowling cricket balls, which on one occasion was used against the Australian cricket team when they were visiting Cambridge.

376: The first daily newspaper to appear in Hull was the *Hull Morning Telegraph*, which started in 1855.

377: Hull's Junction Dock was officially renamed Prince's Dock on Wednesday 7 March 1855 in honour of the previous year's visit to Hull by Queen Victoria and Prince Albert. In 1986 a blue heritage plaque was erected on the end of the warehouse at the southern end of Princes Dock Street to mark the location of the dock. The inscription reads:

> Rapidly expanding trade necessitated the construction of Junction Dock, completed in 1829 and renamed PRINCES DOCK in 1854, to link Queen's Dock and Humber Dock. The designer and engineer was James Walker

378: Hull's first enclosed dock was officially renamed Queen's Dock on Wednesday 7 March 1855 in honour of Queen Victoria's visit to Hull in 1854, during which the Royal party made a tour of the docks aboard the Royal steam-yacht Fairy.

379: On 12 May 1855 William Alfred Gelder was born at North Cave, East Riding of Yorkshire (17 miles west of Hull). He went to school in Elloughton, but at fifteen was apprenticed to his father—also William: a joiner, builder and, later, a timber merchant—before studying under Hull architect Robert Clamp. Clamp and Gelder are jointly credited (Pevsner) as the architects of 67 Whitefriargate, built for the Colonial & United States Mortgage Company in 1886.

380: Having bought the old Custom House at 36 High Street in 1855, Hull Corporation built a new Corn Exchange on the site. The new building was inaugurated with a 'great public dinner' on Tuesday 8 January 1856, and was opened for business on Tuesday 15 January 1856. In 1986 a blue heritage plaque was erected to mark the significance of the building. The inscription reads:

> On the site of the Old Custom House, this building opened as a CORN EXCHANGE in 1856, architects, Bellamy & Hardy of Lincoln. It reopened as the Museum of Commerce and Transport in 1925

381: T.J. Smith was formally elected a member of the Pharmaceutical Society of Great Britain on 6 February 1856.

382: In the summer of 1856 T.J. Smith moved to Hull, where in August of that year he bought a retail chemist shop at 71 Whitefriargate. This was the foundation of the global pharmaceutical and medical equipment company, Smith & Nephew PLC. In 1997 a blue heritage plaque was erected at 10 North Church Side to mark the location of the first production site of T.J. Smith and Nephew before moving to their Neptune Street base on Hessle Road. The inscription reads:

> In a building on this site, SMITH & NEPHEW (founded in 1856 & now a leading world-wide

healthcare company) produced medical supplies from
1861 to 1907, after which they moved to Hessle Road

383: In 1857 Isaac Reckitt & Sons diversified into
manufacturing biscuits, with around 50 varieties being
produced. However, following a fire in the biscuit factory
in September 1866, the company decided to pull out of
manufacturing biscuits and sold the goodwill in that
business to the recently established (1857) Peek, Frean &
Co. Ltd.

384: Emily Maria McVitie (Madame Clapham) was born
in Cheltenham on 22 December 1857. She married Haigh
Clapham on 6 April 1886 at All Saints Church,
Scarborough. The couple established a dressmaking salon
at 1 Kingston Square, Hull in 1887. Shortly thereafter she
reinvented herself as 'Madame Clapham' and built up a
clientele from the higher social classes of Hull and East
Yorkshire, before attracting the attention of the nobility
and royalty—her most famous client being King Edward
VII's daughter Queen Maude of Norway.

385: In January 1858 William Warden, a plumber from
Hessle—challenging the professional opinions and advice
of three civil engineers—predicted that he could procure
for Hull's Waterworks Committee, 5 million gallons of
pure water a day from Spring Head; and in March 1860
the Derringham Springs Committee was appointed to
oversee his works. The initial two artesian bores sunk at
the Julian Well were calculated to raise an estimated 1.4
million gallons a day without pumping; but subsequent
pumping tests indicated that figure could be increased to
4.5 million gallons a day. Warden's predictions were
proved to be correct, and he had identified an abundant
and valuable source of fresh water for the town.

386: The first steam ship ever to sail for the northern
fishing grounds was the whaler Diana, which was owned

by Messrs. William Brown, Atkinson, and Co., and sailed from Hull on 1 February 1857.

387: By December 1858, at the age of 66, Isaac Reckitt had finally paid off all the original family loans that had enabled him to set up his starch business in 1840.

388: William Boyes (the founder of W. Boyes & Co. Ltd.) was born in Scarborough on 4 April 1859. His father was a joiner, and later provided donkey rides for visiting holiday makers during the summer on the resort's south beach.

389: Having been put up for auction by its proprietor, the daughter of John Wilkinson, in May 1859 and failing to attract a bidder, the Theatre Royal on Humber Street, under the management of John Pritchard, was consumed by fire on 13 October that year. The fire had been discovered raging at 7.00am on the Thursday morning; the theatre's roof had collapsed by 8.00am; and by midday only the outer walls remained standing. The cause of the fire was never discovered.

390: On 24 November 1859, at the suggestion of the Rev. G.O. Browne, a curate of the parish, a public meeting, chaired by the Mayor of Hull, Zachariah Pearson, took place at the Mansion House to consider the restoration of Holy Trinity Church, which despite some crucial restorations in the 1830s and 1840s (with nave restoration work, led by Henry Francis Lockwood, being completed in 1846) had fallen into a 'sad condition' of dilapidation.

391: Up to two years before Zachariah Pearson gifted land off Beverley Road for a People's Park, attempts were made to acquire the old Citadel for the purposes of creating a park or public recreation ground for the people of Hull.

392: In 1859 and 1860 Charles Dickens appeared at Hull's New Theatre, to give readings from his works. A blue commemorative plaque was erected on the side of the building in 1990. The inscription reads:

> In this building in 1859 and 1860 the novelist CHARLES DICKENS (1812–1870) gave selected readings from many of his works

(The theatre is said to be haunted by a ghost called Charlie.)

393: In January 1860, with the creation of a People's Park to the forefront of his mind, the then Mayor of Hull Zacharia Charles Pearson bought approximately 37 acres of land adjacent to Beverley Road for £7,400. Having reserved about 10 acres around the northern, eastern and southern boundaries, he gave the central 27 acres of the plot to the Hull Board of Health, on condition that they agree to lay it out as a public park and maintain it. Pearson paid an additional £300 for a road through the field in front of the plot. On Monday 27 August 1860, following a grand procession from the Mansion House, Zacharia Pearson officially signed over the park to the town, formally presenting it to Alderman Moss.

394: When Zacharia Pearson offered to the Hull Board of Health the land that would become Pearson Park, one of the seven conditions stipulated and to be inserted in the Deed of Grant was: 'That musicians shall not be allowed to play in the Park, nor shall refreshment stalls or public games be allowed therein upon a Sunday'.

395: The layout of Pearson Park was designed by the then curator of Hull's Botanic Gardens, James Craig Niven.

396: Zacharia Pearson planted the first tree in Hull's Pearson Park, at the inauguration ceremony. The tree, a Wellington Gigantea (*Sequoiadendron giganteum*) found naturally only in California, had been presented by Captain Wharton. The following afternoon Pearson's eldest son and daughter each planted a tree. The three trees were planted 'in a line east and west, nearly in the centre of the park'. All three trees have since died.

397: In 1860 eminent architect George Gilbert Scott was appointed to supervise the restoration (in the Gothic style) of Holy Trinity Church, including the restoration of the west front of the church, the north side of the nave, and the foundation walls. By 1864 restoration funds had been exhausted and work suspended, with approximately £7,000 more needed to complete the work.

398: The main contractors for the 1860s restorations to the fabric of Holy Trinity Church, carried out under the supervision of George Gilbert Scott, were Hull stonemasons Messrs. Simpson & Malone (Osborne Street); with William Sissons as the Clerk of Works, and carvings by Hull stonemason Thomas Frith.

399: The West Dock Company, a rival to the Hull Dock Company, was formed in 1860 to promote and build new docks to meet the increasing demands of trade and the increasing size of steam ships. The West Dock Company was supported by the Hull Corporation, Trinity House, the North Eastern Railway (NER), and various Hull worthies. The proposed site for the new docks was on the Humber foreshore to the west of the river Hull.

400: In 1860, having changed the focus of his business from retail to wholesale pharmaceuticals, T.J. Smith bought larger premises at 10–11 North Church Street and converted them into a warehouse. The following year, he rented further premises at 10 North Churchside (in 1880 he would purchase the freehold of 10 North Churchside, with the help of a £500 loan from his father).

401: Recognizing the demand for cod-liver oil in the treatment of rickets and consumption, T.J. Smith set about developing a process that would improve both the oil's appearance and its taste. His method was to blend several oils, and then expose the final mix to the sun by placing bottles of the product on a roof where the sun would bleach the oil and at the same time remove some of the strong and unpalatable fishy taste.

402: From around Christmas 1860 to the middle of January 1861 the amount of ice in the Humber was said to be almost unprecedented with navigation of the river being 'rendered very difficult'.

403: In the mid 1860s Thomas Clayton, the Works Manager at Isaac Reckitt & Sons, initiated what would become the company's genuine long-term interest in the social welfare of its employees, including the provision of educational classes, during working hours, for its 'girl workers'.

404: In the 1860s Limekiln Creek (thought to have been the original outlet of the river Hull into the Humber before it was diverted to follow the line of Sayer Creek) was stopped up during the course of the construction of Hull's Western Dock.

405: In 1860, at the age of 13, having been educated at the Belvedere Academy in Bishop Auckland, Thomas Ferens started his first job, at Shildon—as a clerk for the Stockton and Darlington Railway. From when he first started work until the time of his death, Ferens put aside and donated 10% of his income to charitable causes.

406: Construction of the Springhead Pumping Station began in 1861 to designs by Hull Corporation's Surveyor and Resident Engineer, Thomas Dale. The pumping station was officially inaugurated on 14 July 1862, with the works finally being completed in 1864. Until the 1870s, water was pumped from Springhead through pipes to the Stoneferry waterworks, before being distributed around Hull.

407: George Myers completed many contracts for the British government, including work at Windsor Castle, the restoration of the Tower of London and the Guildhall in the City, as well as extending the Royal Military Academy at Woolwich; he also built hospitals and asylums, such as Herbert Hospital (Woolwich), and Broadmoor; and he enlarged and modernised the Bethlem Hospital (Bedlam).

408: In June 1861, in rented premises at 21½ Bishop Lane, Hull, a 25 year-old journeyman currier named Joseph Henry Fenner founded the leather belt and leather currying business that would become the Fenner Group, a worldwide industrial belting manufacturer. The earliest surviving record of an official order, from 1868, is for 50 feet of leather hose at 2 shillings and sixpence a foot.

409: On Wednesday 6 November 1861, at a public meeting in the Music Hall, Jarratt Street, John Ellerthorpe was presented with a white silk purse containing 100 guineas (the proceeds of a subscription from 'a committee of philanthropic gentlemen', along with £20 from the Royal bounty, upon the recommendation of the Prime Minister Viscount Palmerston). The purse also contained a 'gold watch and guard' in recognition of Ellerthorpe having 'saved Twenty-nine Persons from Drowning'. For his humane and heroic acts Ellerthorpe was additionally presented with an especial vote of thanks 'inscribed on Vellum' (from the Royal Humane Society) and a specially struck silver medal from the Board of Trade.

410: Following the untimely death of Joseph Wolfenden in 1861, his widow, Henrietta, and former partner, Robert Melbourne, became business associates, retaining the joint lease on the Queen's Theatre for a further 5 years.

However, increasing financial difficulties eventually took their toll in February 1867 when Melbourne was forced to cease trading. Melbourne's erstwhile rivals at the Theatre Royal in Humber Street came to his assistance by staging two benefit performances for him.

411: In 1861 an Act of Parliament was passed sanctioning a proposal by the Hull Dock Company to build a dock at the same position as had been proposed by the West Dock Company. The new dock was known as the 'Western Dock'.

412: Provision was also made in the Act of Parliament of 1861 for the construction of temporary replacement facilities (Railway Creek) for the railway companies then using Limekiln Creek. Railway Creek (created to the east of Limekiln Creek) was built during the construction work for the new 'Western Dock'. Limekiln Creek was kept in use while the new facilities were under construction.

413: The National Census of 1861 reported the population of the subdivision borough of Hull as 97,661.

414: John Reeves Ellerman was born at 100 Anlaby Road, Hull on 15 May 1862. His father (Jonas Hermann Ellerman), having moved to Hull from Hamburg in his late thirties, became a prominent local ship broker and corn merchant, and was a key figure in the establishment of the Lutheran Church in Hull. Jonas Ellerman died in 1871 when John was nine years old.

415: The construction of the 'Western Dock' began in October 1862, with the foundation stone of the north dock wall being laid by William Wright (Chairman of the Dock Company) in May 1864.

416: Isaac Reckitt & Sons' first London office was taken in 1862 at 40 King William Street; then, following a temporary move to Great Tower Street, the office was relocated to 150 Queen Victoria Street in 1878.

417: From 1862 onwards concerts and an exhibition of waxworks were presented in the saloon of the Mechanics' Institute (the Mechanics' Music Hall) in George Street, with various other music hall and variety entertainments being presented at the venue up to 1890.

418: Following the death of Isaac Reckitt, at the age of 70, on 7 March 1862, the business was bequeathed equally to his sons George, Francis and James. However, in March 1864, by mutual consent, George Reckitt left the firm, taking his £16,000 one-third share of the company and leaving Francis and James to continue the business together. (George returned to the business in 1870 to manage the London office).

419: In 1862 John Bacchus Dykes was appointed vicar of St. Oswald's in Durham; that same year he contributed twenty-eight of the 300 tunes in the second edition of Richard R. Chope's *Congregational Hymn and Tune Book*.

420: John Bacchus Dykes wrote thirty-nine tunes especially for *Hymns Ancient and Modern* and eventually contributed a total of fifty-five, including 'Eternal Father, strong to save' (also known as 'For Those in Peril on the Sea'), 'Nearer, my God , to Thee', and 'Holy, Holy, Holy'.

421: With no success in either the San Francisco or Fraser River gold rushes, and after a brief spell as a Fraser River Pilot, Jack Deighton made a third assault on finding his fortune by trying his luck in the Cariboo Gold Rush of 1862.

422: In 1862 Gleadow, Dibb & Co., which would later become the Hull Brewery Company Limited, built the Malt House, situated near Hengler's Circus on Anlaby Road; and in 1868 the company moved to the purpose-built Anchor Brewery in Sylvester Street. Both premises were designed for the company by William Sissons.

423: In 1863 the turnover of Isaac Reckitt and Sons had reached £40,000, with a trading profit of £4,298. In 1878 the company's trading profit reached £20,000.

424: The Queen's Theatre was capable of being used as an amphitheatre at any time, by removing a section of flooring from the pit in the 42 feet diameter circle.

425: In 1863 the Queen's Theatre was redecorated in an Arabesque style by the theatre's scenic artist, Charles Fox. The theatre had previously been extensively redecorated in 1849.

426: Charles Fox's Act Drop, first introduced at the Queen's Theatre on 28 September 1863, was a rustic scene with a rich broken tessellated foreground depicting figures and goats; a villa fountain with classically dressed figures; a group of bathers in the middle distance, surrounded by rich foliage; and an imposing mass of ruins; all superimposed over the backdrop of a distant bay 'bordered by lofty mountains'.

427: The sculptures of Queen Victoria and Prince Albert in Hull's Pearson Park were produced by Thomas Earle, and were placed in their current positions in 1863 and 1868 respectively. Earle also created a statue of Edward I—the monarch who granted Hull its first charter in April 1299—which was unveiled at the opening of the new Town Hall in January 1866.

428: The former old Corporation Pier, or Jetty (also known as Brownlow's Jetty), situated between Limekiln Creek and the west pier of the Humber dock, was demolished in the 1860s in order to facilitate the expansion of the Humber Dock Basin during the construction of the Western Dock (later named the Albert Dock).

429: In 1863 Hull's Victoria Dock was extended eastwards by about 8 acres.

430: On 29 February 1864 the Alhambra Palace music hall was opened on Porter Street by Mr Charles A. Eyre. The building had formerly been a Dissenting Chapel (later known as St. Luke's Church) and was bought by Eyre following the closure of St. Luke's. Eyre then bought the land immediately to the rear and either side and converted the chapel into what Sheahan describes as an 'elegant place of entertainment'.

431: Between April and July 1864, as part of a scheme to improve the drainage of the River Hull Valley, 16,000 tons of material were removed from the Old Harbour, to assist the flow of the Beverley and Barmston Drain. As a consequence of this scouring, the foundations of adjacent warehouses and mills were compromised and the Beverley and Barmston Drainage Commissioners had to line the affected section of the river bed with three feet of chalk.

432: Frederick Needler, the founder of Needlers Ltd., was born on 12 December 1864 at Arnold near Skirlaugh, about 9 miles north-east of Hull. In 1886, using £100 from his mother, he bought the ailing manufacturing confectionery firm of Edward Buckton (located at the corner of Midland Street and Osborne Street) where he had been employed as a book-keeper, and subsequently moved the firm to premises in Anne Street.

433: The front of the balcony in the auditorium of the Alhambra Palace music hall was formed by metal railings featuring terracotta figures, with further ornamentation on the walls in the form of classical scenes depicted in stucco tablets and medallions. In the ceiling coving were perforated ventilators; and a gas sunlight formed the centrepiece of the ceiling. The capacity of the auditorium was 4,000.

434: The total cost of purchasing the chapel and adjoining land, and the conversion, enlargement and refurbishment of the Alhambra Palace music hall, was somewhere in the region of £8,000. The building was designed by architects Bellamy and Hardy of Lincoln, and the building work was supervised by Mr Langhorn Wardrobe.

435: Sheahan records that the mayor's Gold Chain of Office, presented by Sir William Knowles, Knt., Alderman, in 1564, was 'now [1864] a very fine decoration. A large boss with a blue stone was added to it by Mr Alderman Bannister, on the occasion of his being a second time elected to the office of Mayor, in November, 1855; and the chain was altered, and a handsome centre shield with two shoulder bosses added to it, by, and at the expense of Mr Alderman Moss, at the close of his mayoralty, 1857'.

436: In 1864 Sheahan recorded that there were two Swords of State among the corporate paraphernalia. The oldest, a personal sword of King Henry VIII, presented to the Mayor elect, Sir John Elland 'in honour of the Corporation at large' by the monarch during his visit to Hull in August 1541. The second sword '(that which is now used) appears to be a real sword of state'. Its scabbard is inscribed '1613, J.L., Mayor' in honour of John Lister (who was Mayor of Hull in 1595 and 1612; and, along with John Graves, was elected as a Member of Parliament for Kingston upon Hull in 1601).

437: Hull's Holy Trinity Church is 279 feet long from east to west. The choir is 100 feet long with a breadth of 70 feet; the transept: 96 feet by 28; the nave: 144 feet by 72. The central tower rises to a height of 150 feet. The church covers an area of approximately 25,640 square feet.

438: Rice starch manufacturing plant was installed at Isaac Reckitt & Sons' Kingston Works in 1864, at a cost of £2,600, to supplement wheat flour starch manufacturing.

439: In 1864 the construction works of the 'Western Dock' required the resiting of the goods line and sidings of the North Eastern Railway's Hull and Selby Line.

440: The western side of Hull's Victoria Dock was bounded by the Hull Citadel, which was sold to the Dock company and demolished (with the exception of a stone sentry box) in 1864.

441: James Alderson was the Royal College of Physicians' representative at the General Council of Medical Education and Registration from 1864–66; and he was President of the Royal College of Physicians from 1867–70.

442: In the mid 1860s Reckitt and Sons Ltd. employed a 'pig keeper', who kept more than 160 pigs, fed on starch manufacturing by-products. Pork produced from these animals was made available to employees at affordable reduced rates on Fridays.

443: Hull FC was founded towards the end of 1865 by a group of public-school Old Boys from York, including Anthony Bradley (a former pupil of Rugby School) and five sons of the Reverend John Scott, the priest of St. Mary's Church, Lowgate. Reverend Scott allowed the group to hold regular meetings at the Young Men's Fellowship at St. Mary's. One of the sons, F.A. Scott, was appointed club captain in 1870.

444: Following the destruction by fire in 1859 of the second Theatre Royal (on Humber Street) the site remained derelict until it was bought from the Wilkinson family by the newly formed Hull Theatre and Concert Company. On 19 April 1865 the foundation stone was laid (by Lord Londesborough) for a new Theatre Royal on the same site. Unfortunately this new theatre, which opened on 26 December 1865, was also destroyed by fire—on 6 February 1869. Subsequently, another Theatre Royal was built on Anlaby Road to replace the aforementioned establishment.

445: By 1865 Jack Deighton had married a native Indian and was running the Globe Saloon in New Westminster (Vancouver Island) and piloting a Fraser River paddle steamer.

446: Robert Applegarth became a member of the International Working Men's Association in 1865 shortly after its foundation, and in 1868 was elected Chairman of its General Council. He played a major role in helping to establish the legal status of trade unions, being the first trade unionist to present evidence to the Royal Commission established to look into the matter.

447: While there are strong links (and the holding of a succession of official positions) between Hull and the family of Thomas Walton, Sheriff of Hull in 1783, Walton *Street* was built in the mid 1860s by councillor James Beeton as part of a development of 23 acres of the former Wold Carr in which he named Walton Street, Paisley Street, Longden Street and Pulman Street after the surnames of his female relatives.

448: In 1866 the whaler Diana—which, as mentioned previously, was the first steam ship to sail from Hull to the northern fishing grounds—was also the last whaler to set out on an expedition from Hull—but she became ice-bound and eventually lost thirteen of her crew, including the 64-year-old skipper John Gravill.

449: Following the financial crisis of 1866 (and the collapse of the 'bankers bank' Overend, Gurney & Co.) Joseph Fenner was made bankrupt twice; first in 1867, and again in 1869; but in both instances very quick discharges were granted.

450: Hull FC's first ever match was away at Lincoln during the 1866–67 season. At that time, home games were played at Woodgates Hall (North Ferriby).

451: The 1861 Act sanctioning the construction of what would become Albert Dock (the 'Western Dock') allowed for a dock 2,500 feet long, but an additional Act (1866) increased that length to 3,350 feet.

452: Upon its completion the Western Dock included a connection to the NER network, and had sidings of up to four lines of rails around the dock, with the dock's sidings connecting to the NER system west of the dock.

453: The total construction cost of the Western Dock was £559,479: £113,592 for the work on the excavations, £118,680 for the dock walls, and £88,655 for the lock—excluding the lock gates and their associated machinery.

454: Machinery on the Western Dock (including capstans and the lock gates) was worked by hydraulic power. The dock had its own power supply—to power the hydraulic system, and to pump mains water around the dock. The whole of the hydraulic machinery was supplied by W.G. Armstrong & Co.(Newcastle-on-Tyne).

455: The engineers experienced a number of difficulties (during 1866 and 1867) whilst constructing the Western Dock, including dock walls being breached by the Humber, and 'boils' developing in the lockpit. Consequently the length of the lock, which was originally planned to be 400 feet, was reduced to 320 feet. The width was 80 feet.

456: The resident engineer on the construction of the Western Dock was J. Clarke Hawkshaw, with Sir John Hawkshaw as consulting engineer.

457: In 1866 the 19 year-old Thomas Ferens left home and took up a position as a clerk at Head, Wrightson & Co. in Stockton; and in April 1868 he moved to Hull to take up the post of confidential shorthand clerk to James Reckitt at the family-run business of Reckitt & Sons. By this time Isaac Reckitt had died and his three sons George, Frances & James were running the firm as partners.

458: An additional Act of 1867—obtained while the Western Dock was under construction—granted the Dock Company permission to further expand the dock to the west and south, and sanctioned the purchase of 75 acres of foreshore.

459: In 1867 the saloon built in the grounds to the rear of the Mechanics' Institute at 2 George Street was converted into a theatre and music hall, and was renamed the Mechanics' Music Hall. The newly converted venue was capable of accommodating approximately 1,500 people.

460: The saloon in the grounds of the Mechanics' Institute went through a number of name changes in its first fifty or so years, being variously known as the Mechanics' Music Hall (1867), Ringham's Music Hall (1868), Canterbury Music Hall (1868), the Alexandra Theatre (1869), the Star Music Hall (1878), and the New Mechanics' Theatre (1885).

461: At his Globe saloon, Jack Deighton gained a reputation for relating many adventurous tales to anyone who would listen (or slake their thirst with his whisky), thus acquiring the nickname 'Gassy Jack'.

462: In 1867, returning home after an extended trip away due to health reasons; and having left his saloon, whisky and cash in the care of an American friend, Jack Deighton discovered that his saloon business was bankrupt; he subsequently left New Westminster in a canoe with his wife and her mother, and moved to the Burrard Inlet, near the mouth of the Fraser. Here he set up *another* saloon named the Globe, around which a settlement soon grew up.

463: Proposals for the building of a bridge crossing the Humber at Hull were first made as early as 1867.

464: In June 1868 the Queen's Theatre was relaunched under the name of the Queen's Theatre and Palace of Varieties. Coming after its steady decline, and now competing with the more sumptuous Royal Alhambra Palace of Varieties in Porter Street, it was perhaps inevitable that the Queen's Theatre was doomed. The last performances at the theatre (Pablo Fanque's Monstre Circus Company) took place in April 1869; the building was demolished in 1871, to be replaced by the Imperial hotel, and (where the stage had stood) the city's third Theatre Royal.

465: Hull's second Theatre Royal—on Anlaby Road—opened in November 1869 under the management of a certain Mr White. However, work on the interior was still continuing after the theatre opened for dramatic productions, with the theatre lighting still to be completed; although a hot-air heating system of pipes had been installed.

466: By 1868 Isaac Reckitt & Sons employed between two and three hundred people, an indication of the rate the company had grown from 1840, when it had around 25 employees.

467: Hull's Western Dock was officially opened on 22 July 1869 by Albert Edward, the Prince of Wales (later King Edward VII) and was named Albert Dock in his honour.

468: When it was first opened the Albert Dock was

utilized by Hull's fishing industry, until the construction of St. Andrew's Dock.

469: Upon its completion, Hull's Albert Dock covered an area of almost 23 acres; its entrance lock, at 80ft wide and 320ft long, was one of the largest in the country.

470: 118,000 tons of chalk were used in the construction of Albert Dock, along with 34,396 cubic feet of granite and 66,400 cubic yards of concrete.

471: Thomas Wilson was Chairman of the Hull Seamen's Orphanage in 1866; and became the first Chairman of the Hull Underwriters' Association (founded in 1867). He died on 21 June 1869 at his home, Park House, Cottingham, and was buried in Hull General Cemetery on Spring Bank.

472: The art dealer Joseph Joel (Baron) Duveen was born in Hull on 14 October 1869, the eldest son of Sir Joseph Joel Duveen (d. 1908) and his wife Rosetta (*née* Barnett). Following a private education, the young Joseph entered his father's art dealer business, which became one of the most significant in the British art trade.

473: Mary Charlotte Murdoch, born in Elgin on 26 September 1864, was the first woman to practice medicine in Hull, setting up her private practice here in 1869.

474: Hull-born physician James Alderson (fourth son of Dr John Alderson) was knighted on 11 November 1869; and was appointed Physician-Extraordinary to Queen Victoria in 1874.

475: John Ellerthorpe, the 'Hero of the Humber', died on 15 July 1868, and was buried at Hull General Cemetery, Spring Bank West, not far from the final resting place of John Gravill, skipper of the whaler Diana.

476: The Hull and East Riding School of Medicine and Anatomy, founded by John Alderson, closed in 1869, but the entrance to the old building is preserved as part of the frontage of Kingston House, an apartment block on the west side of Kingston Square (opposite the entrance to Hull New Theatre). In 2004 a blue heritage plaque was erected to mark the site. The inscription reads:

> This Greek revival facade of 1833, designed by Henry R. Abraham (c.1803–77), once formed part of the HULL & EAST RIDING SCHOOL OF MEDICINE & ANATOMY. The school was founded in 1831 & closed in 1869. Restored by Beal Homes in 2003

477: In 1870 Hull FC moved to a ground near the Londesborough Arms public house, Market Place, Selby. This move was aimed at facilitating easier travel to matches for visiting teams.

478: Charles Wilson became Sheriff of Hull in 1870, and represented Hull as a Liberal MP in 1874; representing West Hull from 1885, he continued as an MP until 1905.

479: Thomas Ferens was a lifelong teetotaller, and an energetic and enthusiastic advocate of Methodism, with much of his free time taken up attending chapel, Band of Hope meetings, and teaching in Sunday School.

480: Before she died, Jack Deighton's native American wife arranged for him to marry her 12-year-old niece, Madeline.

481: Following a meeting of 21 primarily London-based rugby clubs, at Regent Street's Pall Mall Restaurant on 26 January 1871, the Rugby Football Union was founded. Hull FC joined the Union in 1872, at which time their home ground was located at the Londesborough Street Rifle Barracks.

482: After fierce opposition from his union's executive to his acceptance of membership of the Royal Commission on contagious diseases, Robert Applegarth resigned his union position in April 1871, bringing his trade union career to an end at the early age of 36.

483: John Ellerman had two sisters (Ida and Emily), but he was an only son. His mother, Anne, was born into the prominent Reeves family, her father Timothy Reeves being a well known local solicitor. After his father's death, Ellerman's mother moved the family to Caen in France. There followed a move back to England, where he became a pupil at King Edward VI School in Birmingham. At the age of 14, he left home to become articled to William Smedley, a Chartered Accountant in Birmingham.

484: Construction work on Hull's third Theatre Royal—in Paragon Street (designed by G.A. Middlemiss)—began in June 1871; the theatre was officially opened later that year (27 November) by its proprietor Mr Sefton Parry.

485: The proscenium of the Theatre Royal in Paragon Street was 26 feet wide and 28 feet high. The interior decorations to the theatre's auditorium were carried out by Messrs. White and Co., London; the Act Drop was by Julian Hicks, with artwork by Mr Absolom (President of the Society of Arts) and William Noble.

486: The Theatre Royal in Paragon Street was constructed to accommodate 1,200 people; its interior was reportedly similar in design to, and about the same size as, that of the Globe Theatre, London, with every seat offering a 'satisfactory view of the performances'. Its stage was 40 feet deep and 60 feet wide, with dressing rooms provided over four floors (two to each floor) to the right of the stage. Workshops were located to the left of the stage.

487: Thomas Ferens was a keen cricketer, but also a keen autodidact committed to the development of his own skills. He taught himself a range of disciplines, including grammar, arithmetic, mechanics, and shorthand. It was his belief that whatever position in life you end up occupying, you should aim to make yourself indispensable.

488: The National Census of 1871 reported the population of the subdivision borough of Hull as 121,892.

489: In their early years Hull FC moved grounds on several occasions. Home grounds after 1872 included the Haworth Arms Field and West Park on Anlaby Road.

490: John Boyes, explorer and merchant adventurer, was born in Hull on 11 May 1873. At the age of 13 he ran away to sea and, after ten years sailing around the world in all kinds of vessel 'from a fishing smack to a Man-of-War', finally landed in Durban in 1896. He became the self-styled King of the Kikuyu people, publishing, in 1912, a memoir of his experiences titled *How I became King of the Wa-Kikuyu*, about which Charles Miller in *The Lunatic Express* (1971) writes 'Virtually none of the experiences he recounts can be authenticated...Yet...the narrative has an unmistakable ring of truth'.

491: In September 1873 Thomas Ferens married Esther Field (the daughter of a wealthy businessman) whom he'd met whilst they were both teachers at the Brunswick Sunday School. They were married at the Sculcoates Registry Office.

492: In 1873 Isaac Reckitt & Sons introduced their *Paris Blue* line; this was the year of the company's first export order to a dominion, with 25cwt of *Blue* being sent to Montreal.

493: As a lad, the earliest jobs of William Boyes were selling newspapers such as the *Scarborough Gazette*, the

Scarborough Express and the *Mercury*. He also worked as an errand boy for several local tradesmen: a tailor named Powley, a hosier named Gibson, painters named Wanless and Hackers, and a confectioner named Shaw.

494: In 1873 John Bacchus Dykes' youngest son was born. He was named John Arthur St. Oswald Dykes (after St. Oswald's church—also, perhaps, with an echo of his grandfather's St. John's Church, Hull). The youngest son was known, at least to family, as Jack, and eventually became a staff member of the Royal College of Music.

495: In 1873 the Ecclesiastical Commissioners agreed to pay the complete stipends of two curates to assist John Bacchus Dykes in his work at St. Oswald's, Durham; however, the Bishop of Durham refused to license their appointment unless they and Dykes pledged agreement to conditions the Bishop sought to impose: not to wear coloured stoles; not to participate in or be present at the burning of incense; and not to turn their backs to the congregation during Holy Communion, except when 'ordering the bread'. For fear of the wider consequences of setting a precedent, Dykes declined to agree, resisting what he considered to be illegal conditions.

496: The construction of Hull's William Wright Dock was begun in 1873, with plans drawn up by the Hull Dock Company engineer R.A. Marillier; Sir John Hawkshaw was appointed as the Consulting Engineer.

497: In June 1873 George Myers retired and handed over the business of George Myers & Sons to the two sons of his first marriage, David and Joseph.

498: John Bacchus Dykes sought judgement from the Court of the Queen's Bench over his dispute with the Bishop of Durham, Charles Baring, regarding the Bishop's insistence that he receive particular written

pledges before he would license two curates to assist
Dykes at Durham. However, on 19 January 1874, the
dispute was settled, with the Court's decision going
against Dykes, inasmuch as the judges refused to interfere
with the discretionary powers of the Bishop.

499: On 28 May 1874 the Albert Hall music hall opened
in the recently (1858) constructed Midland Street. The
venue, designed by W. Thompson, was built for W.M.
Fussey and could accommodate a seated audience of
almost 800.

500: Horatio Nelson Smith was born on 1 June 1874 at
Chorlton upon Medlock, Lancashire. He was the third and
last child of George Frederick Smith (the founder of
Hull's G.F. Smith paper merchants) and his wife, Lucy
Harding. At the age of nine he was sent to live with his
uncle (Thomas James Smith) and his spinster aunt
(Amelia), who shared a house in Hornsea, on the East
Yorkshire coast. He was educated at Hornsea for four
years before being sent to the City of London School.

501: In the boom period following the recession of
1866, the business of Joseph Fenner experienced a
significant upturn, and in 1874 the firm moved
production from 21½ Bishop Lane to larger premises in
Chapel Lane. At this time the company's main product
was leather transmission belting, but it also offered a
range of other related products such as leather fire hose,
seamless woven canvas hose, walrus hide belting, and
hair belting. In 1994 a blue heritage plaque was erected
at the Chapel Lane premises to mark the building where
Joseph Fenner started his machine belt company. The
inscription reads:

> In this building in 1874 JOSEPH H. FENNER 1835–
> 1886 developed the machine belt manufacturing firm
> of J. H. Fenner & Co.

502: Having joined the company in 1868 as a confidential and shorthand clerk to James Reckitt, on a salary of £70 per annum, Thomas Robinson Ferens (while still only in his mid twenties) was appointed Works Manager at Isaac Reckitt & Sons in 1874 in an agreement that offered him a share in the company's profits. His areas of responsibility included the *Blue* and *Blacklead* mills, the Sawmill and the Packing Room.

503: As a boy William Boyes joined Scarborough's Batty Place Band of Hope. At 15 he became apprenticed—starting at 3/- a week (rising in annual increments to 9/- in his final year)—to Messrs. George and Collins, drapers at 27 Westborough, whose establishment was called 'The Golden Tassel'. At about 16 he joined the Jubilee Primitive Methodist Society (his parents were Church of England people), and as a young man he became a regular Sunday School teacher.

504: On the opening night of the Albert Hall music hall, Messrs. Strange and Wilson presented some of the optical illusions of John Henry Pepper during a recital of the poem 'Storm of Thoughts' and Charles Dickens's story *The Haunted Man*. Pepper had first shown his adaptation of Henry Dircks' Dircksian Phantasmagoria during a scene from the Dickens story in 1862, following which the entertainment became known as 'Pepper's Ghost'. In 1877 Strange and Wilson would present a 'Grand Provincial Tour' of their 'Great Pictorial, Scientific, Musical and Illusionary Entertainment', including 'The Original Professor Pepper's Great Optical Wonder, Proteus' and their own 'Newly-invented and Wondrous Aetherscope', along with their version of Dickens's *A Christmas Carol*.

505: The Albert Hall music hall was fitted with a portable proscenium, stage and scenery, and was available to hire for the purposes of general entertainment; but also for balls, lectures, public meetings, presentations or 'any other respectable purpose'. Its proprietor William Fussey lived nearby at 23 Ocean Place with his wife, Mary Ann, a confectioner.

506: T.J. Smith twice served as a town councillor for Hull: first from 1875–82 and again from 1885–92; and he founded the local branch of the Charity Organization Society. He was also a member of the East Yorkshire Conservative Association; and became involve with the Hull Chamber of Commerce, taking on the roles of Honorary Secretary and Treasurer, and serving as the Chamber's President from 1879–80.

507: In the early entries in his diary of 1875 John Bacchus Dykes describes a series of symptoms consistent with him having suffered a minor stroke: 'perplexed', 'bewildered', 'nervous' 'disconcerted', 'Feel all unhinged today', 'incapable'. His doctor advised a complete rest, suggesting a break abroad: so Dykes, accompanied by his wife and other family members, finally ended up in Tellsplatte, on the shore of Lake Lucerne, Switzerland. After nine weeks, and with his health deteriorating further, a Swiss doctor decided he should be brought home to England; at the end of December he and his wife, 'in search of a warmer climate', went to Sussex.

508: In about 1875 the western pier at the front of the Humber Dock Basin was lost when the entrance to the Albert Dock was partially filled in during the creation of Island Wharf, so named because it was once an island isolated from the mainland by the Albert Channel (infilled in the 1960s).

509: After suffering a stroke in the spring of 1874, George Myers died aged 72 at his home, Thanet House, Montague Place, Lambeth, London on 25 January 1875. He was buried in Norwood Cemetery.

510: Jack 'Gassy Jack' Deighton died aged 44 in 1875, in Vancouver. He is interred at the Fraser Cemetery in New Westminster, British Columbia, where the inscription on his headstone reads:

> Here lies John "Gassy Jack" Deighton 1830–1875 Sailor, Prospector, Steamboatman, Pioneer, Hotelman at New Westminster & Granville "I have done well since I came here"

511: On Saturday 22 January 1876, at fifty-two years of age, John Bacchus Dykes died at Ticehurst (near St. Leonards), Sussex. He was buried the following week, on Friday 28 January, in the churchyard at St. Oswald's, Durham, where he had been vicar for thirteen years.

512: Following the death of John Bacchus Dykes, his wife and family being left poorly provided for, a Memorial Fund for the family's benefit was inaugurated. With donations flowing in 'from all parts', the fund quickly reached £10,000, before it was closed.

513: John Bacchus Dykes wrote almost 300 hymn tunes; services for Holy Communion, Morning and Evening Prayer, and a Burial Service; and numerous sacred and secular songs and part songs. He contributed 55 tunes to *Hymns Ancient and Modern*, 28 to Chope's *The Congregational Hymn and Tune Book*, 21 to Grey's *Hymnal*, as well as contributing as many as 13 tunes to various other hymnals, such as Lady Evans-Freke's *The Song of Praise*.

514: The foundation stone of Hull's William Wright Dock was laid by Sir William Wright (Chairman of the Dock Company) on 26 April 1876.

515: Hull-born sculptor Thomas Earle died of valvular disease of the heart, at his home, 1 Vincent Street, Ovington Square, South Kensington, London, on 28

April 1876. He was buried in Hull's Spring Bank Cemetery.

516: On 21 June 1876 (at the age of 77) James Acland, the London-born radical municipal reformer and erstwhile publisher of the *Hull Portfolio*, died at Clapham, Surrey.

517: Thomas Sheppard, museum curator, autodidact and amateur geologist, was born at South Ferriby on 2 October 1876, the eldest of ten children. His father, Harvey, held the position of Master at the Fountain Road Elementary School (1877), the Beverley Road Boys School (1886) and Craven Street Higher Grade (Boys) School (1893), where he remained until his death. Thomas's brothers Harry and Walter became Borough Treasurer of Beverley, and Secretary of Reckitts Ltd. respectively. His sister Mary became Head of the Boulevard Secondary School, Hull.

518: The site near Spring Bank to which Hull's Botanic Gardens was relocated in 1877 (from its six acre Linnaeus Street location) consisted of some 49 acres, and was acquired from the North Eastern Railway Company. The Botanic Gardens remained there until they closed in 1889 as a consequence of financial problems. The site has been occupied by Hymers College since 1893.

519: The Spring Bank site of Hull Botanic Gardens contained a 3.5 acre lake upon which pleasure boats were provided for visitors.

520: In 1877 a floating pontoon was attached to Hull's Corporation Pier. This was replaced in the 1930s and removed completely in the 1980s.

521: On 1 January 1879 Reckitt and Sons Ltd., a private joint stock company (a company whose stock is not traded publicly), was formed to take control of Isaac Reckitt and Sons (Hull) and Reckitt and Sons (London). All the authorised capital of the new company, £200,000, was held by the Reckitt family; with Francis, James and George being named as the directors. The company's first Chairman was Francis, but he and James swapped the role in alternate years.

522: On 28 May 1879, at Hull's Station Hotel, a new scheme was launched for a railway linking the South Yorkshire coal field with a deep water dock (the Alexandra Dock) on the foreshore of the Humber. The line would be an adaptation and combining of the existing Hull and Barnsley Junction to Howden, and the Hull and West Riding Junction, from Howden in to Hull. The scheme, which would cost an estimated £4m, would involve Hull Corporation selling 126 acres of land to the Hull, Barnsley and West Riding Junction Railway and Dock Company (Hull and Barnsley) for its development.

523: John Boyes lived in Hull with his parents until the age of six, when he was sent away to Engelfingen, Germany, to be educated. His schooling ended when he was 13, at which point he returned to his parents in Hull, who wanted him to continue his education here; but he spent much of his time watching the ships come and go at the Hull docks.

524: Still best known in Chile as a landscape painter, Hull-born artist Thomas Jacques Somerscales became a marine artist following the war between Chile and Peru (1879–1883), during which demand for his depictions of naval battles had soared; and his international reputation was built on his skills as a marine artist. In 1890 his daughter died prompting him to return to England in 1892.

525: At the age of 17, following the death of his grandfather, John Ellerman inherited around £14,000. Keen to see some personal benefit from this legacy,

Ellerman lent some of it to his employer in return for the entitlement to take four months of annual holiday while he served his articles; time he used to develop his mountaineering skills, in Switzerland and India.

526: When Reckitt and Sons Ltd. was formed, George Reckitt remained in London in charge of the firm's London office at 150 Queen Victoria Street.

527: In 1879 Thomas Robinson Ferens became the first Secretary of the newly created Reckitt & Sons Ltd., becoming General Manager in 1880. He was one of the major factors in the developing success of the company; and when Reckitts became a public company, in 1888, he was appointed to the Board of Directors.

528: In 1879 Hull-born Sir John Hall (1824–1907) became the 12th Prime Minister of New Zealand, a position he held until April 1882.

529: In January 1880 the documents supporting the plans for a new combined railway and dock (the Alexandra Dock) showed that timber imports at Hull had increased by 36% between 1870–78; and between 1870–79 the coal-export figures had increased by more than 140%: from 193,106 tons to 463,819 tons.

530: As a lad, John Boyes enjoyed piloting a boat round the Hull docks and helping the sailors he knew, by cleaning decks or polishing brass work. He was determined to get away to sea at the first opportunity, and become a sailor. After discovering that a sailing trawler was leaving early one morning, he stole out of the house while the family was asleep and signed on as a cook and cabin boy (with absolutely no knowledge of the work he would be undertaking).

531: John Boyes' first trip to sea was on board a Hull trawler bound for the North Sea fishing grounds. The trip provided him with his first (and last) experience of sea-sickness; and life aboard a working trawler proved to be not as glamorous as he'd expected, and much more tiring—being at the call of the other crew members at any time, night or day.

532: On his first trip to sea John Boyes escaped with his life after being tossed into a heavy sea by a sail whilst 'reefing the lacing'. A fellow crew member hauled him back on board by his belt—with a boat hook.

533: In 1880 Hull FC merged with Hull White Star, keeping the Hull FC name, but using the White Star ground at Hall's Field, Holderness Road (with a capacity of 5,000) as the newly merged club's home ground.

534: In 1880, following the suggestion of a London specialist, T.J. Smith began bottling and selling his cod-liver oil under the brand *Smith's Paragon Cod Liver Oil*.

535: T.J. Smith and his brother George Frederick Smith (founder of the world-leading, Hull-based paper merchants G.F. Smith) shared premises at 10 Churchside, Hull when the two companies first began trading in the late 1800s.

536: Thomas Ferens and his wife remained childless, but in 1880 they adopted her nephew, John Till (known as Till), who became estranged from his adoptive parents during the First World War.

537: The westward extension to the Albert Dock, sanctioned in an 1866 Act of Parliament, was named William Wright Dock (after the Chairman of the Dock Company) and was opened in 1880.

538: Upon its completion William Wright Dock covered an area of 5.75 acres.

539: The Hull, Barnsley & West Riding Junction Railway and Dock Company scheme for a deep-water dock (later named Alexandra Dock) fed by railway from South Yorkshire was proposed by London solicitor Robert Galland, supported by Hull banker Gerard Smith—former High Sheriff of Hull (1880), and later Governor of Western Australia (1895–1900). The privilege of turning the first sod of the dock fell to Gerard Smith in January 1881, which he carried out to the enthusiasm of onlookers during a snowstorm.

540: In preparation for the construction of Alexandra Dock approximately 150 acres of land were reclaimed from the Humber foreshore.

541: In the plans for Alexandra Dock, the dock walls were designed to be constructed of chalk rubble faced with ashlar stone, but a strike by masons during the works led to the walls being constructed of Portland-cement concrete instead.

542: The construction of Hull's Alexandra Dock took place between January 1881 and July 1885. As with both the William Wright Dock and St. Andrew's Dock, Alexandra Dock was built on land reclaimed from the Humber.

543: The construction of Hull's Alexandra Dock—by the Hull, Barnsley & West Riding Junction Railway and Dock Company—broke the prevailing regional monopoly of North Eastern Railways.

544: Almost 80% of the 192 acre site upon which Alexandra Dock was constructed was below the high-water mark, necessitating the construction of an embankment 40 feet high and 6,000 feet long to enable the reclamation of the required amount of Humber foreshore.

545: The sea bank created to keep out water from the works during the construction of Alexandra Dock was one and a quarter mile long and was made of 200,000 tons of chalk, faced with Bramley Fall stone. The curved cofferdam built across the lock entrance was 500 feet long.

546: In order to minimize the amount of silting up, and therefore the amount of dredging required, Alexandra Dock was designed so that fresh water could be pumped into it from the Holderness Drain, a fresh-water stream which drains a large part of Holderness and has its outfall adjacent to Alexandra Dock.

547: Alexandra Dock was designed by James Abernethy; the execution of the design being jointly supervised by the designer (assisted by James Oldham and George Bohn), with Arthur Cameron Hurtzig as the resident engineer.

548: The main contractors for building Alexandra Dock were Lucas & Aird. The total cost of construction being £1,355,392, or £29,147 per acre.

549: In 1881 an upper promenade deck was built on Hull's Corporation Pier. This was removed in the mid 20th century.

550: Amy Johnson's father, John William Johnson (born on the Danish island of Fyn), was employed in the family business: Andrew Johnson, Knudtzon Ltd. (AJK: established in 1881). They were fish merchants in Hull.

551: The National Census of 1881 reported the population of the subdivision borough of Hull as 154,240.

552: James Alderson died at his home, 17 Berkeley Square, London on 13 September 1882 and was buried in Norwood Cemetery.

553: In October 1882, aged 22 years old and with just £10 capital, William Boyes founded what would become W. Boyes & Co. Ltd. when he opened The Remnant Warehouse, a small store at 28 Eastborough, Scarborough, selling 'odd lots and remnants from merchants'. In time, it became apparent that the shop was too small, and Boyes rented a warehouse (formerly occupied by W. Rowntree & Son) in Market Street; the warehouse had been up to-let for the previous three or four years, so Boyes knew he would be able to negotiate a good deal on the rent.

554: In 1882, in a move to counteract difficulties with supply, Reckitt and Sons Ltd. bought land at Morley Street, and the following year built a small factory to produce ultramarine.

555: In 1882 a group of apprentice boilermakers from the Hessle Road area of Hull formed a rugby club named Kingston Amateurs. The club began playing games in 1883 at Albert Street (later Gillett Street), Hessle Road. Their home ground changed several times to various locations west of the river including, Anlaby Road, Chalk Lane, and the Hull Athletic Ground (later The Boulevard). Kingston Amateurs changed their name to Kingston Rovers, briefly, before settling on Hull Kingston Rovers within three years of the club's foundation.

ON TUESDAY 6 MARCH 1883 approximately thirty Hull fishing smacks were lost in the great gale that wreaked havoc across the Dogger Bank grounds of the North Sea. After a mild winter the high pressure over the UK and the North Sea as March began seemed to indicate that spring had arrived. However, on Monday 5 March everything changed when an overpowering Arctic air-stream blasted through to replace the tranquil high pressure as it moved away west towards the Atlantic. By any measure this must surely be the darkest day in the history of the Hull fishing industry, with more than 200 seamen lost to the North Sea, leaving an unprecedented number of Hull maritime families bereft in a single day. The losses included:

556: Andrew Marvel (H1092), built in 1877 by William McCann (Hull) and owned by George Hallatt (Hull), lost with all hands. She was skippered by William Nelson (38) of 40 Goulton Street, Hull.

557: Ann Sins (H615) also lost with all hands. She was skippered by John Huckstep (47) of 2 Milton Terrace, Anlaby Road, Hull.

558: Bernice (H1052), built in 1877 by John Wray & Son (Burton-upon-Stather) and owned by Charles Hellyer (Hull): lost with all hands. She was skippered by Thomas Kingdom (39) of 8 Sarah Ann's Terrace, Walker Street, Hull.

559: Bessie Lewis (H1170), built at Goole in 1878, and owned by John Lewis Potter (Hull): lost with all hands. At least one Hull seaman, 3rd Hand, Hans Hoier, of 10 Wassand Street, was among those lost.

560: Britannia (H686), built in 1871 and owned by Samuel Edwards (Hull): lost with all hands. She was skippered by Thomas Biggins (37) of 1 Victoria Terrace, Bean Street, Hull.

561: Burton Stather (H247), built in 1866 by John Wray & Sons (Burton-upon-Stather) and owned by Henry Toozes (Hull): lost with all hands. She was skippered by George Dale (24) of Goodwin Street, Hull.

562: Clara (H566), built in 1869 by William McCann (Hull) and owned by the Hartlepool Fishing Company (Hartlepool): lost with all hands. She was skippered by Walter Mitchell (27) of Adelaide Street, Hull.

563: John Harker (H1070), built in 1877 by Hunt, Fowler & Co. (Hull) and owned by George Cook (Hull): lost with all hands. She was skippered by John Read (33).

564: North Sea (H926), built in 1875 by John Wray & Sons (Burton-upon-Stather) and owned by Jabez Rutter (Hull): lost with heavy loss of life. The vessel's skipper William Bartlett, who was picked up by the Dayspring (H983), was the only survivor.

565: Other Hull fishing vessels that foundered at Dogger Bank in the North Sea during the violent gale of 6 March 1883 included: Brilliant (H896), Dove (H1003), Friends Goodwill (H711), Harrier (H706), John Rogers (H80), Lily (H904), Lively (H655), Lizzie Gale (H114), Loch Long (H1281), Mary Esther (H1189), Messenger (H4), Prudence Ann (H775), Sunbeam (H632), The Boys (H1084), Vanguard (H1117), and Water Lily (H1197).

566: On 18 December 1883 the Hull smack C.M. Norwood (H1162) was lost with all hands after foundering on The Binks, off the Spurn peninsula. She was skippered by Richard Allen (28).

567: Originally intended to be a coal dock, St. Andrew's Dock, named after the Patron Saint of Fishermen, opened on Monday 24 September 1883.

568: During the construction of St. Andrew's Dock a cofferdam at the west end of the dock collapsed, causing about £20,000 of damage when a number of vessels moored in the dock broke free, resulting in many of them being sunk or damaged. Fortunately there were no fatalities. The collapse was believed to have been caused by the pile driving and excavation works disturbing underground springs.

569: Hull's St. Andrew's Dock was opened by the Chairman of the Hull Dock Company, Mr J.R. Ringrose.

A procession of vessels, including the Trinity House yacht Duke of Edinburgh and the steamer Isle of Axeholme transported local dignitaries to the opening ceremony from the pier.

570: The total cost for the construction of St. Andrew's Dock was £414,707.

571: St. Andrew's Dock was known to the local (Hessle Road) community, and the people employed in the fishing industry, simply as 'Fish Dock'.

572: The fish market on Hull's St. Andrew's Dock was known as Billingsgate, after London's famous fish market.

573: With the completion of St. Andrew's Dock in 1883, the total water area at the port of Hull covered in excess of 85 acres: St. Andrew's Dock (10.5 acres); William Wright Dock (8 acres); Albert Dock (23 acres); Victoria Dock (20 acres); Queen's Dock (9 acres); Prince's Dock (6 acres); Humber Dock (7 acres); Railway Dock (2 acres).

574: On 23 March 1884 Joseph Groves Boxhall was born in Hull. Following the family tradition, Boxhall chose a life at sea (his father was a Master working for the Wilson Line), qualifying for his Mate's Certificate in 1903. He subsequently signed up as Third officer on the Wilson Line's 2,354 ton steam ship, Iago. He obtained his First Mate's Certificate in 1905, and, with further study at Hull's Trinity House, his Master's and Extra-Master's Certificates in 1907 before joining the White Star Line the same year. He served as a junior officer on both Oceanic and Arabic, and joined Titanic as Fourth Officer in Belfast on 27 April 1911.

575: On 5 April 1884 Hull FC finished runners up in the Yorkshire Rugby Football Union Cup when they lost to Bradford Park Avenue at Cardigan Fields, Leeds;

Bradford scoring a single goal, four tries and five minor points, to Hull's single try and three minor points.

576: When William Boyes rented additional premises in Market Street, the warehouse was so much larger than his premises in Eastborough that he had doubts about whether he could adequately stock it, but he soon found he also needed to utilise the second floor as well as the first, and finally had to extend the shop into the warehouse. A year or so later Boyes bought the entire block, including three houses, two shops, and three cottages behind the Wesleyan Chapel; all of these were pulled down in the winter of 1895–96, before being rebuilt and added to the existing premises.

577: The Eastborough premises of The Remnant Warehouse had about 14 feet of counter space, but after the acquisition of further properties and re-configuring, the new premises had 600 feet of counter space. Not satisfied with this expansion, Boyes bought the Old Post Office adjoining the Remnant Warehouse, just in case the need for further extension of the premises arose in the future.

578: William Boyes married Jane Riby in 1884. They had two sons, George Thomas (born 1887) and Robert Riby (born 1889)—who both followed their father into the family business—and five daughters, two of whom became his Mayoress, when he was appointed Mayor of Scarborough in 1921 and 1924.

579: In the summer of 1884 James Reckitt bought the Manor House in Swanland from John Davenport; by 1901 the Manor House had become known as Swanland Manor.

580: In 1884 Arthur Stanley Morrison and Co., distributors of asbestos and rubber supplies, was founded in London. In its early days it made tennis balls for the Wimbledon Tennis Club, and in 1888 changed its name to the Asbestos and Rubber Company. In 1890, to take advantage of the port's growing mercantile shipping trade, it established a shop in Hull. It would eventually become the UK's leading safety company ARCO, whose Registered Office remains at Waverley Street in Hull.

581: Returning to Hull after six months at sea with a fishing fleet (his first trip), John Boyes was disillusioned with life on a trawler and decided he would like to go abroad to 'see something of the world', and that he would be better placed to do this if he were in Liverpool.

582: Having decided to try for a ship in Liverpool, the penniless fifteen-year-old John Boyes set out to walk there from Hull; but with no real idea of the route, he headed first in the direction of York, then Leeds and Manchester, before finally arriving at Liverpool, weary and footsore. He found lodgings in the 'sea-men's quarter' of the town, where an old sailor took him in on trust until he found a ship.

583: During construction of Hull's Alexandra Dock the engineers had to excavate 3,335,000 cubic yards of material, while 661,000 cubic yards of material was removed by dredging; 88,000 cubic yards of cement concrete and 74,000 cubic yards of lime concrete were used in its construction.

584: Upon its completion in 1885, the dock walls to Alexandra Dock were 20 feet wide at the base and 6 feet 9 inches wide at the top; the lock was 550 feet long and 85 feet wide, with a depth of 34 feet. With an area of 46.5 acres, being 2,300 feet long and 1,000 feet wide it was almost twice the size of the town's Albert Dock.

585: With the advent of steam power, Alexandra Dock was the first dock to be built in Hull specifically to accommodate larger cargo vessels.

586: Alexandra Dock, named for H.R.H. Princess Alexandra the Princess of Wales, was opened on 16 July 1885.

587: As Princess Alexandra and the Prince of Wales were unable to attend the opening ceremony for Alexandra Dock, it was opened by the wife of Lt. Colonel Gerard Smith MP, Chairman of the Hull and Barnsley Railway Company.

588: The two graving docks at the north east corner of Alexandra Dock were used to facilitate the general servicing and repair of vessels by local firms.

589: As a consequence of the ending of the Hull Dock Company's monopoly on dock facilities in the port—with the Hull, Barnsley & West Riding Junction Railway Dock Company's construction, ownership and operation of Alexandra Dock—a dock-charges price cutting competition between the two companies was triggered.

590: On 29 August 1885 Hull's West Park, which covers around 31 acres on Anlaby Road, was opened by the then mayor, Sir Albert Kaye Rollit MP. It was constructed on land formerly owned by the North Eastern Railway Company, but acquired by Hull Corporation in 1878 at a cost of £1,400 per acre. The Borough Engineer, Joseph Fox Sharpe, designed the layout of the park, and its construction provided work for 200 unemployed men.

591: The *Hull Daily Mail* was first published from 22 Whitefriargate on 29 September 1885. It's thought the venture began as a means by which a group of local businessmen could get Frederick Brent Grotrian elected to Parliament, a goal achieved on 1 July the following year.

592: On 13 April 1886 Ethel Annie Liggins (later, Ethel Leginska) was born at 22 Pemberton Street, Hull, the only child of Thomas Edward and Anne Liggins (*née* Peck).

Home-educated by her governess mother, Ethel began playing the piano at a very early age and, in Hull, became a student of Mrs Russell Starr (Annie Jane, *née* Martin), with her musical education being developed under patronage from Mary Wilson, the wife of Arthur Wilson of the famous Wilsons of Tranby Croft. She made her musical début at St. George's Hall, Hull on her ninth birthday (13 April 1895), later (14 January 1897) performing at the Assembly Rooms, Jarratt Street. Her London début was at the Queen's Hall in June 1896—she would have been ten years old.

593: On 11 May 1886, at just forty-nine years old, Joseph Henry Fenner died after being thrown from his horse and trap. His two sons Henry John and Walter George, who had been working in the family business alongside their father, took over the running of the company.

594: The last tune composed by John Bacchus Dykes was to Adelaide Proctor's 'The Pilgrims': 'The way is long and dreary', which appeared in Henry Allon's *Congregational Psalmist* (1886).

595: Not long after passing his accountancy exams (with Distinction), John Ellerman moved from Birmingham to London to take up a position with Quilter, Ball & Co. He was offered a partnership in the firm, but turned down the offer in order to found his own accountancy firm J. Ellerman & Co. in 1886, at 10 Moorgate.

596: By the end of 1886, as a result of the rate reduction war between the Hull Dock Company and the Hull and Barnsley, the Hull Dock Company was forced to look into the possibility of selling off or leasing its holdings to one or more of the big railway companies, while the Hull and Barnsley was forced by shareholders to agree to the appointment of a receiver.

597: In 1887 Alfred Gelder became an Associate of the Royal Institute of British Architects, becoming a Fellow in 1892. He entered into partnership with Llewellyn Kitchen—as Gelder & Kitchen—in 1896.

598: On 21 June 1887, to coincide with Queen Victoria's Golden Jubilee, Hull's East Park on Holderness Road opened to the public for the first time. The site chosen for the park by the town's Parks Committee was close to the Holderness Road terminus of the horse-drawn tramway.

599: At the official opening ceremony for East Park, on 21 June 1887—which started in the town centre and was led by the Police Band—it was suggested by Alderman W.F. Chapman that the park be named Victoria Park, in honour of Queen Victoria, who was celebrating her Golden Jubilee. The project to construct the park provided 140 new jobs by 1886.

600: East Park, the largest of Hull's parks, covers approximately 120 acres to the north of Holderness Road, and is sited on land bought from the Trust of Mrs Anne Watson (for £117,000), and the former Summergangs Farm (which was already under the ownership of the Corporation). The design of the park was by Joseph Fox Sharpe, the Borough Engineer.

601: Among the features at East Park was a watchtower from the old Hull Citadel—installed near the entrance to the Khyber Pass feature, but removed in 1998—and part of a tower from the old Town Hall (designed by Cuthbert Brodrick) which was demolished in 1911.

602: Following a decision by the Board of Gleadow, Dibb & Co. to form a new company to take over their existing business, the Hull Brewery Company Limited was incorporated on 9 January 1888 (and incorporated as a public limited company on 18 May 1888). Subsequently, at an Extraordinary General Meeting of Gleadow, Dibb & Co. on 19 June the same year, a resolution was passed 'That the Company be wound up voluntarily'; this resolution was confirmed on 4 July 1888.

603: Mr Sefton Parry, the first manager of Hull's third and final Theatre Royal (in Paragon Street), was succeeded by Mr Wilson Barrett, who was lessee and manager until 17 March 1888, when the theatre was taken over by Mr Alfred Cuthbert.

604: On 17 April 1888 the authentic Hull fish and chip experience of Bob Carver's opened for the first time, on a stall at Hull market. The firm opened their fish and chip restaurant at 9 Trinity House Lane in around 1980, and the family business is now being run by the third generation Bob Carver. Bob Carver's were also a firm favourite with visitors to Hull Fair; but since around 2010 a different firm with (confusingly) the same name occupies the position at the fair traditionally associated with the original Bob Carver's. The original, authentic Bob Carver's should not be confused with the 'fish restaurant & takeaway' of the same name with premises in Chapel Street—the two businesses are not connected.

605: Joseph Arthur Rank (later Baron Rank) was born on 22 December 1888 at Chestnut Villas, Holderness Road, Hull, the youngest son of flour miller and entrepreneur Joseph Rank (also born on Holderness Road, on 28 March 1854) and his wife Emily (*née* Voase). He attended 'The Leys' Methodist boarding school (Cambridge) between 1901–06, and joined the family business straight from school—working initially in its London head office, before gaining experience in a wide range of the company's administrative and production processes. He became a director of the company in 1915.

606: In 1888 Alfred Cuthbert, the manager of Hull's third and final Theatre Royal, oversaw major alterations to the theatre; primarily measures to improve the safety of patrons in the event of a fire. These included increasing the number of exits from the Pit (from two to four); the addition of two stone exit-staircases from the Gallery; the replacement of the wooden staircase to the Dress Circle with one of stone; and fitting all the most recent fire-fighting appliances. Two fire hydrants were located on the stage itself. The manager was confident that the theatre Pit could be evacuated in just three minutes.

607: The manager of The Remnant Store located at 84 Prospect Street (William Boyes' first store in Hull) was a Mr T. Atkinson; Mr Bob Boyes, the son of William Boyes' step-brother, became the first manager of the company's Hessle Road store.

608: When Reckitt and Sons Ltd. was formed into a public limited company in 1888, with a capital of £450,000, 2,500 £10 Ordinary Shares were offered to the public in a move to generate additional capital.

609: Hull became a County Borough in 1888.

610: On 8 February 1889 the Hull steam trawler Adventure (H1500) became the fishing fleet's first steam trawler to be lost, when she sank with the loss of all hands in the North Sea. Built in 1886 by Cook, Welton & Gemmell Ltd. (Hull), she was skippered by Thomas Owens, and owned by Humber Steam Trawling Co. Ltd. (Hull)/Richard Simpson (Hull).

611: Harry Fletcher, the founder of H. Fletcher & Son Ltd., was born on 27 June 1889 at 3 Newton Street, Hull, the son of Harry and Jane Fletcher (*née* Shaw). His father was a Master Butcher, formerly of Bridlington.

612: In 1889 the former Mechanics' Music Hall was renamed the Empire (or Empire Palace) becoming the Empire Theatre of Varieties in 1890. From 1909 to 1913 it was known as the Bijou; in 1913, having become increasingly run down, the venue was finally closed. It was demolished the following year. A boxing arena was later established on the site.

613: In September 1890, at his Tranby Croft home, Arthur Wilson hosted a house party, which the Prince of Wales (later Edward VII) attended. A famous case of slander arose when Sir William Gordon-Cumming (who was also a guest of the Wilsons) was accused of cheating at baccarat. In the ensuing legal case, which was unsuccessful, the Prince of Wales was called as a witness—the first time the heir to the throne had been compelled to appear in court since 1411.

614: In 1890 J.H. Fenner acquired 18 acres of land at Marfleet which was then a small village some three miles outside Hull. A new factory was built, with production starting there in 1893. The company also built houses for its workforce, at rents ranging from three shillings and sixpence to five shillings a week, which represented approximately 14–18% of the weekly wage received.

615: In 1890 Reckitt and Sons Ltd. started a non-contributory pension fund for its employees.

616: In 1890 Frederick Brent Grotrian bought out his fellow directors to become the sole proprietor of the *Hull Daily Mail*.

617: In 1890 Horatio Nelson Smith (the 'nephew' in Smith & Nephew) began working for a London wholesale draper and woollen manufacturer on the salary of £12 a year. In January 1896, after being refused a pay rise, he decided to accept the offer of a trial at his uncle's wholesale cod-liver oil business (his elder brother, Thomas Brooks Smith had taken a position working in his father's paper merchant business G.F. Smith).

618: In 1890 John Ellerman founded his first major business success, the Brewery and Commercial Investment Trust, which in nine years appreciated in value by 1300 per cent.

619: As a mark of respect for his leadership in fierce battles with the Chinga tribe, the three most powerful chiefs in the region (Kururi, Karkerrie and Wagomi) acknowledged John Boyes as their leader (hence his claim to be King of the Wa-kikuyu). Shortly thereafter, Boyes led a representation to meet with Government officials in Mbeere, where he was summonsed to appear before a court on the grounds that: 'during your residence in the Kenia district, you waged war, set shauris, personated Government, went on six punitive expeditions, and committed dacoity'. He was sent first to Nairobi, then on to Mombasa, before being returned to Nairobi for trial, in which all charges against him were dismissed.

620: Sir Henry Cooper died on 21 May 1891, at his home at 12 Albion Street.

621: William Jackson, the founder of the William Jackson Food Group, opened his first bakery in 1891. Since 2004 the company has invested heavily in its current bakery in Derringham Street (which opened in 1907), spending over £20m to turn it into a state-of-the-art bakery.

622: By 1891 it was becoming clear that the fishing trade needed increased facilities at Hull, including additional quay and water space; and that the coal trade needed deeper dock facilities for larger vessels, along with additional quayside coal-shipping appliances. In order to facilitate the required investment, an amalgamation between the North Eastern Railway and the Hull Dock Company was proposed.

623: In 1891 the Hull Dock Company approached North Eastern Railway for capital to improve the Albert Dock, resulting in North Eastern Railway acquiring the shares and debts of the Dock Company in exchange for its shares.

624: Thomas Wilson, Sons & Co. became a private limited company in 1891, with capital of £2.5m and a fleet of over 100 ships. Following the acquisition of Bailey and Leatham (Hull) in 1903, the Wilson Line became the largest privately owned shipping company in the world.

625: The National Census of 1891 reported the population of the subdivision borough of Hull as 200,472.

626: In 1892 Reckitt and Sons Ltd. opened a third overseas branch—in New York (under the management of Henry Johnson).

627: From 1892–95 Hull Kingston Rovers played their home games at the Hull Athletic Ground, Boulevard, Hessle Road; but when Hull FC took over the lease of the ground in 1895 Hull KR moved east of the river to Craven Street, Holderness Road.

628: In 1892, following the death of Frederick Leyland, John Ellerman headed a syndicate (with Henry Osborne O'Hagan and Christopher Furness) which bought the Leyland & Co. fleet and restructured the business, with Ellerman being appointed Managing Director. In 1893, aged 31, John Ellerman became Chairman of the company. The capital value attached to the firm on floatation was £800,000, a figure many regarded as far too high for the market; but in 1901 Ellerman sold most of Leyland & Co. to the American financier J.P. Morgan for £1.2m.

629: From the 1890s on, the Albert Hall music hall in Midland Street functioned mainly as a public house or working men's club, having been acquired by the brewery Worthington & Co. in 1892. It was still operating as a public house in the 1950s and 60s (its address then was No. 10 Midland Street). It was later re-configured as a bingo venue named the 'Fair & Square Club'.

630: Within 5 years of establishing her dressmaking salon at 1 Kingston Square, Madame Clapham had expanded into 2 Kingston Square, and later expanded into No.3.

631: In 1892, rather than opting to spend £22,000 on the deepening of the entrance to Hull's Albert Dock, the NER board decided a better investment would be to spend £1,000,000 constructing a new dock to the east of Alexandra Dock, and so they submitted to Parliament Bills for both the new dock and for the amalgamation of NER with the Hull Dock Company. However, both Bills were rejected.

632: Alfred Gelder designed a wide range of buildings in Hull, though many were destroyed during the Second World War. Those that remain include the Paragon Arcade, Paragon Street (1892) and Hepworth's Arcade, Silver Street (1894); the James Reckitt (1888–9) and Boulevard (1894) libraries; and the former Premier Stores at 152–154 Hessle Road on the corner of Coltman Street (1898), now occupied by Premier Work and Leisurewear.

633: On 9 January 1893 the Grand Opera House opened on George Street, Hull. Despite its name, the venue— designed by the prolific theatre architect Frank Matcham—was primarily a venue for dramatic and theatrical productions, though its opening show was a production of the Comic Opera *Cinderella* by the Burns-Crotty Opera Company.

634: On 18 April 1893 the Hull steam trawler Dogger Bank (H47) sank with the loss of all hands, following (it is believed) a collision with the German barque Theckla. Dogger Bank had left Hull on 13 April, heading for the fishing grounds, but the owners' insurers received reports from Theckla crew members that they had run down an unknown steamer in the same area where Dogger Bank was thought to be at that time. Built in 1888 by Cook, Welton & Gemmell Ltd. (Hull), Dogger Bank was owned by the Cargill Steam Trawling Co. Ltd. (Hull).

635: On 4 July 1893 Hull-born Sir John Robinson (1839–1903) became the first Prime Minister of the South African province of Natal.

636: In 1893, shortly after qualifying as a doctor, Mary Murdoch became the House-Surgeon at Victoria Hospital for Children in Park Street, Hull.

637: Dr. Mary Murdoch established Hull's first crèche— and also encouraged the involvement of working fathers in the upbringing of their children. She is reported to have been the first woman in Hull to own a car.

638: The new factory built at Marfleet by J.H. Fenner, which began production in 1893, had the telephone number 'Hull 8', the numbers 1–6 being reserved for the telephone company.

639: Thomas Jacques Somerscales first exhibited his work at the Royal Academy, London in 1893; and eventually exhibited 23 works there. His *Off Valparaiso* is now housed in the Tate Collection (accession number: N01773) after being presented by the Trustees of the Chantrey Bequest in 1899. The National Maritime Museum at Greenwich has two of his works, and Hull's Ferens Art Gallery has four. Frequently returning to Chile, Somerscales finally settled in Hull for good in

1915, dying here in 1927. A green heritage plaque, erected by the Avenues and Pearson Park Residents' Association, marks his former home at 127 Park Avenue, Hull. The inscription reads:

THOMAS SOMERSCALES marine artist lived here 1910–1920

640: In 1893 the NER/Hull Dock Company amalgamation Bill was resubmitted, this time including clauses to protect the interests of the Hull and Barnsley Railway, who were opposed to the possibility of a rival dock adjacent to their own Alexandra Dock. The North Eastern Railway (Hull Docks) Act was passed and the amalgamation Bill received the Royal assent on 24 August 1893, with the amalgamation taking effect as from 1 July.

641: The 1893 Act allowing the amalgamation of the Dock Company and NER prevented NER from creating a new deep water dock without consulting the Hull and Barnsley Railway company, resulting in a joint proposal being submitted for a dock east of Alexandra Dock. This was passed in 1899, as the 'Hull Joint Dock Act', leading to the construction of the King George Dock.

642: During the debates surrounding the proposed amalgamation of the North Eastern Railway Company and the Hull Dock Company, local shipowner and Member of Parliament Charles Wilson, along with Frederick Brent Grotrian expressed their support for the merger.

643: The 1893 Act sanctioning the amalgamation of the Hull Dock Company and NER stipulated that £500,000 would be spent on dock improvements over the next seven years.

644: The 1893 purchase of the Hull Dock Company added £2,250,000 to the capital value of the North Eastern Railway Company.

645: On the completion of their amalgamation with the Hull Dock Company, the total water area of the docks added to the North Eastern Railway Company's system amounted to over 140 acres.

646: Hymers College, located at Hymers Avenue, Hull, was built by Botterill, Son & Bilson (on the former site of Hull's Botanic Gardens) with money bequeathed 'for the training of intelligence in whatever social rank of life it may be found among the vast and varied population of the town and port of Hull' by the Reverend John Hymers, Rector of Brandesburton—a village approximately 10 miles north of Hull. It opened in 1893 as a school for boys, with its first Headmaster being Charles Gore. A Science wing, added in 1908, and a Memorial Hall in 1924, are both also by Bilson. A Craft, Design and Technology block was added by Gelder & Kitchen in 1988–9.

647: There was a strike at the port of Hull in 1893, with the dockers in a six-week dispute over the use of non-Union labour on the docks to load and unload ships. The dockers, who were supported in their cause by the lightermen, watermen and oil-fillers, brought the port to a standstill; and the effects of the dispute erupted into violence and bloodshed on the streets and around the docks generally, with the police and the military occasionally being forced to intervene with batons and drawn swords respectively to break up the crowds. The dockers eventually lost their struggle and the port returned to normal service.

648: Following the amalgamation of the Hull Dock Company with the North Eastern Railway, Hull's St. Andrew's Dock was extended with the addition of a 10 acre basin, three slipways (for ship repairs), a river wall and jetties at an estimated cost of £70,000–£80,000, with work on these additions commencing in June 1894.

649: The extension to Hull's St. Andrew's Dock (St. Andrew's Dock Extension) was connected to the main dock at the west end via a channel; the slipways were at the extreme west end.

650: In September 1894 John Ellerman and his lifelong partner Hannah Glover (daughter of George Glover) had a daughter, Annie Winifred Glover, in Margate, Kent. Annie, who changed her name to Annie Winifred Bryher, became a novelist, writing under the pen name Bryher, and later entered into a marriage of convenience with American poet and publisher Robert MacAlmon.

651: During the Great Storm of 22 December 1894, which battered the north of England, Hull lost six steam trawlers and at least 108 men in the North Sea in one day: City of Birmingham (H162), Economy (H221), Energy (H218), England (H255), Express (H237), and Staghound (H85) were all lost with all hands.

652: In 1894, having previously declined the honour, James Reckitt was created a baronet, becoming Sir James Reckitt, in recognition of both his public service and services to the Liberal Party in Hull.

653: With the opening of the Manchester Ship Canal in 1894, and the competition it posed, it was considered essential to improve the accommodation offered by the port of Hull: the deepening of Victoria Dock was undertaken, and it was proposed that the entrances to the old docks should be improved; but with restrictive agreements already in place preventing NER from proceeding with any arrangements that might jeopardise the operations of the Hull and Barnsley, thoughts once again turned to the possible amalgamation of the two companies.

654: In 1894 the general public response to a proposed amalgamation between NER and the Hull and Barnsley companies was negative, with the prospect generating hostile responses from both the Hull Corn Trade Association, and the Hull Chamber of Commerce. Despite the positive support of the main shipping interests of the port the Bill was ultimately dropped.

655: In 1894 Thomas Ferens was appointed a J.P. and thereafter became increasingly involved in public affairs. He was defeated when he stood as a Liberal parliamentary candidate for Hull East in 1900, but was elected as representative for Hull East in 1906 and held the seat for thirteen years. As an MP, he could no longer attend to the day-to-day running of Reckitt & Sons Ltd., but kept in regular contact with the company's management, and closely followed its direction and development.

656: In the early 1890s Hull FC began making enquiries about moving to the Athletic Ground, located off the Boulevard and owned by the Hull Athletic Company. The ground had become home to Hull Kingston Rovers in 1892, but a rent increase imposed by the owners left Rovers unable to continue at the venue. Hull FC agreed a lease with the owners at a cost of £150 per annum (three times the sum Rovers had been paying).

657: The beginning of Hull FC's association with what became known as The Boulevard—with the venue becoming the club's 'home' in 1895—coincided with the club's first season in the Northern Rugby Football Union, founded at the George Hotel, Huddersfield on 29 August 1895.

658: On 7 September 1895, just nine days after the founding of the Northern Rugby Football Union, Hull FC visited Batley for their first game in the Northern Union league. The match, played at Batley's Mount Pleasant ground, finished with Hull FC losing 7-3. Hull's 3 points were scored by Jack Holmes, who became the first Hull

FC player to score a try in the newly formed Northern Union.

659: On 14 September 1895 Hull FC took their first victory in the Northern Union when they travelled to Warrington's Wilderspool ground for their second game of the league's inaugural season. Feetham, Thompson and Townend scored the points in an unexpected 9-3 win for the Airlie Birds.

660: Hull FC played their first home game at the Athletic Ground (later to become The Boulevard), in front of a record crowd of 8,000, on 21 September 1895, beating Liversedge 3-0. The club's first ever try at their new spiritual home was scored by George Jacketts early in the second half.

661: Former Chairman of the Hull and Barnsley Railway Company and High Sheriff of Hull (1879) Lt. Colonel Gerard Smith J.P., of the Hull banking family Abel Smith & Sons, was appointed KCMG (Most Distinguished Order of Saint Michael and Saint George), and became Governor of Western Australia in October 1895.

662: In January 1896 Horatio Nelson Smith began a trial period working in his uncle's pharmaceutical business; and on 1 July 1896 was made a partner in the business, which was then renamed T.J. Smith and Nephew. By this time T.J. Smith was suffering increasing health problems and infirmity; and he died at home on 3 October, just three months after the partnership was formed.

663: The astrophysicist, mathematician and cosmologist Edward Arthur Milne, best known for developing the theory of kinematic relativity, was born in Hull on 14 February 1896. Milne attended Hymers College before winning an open scholarship in Mathematics and Natural Science to study at Trinity College, Cambridge in 1914;

he achieved the highest score of marks ever awarded in the examination.

664: At the end of the inaugural Northern Rugby Football Union season, in April 1896, Hull FC finished in eighth position with 49 points; Manningham (Bradford) took the Championship title with 66 points, whilst Rochdale Hornets finished bottom of the league with just 16 points.

665: T.J. Smith never married, and lived at 7 Wilton Terrace, Hornsea, on the East Yorkshire coast with his spinster sister, Amelia. It was she who invited Smith's 22 year old nephew Horatio Nelson to leave his job with a London firm of drapers to work with his uncle in the pharmaceutical industry.

666: T.J. Smith was buried at St. Nicholas Church, Hornsea. He left his share of the business to his sister Amelia who, not wanting to be a part of it, had within a few years transferred it over to Horatio Nelson.

667: At the time of T.J. Smith's death, the company had a staff of just three and a turnover of £3,000 (around 85% of which was from its cod-liver oil business).

668: In 1896, following the death of his uncle, Horatio Nelson Smith assumed complete control of T.J. Smith & Nephew.

669: Under the control of Horatio Nelson Smith, Smith & Nephew began its development from a wholesale supplier of cod-liver oil into one of the largest companies in the global health-care market. It was he who steered the company towards the production of medical and surgical dressings.

670: In 1896 Thomas Robinson Ferens bought the Dansom Lane Recreation Ground and eventually, after offering the land to Reckitt & Sons, gifted it to the Corporation of Hull for use as a children's playground.

671: Margot Bryant, famous for her portrayal of Minnie Caldwell in the world's longest running soap-opera, *Coronation Street*, was born in Hull on 8 March 1897.

672: The patronage of the Wilsons of Tranby Croft enabled Ethel Annie Liggins (later, Ethel Leginska) to study piano and composition at Frankfurt's Hoch Conservatoire (1897–1902); and piano, under Theodor Hermann Leschetizky, in Vienna (1902–4).

673: Hull was given the status of 'City' on 22 June 1897.

674: On 6 December 1897 the New Palace Theatre of Varieties opened on the south side of Anlaby Road, approximately opposite Park Street. Designed by Frank Matcham for the theatre impresario Edward Moss's Liverpool, Leeds, and Hull Empire Co. Ltd., the New Palace could seat 1,800 people. Living up to its name, the opening-night bill featured the popular music hall singer and comedian Gus Elen, and a variety of other acts including a ventriloquist, a juggler, musical grotesques and an international dance troupe. Edward Moss later became founder and Chairman of Moss Empires Ltd.

675: In 1897 NER put forward an application to Parliament for permission to make a range of improvements at Hull, with an estimated cost of £781,000: a river-wall extending from the William Wright Dock to the basin of Victoria Dock, incorporating additional quay-room within the area created by the wall; a new 10 acre dock on the site of the Island Wharf; and new entrances and locks to the Albert and Humber Docks.

676: The New Palace Theatre of Varieties would presumably have been named the 'Empire Theatre of Varieties', in keeping with the Moss tradition, had it not been for the fact that Hull already had an Empire Theatre of Varieties (originally the Mechanics' Music Hall) situated on Grimston Street.

677: The New Palace Theatre of Varieties on Anlaby Road was situated next to Hengler's Circus.

678: The Moorish style decorations to the interior of the New Palace Theatre of Varieties were created by De Jong of London, with artistic panel painting and gilding by Messrs. Binns of Halifax. Upholstery was by Morton and Sons of Liverpool.

679: The proscenium of the New Palace Theatre of Varieties was 30 feet wide, and the stage was 30 feet deep. The theatre also contained a winter garden with a fountain. Subsequent to its opening it was equipped with a screen to enable films to be included in the programme.

680: On 15 February 1898 the Hull steam trawler European (H355) foundered in the North Sea and was lost with all hands. She was skippered by James Ashton (39) of Witty Street, Hull.

681: On 15 February 1898 the Hull steam trawler Newfoundland (H292) went missing and was lost with all hands after leaving Hull bound for the North Sea fishing grounds. Built in 1895 by Cochrane, Hamilton, Cooper & Schofield (Beverley), for the Hull Steam Fishing & Ice Co. Ltd. (Hull), the Newfoundland was skippered by John Jewsbury (40) of 11 Victoria Avenue, Conway Street, Hull.

682: On 18 November 1898 the Hull steam trawler Boyne (H424) went missing in the North Sea, and was lost with all hands. She was skippered by Henry Harber (38) of 5 Ashton Villas, Eton Street, Hull.

683: By 1898, continuing his expansion strategy for The Remnant Warehouse, William Boyes had opened a branch at 84 Prospect Street, the first presence of a Boyes store in Hull. 84 Prospect Street was occupied by The Remnant Warehouse under lease, which was sold in 1901 for £114 to Taylors Drug Store, a company owned by William Barker Mason, one of the directors of W. Boyes & Co. Ltd.

684: In 1898 Horatio Nelson Smith married builder's daughter Margaret Syme at Bromley, Kent. They had three children: Alister, Margaret and Neil. Margaret became the company's first female director, but only Alister held an executive position within the firm.

685: In 1898 the trading profit of Reckitt and Sons surpassed £100,000 for the first time, reaching £115,225; in 1907 the trading profit reached £259,576; and by 1911 the trading profit had reached £521,709.

686: In 1898 Frederick Needler, the founder of Needlers Ltd., bought premises at 9 and 11 Spring Street; and by 1900 his firm had a turnover of £15,000 with a profit of almost £900, had about 33 employees, and was producing more than 200 different product lines (boiled sweets, toffees, health sweets, pralines, rock, and various Spring Sweets).

687: The improvements Bill sought from Parliament by NER in 1897 was withdrawn, but resubmitted in 1898 with further extensive proposals for improvements to provisions at Victoria Dock. Once again, in the face of vigorous opposition, the Bill was withdrawn.

688: In 1899 Hull KR were admitted as full members of the Northern Rugby Football Union. They lost their first match in the Northern Union, in September 1899, 3-0 away to Bradford.

689: Following the decision of the Northern Union in 1896 to split into two county leagues, Lancashire and

Yorkshire (to accommodate several more clubs from the Rugby Football Union)—with each county league consisting of 14 clubs—Hull FC achieved their highest league position up to that point, when they finished runners-up to Batley in the 1898–99 season. Batley took the Yorkshire Senior Competition league title with 48 points, just one point ahead of Hull FC on 47 points.

690: On 16 September 1899, in Hull Kingston Rovers' first season in the Northern Union, Hull FC visited Craven Street for the first ever Hull v Rovers local derby game. Rovers took the glory, winning 8-2 in front of a crowd of more than 12,000. Billy Jacques scored Hull FC's points with a drop goal early in the second half. Rovers' Anthony Stark became the very first player to score in a Hull v Rovers local derby, with a try in the first minute of the game.

691: William Boyes stood for election to Scarborough Town Council in 1895, for the Liberals in the North Ward, but was defeated by the established Conservative candidate; however, when he stood again in a different ward, in 1899, he was elected and remained on the Council for nine years.

692: John Boyes claimed to have been 'given' ownership of Mount Kenya (following a blood-brother-hood ceremony) by two of the region's tribal chieftains, namely Wagombie, and Olomondo (chief of the Wanderobo tribe). The tribal chiefs had assaulted Sir Halford John Mackinder's expedition on Mount Kenya, killing some of Mackinder's party; and since Boyes was the only white man they knew, and was now a blood-brother, they wanted him to have the mountain. The Government refused Boyes' claim of ownership when he brought the matter to the attention of Sir William Morris Carter, of the Kenya Land Commission, in 1932.

693: In 1899 an Act of Parliament (the Joint Dock Act) was passed authorising the North Eastern Railway Company and the Hull, Barnsley and West Riding Junction Railway and Dock Company to construct a new dock with a lock and entrance from the river Humber, to be sited on the north bank of the river between the Holderness Drain on the west, and the Old Fleet drain and the Salt End pasture on the east, and between the river embankment to the south and Hedon Road to the north.

694: In their 1899 application for an Act to construct Hull's Joint Dock, the NER and Hull and Barnsley companies estimated the cost at £1,419,555 (£1,194,160 of which would be for the new dock and the entrance lock from the Humber). 306 acres of land were required, with 4,535,354 cubic yards of earth to be excavated. They estimated the cost of the river wall at £99,763, with the railways connecting the dock with the railway system costing an additional £90,155. The time needed for the construction work was estimated at seven years.

695: The application to Parliament for the Joint Dock included the taking of thirty-three acres of Marfleet Common for use in the dock's construction.

696: The 1899 application also stated that the dock would measure 1,050 yards from east to west, and 320 yards from north to south at its western end, and 340 yards from north to south at its eastern end; the centre of the dock being 'at a distance of four hundred and ninety yards, or thereabouts, measured in a straight line southwards from a point in the Hedon-road seven hundred and fifty-five yards, or thereabouts, westward of the mile post indicating three miles from Hull'.

697: In 1899 an extension, designed specifically for the shipment of coal and mining timbers, was opened at Hull's Alexandra Dock. The dock was expanded by 7 acres, adding nearly half a mile of extra quayside. The contractors who built the extension were Whitaker and Sons, Horsforth, Leeds.

698: By the end of the 19th century the combined recent investment in Hull by the amalgamated Hull Dock Company and the North Eastern Railway Company was around £1m, with the Dock Company having spent well in excess of £400,000 on construction work at William Wright and St. Andrew's docks, and NER approximately £450,000 between 1872–79 developing and improving their railway facilities.

20th century

699: On 6 February 1900 the steam trawler Indian (GY184), built by John Duthie, Sons & Co. (Aberdeen) for the Great Grimsby Albion Steam Fishing Co. Ltd. (Grimsby), foundered in the North Sea and was lost with all hands. (Brian Langley's *Lost Trawlermen of Hull* lists three members of the crew of Indian, but with no addresses traced.)

15 FEBRUARY 1900 WAS ANOTHER GRIM DAY for the fishing community of Hull, with the following steam trawlers and their crews being lost:

700: Bermuda (H296): lost with all hands. Built in 1895 by Cochrane, Hamilton, Cooper & Schofield (Selby), she was skippered by John Berry (44) of 2 Alma Avenue, Woodcock Street, Hull; the owners were Hull Steam Fishing & Ice Co. Ltd. (Hull).

701: Cyprus (H198): lost with all hands. Built in 1892 by Cook, Welton & Gemmell Ltd. (Hull), the Cyprus was skippered by Edwin Watson (30). Her last owners were the Hull Steam Fishing & Ice Co. Ltd. (Hull).

702: Deerhound (H81): lost with all hands, off Unst, Shetland—Shetlanders described the storm that hit the island in terms of unprecedented severity. Built in 1889 by Cook, Welton & Gemmell Ltd. (Hull), Deerhound was skippered by Charles Munzer, of Subway Street; and owned by the Humber Steam Trawling Co. Ltd. (Hull).

703: Falcon (H321): lost with all hands. Built in 1896 by Cook, Welton & Gemmell Ltd. (Hull) for Pickering & Haldane's Steam Trawling Co. Ltd. (Hull), the Falcon was skippered by John Swain (29).

704: Indian Empire (H369): lost with all hands. Built in 1897 by Cook, Welton & Gemmell Ltd. (Hull) for the Cargill Steam Trawling Co. Ltd. (Hull), the Indian Empire was skippered by Harold Elliot (32).

705: Emperor (H325): lost with all hands. Built in 1893 by Robert Craggs & Sons Ltd. (Middlesbrough) for the East Coast Steam Fishing Co. Ltd. (Aberdeen), her last owners were David M. Gammie (Edinburgh), and she was skippered by George Pearson.

706: W. Boyes & Co. Ltd. was incorporated as a Limited Company (company number 00066251) on 18 June 1900, with William Boyes becoming Managing Director. Three of William Boyes' friends became directors of the company: James Pirie (Chairman), Henry Merry Cross, and W. Barker Mason. J.H. Harrison was appointed Company Secretary. After the incorporation, and the sale of shares, the company had £42,500 to begin its expansion plans.

707: Joseph Leopold (Sir Leo) Schultz was born on 4 February 1900 at 95 Holderness Road, Hull the third generation son of Polish immigrants Solomon and Hinda (*née* Hiller) Schultz. When Leo was born his father was a pawnbroker, on Holderness Road—where Leo attended

Craven Street School. In 1926, aged 26 years old, he was elected a Labour councillor (for Myton Ward) for the first time; he was Lord Mayor of Hull from 1942–43, and later went on to serve as Leader of Hull City Council for an unprecedented 34 years (1945 to 1979). He became known both as 'Mr Hull' and 'The lion of Hull'. He died in 1991, aged 91.

708: At the end of the 1899–1900 season (their first season in the Northern Union) Hull KR finished 6th in the Yorkshire Senior Competition league table with 32 points; one place above Hull FC on 30 points.

709: On 17 September 1900 'Eight Lancashire Lads', a troupe of clog-dancers of which Charlie Chaplin was the youngest member, appeared at the Palace Theatre on Anlaby Road, though it is not absolutely certain that Chaplin performed with the group on that particular occasion. It is also believed that Chaplin appeared in a production of *Sherlock Homes*, staged at the Theatre Royal, Paragon Street during the week commencing 21 August 1905; and as a villain who bribes the goalkeeper in a production of *Fred Karno's Football Match* at the Palace Theatre during the week commencing 16 January 1909.

710: In 1900 local engineering company Rose, Downs and Thompson—having acquired a licence from Louis-Gustave Mouchel, the British agent of François Hennebique, permitting the company to build structures using Hennebique's patented ferro-concrete system—constructed an extension to its Caroline Street works. Using the same system, the company subsequently constructed a bridge over the former Foredyke Drain at New Cleveland Street. In 1986 a blue heritage plaque was erected on the former factory to mark its construction. The inscription reads:

> From an iron foundry established in the late 18th century
> Rose Downs and Thompson developed an engineering

business specializing in machinery for the edible oil industry. Constructed in 1900, this FERRO-CONCRETE WORKSHOP was the first using the Hennebique system

711: The person to have held the office of Mayor of Hull the most times is John Bedford, who was elected Mayor on six occasions: 1412, 1414, 1420, 1428, 1435, and 1443; while John Tutbury served as Mayor five times: 1399, 1408, 1413, 1425, and 1432. A little more recently, Alfred Gelder was elected Mayor in the five consecutive years from 1898–1902.

712: The site and wider district of Hull's St. Andrew's Dock was host to the full range of activities associated with the running and maintenance of the region's fishing fleet and its labour force and community, with its own ice plant, ship maintenance slipways, a post office, banks, shops, cafes, a doctor's surgery and a police station—complete with cells.

713: From 1900 onwards, Thomas Ferens donated generously to a range of causes, including the Middlesex Hospital and the Victoria Hospital for Sick Children. He supported, among others, the Hull Institute for the Deaf and Dumb, the NSPCA, and Yorkshire Cancer Research.

714: On 11 October 1901 the Hull steam trawler St. Bernard (H501) was wrecked with the loss of all hands, after being stranded off the Faroe Islands. Built in 1900 by Cook, Welton & Gemmell Ltd. (Hull), St. Bernard was skippered by Richard Moore (37). Her last owners were the Humber Steam Trawling Co. Ltd.

715: Hull Central Library in Albion Street was built to a design by J.S. Gibson in 1900–01, and was opened on 6 November 1901 by Sir John Lubbock, Lord Avebury. The total cost of construction was £20,000, including the purchase of the site and fittings.

716: On 12 November 1901 the Hull steam trawler Aden (H250) foundered and was lost with all hands, in the North Sea. Built in 1894 by Edwards Brothers (North Shields), Aden was owned by the Hull Steam Fishing & Ice Co. Ltd. (Hull). She was skippered by Samuel Knowles (28) of Camberwell Avenue, Brighton Street, Hull.

717: When John Ellerman sold most of Leyland & Co. to J.P. Morgan in 1901, he retained ownership of 20 ships and subsequently bought the inactive Liverpool-based Papyanni Co. to operate these. The company was initially operated as Ellerman & Papyanni, and continued to trade on the European routes formerly operated by Papyanni Co.

718: Thomas Sheppard married his wife, Mary Isobel, in Leeds in 1901; they had one son, Thomas Harvey, but the couple separated in 1930–31. Mary died at Colwyn Bay in 1947. Sheppard lived at various addresses in Bridlington between 1910 and 1919. He became President of a number of local societies, including the Hull Shakespeare Society, the Hull Playgoers' Society, the Hull Geological Society, and the Yorkshire Numismatic Society.

719: In 1901, aged 24, Thomas Sheppard became the first curator of the Hull Municipal Museum (based on the Hull Literary and Philosophical Society collections) at the Royal Institution in Albion Street. The museum, having been closed for 18 months for extensive refurbishments, carried out under Sheppard's direction, re-opened on 2 June 1902, with Sheppard abolishing admission charges, thereby ensuring over 2,000 visitors a week.

720: In 1901 the country's first municipally owned crematorium was opened at Hull's Hedon Road Cemetery. It was designated a Listed Building (English Heritage Building ID: 387572) on 21 January 1994.

721: In 1901 Ellerman & Papyanni was renamed the London, Liverpool and Ocean Shipping Co. Ltd., and John Ellerman expanded his shipping interests with the acquisition of the City Line (Glasgow), and the Hall Line (Liverpool). In each case, the London, Liverpool and Ocean Shipping Co. Ltd. bought 50% of the shares and Ellerman personally bought the remaining 50%. A restructuring saw Ellerman selling his personal holdings to the parent company, in return for additional shares, towards the end of 1901.

722: The National Census of 1901 reported the population of the county borough of Hull as 240,259.

723: In January 1902 the London, Liverpool and Ocean Shipping Co. Ltd. was renamed Ellerman Lines. Subsequently all its employees were issued with a company uniform. A new company pennant bearing the letters JRE was introduced in October 1904.

724: On 8 January 1902 the Hull steam trawler Jupiter (H432) was lost with all hands in the North Sea, off Whalsay, Shetland, after becoming stranded at Rumble Holm. Built in 1898 by Mackie & Thomson (Govan) and launched on 1 September that year, she was skippered by James Bell, and owned by William Widdowson (Hull).

725: On 14 January 1902 the Hull steam trawler Anlaby (H437) was lost with all hands after foundering in a snow storm off Grindavik, on Iceland's south-western peninsula. Built in 1898 by Cochrane & Cooper Ltd. (Selby), she was skippered by Carl Nielson (38); she was owned by James Henry Collinson (Hull).

726: On 25 January 1902 the Hull steam trawler Linnet (H363) was lost with all hands after going missing while heading for the Icelandic grounds. Built in 1897 by Cook, Welton & Gemmell Ltd. (Hull), for Pickering &

Haldane's Steam Fishing Co. Ltd. (Hull), the Linnet was believed to have foundered off the north coast of Scotland. She was skippered by Alfred Snowden (31).

727: On 26 January 1902 the Hull steam trawler Orkney (H386) went missing and was lost with all hands off Horn Reef, Jutland. Built in 1898 by Thomas Scott (Goole), for the Hull Steam Fishing & Ice Co. Ltd. (Hull), the Orkney was skippered by Charles Leverson (39).

728: On 25 March 1902 Arthur Richardson became the first person to be executed by hanging at Hull's Hedon Road prison. Richardson was 30 years old when he was executed for murdering his aunt, Sarah Hebden (62) at 97 Hodgson Street, Hull on 28 November 1901.

729: On 22 August 1902 Hull Corporation was granted a licence under the Telegraph Act 1899 to operate a municipal telephone system in Kingston upon Hull.

730: Florence Margaret (Stevie) Smith, poet and novelist, was born on 20 September 1902 at 34 De La Pole Avenue, Hull, the second daughter of Charles Smith and his wife Ethel. Following the collapse of her marriage, Stevie Smith's mother moved the family (along with Stevie's aunt, Margaret Annie Spear) to London when Stevie was four years old. They lived at 1 Avondale Road, in Palmers Green; and Stevie lived there all her adult life. In 1997 a blue heritage plaque was erected at 34 De La Pole Avenue to identify it as the house in which Stevie Smith was born. The inscription reads:

> Poet & writer STEVIE SMITH (1902–1971) was born here 20th September 1902

731: On 27 October 1902 the company founded by Fred Needler (which would eventually become Needlers Ltd.) was incorporated as Fred Needler Ltd., then, in 1906, to cope with increasing growth and expansion, Needler bought land off Sculcoates Lane and built a purpose designed factory in Bournemouth Street; it was at this time the company name was changed to Needlers Ltd.

732: Hull Boys' Club was founded on Tuesday 18 November 1902. It has been visited by Royalty on four occasions: 1936 (HRH The Duke of Gloucester); 1937 (Queen Elizabeth and King George VI); 1972 (HRH The Duke of Kent); 2002 (The Duke of Gloucester).

733: On 26 December 1902 the Alexandra Theatre, situated on George Street (on the corner of Bourne Street) opened its doors to the public for the first time, with a production of *A Royal Divorce*, a play by C.C. Collingham. Designed in the Renaissance style by Thomas Guest, and owned by William Morton, the Alexandra Theatre's auditorium extended to four levels, and had a total capacity of 2,700 with seating accounting for 2,200 of that total.

734: On 20 February 1903 the Hull steam trawler Fides (H372) was lost with all hands after foundering off North Orkney. She left the Orkney Islands on 16 February, and was last seen on 18 February. Built in 1906 by Alexander Hall & Sons Ltd. (Aberdeen), the Fides was skippered by Albert Butcher (35) of 1 Napier Terrace, Tyne Street, Hull. Her last owners were the Anglo-Norwegian Steam Fishing Co. Ltd. (Hull).

735: Hollywood actress Dorothy Mackaill was born on 4 March 1903, at 20 Newstead Street, off Chanterlands Avenue, Hull and attended the nearby Thorseby Street School.

736: Aviator Amy Johnson was born at 154 St. George's Road, Hull on 1 July 1903. In 1988 a blue heritage plaque was erected at the house to identify it as Amy Johnson's birthplace. The inscription reads:

Pioneer Aviator AMY JOHNSON (1903–1941) was
born here 1st July 1903

737: The youngest person to be hanged at Hull Prison
was 19-year-old Charles William Ashton, who was
executed on 22 December 1903 for the murder of 16 year-
old Annie Marshall. Ashton's victim had been brutally
raped, and shot in the head, before being thrown in the
river.

738: John Ellerman continued to expand his shipping
interests in the first two decades of the 20th century,
acquiring several long-established companies, including
Bucknalls (London) and the Glen Line (Glasgow).

739: Hull City Association Football Club was founded
on 28 June 1904—too late to apply for entry into the
Football League. So, in their first season as a professional
club, City played friendly matches: at Dairycoates, the
Anlaby Road Cricket Ground (the Circle), and The
Boulevard.

740: Hull City's first match, played on 1 September 1904
in front of 6,000 spectators at The Boulevard, was a
friendly against Notts County. The score finished 2-2,
with George Rushton scoring the club's first goals.

741: Hull City's first competitive match was an FA Cup
Preliminary Round game against Stockton, on Saturday
17 September 1904. While City were drawn as the home
team, Hull FC were scheduled to play Warrington Wolves
at The Boulevard on that date (a game they won 8-7), so
City agreed to forgo their home advantage and played at
Stockton. The final score was 3-3; but the replay, on 22
September (again at Stockton), saw City being eliminated
from the competition when they were beaten 4-1.

742: Established in 1904, the same year as Hull City
AFC, Hull Golf Club was the first golf club in the Hull

area. It was founded by 9 local golfers, including solicitor Haggit Colbeck, who became the club's first captain. The club was initially located just off Anlaby Road, on the site that was later occupied by Boothferry Park, the home ground of Hull City until they moved to the Kingston Communications Stadium in December 2002.

743: On the night of 21–22 October 1904 Hull's Gamecock Fleet, fishing at Dogger Bank, was attacked by the Baltic Fleet of the Russian Imperial Navy. The Baltic Fleet included new battleships crewed by inexperienced and untrained naval personnel; and the Gamecock Fleet were fired upon when its trawlers were mistaken for Japanese torpedo boats. The incident, which became known as the 'Dogger Bank Incident', strained diplomatic relations between Russia and Britain to their limit, resulting in an International Commission, held in Paris, to investigate the actions of Admiral Zinovy Rozhestvensky, the commander in charge of the Baltic Fleet.

744: The three main targets of the October 1904 attack on Hull's Gamecock Fleet were the Crane (H756), the Moulmein (H61), and the Mino (H799); but it was the Crane that sustained the most severe shelling, resulting in the loss of the lives of its Skipper: George Henry Smith (40) of 7 Ripple Street, Hull; and Third Hand: William Richard Leggett (28) of 16 Flora Avenue, Carlton Street, Hull, before the vessel eventually sank. The surviving crew members of the Crane were rescued by the Gull (H241), skippered by George Green. Walter Whelpton, the skipper of the Mino, died almost seven months later as a result of injuries sustained during the attack.

745: The first exchange of Hull's municipally owned telephone system, which opened on 28 November 1904, was located at the site of the former Trippett Street Baths; then in 1914 the Corporation acquired the former National Telephone Company exchange at 65 Mytongate.

The construction of Telephone House on Carr Lane in 1964 resulted in both the Trippett Street and the Mytongate exchanges being superseded. In 2000 a blue heritage plaque was erected at Castle Street, Hull to mark the site of the city's unique municipally owned Telephone Department. The inscription reads:

> From 1914 to 1963 the headquarters of the Hull Corporation Telephone Department was here at 65 MYTONGATE. In 1987 the department became Kingston Communications (Hull) PLC

746: In their first season (1904), Hull City played forty-seven matches (including their two FA Cup Preliminary Round matches against Stockton): thirty-one home games and sixteen away games. They won twenty-seven matches, lost eleven, and drew nine.

747: Some time around 1904 Hull-born Ethel Annie Liggins, acting on advice given by Lady Maud Warrender, changed her surname to the Polish-sounding Leginska; and was later dubbed the 'Paderewski of women pianists'—a comparison with Polish piano virtuoso Ignacy Paderewski (who went on to become the Polish Prime Minister in January 1919).

748: In 1904 the North Eastern Railway (NER), then the main owner of the Hull docks, applied to Parliament for powers to build 'A river wall or quay' 'on the foreshore of the river Humber commencing at the south-eastern corner of the Albert Dock'. This would become the Riverside Quay.

749: Hull's Carnegie Library, situated adjacent to the main gates at the Anlaby Road end (south) of West Park, was built with funds provided by the Scottish-American industrialist Andrew Carnegie—thought to have been the richest American of all time and among the 10 richest people who ever lived. The site was provided by Hull

Corporation, with construction commencing towards the end of 1904.

750: Celebrated Hull architect Cuthbert Brodrick died at Gorey, Jersey on 2 March 1905. He was buried in St. Martin's churchyard, near Gorey.

751: The Hull Kingston Rovers record for the most individual points scored in a match is held by George Henry West, who scored 53 points in a 73-5 Challenge Cup First Round win over Brooklands Rovers on 4 March 1905.

752: The Hull Kingston Rovers record for the most individual tries scored in a match is held by George Henry West, who scored eleven tries against Brooklands Rovers in the same match mentioned above.

753: Frederick B. Grotrian, parliamentary representative for Kingston-upon-Hull East from 1886–92, and once sole proprietor of the *Hull Daily Mail*, died on 8 April 1905 at his home Ingmanthorpe Hall, Wetherby.

754: Sir James Reckitt was instrumental in securing a £3,000 donation from Andrew Carnegie towards the establishment of Hull's Carnegie Library. The library, which was designed by the City Architect Joseph Hirst, was officially opened by Sir James Reckitt (Chairman of the Libraries Committee) on Tuesday 18 April 1905, with the doors opening to the public at six o'clock that evening.

755: The Reckitt's Orchestral Society was formed in July 1905: programming concerts at the Reckitt Social Hall; both East Park and West Park; the Queen's Hall, and the Assembly Rooms. Its Musical Director was Percival Leech.

756: On 17 December 1905 the Hull steam trawler Golden Era (H798) was posted missing and lost with all hands after foundering off the coast of Iceland. Built in

1903 by Cook, Welton & Gemmell Ltd. (Beverley), for Hall, Leyman & Co. Ltd. (Hull), she was skippered by Samuel Mitchell (47) of 49 King's Bench Street, Hull.

757: The company's first full-time Welfare Worker, Miss Martha Jones, was appointed by Reckitt and Sons Ltd. in 1905. Miss Jones retired in 1917.

758: In 1905 *Brasso* liquid metal polish was marketed by Reckitt and Sons Ltd. for the first time.

759: The family of Arthur Milne moved to Hessle when he was 9 years old. Up to that point, he had attended the Church of England school in Hull at which his father was Headmaster.

760: In 1905, when both the First and Second divisions of the Football League expanded from eighteen to twenty clubs, Hull City were elected to the Second Division. In the 1905–06 season they played most of their home matches at The Circle, Anlaby Road.

761: In 1905, in recognition of his contribution to Britain's shipping requirements during the South African War, John Ellerman was given a baronetcy; and in 1921 he was made a Companion of Honour.

762: The Alhambra Palace music hall on Porter Street was acquired by Thomas Barrasford in 1905, and became part of his ever expanding 'Barrasford Circuit'. It was subsequently refurbished as the New Hippodrome.

763: In 1905 an Act was passed sanctioning the construction of a quay (Riverside Quay) of up to 5,580 feet (1,700 m), and to dredge to a depth of 16 feet (4.9m) below low water of ordinary spring tides.

764: The Act sanctioning the construction of Riverside Quay allowed for it to be built in two stages: the first section to be constructed stretched 2,500ft westward from the entrance to Albert Dock.

765: During the dredging operations for the construction of Riverside Quay, approximately 2m tons of material were removed and deposited four miles down the river Humber on the south bank.

766: Riverside Quay was designed as a deep water quay for the processing of perishables requiring quick handling and discharge, avoiding the kinds of delays previously experienced due to the variations of the tide times.

767: Hull's Royal Station Hotel was extended, with wings and a fourth floor being added, in 1903–05. The architect for these additions was William Bell.

768: The world's oldest surviving steam trawler with its steam engines intact is the Viola (H868), built by Cook, Welton & Gemmell Ltd. (Beverley) for the Hellyer Steam Fishing Co. Ltd. (Hull). One of around 50 trawlers built at that time for Hellyer's new North Sea boxing fleet, the Viola was launched into the river Hull at Beverley early in 1906 before being floated down the river to Hull to be fitted with triple-expansion steam engines by Amos & Smith of Neptune Street, Hull.

769: Horatio Nelson Smith drew on his experience in the textile industry to begin the company's expansion into surgical dressings. He bought a machine from Germany for cutting and rolling bandages, and in 1906 won a contract to supply surgical dressings to Canadian hospitals.

770: The Fishermen's Memorial commemorating the Hull trawlermen who lost their lives as a result of the Dogger Bank incident cost £245 and was assembled by local stone mason and sculptor Albert Leake of Spring Bank West. The standing fisherman was carved in Italy from a photograph of Leake posing in oilskins and a sou'wester. The members of the memorial committee were elected for the Blythe Boys Lodge of the Royal Antediluvian Order of Buffaloes, of which the Crane's skipper George Smith was a member.

771: The Fishermen's Memorial commemorating the Hull trawlermen who lost their lives as a result of the Dogger Bank incident, was unveiled on 30 August 1906. The statue, erected by public subscription, depicts George Smith, the skipper of the sunken vessel the Crane (H756), and stands at the junction of Hessle Road and Boulevard (south).

772: Although the inscription it bears states: 'Unveiled by Lord Nunburnholme August 30th 1906', the memorial commemorating the trawlermen who lost their lives as a result of the Dogger Bank incident was actually unveiled by John Watt J.P., as Lord Nunburnholme [Charles Henry Wilson]—nearing the end of his life—was 'indisposed on the morning of the unveiling'.

773: At the beginning of the 12th season of the Northern Rugby Union, in 1906, the rules were changed in two significant areas: to reduce the number of players on each side from 15 to 13; and to introduce the 'play-the-ball' rule, whereby a tackled player stands up and rolls the ball backwards (back into play) using his boot. By the end of the 1906–07 season Hull FC had accrued just 22 points, and finished in 23rd position in the league of 27 teams.

774: On 12 March 1906 the Hull steam trawler Antonio (H857) was lost with all hands whilst fishing in the North Sea. The Antonio was built in 1906 by Cook, Welton & Gemmell Ltd. (Hull), for the Hull Northern Fishing Co. Ltd. (Hellyer Bros. Ltd.). She was skippered by William Level (59) of 4 George Terrace, Tadman Street, Hull. George Renardson of 234 Hawthorne Avenue, Hull was the vessel's Chief Engineer.

775: In 1906 Hull City finished 5th in their first season in the Second Division of the Football League, and after a brief period with The Circle as their home ground, they soon moved to a new home ground adjacent to (and east of) The Circle. Here they stayed until the Second World War disrupted fixtures and City returned, albeit briefly, (in 1941) to The Boulevard.

776: The 1899 Act authorising the construction of Hull's Joint Dock sanctioned it covering an area of 60 acres, but the Hull Joint Dock Act, 1906, reduced that to 32 acres. The completion date was also extended to 1910.

777: In March 1906 the £850,000 contract for Hull's Joint Dock was awarded to S. Pearson and Son Ltd. of Westminster.

778: Hull's Joint Dock was designed by eminent engineer Sir Benjamin Baker, who also consulted on the Aswan Dam, the Forth Bridge and London's Metropolitan Railway.

779: Commencement of the construction of the Joint Dock was delayed until 1906 due to opposition to the original plans from the Humber Conservancy Board, who objected on the grounds that the new dock would divert the flow of the river Humber.

780: In 1906, having been elected MP for the first time, Thomas Ferens sent each of Reckitts' employees a sovereign, explaining that he'd made provisions in his will for the payment of £1 to each of the company's employees, but had decided to 'celebrate [becoming an MP] by making the presentation now, instead of leaving it to my executors', requesting, in line with his belief in total abstinence from alcohol, that 'no portion of it be spent on intoxicating liquor'. This gesture cost him around £3,000.

781: In 1906 Thomas Ferens donated grounds to the Young People's Christian and Literary Institute in Hull, and the following year helped to establish the city's Garden Village.

782: Thomas Ferens was elected as Liberal Member of Parliament for East Hull between 1906–18, winning for the first time in 1906 with a majority of 2,362 votes.

783: In February 1907 Sir James Reckitt wrote from his Swanland Manor home to T.R. Ferens, setting out a proposal 'to establish a Garden Village, within a reasonable distance of our Works, so that those [of the Reckitt and Sons Ltd. employees] who are wishful might have the opportunity of living in a better house, with a garden, for the same rent that they now pay for a house in Hull', thereby sowing the seeds for the formation of The Garden Village (Hull) Ltd. and the subsequent construction of the Hull Garden Village (also referred to as the Hull Garden Suburb) to the north of Holderness Road, designed for The Garden Village (Hull) Ltd. by Hull architects Runton & Barry.

784: On 13 February 1907 the Hull steam trawler Setter (H163) foundered and was lost with all hands, in the North Sea. She was built in 1891 by Cook, Welton & Gemmell Ltd. (Hull) for the Humber Steam Trawling Co. Ltd. (Hull).

785: On Monday 18 February 1907 the Hull steam trawler Celia (H863) was lost with all hands after foundering in the North Sea. Built for the Hellyer Steam Fishing Co. Ltd. by Mackie & Thomson (Govan), Celia was just a few weeks old, having been built the previous year and launched on 28 December 1906. She was skippered by James Parrot of 55 Waverley Street, Hull.

786: On 13 July 1907, three months after her 21st birthday, Hull-born Ethel Annie Liggins (Ethel Leginska) married a former fellow pupil of Leschetizky, Roy Emerson Whittern (later known as Emerson Whithorne, the composer) at Paddington register office. They had one child, a son named Cedric, born on 12 September 1908; and, after officially separating by 1912, the couple were eventually divorced on 11 February 1918. Her marriage to Whithorne had qualified Leginska for American citizenship, and she became a resident of New York in 1913.

787: Charles Wilson—who had received the freedom of Hull in 1899, and was made a peer (Baron Nunburnholme) in 1906—died on 27 October 1907 at his home, Warter Priory, where he was buried on 31 October.

788: On 4 December 1907 the steam trawler Rowena (GY915) went missing and was lost with all hands after leaving Grimsby for the North Sea fishing grounds. She was built in 1898 by Cochrane & Cooper Ltd. (Beverley), for the United Steam Fishing Co. Ltd. (Grimsby); Hull seaman T. Priestley of 219 Bean Street, Hull was the vessel's Chief Engineer.

789: As early as 1907 Hull City Council had discussed the possibility of establishing a municipal training college for men and women. This finally happened with the opening of the Hull Municipal Training College, on Cottingham Road, in September 1913. With just 126 students and a staff of 9, the Principal was Ivor B. John, with Miss C.T. Cumberbirch as vice-Principal.

790: T.J. Smith & Nephew was registered as a limited liability company (company number: 00093994), with its Registered Office at 101 Hessle Road, Hull, on 2 July 1907.

791: In 1907, 19 year-old Harry Fletcher junior opened a butchers shop at 482 Hessle Road, Hull. The business he established would eventually become H. Fletcher & Son, the much respected beef and pork butchers, and confectionery retailer, whose flagship branch was located at 41–45 King Edward Street (at the corner of King Edward Street and Jameson Street). He was originally set up in business by his father.

792: In 1905 the Board of Reckitt and Sons Ltd. discussed the possibility of providing a number of social welfare facilities for its employees, including a Social Hall, a Girls Rest Room, and both a Works Doctor and Works Dentist. As a result of these Board Room discussions the company's first Social Hall was opened in 1907.

793: In 1907 Thomas Martin became Managing Director of the Asbestos and Rubber Company and the Martin family took control of the company. The company has been owned by the Martin family ever since, with the fourth generation of the family now running the business.

794: Hull's Riverside Quay was first used in 1907 by a steamer (jointly owned by the North Eastern Railway Company and the Lancashire and Yorkshire Railway Company) bound for Zeebrugge.

795: Riverside Quay projected into the river approximately 90ft beyond the old 'coping line'.

796: In 1907 Hull's National Avenue was named after the National Radiator Company, who established a production facility there in 1905. Prior to the construction of the factory the site was mainly open country, being only partially occupied, by one of the city's brick works.

797: In 1908 Hull FC reached the final of the Northern Rugby Football Union Challenge Cup for the first time when they played Hunslet at the Fartown Ground, Huddersfield on 25 April. Hunslet took the honours, beating Hull 14-0. This was the first of three successive

Challenge Cup final appearances for the club: they were beaten 17-0 by Wakefield Trinity (at Leeds) in 1909; and 26-12 by Leeds (at Huddersfield) in a replay, following a 7-7 draw, in 1910.

798: In October 1908 John Ellerman 'married' Hannah Glover under an obscure Scottish law allowing a couple to be legally married by mutual consent if they cohabit for twenty-one successive days. On 21 December 1909 Ellerman's son (and heir to his baronetcy as well as his fortune), also John Reeves Ellerman, was born at Folkestone, Kent. The baronetcy would not have succeeded to Ellerman's son had the child been illegitimate.

799: On 24 November 1908 the Hull steam trawler Paragon (H56) was lost with all hands, after becoming stranded in thick fog at Aðalvík, Iceland. Built in 1899 by Alexander Hall & Sons Ltd. (Aberdeen), she was skippered by Holger Pederson and owned by City Steam Fishing Co. Ltd. (Hull).

800: Geoffrey Dummer, generally accepted as being the first person to conceptualize the integrated circuit (the basis of all computer processors, and used in virtually all electronic devices) was born in Hull on 25 February 1909.

801: On 22 July 1909 the Hull steam trawler Prome (H88) sank with the loss of all hands in the Dogger Bank fields of the North Sea. After being struck amidships by the Bristol barque, Gladys, at around 9am, the Prome sank within three minutes, taking all her crew with her. She was skippered by William Allon (45) of 8 Myrtle Grove, Brighton Street, Hull; it was his first trip with the vessel. Built in 1897 by Edwards Brothers (North Shields), the Prome was launched on 2 March 1897. She was owned by Kelsall Brothers & Beeching Ltd. (Manchester).

802: Arthur Wilson—who took control of the famous Wilson Line shipping company when his brother Charles died in 1907—died of cancer on 21 October 1909 at his home Tranby Croft, Anlaby. He was buried at Kirk Ella.

803: The Theatre Royal in Paragon Street closed in 1909, re-opening in 1912 as the Tivoli music hall, which was remodelled and refurbished in 1929. Following an air raid in 1943, which caused serious fire damage, the building closed, but was re-opened in 1944.

804: T.R. Ferens was a vocal advocate for Women's Rights, supporting women's suffrage at home and highlighting the trade of trafficking in women and young girls in the colonies. In 1910 he presented to Parliament a petition signed by 4,123 citizens of Hull calling for 'the extension of the franchise to women as it is or may be granted to men'.

805: The Hull Kingston Rovers record for the most individual goals scored in a match is 14, and is jointly held by Alfred Carmichael (10 placed and 4 drop-goals), against Merthyr Tydfil, 8 October 1910; Mike Fletcher, against Whitehaven, 18 March 1990; Colin Armstrong, against Nottingham City, 19 August 1990; and Damien Couturier, against Halifax, 23 April 2006.

806: On 24 December 1910 the Kinemacolour Palace opened on the south side of Anlaby Road (No. 21–25) near the city centre. The single-screen, 650-seat theatre (by J.M. Dossor) was built over a seven week period and received an early name change (prior to 1914) to Kinema Picture Palace, before being renamed Regent Picture Theatre (or simply 'Regent Cinema') in 1919. Along with the Tower Cinema, the Regent was owned and operated by a family named Freeman until both were closed in September 1978.

807: On 31 December 1910 the Hull steam trawler Grebe (H906) was posted missing and lost with all hands after foundering in the North Sea. Built in 1906 by Goole Shipbuilding & Repairing Co. Ltd. (Goole), for Kelsall Bros. & Beeching Ltd. (Hull), the Grebe left port on 29 December on her way to join the fishing fleet. She was skippered by George Radford of 342 Hessle Road, Hull.

808: The highest position reached by Hull City between their first season in the Second Division of the Football League (1905–06) and the suspension of the Football League due to the First World War, was when they narrowly missed out on promotion by coming third, behind Manchester City (1st) and Oldham Athletic (2nd) in the 1909–10 season. Hull City finished on the same number of points (53) as Oldham, and had an identical record of wins (23), losses (8) and draws (7); and even scored more goals: 80 to Oldham's 79. However, Oldham's goal average was 2.03. and City's was 1.74, so Oldham won the second promotion place. Incidentally, City lost 3-0 to Oldham on the last Saturday of the season; and Hull City's Jackie Smith was the Division's leading goalscorer in that year, with 32 goals.

809: The 1,500-seat Princes Hall cinema on George Street, Hull opened in July 1910, directly opposite the 1,507 seat Grand Opera House (later, the Dorchester Cinema). Princes Hall was renamed the Curzon Cinema almost a decade before it closed, and was converted into a club in February 1960. The building was demolished in the mid 1980s.

810: The Albert and William Wright docks were joined together in 1910.

811: Stevie Smith was educated at Palmers Green High School (1910–17) and North London Collegiate School (1917–20), but she did not progress to university. She trained at Mrs Hoster's Secretarial Training College, on London's Cromwell Road, and after a year working for a consulting engineer, took a position with the firm of C. Arthur Pearson in 1922, being appointed personal secretary to Sir Neville Pearson, 2nd Baronet (who Smith fictionalised as Sir Phoebus in her first two novels).

812: In October 1911 Thomas Ferens was presented with the Freedom of the City of Hull.

813: On 4 November 1911 Hull City suffered their heaviest defeat when they lost 8-0 to Wolverhampton Wanderers at Molineux in the Football League Second Division.

814: On 14 December 1911 the steam trawler Persian (GY1226) went missing and was lost with all hands after sailing from Grimsby for the North Sea fishing grounds. She was built by Cook, Welton & Gemmell Ltd. (Hull) for Thomas Robinson (Grimsby). Hull seaman William Sallis of 56 Adelaide Street was the vessel's 3rd Hand.

815: The early acquisition of the smaller (local) competitor Lambert & Lambert in around 1911, was the first of many strategic acquisitions by Smith & Nephew. The following year (1912) the company bought Sashena Limited, manufacturers of the *Sashena* sanitary towel brand, which later became the *Lilia* brand.

816: Early orders from the Turkish War Office at the start of the Turkish-Bulgarian War (1911), and from the governments of the Allied Forces during the First World War, were major contributing factors to the rapid expansion and successful development of Smith & Nephew.

817: In the 1910–11 season Hull City reached the last 16 (Third Round) of the FA Cup for the first time, going down 3-2 away to the Cup holders Newcastle United. Newcastle went on to reach the final where they drew 0-0 with Bradford City at Crystal Palace, London, before losing 1-0 to a goal by Jimmy Speirs in the replay at Old Trafford, Manchester.

818: In 1911 the Hull and Barnsley Railway Company built a pier on the river Humber, west of the entrance to Alexandra Dock. The pier stood 400 feet out into the Humber and was 1300 feet long, having a minimum depth of 18 feet and being connected to the shore by two gantries with an electric conveyor belt capable of moving 600 tons an hour.

819: Thomas Ferens believed in leadership by example and expected employees to be as energetic and punctual as he himself was. His determination to see improvements in productivity led to increasing success for Reckitt & Sons, with significant gains in turnover, profits, and capital; and therefore the value of shares in the company multiplied. As a consequence, of course, so did Ferens's personal fortune, which by his own estimation was £650,000 in 1911.

820: The National Census of 1911 reported the population of the county borough of Hull as 277,991.

821: On 15 April 1912 Hull-born Joseph Boxhall (28), the Fourth Officer on the Titanic, was on watch when the collision with the iceberg occurred, but he was just approaching the bridge, not actually on it. After hearing the three bells struck from the crow's nest, warning of the iceberg straight ahead, he joined the Captain and the First and Sixth officers, on the bridge. His main responsibility during the evacuation process was working out the position of the ship so it could be included in the wireless operators' SOS transmissions. On leaving the Titanic he was put in charge of lifeboat No. 2, and survived the disaster. Along with the two more senior surviving officers—Charles Lightoller and Herbert Pitman—Boxhall gave evidence at both the British and American enquiries into the tragedy.

822: On 22 April 1912 the Hull steam trawler Kingfisher (H830) was wrecked and lost with all hands off Cape Portland, Iceland. Built in 1905 by Cook, Welton & Gemmell Ltd. (Hull), for the St. Andrew's Steam Fishing Co. Ltd. (Hull), the Kingfisher was skippered by John Holroyd (47) of 198 St. George's Road, Hull.

823: Dr Eva Crane—who founded what would become the International Bee Research Association (IBRA) whilst living at 55 Newland Park, Hull—was born in London on 12 June 1912, and earned a PhD in Nuclear Physics at King's College London in 1937. She subsequently took up lectureships in Physics at both Hull and Sheffield universities. She continued as Director of IBRA for 35 years until her retirement at the end of 1983, when she became Scientific Consultant to the organization.

824: Legendary Hull FC winger Jack Harrison was born on Holderness Road on 12 November 1890, and was educated initially at Craven Street School before attending York Training College to embark on teacher training. On completion of his teacher training, he took a position at Hull's Lime Street School. He joined Hull FC in September 1912, playing his first match for the club against York that month.

825: On 28 November 1912 the Hull steam trawler Stork (H498) was lost with all hands when she ran aground and was wrecked on the west coast of Iceland. Built in 1900 by Cook, Welton & Gemmell Ltd. (Hull), she was skippered by Hans Arthur Hoier (35) of 14a Victoria Avenue, Conway Street, Hull; the owners were the St. Andrew's Steam Fishing Co. Ltd. (Hull).

826: John Bacchus Dykes' 'Nearer, my God, to Thee' is strongly associated with the RMS Titanic and the bravery of the musicians that are reputed to have continued playing as the ship went down. Some survivors reported hearing the tune being played; though the assertion that the tune was being played as the ship was actually sinking has been disputed. Several passengers also recalled that 'Eternal Father, strong to save' was sung at the ship's only hymn service, conducted by the Rev. Ernest Carter the night before the ship sank. In the American film version of the disaster, *Titanic* (1943), the Lowell Mason tune 'Bethany' was used; but in the British film version, *A Night to Remember* (1958), the Dykes tune 'Horbury' featured. The American Mason's tune was favoured once again in James Cameron's 1997 film version, *Titanic*.

827: Thomas Sheppard authored many books of local interest, including: *The Lost Towns of the Yorkshire Coast, and other chapters bearing upon the geography of the district* (1912), *William Smith: his maps and memoirs* (1917), *Kingston-upon-Hull before, during and after the Great War* (1919), *Handbook to Hull and the East Riding of Yorkshire* (1923), and *Wilberforce House: its history and collections* (1927).

828: Subsequent to being curator of the Hull Municipal Museum, Thomas Sheppard established a further seven museums in the city, including the Wilberforce House Museum; the Railway Museum (located at Paragon Station, and destroyed by enemy bombs in 1941); the Natural History Museum (destroyed by enemy fire in 1943); and the Museum of Fisheries & Shipping, at Pickering Park (now the Maritime Museum in the city centre).

829: The single-screen Eureka Picture Palace at 562 Hessle Road opened in the heart of the city's fishing community in September 1912, just 17 years after the first public screening of moving pictures by the Lumière brothers at the Grand Café in Paris on 28 December 1895. In 1921, in response to its increasing popularity, the venue was enlarged with the addition of a balcony.

830: On 7 September 1912 the East Hull Picturedrome was opened on the corner of Holderness Road and Brazil Street. This single-screen cinema had a seating capacity of 600 and was run by East Hull Picturedrome Ltd.

831: The Holderness Hall Cinema, on the corner of Witham and Clarence Street, opened on 16 November 1912. Costing £12,000 to build, the venue's interior décor featured ornate fibrous plaster mouldings and a barrel vaulted ceiling; it also boasted three cafés. The theatre's seating capacity, originally 2,000, was later reduced to 1,850.

832: In the ten years up to 1912 the net registered tonnage of shipping entering the docks at Hull increased by 72%, from 3,595,233 to 6,168,500; in the same period the shipments of coal had increased 129%, from 2,627,098 tons to 6,026,645 tons.

833: In 1912 Thomas Ferens built twelve almshouses at East Park and donated them to the Hull City Council to be administered as a Trust under the Ferens Haven of Rest (later as Ferens Haven). This Trust subsequently developed further properties at various locations in East Hull.

834: In 1912 Thomas Ferens was appointed by King George V to the Privy Council and was made High Steward of Hull.

835: The Hull Maritime Museum, originally known as the Museum of Fisheries & Shipping, first opened in 1912 at Pickering Park. It now occupies the old Dock Office, built by the Hull Dock Company in 1871.

836: The cupola from the old Hull Town Hall, designed by Cuthbert Brodrick, was rescued and resited in 1912 (and now stands, folly-like) at Pearson Park, near its western boundary. The cupola was registered as a Grade II Listed structure on 21 January 1994.

837: Renowned escapologist Harry Houdini appeared five times at the Palace Theatre, Hull (he once jumped, wrapped in chains, off Corporation Pier into the Humber!). In an appearance at the theatre early in 1913, he accepted a challenge from three Hull seamen in which he was to escape from a 'sea-bag, which is made of sail cloth [and] broad belting straps'. The challenge, which became known as the 'Seamen's Challenge', was accepted by Houdini for the second performance of his show on Thursday 30 January. The three seamen who offered the challenge were Dan Morris of 6 Norwood Street (Spring Bank), Tom Carr of 45 Craven Street, and Robert Mason of the Hull Sailor's Home on Alfred Gelder Street.

838: On Friday 7 March 1913 the Hull trawler Admiral Togo (H259) was lost with all hands after running aground and being wrecked off Iceland's southern peninsula. The crew took to the lifeboat in an attempt to reach safety, but the lifeboat capsized and all twelve crew were lost. Built in 1904 by Cook, Welton & Gemmell Ltd. (Hull), she was skippered by William Ponder (24) of 64 Walcott Street, Hull, and owned by Pickering & Haldane's Steam Fishing Co. Ltd. (Hull).

839: On 18 March 1913 the Hull steam trawler Oberon (H851) was lost with all hands in the North Sea. Built in 1905 by Cook, Welton & Gemmell Ltd. (Beverley), she was skippered by Horace Canning (26) of 74 Flinton Street, Hull; the owners were the Hellyer Steam Fishing Co. Ltd. (Hull).

840: On 3 April 1913 the Hull steam trawler Dauntless (H840) was posted missing and lost with all hands. Built in 1905 by Earle's Shipbuilding and Engineering Co. Ltd. (Hull), the Dauntless left Hull in early March for the Icelandic grounds, but no contact was made with the vessel after she left Stornoway on 4 March. Her last owners were J. Hollingsworth (Hull). She was skippered by Nicholas Michael (48) of 51 Cholmley Street, Hull.

841: On 18 November 1913 the Hull steam trawler Angus (H895) was lost with all hands after going missing in the North Sea. Built in 1897 by Mackie & Thomson (Govan) for the Hellyer Steam Fishing Co. Ltd., the Angus was skippered by William Johnson, of 7 Myrtle Grove, Brighton Street, Hull.

842: On 3 December 1913 the Hull steam trawler Desdemona (H904) was declared lost with all hands after wreckage and bodies from the vessel were found in the Dogger Bank region, where she had been headed. Built in 1906 by Mackie & Thomson (Govan), the Desdemona was skippered by David Lloyd (27) of Wilfred Terrace, Westbourne Street, Hull. Her last owners were Hull Northern Fishing Co. Ltd. (Hellyer Bros. Ltd.).

843: In 1913 the Alhambra Palace music hall, on Porter Street, was reconfigured as a cinema. It was destroyed by enemy bombing in 1941.

844: In 1913 the Gaiety Picture House opened in Hull's Market Place. Converted from a Georgian house (51/52 Market Place) to a design by Hull architect B.S. Jacobs, the theatre provided a total of around 600 seats, but closed on 20 March 1915, just two years after opening.

845: Prior to the First World War, Thomas Ferens made several gifts of land for the expansion of Hull's East Park, and in 1913 paid for the construction of the Ferens

Boating Lake within the park, this being further extended in 1923.

846: The Asbestos and Rubber Company was incorporated as a private limited company on 6 February 1914.

847: On 1 June 1914 the Tower Picture Palace was opened on the north side of the city centre end of Anlaby Road. This single-screen, 1,200-seat cinema was designed by Hull architect H. Percival Binks, in the Baroque Revival style with *Art Nouveau* details that Pevsner described in 1972 as 'undeniably debased in the extreme'.

848: The title of 'Mayor' of Hull was superseded by 'Lord Mayor' when a declaration by King George V, carried in the *London Gazette* of 26 June, announced that 'henceforth the Chief Magistrate and officer of the city shall bear the style and title of Lord Mayor of Kingston-upon-Hull'.

849: On 2 September 1914 the steam trawler Ajax (GY18), sailing out of Grimsby, was lost with all hands after striking an enemy mine off the mouth of the river Humber. Built in 1896 by Cochrane, Hamilton, Cooper & Schofield (Beverley), for Baker & Grant Steam Fishing (Grimsby), she was skippered by Edward Grant. Hull seaman J.W. Pettman (50) was a Deckhand on the vessel.

850: On Sunday 6 September 1914 the trawler Imperialist (H250) became the Hull fishing fleet's first casualty of the First World War due to enemy mines when she was lost after striking a mine in the North Sea, 40 miles east-north-east of Tynemouth, whilst on her way back to port from the Icelandic grounds, resulting in the loss of two of her crew.

851: On 10 September 1914 the steam trawler Oxford (GY233) went missing after sailing from Grimsby and was lost with all hands (presumed to be as a result of enemy action). Built in 1897 by Mackie & Thomson (Govan) for Hagerup & Doughty Ltd. (Grimsby), her last owners were the Consolidated Steam Fishing & Ice Co. Ltd. (Grimsby). Hull seaman Oswald Robson (29) of 5 Lizzie Grove, Liverpool Street, was a Deckhand on the vessel.

852: On 29 September 1914 the steam trawler Salvia (GY1164) was reported missing (presumed to be as a result of enemy action) and was lost with all hands. Built in 1900 by Schofield, Hagerup & Doughty Ltd. (Grimsby) for the North Eastern Steam Fishing Co. Ltd. (Grimsby), she was skippered by Richard Jones (43). Hull seaman Herbert Meanwell (32) of 38 Division Road was the vessel's 2nd Engineer.

853: On 30 September 1914 the Hull steam trawler St. Lawrence (H939) sailed from Hull, bound for Iceland. She went missing (presumed to be as a result of enemy action) and was lost with all hands. Built in 1907 by Mackie & Thomson (Govan), she was skippered by Henry Fletcher (42) of 1 St. Andrew's Street, Hull; the owners were the St. Andrew's Steam Fishing Co. Ltd. (Hull).

854: In September 1914 the Hull steam trawler Viola (H868) was requisitioned by the Admiralty to serve in the First World War. She was armed with a 3 pounder gun (she would later be fitted with a 12 pounder gun) and then sent to patrol waters around the Shetland Isles. The Viola's first crew after being requisitioned was made up of local seamen, with Charles Allum of Rosamond Street, Hull, skippering the vessel for much of her Admiralty duties.

855: On 2 November 1914 the West Park Picture Palace was opened at 419–421 Anlaby Road. This single-screen, 742-seat cinema, part of a portfolio of cinemas owned by Hull Picture Playhouses Ltd., closed on 4 January 1959. However, the venue has been re-configured at various stages of its existence into other kinds of establishments, such as the Charleston Club, the Granada, and the West Park Club. It was refurbished and reconfigured once again in the mid 1990s as the Steam Tavern. More recently it became the Premier Bar. A 2009 Hull City Council report, *Prioritisation and funding of the Council's Demolition Programme to March 2010*, put the cost of demolishing the venue at £54,000. The building had been removed from the 'Empty Building Rates' list.

856: On 26 November 1914 the Monica Picture House opened on Newland Avenue. By the end of the 1920s the single-screen, 894-seat theatre had been equipped with a Western Electric sound system; and by the mid 1950s CinemaScope had been installed, and its proscenium was accordingly widened to 31 feet.

857: On 23 December 1914 Hull's National Picture Theatre opened on Beverley Road, near the junction with Fountain Road. The single-screen, 1,050-seat theatre, designed in a Baroque revival style by architects Runton and Barry (for the De-Luxe Theatre Company) had a 24 feet wide proscenium and, in the early days, a resident orchestra; a Western Electric sound system was installed in 1930.

858: In 1914 Hull FC won the Challenge Cup for the first time in the club's history (on their fourth attempt), when they beat Wakefield Trinity 6-0 at Thrum Hall, Halifax on 18 April. The sides were even at 0-0 with about five minutes of the match remaining, but Hull (captained by Bert Gilbert) ultimately triumphed with late tries by Jack Harrison and Alf Francis.

859: In the 1913–14 season, winger John (Jack) Harrison scored 52 tries for Hull FC—still the club record for the most tries in one season by a single player. Harrison, a former teacher whose father worked as a plater and boilermaker at Hull's Earle's Shipyard, scored a remarkable 106 tries in his 116 matches for the club.

860: The front of the Tower Picture Palace on Anlaby Road is faced with white and green faience tiles, with a decorated balcony (with columns and wrought-iron balustrade), and is topped by an allegorical female figure. The two corner rounded towers are topped by spectacular mosaic-covered onion globes.

861: In 1914 a jetty (No.1 Oil Jetty) was constructed at Salt End, by the North Eastern and Hull and Barnsley railway companies, for the importation of bulk mineral oil. The jetty extended 1,500 feet into the Humber, and thus provided a water depth of 30 feet at low spring tides. These bulk mineral oil importation facilities eventually led to the establishment of the BP Saltend chemicals industrial site.

862: Hull's King George Dock, initially referred to as the Joint Dock because of the Joint Dock Act sanctioning its construction, was built to a design by Sir Benjamin Baker and Sir John Wolfe Barry. It became officially known as King George Dock following its opening in June 1914.

863: The electrically powered hydraulic plant installed at King George Dock was supplied by Hawthorn, Davey and Co. Ltd., Leeds.

864: The contractor for the main silo building at King George Dock was the British Reinforced Concrete Engineering Company.

865: The office buildings at King George Dock were designed by William Bell, the North Eastern Railway Company's Chief Architect between 1877 and 1914.

866: The 440 volt DC electricity supply used to power the operations at King George Dock (including the pumps used to power the hydraulic systems for such as the gates to the lock and the graving docks) was provided by the Hull Corporation.

867: Upon its completion in 1914 the quays of King George Dock were equipped with four 7-ton cranes, nine 10-ton cranes (supplied by Craven Brothers Ltd., Manchester, and fitted with Musker-Davidson luffing gear); thirty 3-ton electric cranes (built by Royce Ltd., Manchester); along with an 80-ton floating crane by Werf Gusto (A.F. Smulders). Also provided, on the roofs of the warehouses, were six 1.5-ton electric travelling cranes (built by Craven Brothers Ltd.) for use in the transfer of goods from rail to ship or vice versa.

868: Upon its completion King George Dock was equipped with six diagonally positioned berths dedicated solely to the processing of coal vessels, each berth's coaling appliances capable of handling 800 tons an hour.

869: King George Dock was built under the direct supervision of T.M. Newell and R. Pawley, with W. Ebdon acting as resident engineer, and the construction of the equipment being supervised by T.L. Norfolk.

870: Upon its completion King George Dock provided two graving docks (made entirely of concrete) situated at the eastern end of the north-east arm, their dimensions were: 550 feet by 72 feet; and 450 feet by 66 feet.

871: Upon its completion King George Dock provided six ferro-concrete warehouses, occupying almost all the quay on both sides of the dock's north-west arm: three single-storey blocks of 375 feet by 90 feet on the north side; three two-storey blocks of 375 feet by 70 feet on the south side; with a total capacity of 73,000 tons of general goods, all the warehouses were constructed with flat asphalted roofs which could be used for storage.

872: Upon its completion King George Dock consisted of a central basin measuring 1,050ft by 1000ft, a north-west arm measuring 1,350 feet by 312 feet (mainly for general commerce), and a north-east arm measuring 1,356 feet by 450 feet (mainly for the shipment of coal and the importation of timber).

873: Upon its completion King George Dock covered a water area of 53 acres, with provision for future extension to 85 acres; the total length of the quays extended to 8,162 feet; and the coaling appliance facilities provided a total shipping capacity of 5,000 tons per hour.

874: The entrance lock to King George Dock was 750 feet long, and 85 feet wide. Consisting of three pairs of gates, the lock was divided into two pens: the inner pen being 250 feet long, and the outer pen being 500 feet long.

875: King George Dock was constructed to provide berths and facilities for the largest vessels using the port of Hull, its primary initial use being for the export of coal.

876: King George Dock was the first fully-electrified dock in the country.

877: King George Dock was officially opened on 26 June 1914 by H.M. King George V and H.M. Queen Mary.

878: In 1914 the construction of a ferro-concrete grain silo, with a capacity of 40,000 tons, was begun at the western end of the north-west arm of the King George Dock. The silo, consisting of two blocks, each 96 feet wide by 241 feet long, and containing a total of 288 bins, each 12 feet square by 50 feet deep, was completed by 1919.

879: Hull's King George Dock was constructed with the north-west arm having three quays and—since it was initially conceived as being primarily for the exportation of coal (from Derbyshire, Nottinghamshire and Yorkshire)—a direct connection to the rail network. However, with the addition of the grain silo, plus a further two berths, the dock was well equipped for the shipment of wool and perishable foodstuffs when coal exports declined.

880: The two grain silo blocks at Hull's King George Dock were designed each with a receiving house standing 98ft above the quay, containing all the necessary machinery for handling large shipments of grain; the basements of the receiving houses linking to an underground distributing-chamber connected to two subways extending 900 feet along their respective quayside, thereby providing four 450 feet grain-ship berths.

881: Dorothy Mackaill's father, John Mackaill, was a store manager for the Maypole Butter Company; and M.C. at the Newington Dance Hall, Albert Avenue; however, her parents divorced when Dorothy was eleven years old, and she was placed in the custody of her father. They lived together at 15 Newstead Street, a short distance from the former family home at 20 Newstead Street.

882: On 8 January 1915 the Hull steam trawler Celia (H989), another Hellyer ship, was lost with all hands after going missing as a result of enemy action in the North Sea. The vessel, skippered by Wilfred Longthorne (27) of 8 St. George's Avenue, Selby Street, Hull, was built by Earle's Shipbuilding and Engineering Co. Ltd. (Hull) in 1908.

883: On 24 February 1915 the steam trawler Stirling (GY765) left Grimsby, went missing, and was lost with all hands. Built in 1898 by Mackie & Thomson (Govan) for Hagerup, Doughty & Co. (Grimsby), her last owners were the Consolidated Steam Fishing & Ice Co. Ltd. (Grimsby). She was skippered by Robert Cressey (52) of 11 Shaw Street, Holderness Road, Hull.

884: On 25 February 1915 the steam trawler Resto (GY1209) went missing and was lost with all hands in the North Sea; she was first posted missing on 25 January. The Resto was built in 1900 by Cochrane & Cooper Ltd. (Beverley), for George F. Sleight (Grimsby). She was skippered by Christopher Bishop, and the vessel's 2nd Engineer was William Matthew Gill (39) of 630 Hessle Road, Dairycoates, Hull.

885: On 26 February 1915, Scarborough's The Remnant Warehouse, the forerunner of W. Boyes & Co. Ltd., was destroyed by a ferocious fire in Queen Street (the blaze also destroyed the adjoining Queen Street Methodist Chapel). William Boyes reassured the staff of 80 that none of them would be laid off as a result of the fire, and within two weeks had made arrangements for the firm to continue trading from the St. Nicholas Hall in St. Nicholas Street.

886: Following its closure on 20 March 1915, Hull's Gaiety Picture House was converted into the Gaiety Theatre, and was subsequently re-named the Playgoers Theatre (1928), but it closed once again in 1934.

887: On 7 April 1915 the steam trawler Zarina (GY573) foundered and was lost with all hands 72 miles east by north off Spurn Point after being blown out of the water by either an enemy torpedo or an enemy mine. The Zarina was built in 1894 by Earle's Shipbuilding and Engineering Co. Ltd. (Hull), for Henry L. Taylor & Co. (Grimsby). She was skippered by Walter Bracewell Cooper (34) of 5 Thesiger Street, Grimsby. Hull seaman Edward Forest (50) of 21 Porter Place, Porter Street was the vessel's Chief Engineer.

ON 3 MAY 1915 SEVEN HULL TRAWLERS WERE LOST when they were targeted by a single enemy U-boat, U9, commanded by Johannes Spieß. The vessels were:

888: Bob White (H290): built in 1915 by the Goole Shipbuilding & Repairing Co. Ltd. (Goole), for Kelsall Brothers & Beeching (Hull). She was stopped before being sunk at 7.15pm.

889: Coquet (H831): built in 1905 by Earle's Shipbuilding & Engineering Co. Ltd. (Hull), for the Hull Steam Fishing & Ice Co. Ltd. (Hull). She was stopped—and the crew ordered to leave the ship—before being sunk at 4.45pm, 160 miles east-north-east of Spurn. There were no casualties.

890: Hector (H896): built in 1906 by Mackie & Thomson (Govan) for Hull Northern Fishing Co. Ltd. (Hellyer Bros. Ltd). She was stopped and then sunk at 6pm, 160 miles east-north-east of Spurn.

891: Hero (H886): built in 1906 by Cook, Welton & Gemmell Ltd. (Hull), for Hull Northern Fishing Co. Ltd. (Hellyer Bros. Ltd.). She was stopped and then sunk at 3.15pm, 150 miles east-north-east of Hornsea.

892: Iolanthe (H328): built in 1896 by Cook, Welton & Gemmell Ltd. (Hull), for the Hellyer Steam Fishing Co. Ltd. (Hull). She was stopped and then sunk, 140 miles east-north-east of Hornsea.

893: Northward Ho (H455): built in 1896 by Cook, Welton & Gemmell Ltd. (Hull), for S.T. White & Co. (Hull) Ltd. She was stopped and then sunk, 125 miles north-east of Hornsea.

894: Progress (H475): built in 1899 by Hawthorns & Co. (Leith), for the Great Northern Steam Fishing Co. Ltd. (Hull). She was stopped and then sunk at 5.30pm, 155 miles east-north-east of Spurn.

895: On 6 May 1915 commander Johannes Spieß and his U-boat U9 stopped the Hull trawler Merrie Islington (H183). Built in 1891 by Cook, Welton & Gemmell Ltd. (Hull), for the Humber Steam Trawling Co. Ltd. (Hull), she was sunk, 6 miles north-north-east of Whitby.

896: On 17 May 1915 the Hull steam trawler Mauritius (H547) was lost (presumed mined) with all hands, in the North Sea. The vessel left Hull bound for the North Sea fishing grounds on what should have been a ten day trip. Built in 1902 by Cook, Welton & Gemmell Ltd. (Hull), the Mauritius was skippered by Andrew Summer, and owned by Hull Steam Fishing & Ice Co. Ltd. (Hull).

897: On 18 May 1915 the Hull steam trawler Titania (H903) was lost with all hands after being struck by an enemy torpedo at the north-west corner of Dogger Bank. Built in 1906 by Mackie & Thomson (Govan), she was skippered by William Worrel (55) of 1 Belgrave Terrace, Eton Street, Hull; the owners were the Hellyer Steam Fishing Co. Ltd. (Hull).

898: On Friday 21 May 1915, after colliding with enemy mines laid by the cruiser Hamburg, the Hull trawler Sabrina (H346) sank in the North Sea. Built in 1897 by Cook, Welton & Gemmell Ltd., Beverley (Hull) for the Hellyer Steam Fishing Co. Ltd. (Hull), the Sabrina went down with the loss of all hands 160 miles east-north-east of Spurn Point. The vessel was skippered by William Blanchard (43) of 39 Clifton Terrace, Hull.

899: On 21 May 1915, the same day as the Hull trawler Sabrina (H346) was lost, her Hellyer's sister ship, Angelo (H890), went down in the Dogger Bank field, the most likely cause was thought to be striking enemy mines.

900: On 22 May 1915 the Hull steam trawler Sebastian (H888) went missing and was lost with all hands (presumed lost to enemy action), after leaving Hull. She was skippered by John Jackson (38) of 45 Harrow Street, Hull.

901: On 27 May 1915 the Hull steam trawler Southward Ho (H456) was lost with all hands (due to enemy action) 88 miles north-east of Spurn Point. The vessel was built by Doig & Broadley (Grimsby), and was owned by S.T. White & Co. (Hull) Ltd. She was skippered by Thomas Ellis (29) of 344 South Boulevard, Hull.

902: On 29 May 1915 the steam trawler Condor (SH12) sank and was lost with all hands after striking an enemy mine off Cloughton. Built in 1907 by Cook, Welton & Gemmell Ltd. (Hull), for the Ramsdale Steam Trawling Co. (Scarborough), her last owners were Pickering & Haldane's Steam Fishing Co. Ltd. (Hull). The Condor was skippered by Bob Heritage. Hull seaman James Hunter (25) of 12 Lockwood Street was the vessel's 2nd Engineer.

903: Prior to the start of the First World War, exports accounted for 70% of J.H. Fenner's sales, but by 1915 the company's export sales had slumped by more than 90%.

904: On 30 July 1915 the steam trawler Tors (FD114) sank, with the loss of at least eight crew members, after striking an enemy mine 43 miles east of Spurn Point. Tors was built in 1891 by Cochrane, Hamilton, Cooper & Schofield (Beverley), for William R. Leyman (Hull). Her last owners were H. Woods (Grimsby). She was skippered by Charles Dix of 57 Park Street, Hull. Christopher Harboard (50) of 24 Tyne Street, Hull was a Trimmer on the vessel.

905: In the 1914–15 season Hull City reached the last 8 (Fourth Round) of the FA Cup for the first time, losing 4-2 away to Bolton Wanderers. Bolton lost 2-1 in the semi-final to Sheffield United, who went on to beat Chelsea 3-0 in the final at Old Trafford, Manchester.

906: Australian Jimmy Devereux, who played in the same 1914 Challenge Cup final winning team as Billy Batten and Jack Harrison, became the first ever player to score 100 tries for Hull FC. He scored 101 tries in 181 appearances for the club between 1909–15.

907: Following the Titanic disaster, Hull-born Joseph Boxhall returned to sea as Fourth Officer on the White Star Line's Adriatic. He was commissioned to serve for a year on HMS Commonwealth, before being promoted from Sub-Lieutenant to Lieutenant in the Royal Naval Reserve in 1915 and then given command of a torpedo boat in Gibraltar the same year. After the war he was promoted to Lieutenant Commander.

908: On 15 November 1915 the Hull steam trawler Edward B Cargill (H412) was lost with all hands after striking a mine in the North Sea, off Spurn Point. The vessel left port on 13 November, bound for the North Sea fishing grounds on what should have been a ten day trip. Built in 1898 by Cook, Welton & Gemmell Ltd. (Hull), the vessel was skippered by Henry Lynn of Anlaby Park, Hull, and owned by Cargill Steam Trawling Co. Ltd. (Hull).

909: Legendary Hull FC winger Jack Harrison's last match for the club was against Broughton Rangers on 27 December 1915, two days after his team's 27-5 Christmas Day victory over Hull Kingston Rovers.

910: Between 1915–19, due to the First World War, the competitive Football League was suspended and two regional league competitions were set up instead. Hull City were placed into the Midlands Group, which consisted of 14 teams.

911: Film director Ralph Thomas was born at 139 Coltman Street, Hull on 11 August 1915. His father, Samuel Thomas, worked for the Shell petroleum company. His mother's name was Freda (*née* Cohen). The family moved to Bristol in 1929, which was where both he and his brother were educated. Ralph Thomas attended Tellisford School, Clifton, before progressing to Middlesex University College.

912: Up to 1916, as they shared business premises at 10 Churchside, Horatio Nelson Smith would represent the interests of his father's paper merchant business, G.F. Smith, on his company visits to the USA for Smith & Nephew.

913: On 14 January 1916 the Hull trawler Cornelian (H506) left port to head for the fishing grounds. On 8 February she was officially classified as missing in the North Sea: lost with all hands. The vessel was skippered by James Marshall (37) of 197 North Boulevard, Hull. Her owners were the Kingston Steam Trawling Co. Ltd. (Hull).

914: On 19 January 1916 the Hull steam trawler Malabar (H754) was officially given up as lost with all hands, after leaving Hull on 20 December and going missing (presumed enemy action). Built by Cook, Welton & Gemmell Ltd. (Hull) for the Hull Steam Fishing & Ice Co. Ltd. (Hull), she was skippered by John Crane of 2 Huntington Street, Hull.

915: In January 1916 the Hull steam trawler Earl (H436) was posted missing and lost with all hands in the North Sea (presumed enemy action). Built in 1898 by Mackie & Thomson (Govan), for the Great Northern Steam Fishing Co. Ltd. (Hull), she left Hull on 21 January on what was intended to be a 10–12 day trip. She was skippered by William Darby Coates (59) of 25 Buxton Terrace, Daltry Street, Hull.

916: On 3 November 1916 the Hull steam trawler Quair (H237) was posted missing (presumed enemy action) with all hands lost, off Iceland. Built in 1904 by Mackie & Thomson (Govan), she was skippered by George Pawlett (39) of 1 Dee Street, Hull; the owners were the Great Northern Steam Fishing Co. Ltd. (Hull).

917: In 1916 John Ellerman paid £4.1m for Thomas Wilson Sons & Co. of Hull (which, at the turn of the century was the largest privately owned ship company in the world, but had since fallen into decline). The company was renamed Ellerman's Wilson Line Ltd. in 1917.

918: The Hull-born astrophysicist, mathematician and cosmologist Arthur Milne was prevented from engaging in active service during the First World War due to his defective eyesight, but in 1916 he abandoned his studies at Cambridge to work on ballistics as part of a team led by A.V. Hill for the Anti-Aircraft Section of the Ministry of Munitions. The team were to become known as 'Hill's Brigands'.

919: In 1916 the butchers business set up by Harry Fletcher in 1907 expanded into cooked meats following the acquisition (for a nominal sum) of the premises of Johann Steeg, a German pork butcher who left the town in fear of his life after his shop at 470 Hessle Road was stoned by an angry crowd following the heavy loss of local lives in the Battle of the Somme.

920: Dorothy L. Sayers lodged at number 80 Westbourne Avenue, Hull from 1916–17 while a teacher in Modern Languages at Hull High School for Girls. On 27 August 2006 Hull-born actor Ian Carmichael unveiled a plaque at the house to commemorate its former resident. Carmichael, who lived on Westbourne Avenue as a boy, portrayed the crime writer's best known creation Lord Peter Wimsey on television and radio.

921: On 1 February 1917 the steam trawler Fanny (FD89) went missing, and was lost with all hands after leaving Fleetwood on 25 January for the west of Scotland fishing grounds. Last seen on the fishing grounds on 1 February, it is believed she was sunk by a German U-boat near the Dubh Artach lighthouse off the west coast of Scotland. Built in 1906 by John Duthie, Sons & Co. (Aberdeen), the vessel was owned by the Rossall Steam Fishing Co. (Fleetwood). She was skippered by Denis Nolan; Hull seaman Thomas Morley (52) of 34 Goulton Street was the vessel's Chief Engineer.

922: On 7 February 1917 the Hull steam trawler Shakespeare (H994) was lost after being hit by an enemy U-boat off the Firth of the Forth. Three of the crew were taken as prisoners of war, but the other nine were lost. Built in 1908 by Earle's Shipbuilding and Engineering Co. Ltd. (Hull) for the Hellyer Steam Fishing Co. Ltd. (Hull), the vessel was torpedoed by the U-boat U22 (commanded by Bernhard Putzier). The Shakespeare was skippered by Arni E. Bryon (38) of 346 St. George's Road, Hull.

923: On 19 February 1917 the Hull steam trawler Halcyon (H408) was lost with all hands after striking a mine off the Butt of Lewis, Outer Hebrides. Built in 1898 by Cochrane & Cooper Ltd., Beverley (Hull) for James Leyman & Co. Ltd. (Hull), and owned by East Coast Steam Trawling Co. Ltd. (Hull), she was skippered by James Bland of 281 Hawthorne Avenue, Hull.

924: On 28 March 1917 the Hull steam trawler Expedient (H219) was lost with all hands after being stopped and scuttled in the North Sea by the German U-boat UC75 (commanded by Johannes Lohs). Built in 1893 by Mackie & Thomson (Govan) for the Great Northern Steam Fishing Co. Ltd. (Hull), Expedient was skippered by Benjamin Ellis.

925: On 14 April 1917 the steam trawler Andromache (GY31) was stopped by the U-boat U78 (commanded by Otto Dröscher) west of Shetland while on her way back to port from the Icelandic grounds. Her skipper J.W. Cutsworth was taken prisoner and the crew were ordered into the lifeboats before the ship was scuttled. The crew and the lifeboats were never seen or heard of again The Andromache was built in 1904 by Cochrane & Sons Ltd. (Selby) and operated by A. & M. Smith Ltd. (Grimsby). At least nine Hull seamen were among the crew.

926: On 9 May 1917 the Hull steam trawler Windward Ho (H692) was wrecked with the loss of all hands, after striking an enemy mine laid by the coastal mine layer UC49 (commanded by Alfred Arnold), three miles off Peterhead. Built in 1902 by Cook, Welton & Gemmell Ltd. (Hull), Windward Ho was skippered by George Eddom of Penlee House, Eton Street, Hull. Her last owners were S.T. White & Co. (Hull) Ltd.

927: Following his single-handed act of bravery in the face of enemy fire (on 7 May 1917) Jack Harrison, the legendary Hull FC winger, was posthumously awarded the VC. His body was never recovered.

928: J. Arthur Rank married Laura Ellen Marshall on 18 October 1917. An ardent Methodist, like his father, he founded the Religious Film Society in 1933 to distribute films whose religious and moral message he wanted to promote. In 1934 he formed, with Annie Henrietta (Lady) Yule, the British National film production company; and in 1935 he formed the General Cinema Finance Corporation, with a 25% share in the American production company Universal Pictures, and a controlling interest in General Film Distributors. He later bought—again with Lady Yule—Heatherden Hall in Buckinghamshire, which he transformed into Pinewood Studios.

929: In 1917 Muriel Thetis Wilson, daughter of Arthur Wilson of Tranby Croft, was married (to Richard Edward Warde) in a Madame Clapham dress; the bridesmaids dresses were also by Madame Clapham.

930: In 1917 Thomas Ferens offered £35,000 and the site of St. John's Church, Queen Victoria Square for the construction of a new art gallery, later named the Ferens Art Gallery in his honour.

931: Dorothy Mackaill left school at 14 and began her working life as a typist for the *Hull Evening News* at their offices in Whitefriargate; and in 1918 she persuaded her father to finance her on a two year course at the Thornton Academy ballet school, Wigmore Street, London.

932: On 1 June 1918 the Hull steam trawler Egret (H21) was lost with all hands after being torpedoed by an enemy U-boat. Built in 1899 by Mackie & Thomson (Govan), for the Great Northern Steam Fishing Co. Ltd. (Hull), the Egret was requisitioned by the Admiralty in 1918. She was skippered by William McFee (54) of 75 Ena Street, Boulevard, Hull.

933: Hull-born Sydney Carlin, MC, DCM, DFC (1889–1941)—known to his mates as 'Timbertoes' because of the wooden prosthetic he used following the loss of a leg while fighting on the Western Front—became a First World War flying Ace, scoring a total of ten victories between 13 June and 15 September 1918. Shot down and captured by the Germans on 21 September, just 6 days after his final victory, Carlin was repatriated on 13 December 1918. He died on 9 May 1941, while serving with 151 Squadron, as a result of an air raid on the squadron's base at RAF Wittering. He was 52 years old.

934: The Hull steam trawler Viola has an illustrious history, being instrumental in the sinking of at least two

U-boats during the Great War: in August 1918, U30 (which had sunk at least 17 Allied vessels); and, in September 1918, UB115. This latter incident was the first time that an airship had been involved in the sinking of a submarine.

935: John Ellerman's success in shipping provided him with the resources to expand his business interests into other areas, including brewing (with shares in over seventy breweries by 1918), coal (he held shares in over twenty collieries by the early 1920s); and newspapers (in 1904 he became the largest single shareholder in *The Financial Times*; and acquired further interests in the *Daily Mail*, *The Illustrated London News*, *The Evening News* and *The Sphere*).

936: Brian Rix's sister, Sheila Mercier (*née* Rix), who played Annie Sugden for over twenty-two years in ITVs *Emmerdale Farm* (titled *Emmerdale* since 1989), was born in Hull on 1 January 1919.

937: On 1 March 1919 the steam trawler Southward (GY288) went missing and was lost with all hands (presumed after striking an enemy mine) on her return trip from the Faroes. Southward was built in 1907 by Cochrane & Sons Shipbuilders Ltd. (Selby), for Forward Steam Fishing Co. Ltd. (Grimsby). She was skippered by Joseph Fish (50). Hull seaman William Hardiment (37) of Claremont Avenue, Scarborough Street was the vessel's Chief Engineer.

938: On 7 March 1919 the Hull steam trawler Scotland (H348) was lost with all hands after striking a mine in the North Sea, off Flamborough Head. Built in 1897 by Cook, Welton & Gemmell Ltd. (Beverley), she was skippered by Thomas Baxter (31) of 753 Hessle Road, Hull. She was owned by Benjamin Knowles (Hull).

939: On 15 March 1919 the Hull steam trawler Durban (H378) was posted missing with all hands lost (possibly after striking an enemy mine) in the North Sea. Built in 1897 by Cook, Welton & Gemmell Ltd. (Hull), she was skippered by Charles Bryant (31) of 109 Coltman Street, Hull; the owners were the Hull Steam Fishing & Ice Co. Ltd. (Hull).

940: Hull's Joseph Boxhall married Marjorie Bedells at St. Andrew's Church, Sharrow, Sheffield on 25 March 1919, though they remained childless. He then joined the White Star Line's RMS Cedric (running between Liverpool and New York) as Second Officer. Despite his experience, Boxhall never commanded his own vessel for the White Star Line. He retired in 1940, but acted as technical advisor on the 1958 film *A Night to Remember* and agreed to help promote the film, attending the première at the Odeon Theatre, Leicester Square on Thursday 3 July.

941: On 13 August 1919 the steam trawler Helcia (GY152) went missing, presumed lost with all hands, in the North Sea. Built by Cochrane & Sons Shipbuilders Ltd. (Selby) for the Sylvia Steam Fishing Co. Ltd. (Grimsby). Her last owners were the Rushworth Steam Fishing Co. (Grimsby). Hull seaman Robert Cooper (30) of Souttergate, Hedon was the vessel's Chief Engineer.

942: On 24 August 1919 the steam trawler Fawn (GY1008) was posted missing and lost with all hands (presumed having struck an enemy mine) off Hartlepool. Built in 1898 by Cook, Welton & Gemmell Ltd. (Hull), for Thomas E. Fisher & Henry Morris Co. Ltd. (Grimsby), her last owners were Henry Croft Baker & Sons Ltd. (Grimsby). She was skippered by Hull-born Thomas Mothersdill (53), and was on her homeward trip from Faroe. Thomas Taylor (23) of 111 Havelock Street, Hull was the vessel's 2nd Engineer.

943: In 1919, after the end of the Great War, the fifth season of the Northern Rugby Football Union's Wartime Emergency League was truncated, running from February to May. Hull FC won the Yorkshire League championship with 26 points from 16 games, the club's first ever League Championship title.

944: On 14 December 1919 the Hull steam trawler Isle of Man (H826) went missing, presumed lost with all hands, in the North Sea. Skippered by John Greenhill (48) of 50 Glencoe Street, Hull, she was built in 1905 by Earle's Shipbuilding and Engineering Co. Ltd. (Hull) for Hull Steam Fishing & Ice Co.Ltd. (Hull).

945: The Hull steam trawler Viola (H868) was decommissioned by the Admiralty in 1919, and briefly returned to fishing before being sold by Hellyers to shipbrokers W.A. Massey & Sons (Hull) Ltd. The vessel was sold on by W.A. Massey & Sons to L. Thorsen of Norway, who renamed her Kapduen. L. Thorsen was subsequently acquired by Nils Torvald Nielsen Alonso, who converted the vessel for whaling and, in 1924, renamed her Dias. The Dias was active for several years as a whaler off the coast of Africa, before eventually being laid-up at Sandesfjord in Norway.

946: In Paris, while Dorothy Mackaill was still a teenager, American choreographer Ned Wayburn advised her to try her luck on the New York theatre scene. In New York, she marched into the office of Florenz Ziegfeld, announcing to the impresario's secretary: "Miss Dorothy Mackaill of London to see Mr Ziegfeld". Ziegfeld saw her and she appeared in his *Midnight Frolic* the same night.

947: On 26 January 1920 the Hull steam trawler Amber (H398) was officially given up as lost with all hands (presumed having struck an enemy mine), after leaving Hull on 1 January. Built by Mackie & Thomson (Govan) for the Kingston Steam Trawling Co. Ltd. (Hull), her last owners were the Trident Steam Fishing Co. Ltd. (Hull). The Commonwealth War Graves Commission have recorded the date of loss as 1 January 1920. She was skippered by Harold Hannah (40) of 261 St. George's Road, Hull.

948: In 1920 W. Boyes & Co. Ltd. bought the business of Johnnie Wardell at 232 & 234 Hessle Road, and instantly held a sale to attract the Hessle Road clientele. The bill announcing the sale read:

> W. BOYES & Co. Ltd. beg to announce that they have purchased the well-known Business of Mr J. Wardell – 232 & 234 HESSLE ROAD – Corner Constable Street.
>
> Mr W. BOYES commenced business in a very small way 38 years ago and we now have two large stores in Scarborough and York where "Boyes" has become a household name

The sale began at 9 a.m. on Friday 25 February. As with their first Hull store in Prospect Street, the Hessle Road store was leased, but this time with an option to buy.

949: On 24 April 1920 Hull FC won their first Championship Final when they beat Huddersfield 3-2 in the Championship play-off final at Headingley, Leeds, becoming Northern Union champions. Although Huddersfield took the lead with a penalty in the twenty-seventh minute, Billy Batten scored a late match-winning try to steal it for Hull.

950: Ian Gillett Carmichael, who portrayed James Dixon in the Boulting brothers' 1957 film adaptation of the Kingsley Amis novel *Lucky Jim*, was born at 114 Sunnybank, Hull on 18 June 1920.

951: On 6 November 1920 the Hull steam trawler Barbados (H938) went missing and was lost with all hands (presumed having struck an enemy mine) after leaving Hull bound for the North Sea fishing grounds. Built in 1907 by Earle's Shipbuilding and Engineering Co. Ltd. (Hull), for the Hull Steam Fishing & Ice Co. Ltd. (Hull), Barbados left Hull on 21 October, and was last sighted on 6 November in an area that was known to be mined; she was skippered by J.H. Reynolds (45) of 41 Carrington Street, Hull.

952: On 27 November 1920 Hull Kingston Rovers played Hull FC in the Yorkshire Cup final, at Headingley—the first time the two clubs had met in any final. Hull KR won their first official trophy when they beat Hull FC 2-0. Billy Bradshaw's 40-yard drop goal in the final gasps of the game won it for KR.

953: On 10 December 1920 Gerald Thomas was born at 139 Coltman Street, Hull. His father, Samuel Thomas, worked for the Shell petroleum company. His mother's name was Freda, *née* Cohen. His older brother Ralph had been born (at the same address) five years earlier. The family moved to Bristol (1929), which was where both Thomas brothers were educated. Gerald Thomas began to study for a career in medicine, before the Second World War intervened: he served with the Sussex regiment. A green heritage plaque, erected at 89 Westbourne Avenue by the Avenues and Pearson Park Residents' Association identifies the house where Gerald and Ralph Thomas lived as children in Hull. The inscription reads:

> RALPH & GERALD THOMAS Film Directors lived here 1926–1929

954: In 1920 Sir John Ellerman bought part of London's Covent Garden estate (including the Drury Lane Theatre) from the Duke of Bedford; in 1925 he bought 21 acres of Marylebone (including Great Portland Street—later, the Langham Estate) from Lord Howard de Walden for £3m;

in 1929 he bought 14 acres in Chelsea, from Fulham Road in the west to Draycott Place in the east (including 600 properties) from the Cadogan and Hans Place estate; and in 1930, following the death of Lord Iveagh, he bought 82 acres of freehold land in South Kensington from the Iveagh Trust. At the beginning of the 1930s Sir John Ellerman was among the major private land owners in London.

955: Minerva Pier, an L-shaped pier to the east of Island Wharf, dates from the late 20th century and replaced an earlier 19th century timber pier originally known as the East Pier, but renamed in the 1920s.

956: By 1920 Thomas Ferens was making donations to the value of around £47,000 from his annual income of £50,000; he donated over £1m during the last years of his life.

957: Dorothy Mackaill played in a musical revue in Paris with Maurice Chevalier; and appeared alongside several of Hollywood's biggest stars of the period, including John Barrymore, Douglas Fairbanks Jnr, Clark Gable, Humphrey Bogart and Frank Fey.

958: Amy Johnson attended the Boulevard Secondary School, and went on to read Economics at Sheffield University. She graduated with a BA in 1925, before finding work in a solicitor's office.

959: Ian Carmichael—along with Richard Stone (an Entertainments Officer and a Major in the British Army, who was to become Carmichael's agent)—was instrumental in the initial breakthrough of both Terry Scott and Tommy Cooper.

960: On Saturday 29 January 1921 Jimmy Kennedy set the Hull FC club record for scoring the most points in a match when he contributed 36 points to Hull's 80-7 victory over Keighley, at The Boulevard.

961: On 7 May 1921 Hull FC won the Championship Final, becoming Northern Union champions for a second, successive year when they beat Hull Kingston Rovers 16-14 in the Championship play-off final at Headingley, Leeds. Despite Hull FC finishing the season with 54 points to Rovers' 49 points, Rovers finished top of the table because they had played fewer games (32 to Hull's 36) and therefore had a better percentage (76.56 to Hull's 75). Hull FC had beaten Halifax 27-10 in their play-off semi-final; Rovers had beaten Wigan 26-4.

962: At 5.37pm on 24 August, 1921, on only her fourth flight, the R38 airship failed structurally and fell into the Humber estuary, killing 44 of the 49 crew aboard. Eye-witnesses had observed creases in her outer skin, before both ends drooped and collapsed. This was followed by a fire in the bow and a large explosion which broke many of the airship's windows. The five survivors had all been positioned in the tail section of the airship.

963: Besides buying individual items at auction, Hull-born art dealer Joseph Joel Duveen bought whole collections of increasingly large value, such as the J.P. Morgan collection of Chinese porcelain. In 1921 he bought Gainsborough's portrait of Jonathan Buttall—more widely known as *The Blue Boy*—from the Duke of Westminster, and sold it to Henry Huntington; and in 1929 he sold Raphael's *Madonna* to Andrew Mellon for $970,000.

964: The original Hull Golf Club, founded in 1904, was 'wound up' in 1921, and re-established as Hull Golf Club (1921) Ltd., a private limited company (company number 00177772) incorporated on 11 November 1921.

965: Sydney Hainsworth—under whose leadership the expansion of J.H. Fenner & Co Ltd., from a small leather belting manufacturer into an international organisation, was undertaken—joined the company as manager of the

Weaving Department in 1921; he was appointed a director in 1930 and Managing Director in 1945, before eventually becoming Chairman of the company. He was appointed CBE in 1972 and retired as Group Chairman in 1974, when he was replaced by Joseph Palmer. He continued to serve J.H. Fenner & Co Ltd., as President, until he died on 24 October 1992.

966: The National Census of 1921 reported the population of the county borough of Hull as 287,150.

967: As well being a renowned art dealer, Hull-born Joseph Duveen was a significant benefactor, donating many works to a range of British galleries, including Hogarth's *The Graham Children* to the National Gallery, and John Singer Sargent's study of Mme. Gautreau to the Tate Gallery. He died in London on 25 May 1939.

968: By the early 1920s the turnover of Hull-based sweet and chocolate manufacturers Needlers Ltd. was averaging £570,000, and the company had 1,700 (mainly female) employees; however, turnover dipped to its lowest in the recession year of 1931 (£328,000) when the company made a profit of just £5,000.

969: On 1 April 1922 the Hull and Barnsley Railway became part of North Eastern Railway and the docks in Hull became the responsibility of a single company once again.

970: On 29 April 1922, in their 5th Northern Union Challenge Cup final, Hull FC lost by a single point to Rochdale Hornets, at Headingley, Leeds. A record 32,596 crowd (approximately 7,000 Hull FC fans had made the trip to Leeds) witnessed Hull go down 10-9 to Rochdale in what was to be the last match under the auspices of the Northern Rugby Football Union before the name change to the Rugby Football League.

971: Jack Irwin Hale—the swimmer who is credited with revolutionising the butterfly stroke by creating the dolphin-style kicking technique, and who at various times held every British freestyle, backstroke and butterfly swimming record—was born in Hull on 8 June 1922. He died on 29 February 2008, aged 85; his funeral service took place at Willerby's Haltemprice Crematorium on Wednesday 12 March.

972: Philip Larkin was born in Coventry on 9 August 1922. He wrote many of his best-known poems in Hull, including his final great contemplation on death 'Aubade'. With his early education taking place in Coventry, Larkin went on to study at St. John's College, Oxford, where he forged a few lifelong friendships, including that with Kingsley Amis. After Oxford, Larkin's first job was Librarian at Wellington, Shropshire, where he studied for professional library qualification via a correspondence course. Once qualified, he applied for the job of assistant Librarian at University College, Leicester, a position he took up in June 1946. He was appointed Sub-Librarian at Queen's University, Belfast in 1950, before applying for the position of Librarian at Hull University, a job he accepted in 1955.

973: Hull Kingston Rovers moved from their Craven Street ground to Craven Park at the start of the 1922–23 season: their first game at the new ground took place on 2 September when they lost 3-0 to Wakefield Trinity.

974: Stevie Smith was known to her family as 'Peggy', only acquiring the nickname 'Stevie' in her twenties after a friend with whom she was out riding said she reminded him of the jockey Steve Donaghue.

975: After acquiring their Hessle Road premises in 1920, W. Boyes & Co. Ltd. made alterations to the building in 1922, and finally bought the property in 1924. In 1927 the company bought 230 Hessle Road; and, subsequently, further property—268 Hessle Road; a shop in Constable Street; and 226 Hessle Road—was acquired enabling the extension of the store. The company also acquired land (the former site of Rose and Spring terraces) at the rear of the Hessle Road premises, where the store's car park now stands. The Hessle Road store was rebuilt in 1956 and extended further in 1973.

976: The trading profit for Reckitt and Sons Ltd. first broke through the £1m barrier in 1922—sixty years after the death of the company's founder Isaac Reckitt—when the recorded figure was £1,137,465.

977: Sir John Ellerman's daughter, Annie Winifred Ellerman (later 'Bryher') became a key supporter of the Modernist circle of intellectuals associated with the Shakespeare and Company book store in Paris, such as James Joyce, Ernest Hemingway, Gertrude Stein and Marianne Moore. Bryher's lifelong partner was Hilda Doolittle (H.D.). In 1922 Bryher and her husband Robert McAlmon helped to finance the publication of Joyce's *Ulysses*.

978: At the end of the 1922–23 season Hull KR finished fourth in the league with 53 points, behind Hull FC (60 points), Huddersfield (52), and Swinton (54). They beat Hull FC 16-2 in the play-off semi-final on 21 April 1923, before going on to beat Huddersfield 15-5 in the play-off final on 5 May, to secure their first Championship title.

979: Hull-born mathematician, logician and philosopher John Venn died in Cambridge on 4 April 1923. He was 88 years old.

980: On 28 April 1923 Hull FC lost 28-3 to Leeds in their 6th Challenge Cup final, at Belle Vue (Wakefield).

981: The Hanson PLC entrepreneur Sir Vincent Gordon

Lindsay White, Baron White of Hull, was born on 11 May 1923 at 124 College Grove, Drypool, Hull. He died in a Los Angeles hospital on 23 August 1995.

982: On 29 October 1923 the Savoy Picture Theatre opened on Hull's Holderness Road. This single-screen, 1,337-seat cinema was equipped with a Western Electric sound system, and had a 40 feet wide proscenium, a 6 feet deep stage and two dressing rooms.

983: On 24 November 1923 Hull FC won the Yorkshire Cup for the first time when they beat Huddersfield 10-4 at Headingly, Leeds. This was the club's fourth appearance in a Yorkshire Cup final, having previously been beaten by Batley (17-3) on 23 November 1912; Huddersfield (31-0) on 28 November 1914; and Hull Kingston Rovers (2-0) on 27 November 1920.

984: On 18 December 1923 the Hull steam trawler Wren (H215) foundered and was lost with all hands, in severe gale conditions south of Dogger Bank in the North Sea. Wren was built in 1897 by Edwards Brothers (North Shields), for Kelsall Brothers & Beeching Ltd. (Manchester). Having been requisitioned by the Admiralty in November 1914, and renamed HMT Whitethroat in July 1918, she was returned to Kelsall Brothers & Beeching in 1919 with her name reverting to Wren. She was skippered by Francis Mobbs (39) of 30 Lincoln Street, Hull.

985: Despite finishing top of the Championship table at the end of the 1922–23 season, following their 16-2 defeat at the hands of Hull KR in the play-off semi-final, Hull FC became the first top of the league team not to reach the Championship play-off final. However, there was some consolation for the club and the fans when they became Yorkshire League champions for the second time in the club's history.

986: In 1923 the Hull Repertory Theatre Company was founded by a group of enthusiasts led by A.R. Whatmore. The company used Morton's Lecture Hall (next to the Assembly Rooms in Kingston Square) for their productions, renaming it the Little Theatre. In 1928 the Hull Repertory Theatre Company became a private company, and the Little Theatre (Hull) Ltd. public limited company was formed for the purpose of buying the lecture hall. This was accomplished in 1930.

987: Brian (Norman Roger) Rix was born in Cottingham on 27 January 1924, the son of Herbert Dobson Rix whose father had founded what would become J.R. Rix & Sons Limited. Despite early ambitions to play cricket for Yorkshire and a general (lifelong) enthusiasm for the sport, Rix became a professional actor at eighteen. While still only in his early twenties he formed his own theatre company, beginning a thirty year career as an actor/manager, running repertory companies at Ilkley, Bridlington and Margate. He first found fame in the 1950s in the *Whitehall Farces*.

988: Hull-born trade unionist, abolitionist and radical reformer Robert Applegarth died at his home in Thornton Heath, Surrey on 13 June 1924, aged 90.

989: Ebenezer Cobb Morley—acknowledged as the founding father of the Football League, who was born in Hull in 1831—died of pneumonia at the age of 93, at his Barnes home on 20 November 1924. He was buried in Barnes Cemetery on 25 November.

990: As a consequence of an urban development programme by Hull City Corporation, the Hull Golf Club was forced into relocating in 1924, and moved to its current home at Kirk Ella; with Kirk Ella Hall becoming its new clubhouse, and the new 18 hole course being designed by the Scottish former professional golfer James

Braid (who built up a successful career in golf course design after retiring from Championship golf).

991: In 1924 a memorial was erected at the south-western side of Hull's Western Cemetery to commemorate those who died in the R38 disaster of 24 August 1921. Made of Portland Stone with two bronze plaques (one on either side), the memorial bears a stone cross; and the names of all those who died in the disaster are listed on the plaques: the 28 British servicemen on the left-side plaque; the 16 American servicemen on the right-side plaque.

992: The Hull Kingston Rovers record for the longest unbroken sequence of appearances for the club is held by Gilbert Austin, who made 190 appearances between the 1918–19 season and the 1923–24 season. Austin ended this sequence himself when he was selected for, and agreed to represent, Yorkshire.

993: Dorothy Mackaill was one of 13 young actresses selected by the Western Association of Motion Picture Advertisers (WAMPAS) when she became one of the WAMPAS Baby Stars of 1924.

994: On 28 January 1925 the Hull steam trawler Scapa Flow (H1016) was lost with all hands, off Iceland. Built in 1913 by Cochrane & Sons Shipbuilders Ltd. (Selby), the vessel was originally called Peary, but was renamed Scapa Flow in 1920. On her final trip she was skippered by Jacob Martin (35) of Bridlington, with Thomas Netherton (31) of 80 Devon Street, Hull as his Mate; the owners were Jutland Amalgamated Trawlers Ltd. (Hull).

995: Over the weekend of 7/8 February 1925, in severe weather, Hull steam trawler Field Marshall Robertson (H104) was lost with all hands. No trace of the vessel—which sailed from Hull with a minimal crew, but took on 29 native crew members to complement the Hull men when she reached Iceland—was ever found. A carved memorial tablet, supplied by Hellyer Bros., recording the names of all 35 hands lost, is mounted on the north wall of the choir in the National Church, Hafnarfjordur, on Iceland's southern peninsula, not far from Reykjavik. Built in 1919 by Cochrane & Sons Shipbuilders Ltd. (Selby), Field Marshall Robertson was skippered by Chas. Beard, of 11 Marlborough Avenue, Hampshire Street, Hull. She was owned by the Hull Northern Fishing Co. Ltd. (Hellyer Bros. Ltd.).

996: At the end of the 1924–25 season Hull KR finished 2nd in the league with 53 points, behind Swinton on 60 points. They beat Wigan 13-4 in the play-off semi-final on 18 April 1925, before going on to beat Swinton 9-5 in the play-off final on 2 May to secure their second Championship title. This was also the year they won the Yorkshire League for the first time in the club's history.

997: The course at the Hull Golf Club's new site in Kirk Ella was opened on 21 May 1925 by club captain R.B. Johnston, with an exhibition match—featuring James Braid (the course designer) and three professional golfers: John Henry Taylor, Charles Albert Whitcombe and Arthur Gladstone Havers—being played later that day.

998: The Hull FC player with the record for the most career appearances is Edward 'Ned' Rogers who played 500 games for the club in the period 1906–25.

999: On Monday 28 September 1925 the original Cecil Theatre opened on the north/west corner of the junction of Anlaby Road and Ferensway. Built on the site of the 600-seater Theatre De-Luxe (built in 1911 for National Electric Picture Theatres Ltd.), but with a much altered footprint, the Cecil had a seating capacity of 1,700, and a full orchestra pit. It also boasted of having 'The most luxurious café in the city'.

1,000: On 10 December 1925 the Hull steam trawler Axenite (H183) went missing, presumed lost with all hands. She was skippered by Harold Marwood of 765 Anlaby Road, Hull.

1,001: Norman Collier, considered by many comedians to have been the 'comedians' comedian' was born in Hull on 25 December 1925. He stayed in the area his whole life, living in Welton to the west of the city. He died at Welton on 14 March 2013. His funeral service took place at Welton's St. Helen's church on 27 March 2013.

1,002: William Boyes died on 30 December 1925, 35 days after completing his term of office as Mayor of Scarborough. His wife, Jane, had passed away six years earlier, in 1919.

1,003: Hollywood actress Dorothy Mackaill's contract with First National Pictures guaranteed her a salary of £40,000 a year, which at that time (1924) was the highest ever paid to a film star; and while still in her early twenties she made some shrewd investments in property on Wilshire Boulevard, Los Angeles, which secured an income for the rest of her life.

1,004: Adrian Hill, better known as singer and entertainer Ronnie Hilton, who had a Number One UK hit with 'No Other Love' in May 1956 and later in his career presented BBC Radio 2's *Sound of the '50s*, was born at 65 North Road, Gipsyville, Hull on 26 January 1926.

1,005: Hull-born Adrian Hill was born with a hairlip (later operated on at the suggestion of HMV A&R man Walter Ridley). He made his stage debut as Ronnie Hilton in July 1954 at the Dudley Hippodrome, and went on to have nine top 20 chart hits between 1954 and 1957, and appeared in three Royal Variety Performance shows. In 1965 he released 'A Windmill in Old Amsterdam'—many people from Hull will remember this song being a favourite in Christmas pantomimes at the Hull New Theatre—which, although only reaching No. 23 in the charts (and was Hilton's last chart hit), would eventually go on to become a million seller.

1,006: David Whitfield was born on 2 February 1926. At that time the Whitfield family were living at No. 3 Albert's Terrace, East Street, which was off Clarence Street, in the Drypool area of the city. After being de-mobbed from the Royal Navy in 1950, he worked as a coalman's mate and then in the concrete business. His singing career took off when, in May 1950, he appeared in Radio Luxembourg's *Opportunity Knocks* talent show. Within a very short space of time, his weekly earnings rose from £7 to around £450, and he became one of the most popular tenors of his day, achieving great chart success during the 1950s, with more records in the British charts than any other British artist, and more than ten singles entering the top twenty. He was the first British recording star to break into the American top ten; and the first British artist to achieve a million seller in the United States.

1,007: At the end of the 1926–27 season Hull FC finished in 5th position in the Championship, but became Yorkshire League Champions for a third time.

1,008: Dorothy Mackaill was married three times: first to screenwriter and film director Lothar Mendes (1926); then to Neil Miller, a Hawaiian sugar planter, orchestra leader, and singer (1931); and finally, to Harold Patterson a horticulturist orchid grower (1947).

1,009: In 1926 the *Hull Daily Mail* moved from 22 Whitefriargate to new premises at 84–86 Jameson Street.

1,010: On 4 September 1926 George William Gray was born at Denny, Falkirk, Scotland. The son of a pharmacist,

Gray went on to study Chemistry at Glasgow University (graduating with a BSc. in 1946) before moving to University College Hull—then an outpost of the University of London—to take up the post of Assistant Lecturer and to study for a PhD (supervised by Brynmor Jones) in the nascent field of liquid crystals. The work of his research team led to the development of the liquid crystal industry, with 90% of liquid crystal materials manufactured during the 1970s being held in the UK.

1,011: On the morning of 14 February 1927 Hull's worst ever train accident occurred when the incoming 8:22am express train from Withernsea to Hull's Paragon Station was involved in a head-on collision with the outgoing 9:05am service to Scarborough. The Scarborough train had slowed almost to a stand-still and the Withernsea train was travelling at around 13 mph; yet 12 people lost their lives, with 24 passengers being seriously injured and a further 22 suffering minor injuries. The two train drivers involved were Samuel Atkinson (driving the Scarborough-bound train) and Robert Dixon (driving the Withernsea to Hull train).

1,012: Within days of the horrific 1927 Valentine's Day train crash that occurred under the Argyle Street bridge, on the approach to Paragon Station, an investigation into the accident was launched by the Ministry of Transport. Headed by Colonel J.W. Pringle, the investigation reported that the accident happened as a result of human error; concluding that the primary cause was a mistake by signalman of 46 years John Clark (who was responsible for levers 70–130), who pulled lever 95 instead of lever 96.

1,013: Film and stage actor Tom Courtenay was born Thomas Daniel Courtenay in Hull on 25 February 1927, the son of Thomas Henry (a boat painter) and Anne Eliza Courtenay (*née* Quest), whose family home was at 29

Harrow Street, Hessle Road. He married the actress Cheryl Kennedy on 12 November 1973, but the couple later divorced (1982); he subsequently (1988) married Isabel Crossley, a stage manager at the Royal Exchange Theatre in Manchester.

1,014: The Ferens Art Gallery officially opened its doors to the public on 29 November 1927. The following year Thomas Ferens provided £20,000 for the purchase of new works of art. In 1994 a blue heritage plaque was erected on the gallery to commemorate Thomas Robinson Ferens. The inscription reads:

> Businessman Liberal M.P. and Philanthropist
> THOMAS R. FERENS J.P. 1847–1930 This Art
> Gallery is one of his many benefactions

1,015: The Labour Party won its first parliamentary seat in Hull in 1926 when Joseph Montague Kenworthy— elected for the Liberals as representative for Central Hull at a by-election in 1919—resigned from the Liberal Party, resigned his parliamentary seat, joined the Labour Party, sought re-election in a by-election on 29 November, and was returned with almost 53% of the vote. He held the seat for Labour until 1931, when he was defeated by Hull-born Conservative Basil Kelsey Barton.

1,016: In 1927 Robert Rix & Sons began importing tractor vaporising oil for the post-war agricultural revolution—as well as lamp oil from Russia, packed in oak casks—thereby beginning the association of the family business with petroleum and fuel products. By 1939 the fleet owned by Robert Rix & Sons had expanded to eleven ships across four companies.

1,017: In 1927 the Dias (formerly the steam trawler Viola H868) was sold to a company who needed a vessel at their Grytviken base for sealing, and the vessel was put into the service of hunting Elephant seals.

1,018: The University of Hull was founded as University College Hull in 1927. The foundation stone was laid in 1928 by Prince Albert, the Duke of York (later King George Vl). The college opened in October 1928.

1,019: By 1927 the East Hull Picturedrome was under the control of Sherburn Pictures (Hull) Ltd. In 1928 the venue was modernised and extended by local architects Blackmore & Sykes, and re-opened as the Ritz Cinema on 17 April 1928. The Ritz was equipped with a Wurlitzer 2 Manuals and 6 Ranks organ, along with rear screen projection.

1,020: Thomas Robinson Ferens donated £250,000 towards the founding of University College Hull as well as providing the 18 acre site on Cottingham Road upon which it was built.

1,021: The main administrative department of Hull University, housed in what was the original building of University College Hull, is now named the Venn Building in honour of Hull-born mathematician John Venn.

1,022: On 18 March 1928 the Hull steam trawler Lord Devonport (H273) was wrecked and lost with eight crew members, on her way back from the Icelandic grounds, when she ran aground and foundered in treacherous seas off Hoy, west Orkney. The Stromness lifeboat (on her first call to service) rescued 6 of the crew. Built in 1925 by Cochrane & Sons Shipbuilders Ltd. (Selby), for Pickering & Haldane's Steam Fishing Co. Ltd. (Hull), the Lord Devonport was skippered by John Hanson of 3 Beaumont Avenue, St. George's Road, Hull.

1,023: In October 1928 full-back/centre Joe Oliver joined Hull FC from Huddersfield for a transfer fee of £800. Oliver was so consistent as a goal kicker that the Hull fans gave him the nickname 'Old Faithful' and adopted the Gene Autry song 'Ole Faithful', from the film *The Big Show* (1936) as a tribute to him. 'Old Faithful' became the club's official anthem in September 1936. Oliver holds the record as the club's all-time highest scorer with 1,842 points amassed over 426 games.

1,024: When University College Hull opened in October 1928 it had just 39 students and 14 'one-man' departments. By 1931 the college had 100 students.

1,025: When it opened, University College Hull, located at its current site on Cottingham Road, boasted just one building (now the Venn Building). As an outpost of the University of London, the College offered courses in the arts and pure sciences.

1,026: The University of Hull coat of arms was designed by Sir Algernon Tudor-Craig in 1928. The symbols featured are the torch for learning, the rose for Yorkshire, the ducal coronet from the arms of the City of Hull, the fleur-de-lys for Lincolnshire and the dove (symbolising peace) from the coat of arms of the Ferens family.

1,027: In 1928 Hull City Council created a plan to construct a multi-span truss bridge across the Humber between Hessle and Barton-upon-Humber, but the financial crisis arising from the 'Great Depression' in the UK in the 1930s meant that the plan was never implemented.

1,028: The 1,671 seating capacity Carlton Picture Theatre, at 474 Anlaby Road, Hull, opened on 9 September 1928. The first film to feature at the new theatre was the silent movie *Lonesome Ladies*. Designed by Blackmore & Sykes, and built by Greenwood and Sons, the Carlton belonged to the stable of Hull Picture Playhouse Ltd.

1,029: The Carlton Picture Theatre had two entrances, one in each of the two bays on the front corners of the building. There was a single balcony inside the theatre, and an inscription in large capital letters above the proscenium stating: 'A PICTURE IS A POEM WITHOUT WORDS'.

1,030: In 1928 the New Palace Theatre of Varieties on Anlaby Road was enlarged, but after becoming a casualty of the Hull Blitz of 1940, it remained closed until 1951 when it was leased to Kingston Varieties, owners of Hull's Tivoli Theatre.

1,031: Lillian Bilocca (*née* Marshall) was born on 26 May 1929 at 7 Welton Terrace, Wassand Street, Hessle Road, Hull, in the centre of the community whose men's safety she would fight for. Her father was a seaman; and both her husband Charlie and her son Ernie made their living at sea. After the trawlers St. Romanus, Kingston Peridot, and Ross Cleveland went down in early 1968, resulting in the loss of 58 men, 'Big Lil' began her war against some of the most powerful names in the fishing industry. This battle, and the high profile she achieved, was to turn her into a national figure and a local folk-hero.

1,032: Amy Johnson obtained her pilot's licence on 6 July 1929 (after sixteen hours of flying) at the London Flying Club.

1,033: Aviator Amy Johnson learned to fly partly with the help of the renowned comedian Will Hay, who was already an experienced pilot.

1,034: The water chute at East Park (a Grade II listed structure) is a rare surviving example of a Wicksteed splash boat. Built and supplied by Charles Wicksteed & Co. at a cost of £1,400—with the tower of the structure having been built by the City Engineers at a cost of £474 2s 5d—the water chute was installed in 1929, opening to the public for the first time on Tuesday 13 August.

1,035: On 25 August 1929 Hull's St. Andrew's Dock suffered a ferocious fire (which started in the newly constructed but still unfinished landing sheds) with more than 200 wooden dock-side structures razed to the ground, and no less than three trawlers completely burned out.

1,036: On 7 October 1929 Hull's Mayfair Cinema was opened on Beverley Road. Designed by H.F. Wharf, and featuring a Standaart 2 Manual 10 Ranks organ with illuminated console, the 1,936-seat cinema was fitted with a Western Electric sound system. The proscenium was 30 feet wide, and the stage 9 feet deep, with 2 backstage dressing rooms. Refreshments were available from an integral café.

1,037: At the end of the 1929–30 season Hull KR finished 6th in the league with 48 points, behind St. Helens (55 points), Huddersfield (52) Salford (49), Leeds (52) and Dewsbury (49); but they beat Hunslet 13-7 at Headingley on 30 November 1929 to take the Yorkshire Cup for a second time.

1,038: In December 1929 Amy Johnson became the first woman in England to qualify for an Air Ministry ground-engineer's 'C' licence.

1,039: One of Amy Johnson's ambitions was to make a living as a professional pilot, but at a time when men dominated the profession, she was unable to do so.

1,040: Amy Johnson received constant encouragement and support from her father, and it was he (along with Lord Wakefield) who provided the financial backing that enabled her to buy a second-hand De Havilland Gypsy Moth biplane.

1,041: Sir John Ellerman was included in a list drawn up by the Inland Revenue in 1929 to predict how much Estate Duty might be raised upon the death of the wealthiest people in Britain. Ellerman was calculated to earn twice as much as his nearest rival. At today's values, his earnings were put at £389m, and he had liquid assets of approximately £9bn.

1,042: In 1929 a Western Electric sound system was installed at the Tower Picture Palace on Anlaby Road. Prior to this, silent films were accompanied by a 'live' orchestra. At some point, the venue's original wooden benches were replaced by individual seats (and more personal space for the patrons) thereby reducing the seating capacity from 1,200 to 773.

1,043: On 11 February 1930, more than a week before the Hull trawler St. Louis (H153) was officially declared lost with all hands, the *Glasgow Herald* reported that the Admiralty had received reports from Bergen that two lifebuoys bearing the name of the vessel had been picked up at different locations along the Norwegian coast.

1,044: On 20 February 1930 the Hull trawler St. Louis (H153) was officially declared lost with all hands, after leaving port on 8 January on a trip to the Norwegian fishing grounds. A service, led by Pastor Joseph Summers, was held on 9 March 1930 at the Hessle Road Fishermen's Bethel, for the sixteen lost crew members.

1,045: Textile designer Pat Albeck was born in Anlaby on 17 March 1930, the youngest of four daughters of Polish immigrants. At sixteen she attended the College of Arts and Crafts in Hull, where she spent four years, before going on to study at the Royal College of Art, London, in 1950. She has designed tea towels for the National Trust, and her Daisy Chain fabric was a best-seller at John Lewis for more than 15 years. She is married to set designer Peter Rice; her daughter-in-law is ceramicist Emma Bridgewater.

1,046: At the end of the 1929–30 season, Hull City experienced relegation for the first time, from the

Second Division of the Football League to the Third Division North. That same season, City reached the semi-final of the FA Cup for the first time, drawing 2-2 with Arsenal at Elland Road (Leeds), before losing 1-0 in the replay at Villa Park. Arsenal went on to win the final 2-0 against Huddersfield Town, at Wembley Stadium on 26 April.

1,047: Speedway racing began in the Hull area in July 1929 when an eleven acre site at the rear of the skating rink of the White City pleasure park on Anlaby Road was developed into a track. An open licence was granted, with the first meeting taking place on 3 May 1930. At least 17 meetings were held between May and August that year.

1,048: On 5 May 1930, with only her father and a few friends to see her off, Amy Johnson took off from Croydon Airport in her De Havilland Gipsy Moth (christened *Jason* in honour of her family fish-firm's trademark) in her attempt to create a new record for a solo flight from England to Australia.

1,049: Following a few weeks of illness, Thomas Ferens died on Friday 9 May 1930. Two funeral services were held at the same time in the city: at Ferens' local Brunswick Church and at Holy Trinity Church in the city centre. As his wife's death had preceded his and they had no children, their home was left to be used as a 'home for poor gentlewomen'.

1,050: The Shakespearean scholar Stanley Wells was born in Hull on 21 May 1930. The son of a bus company traffic manager, Wells—who has been called 'the world's greatest living expert on William Shakespeare'—attended Kingston High School before going on to take a degree in English at University College, London. He was appointed Commander of the British Empire (for services to Literature) in the Queen's 2007 Birthday Honours, and knighted (for services to scholarship) in the Queen's 2016 Birthday Honours.

1,051: Amy Johnson completed her attempt at beating Hinkler's record when she landed at Port Darwin, Australia at 3.30pm on 24 May 1930, 19½ days after taking off from Croydon Airport. While she hadn't created a new record for a solo flight from England to Australia, she had become the first solo woman to successfully complete that flight, covering approximately 11,000 miles in 19½ days; attracting the attention of the media across the world, and becoming an international celebrity.

1,052: The Grand Opera House on George Street closed on 30 May 1930 to be remodelled as a cinema venue. It re-opened as the Grand Theatre Cinema on 1 September.

1,053: When Amy Johnson arrived back at Croydon she was welcomed by thousands of people; and an estimated 1m people lined the 12 mile route from Croydon Airport to the Grosvenor House Hotel in London. King George V honoured her achievement by appointing her CBE.

1,054: In 1930 Hull-based J.H. Fenner & Co. Ltd. became the first company in the world to manufacture latex impregnated solid-woven belting.

1,055: Horatio Nelson Smith was fluent in German and had many contacts and friends in Germany. It was from one of his German associates, Johannes Lohmann, that, in 1930, Smith & Nephew acquired the rights to *Elastoplast* (invented in 1924 by Georg Teske) and, in 1932, *Gypsona*, the plaster of Paris bandage (also invented by Teske, in 1930).

1,056: Ralph Thomas began his working life as a journalist on the *Bristol Evening World*, though he had a keen interest in the film industry: his uncle was Victor Saville (film producer, director and screenwriter whose original surname was Salberg), who went on to produce *Goodbye, Mr. Chips!* (1939), directed by Sam Wood, and starring Robert Donat, Greer Garson and John Mills.

1,057: Following its closure in 1930, Hull's first enclosed dock (latterly known as Queen's Dock) was sold to Hull Corporation, filled in, landscaped and transformed into Queen's Gardens.

1,058: Upon his death in 1930 Thomas Ferens left most of his £292,843 to charity, requesting that his shares in Reckitts be kept as an investment to provide future income for his bequests. Following his cremation his ashes were placed next to his wife's in a vault in the grounds of their home, Holderness House.

1,059: On more than one occasion Thomas Ferens was offered a title, but turned down all such honours, preferring instead to be known as 'Mr Ferens'.

1,060: Thomas Ferens and his wife Esther were active members of the nearby Brunswick Methodist Church and taught at the Sunday School every week. Ferens thought this so important that he continued to teach to the end of his life, taking his last classes in his own home shortly before he died.

1,061: A Hollywood publicist dubbed Dorothy Mackaill's lips 'The most kissable lips in Hollywood'. When she returned to Hull in 1930, Pathé News produced a short news item titled: *Hull: "The most kissable girl in Hollywood": Dorothy Mackaill, England's "own" Film Star, has "overwhelming" reception on return to her native city after 11 years in America.*

1,062: In January 1931, when she was just twenty-eight, *New Movie Magazine* featured Dorothy Mackaill on its cover, referring to her as 'the richest woman in Hollywood'.

1,063: In 1931 a new main road—the development of which had been proposed as early as 1914—was opened in the city centre. Originally, the plan was to name the road Quality Street, but this idea was scrapped in favour of naming it Ferensway, in honour of Thomas Robinson Ferens, one of Hull's most generous benefactors who had died the previous year. The development of Ferensway followed the clearance of the Mill Street area during a major slum-clearance programme begun in the 1920s. The necessary parliamentary powers for the Ferensway project were granted in 1924.

1,064: The Holderness Hall Cinema was sold to Gaumont British Theatres in 1931.

1,065: On 18 December 1931 the Hull steam trawler Girdleness (H782) was wrecked with the loss of all hands, off Sudero, in the southern Faroe Islands. Built in 1919 by Cochrane & Sons Shipbuilders Ltd. (Selby), the Girdleness was skippered by Arthur Edward George (23) of 268 St. George's Road, Hull. Her last owners were the Trident Steam Fishing Co. Ltd. (Hull).

1,066: The National Census of 1931 reported the population of the county borough of Hull as 313,544.

1,067: At the end of the 1932–33 season (under the management of Haydn Green), after three seasons in the Third Division North, Hull City topped the league table with 59 points—and 100 goals—to win promotion back into the Second Division.

1,068: Amy Johnson married Jim Mollison on 29 July 1932. Mollison's proposal of marriage came just eight hours after he and Amy Johnson had met.

1,069: In 1932 Ralph Thomas was offered a traineeship with Oscar Deutsch (the founder of the Odeon Cinema chain) at Sound City studios, Shepperton after Deutsch had read an article by Thomas about the Odeon cinema circuit. Thomas began work at Sound City as a clapper boy, with stints in various other departments before settling into the role of film editor.

1,070: Frederick Needler died from Parkinson's Disease on 30 September 1932, aged 67. He was a much-respected employer and local benefactor, one of his legacies being a house (gifted to the then recently established University College Hull) which became a student hall of residence, named Needler Hall in his honour.

1,071: On 4 January 1933 the Hull steam trawler Endon (H161) was lost with all hands. The seemingly abandoned vessel was discovered—with a large gash in her side and with the lifeboat missing—by the St. Kilda (H355), whose skipper valiantly tried to tow the Endon back to Hull, but was forced to abandon the attempt because of the prevailing conditions. Built in 1914 by Smith's Dock Co. (Middlesbrough), the Endon was skippered by Frederick Parkes (62) of 29 Tyne Street, Hull, and owned by the Great Northern Steam Fishing Co. Ltd. (Hull).

1,072: On 25 January 1933 the Hull steam trawler Cape Delgado (H47) was officially declared missing: lost with all hands, after being caught in a hurricane off the Norwegian coast on her way back to port from a trip to the White Sea. Built in 1929 by Cochrane & Sons Shipbuilders Ltd. (Selby), she was skippered by Robert Gillard of 27 Priory Grove, Hull, and owned by Hudson Steam Fishing Co. Ltd. (Hull).

1,073: On 18 February 1933 the Hull steam trawler James Long (H141) was lost with all hands after going missing on her way back to port following a trip to the Icelandic grounds. She was skippered by Horace Calvert (28) of 44 Essex Street, Hull.

1,074: Jean Hartley (*née* Holland) was born in Hull, in inauspicious circumstances, on 27 April 1933. She became an 'unmarried mother' at eighteen, giving birth to daughter Laurien, whose father was Peter Everett—later the author of several novels including *Negative* (1964) and *Matisse's War* (1996); and founder, with John Rety, of the literary journal *The Fortnightly* (1958). Jean first met George Hartley in 1947 at the Rhythm Club, at the Wheeler Street Youth Club. They were both fourteen years old. Several years later, after the birth of Laurien, they met up again; Jean became pregnant by George and they married in 1953.

1,075: After suffering a minor stroke earlier in the year, John Ellerman died on 16 July 1933 at the Hotel Royale in Dieppe, France. His estate was valued for probate at £36,685,000, almost three times that of the second ever largest estate valued for probate, that of Guinness brewery magnate Lord Iveagh. Ellerman, who in 1917 was estimated to be worth four times as much as the Duke of Westminster, is considered to have amassed the greatest ever business fortune in British history.

1,076: When Sir John Ellerman died in 1933, leaving the largest estate in British probate history, the probate chargeable to his estate amounting to almost 40% of the total wealth passing through probate in Britain that year.

1,077: Following his death on 16 July 1933, Sir John Ellerman's coffin was returned to London from Dieppe draped with the Merchant Marine flag; he was buried at Putney Vale Cemetery in south-west London.

1,078: In 1933 the Hull Repertory Company and Little Theatre (Hull) Ltd. were amalgamated, acquiring the neighbouring former Assembly Rooms premises in 1939. The Assembly Rooms (with a Music Room and Museum on the first floor) were built in 1830; the Music Room was enlarged in 1877; and by 1910 the premises had been given a cinema license. In 1939 the cinema closed and the Assembly Rooms and the Little Theatre were converted into the New Theatre. In 1990 a blue heritage plaque was erected on the theatre to mark its origins, and the building's original designer. The inscription reads:

> Built as the Assembly Rooms in 1830 (design by R. H. Sharp under the direction of Charles Mountain, Arch.) this building became the New Theatre in 1939 and is now owned and run by Hull City Council

1,079: The appointment of Peppino Santangelo in 1933 to take control of Little Theatre (Hull) Ltd. was a turning point in the company's fortunes. It was under his guidance that the Hull Repertory Company and Little Theatre (Hull) Ltd. were brought together and a new theatre was founded. The New Theatre, Hull officially opened on Saturday 16 October 1939 with a production of Noel Gay's *Me and My Girl.*

1,080: On 14 January 1934 the steam trawler Loch Ard (A151) sailed from Hull, bound for the Icelandic fishing grounds. On 16 January she called in at Aberdeen—the vessel was Aberdeen owned and registered—for minor repairs, but no further contact was made with the ship after she left Aberdeen. On 2 March she was officially declared lost with all hands. Built in 1895 by John Lewis & Sons Ltd. (Aberdeen), she was skippered by William Shears (34) of 24 Liverpool Street, Hull; the owners were the Glasgow Shipping Co. (Glasgow), but she was working out of Hull under the management of Hellyer Bros. Ltd. Besides skipper William Shears, at least eleven other Hull seamen were among the crew.

1,081: The Regal Cinema at 132 Ferensway was opened on 26 January 1934. Built for County Cinemas, and designed in the Art Deco style, the venue (with a seating capacity of 2,553) cost £95,000 to complete. It was home to a Conacher 4 manuals and 22 ranks organ with illuminated surround.

1,082: On 30 July 1934 the Astoria Cinema opened at 669 Holderness Road (on the corner of Lake Drive). Designed in the Art Deco style by James E. Adamson, and built by Messrs. Markwell, Holmes and Hayter Ltd., the single-screen Astoria had a total capacity of 1,546, and boasted a 3 Manual/ 8 Rank organ, built by the John Compton Organ Company (who in 1938 totally rebuilt the organ in Hull's Holy Trinity Church).

1,083: In 1934 the butchers business set up by Harry Fletcher in 1907 moved into pies and confectionery after the founder's son began baking in his mother's oven in the living quarters behind the shop. The popularity and consequent sales of the products allowed the firm to acquire the adjoining premises to accommodate the expanding business.

1,084: Hull author Valerie (Val) Wood, who won the inaugural Catherine Cookson Prize for Romantic Fiction in 1993—and writes novels based around Hull and its environs—was born Valerie Beardshall in Glasshoughton, Castleford on 12 November 1934. She moved to Hull in 1947 at the age of 13 when her father came to work as a war damage assessor. Winning the Cookson prize led to the subsequent publication of her first novel *The Hungry Tide*, since which she's published at least twenty-three more.

1,085: On 19 December 1934 Ethel Lillie Major became the first female to be hanged at Hull Prison. Major (43), who had killed her husband by poisoning him with strychnine in May 1934 at their home near Horncastle, Lincolnshire was executed by Thomas William Pierrepoint (assisted by his nephew Albert Pierrepoint). She was the last person to be executed at the prison.

1,086: On 9 January 1935 after three weeks trawling the Bear Island fishing grounds (and with a full hold) the Hull trawler Edgar Wallace (H262) keeled over in the Humber, resulting in the loss of fifteen of the eighteen crew. The vessel was waiting to enter St. Andrew's Dock; and having continued beyond the dock entrance up to Hessle Sands, had manoeuvred round to make her way back down the Humber when she struck sand banks on three separate occasions, before the six knot spring tide rolled her over with little or no warning.

1,087: The 336 ton trawler Edgar Wallace was owned by the Newington Steam Trawling Co. Ltd. Her skipper was John Stevenson (32) of 165 St. George's Road, Hull. The three survivors were: Clarence Wilcockson (Harrow Street), Charles Hendrick (Wellsted Street), and William Cameron (Coltman Street).

1,088: A fortnight after the sinking of Edgar Wallace another life was lost when Gainsborough seaman James Vessey—the engine-man on a vessel assisting with the salvaging operations—was the only crew member unaccounted for when the Boatman capsized after colliding with a lighter in the treacherous tides of the Humber.

1,089: Following the sinking of Edgar Wallace a fourteen-year-old pupil at Boulevard High School, Lucy Warren, who had witnessed its aftermath, recorded the tragic event in a poem titled 'The Six-Knot Tide'. The poem—which came into the possession of local maritime historian Robb Robinson (a second cousin of the poet)—was recorded decades later by pupils of Newland High School for Girls especially for BBC Radio Humberside.

1,090: The transformation of Hull's Grand Opera House into a cinema venue was so successful that the theatre was closed for three months from July 1935 for extensive renovations and radical internal restructuring by architects

Blackmore & Sykes, the consequence being a decimation of Frank Matcham's richly ornate original auditorium.

1,091: During the 1935 transformation of the Grand Opera House, the original three-tier theatre was re-modelled into a 1,806-seat cinema, with one large balcony; peach, gold and silver décor; a new Binns, Witton & Haley theatre organ, and a new stage with a more comprehensive and elaborate lighting system. Following the alterations the venue was renamed the Dorchester Cinema and re-opened on 30 December 1935.

1,092: On 3 August 1935 the Rex Cinema opened on Endyke Lane, Hull. This single-screen 1,045-seat cinema, equipped with a Western Electric sound system and with a proscenium 38 feet wide, was built for Hull City and Suburban Cinemas (Hull) Ltd., but was controlled by County Cinemas Ltd. It was later (8 November 1937) acquired by Associated British Cinemas.

1,093: On 17 August 1935 the Royalty Cinema was opened on Southcoates Lane, near the corner of Bedale Avenue. Built for Hull City and Suburban Cinemas Ltd., this single-screen, 1,045-seat cinema was equipped with a Western Electric sound system, and had a 40 feet wide proscenium.

1,094: During the months April to September 1935 the 102 feet William Wilberforce monument was resited from its original location at the corner of St. John's Street to what was then the eastern boundary of Queen's Gardens. The monument was re-dedicated by William Wilberforce's great granddaughter, Mrs Arnold Reckitt, on 19 September. The relocation was carried out by Tarran Industries Ltd., the company of councillor Robert Greenwood Tarran.

1,095: On 19 September 1935, Queen's Gardens opened on the site of the former Queen's Dock.

1,096: On 24 September 1935 the Hull steam trawler Skegness (H14) foundered and was lost with all hands after running aground in darkness, and in the grip of a tremendous gale, at Speeton during her return trip from the Faroes. Built as the James Peake (for the Admiralty) in 1917 by Smith's Dock Co. Ltd. (Middlesbrough), her last owners were the Trident Steam Fishing Co. Ltd. (Hull). She was skippered by Richard Wright (28) of 596 Spring Bank West, Hull.

1,097: During the slum clearance in the early decades of the 20th century the number of public houses in Hull fell by more than 35%—from 452 in 1901 to 288 in 1935. This fall can be directly attributed to the teetotal council refusing to issue new licences to replace the public houses demolished after being destroyed by bombing.

1,098: In 1935 the Regis Cinema was opened at the Gipsyville end of Hessle Road. This single-screen 1,045-seat cinema, equipped with a Western Electric sound system and with a proscenium 45 feet wide, was built for Hull City and Suburban Cinemas (Hull) Ltd., but was later (8 November 1937) acquired by Associated British Cinemas.

1,099: In 1935 the Astoria Cinema, on Holderness Road, was taken over by County Cinemas, but was operating independently once again in 1936. After closing on 7 June 1963, the venue was almost immediately reinvented as a bingo hall. The Astoria Bingo Club continues to operate successfully today.

1,100: The Regis (Hessle Road), Rex (Endyke Lane) and Royalty (Southcoates Lane) cinemas were each built to the same Robert Cromie design—in the Art Deco style.

1,101: Pioneering aviator Amy Johnson was the President of the Women's Engineering Society from 1935–37.

1,102: In the Third Round of the Rugby League Challenge Cup, on 7 March 1936, 28,798 spectators (the all-time attendance record at The Boulevard) saw Hull FC go down 4-5 to Leeds. After a series of contentious decisions by the referee Frank Fairhurst, Hull FC players Joe Oliver and George Barlow were both sent off, leaving Hull with eleven men for the last quarter of the match, with Freddie Miller taking over goal kicking duties following Oliver's dismissal.

1,103: At the end of the 1935–36 season Hull FC finished top of the table (with 61 points), five points above Liverpool Stanley. Having beaten Wigan 13-2 in the semi-final, they won the Championship for the third time with a 21-2 victory over Widnes in the Championship final at Fartown, Huddersfield. In what would become known as 'Joe Oliver's match', the Hull full-back scored two tries and five goals. Also in the same year, Hull FC became the Yorkshire League Champions for a fourth time.

1,104: At the end of the 1935–36 season, after just three seasons in the Second Division, Hull City were relegated back to the Third Division North after conceding one hundred and eleven league goals and accumulating only twenty points.

1,105: On Thursday 31 December 1936 Fred Danton, the skipper of the Admiral Collingwood (H341) sent a wireless message back to port (but addressed to his wife) stating he hoped to be 'Home on Sunday' [3 January]. It was the last anyone heard from the skipper or the vessel. The ship was setting off with her catch from Bear Island on her homebound journey, after two weeks fishing in the Barents Sea.

1,106: The Admiral Collingwood, owned by C.H. Smith & Co. (Hull) Ltd., and built by Cochrane & Sons Ltd. of Selby, was one of Hull's biggest and most modern trawlers. She had sailed from Hull (on just her fifth trip) on 12 December, with the crew spending Christmas at sea. Her maiden voyage was in October, three months earlier. The owners of the trawler created maritime history when they persuaded the BBC to broadcast an announcement to shipping in the North Sea to look out for the ship, the BBC's first ever broadcast of this kind.

1,107: John Ellerman's Ellerman Lines lost 67 ships during the First World War, and 85 ships during the Second World War including, in 1936, the SS City of Benares which was being used as part of the Children's Overseas Reception Board (CORB) programme to evacuate 90 British children to Canada. The ship was torpedoed by a German submarine, with the loss of seventy-seven of the children. The sinking resulted in the cancellation of the CORB programme.

1,108: On 24 January 1937 the Hull trawler Amethyst (H455) sank on her way home from Lodingen, in the Norwegian Sea, after a trip to the White Sea in the southern Barents Sea. As the vessel sailed further into the North Sea the gale-force winds strengthened into hurricane force. The Kingston Chrysolite (H205) was also heading back to port after a trip to the White Sea, and was a few miles ahead of Amethyst when she received a call on the radio from the Amethyst saying her boiler had shifted and she was in trouble. Before the radio message could be completed, the call was cut, in mid sentence. The Amethyst, skippered by Richard Baker (28) of 61 Bernadette Avenue, Anlaby, was lost with all hands, off Kinnaird Head.

1,109: A company (company number: 00324357) named Smith and Nephew Associated Companies (SANACO) was incorporated as a limited company on 15 February 1937. One of its stated objects was to 'acquire not less than ninety percent of the issued share capital of T.J. Smith &

Nephew Limited, Smith & Nephew (Manchester) Limited, and Sashena Limited'. SANACO changed its name to Smith & Nephew PLC on 16 June 1988. T.J. Smith and Nephew Limited still survives as a private limited company, with its Registered Office remaining at 101 Hessle Road, Hull.

1,110: On 1 July 1937 J.H. Fenner & Co. Limited was incorporated and became a public limited company, with a share capital of £250,000 made up of 125,000 5½% Cumulative Preference shares of £1 each and 500,000 Ordinary shares of 5/- each.

1,111: On 8 November 1937 Hull's Regal Cinema was acquired by Associated British Cinemas.

1,112: On 8 November 1937 the Royalty Cinema on Southcoates Lane was acquired by Associated British Cinemas, who eventually closed the venue on 2 April 1966, since when the original facade has been demolished. The auditorium, however, remains and has been utilized by the most recent business occupier of the premises, United Carpets and Beds.

1,113: In 1937 J. Arthur Rank bought out Lady Yule's share in Pinewood Studios and subsequently acquired the Gaumont-British Picture Corporation (1941), Odeon Theatres (1942), and Ealing Studios (1944).

1,114: In 1937, at the age of 34, Dorothy Mackaill made her last film: *Bulldog Drummond at Bay*. She subsequently cared for her mother (whose health was failing) until her death in 1956.

1,115: Although she became one of the biggest stars in Hollywood, Dorothy Mackaill's first film (*The Face at the Window*) and her last (*Bulldog Drummond at Bay*) were both made by British companies.

1,116: After reaching an agreement in 1931 to market rubber V-belts by Gilmer (Philadelphia), in the UK, South Africa, Australia and New Zealand, J.H. Fenner invested in its own V-belt manufacturing plant, with the first Fenner-manufactured V-belt leaving the Marfleet factory in 1937.

1,117: As a consequence of his various other interests and numerous absences, following the incorporation of Smith and Nephew Associated Companies Ltd. in 1937, Horatio Nelson Smith had his executive authority removed by the company's Board, but continued as Chairman. The management and day-to-day running was passed on to the company's Chief Executive.

1,118: On 5 March 1938 the Hull steam trawler Lady Lavinia (H160) was lost with all hands when she foundered off the Sula Lighthouse on the west coast of Norway; she was returning to Hull after a trip to the Bear Island fishing grounds. Built in 1935 by Cook, Welton & Gemmell Ltd. (Hull), she was skippered by Jacob Walker (29) of St. Matthew Street, Hull; the owners were Jutland Amalgamated Trawlers Ltd. (Hull).

1,119: Edwin Dyson (Eddie) Healey was born on 22 April 1938. He built his fortune in property development, including out-of-town retail parks such as Meadowhall, the sale of which, in 1999, added more than £400m to his wealth.

1,120: The possibility of an amalgamation between Reckitt and Sons Ltd. and J.J. Colman Ltd. was first discussed in 1909. The two companies finally merged in 1938 with Reckitt & Colman (UK) Ltd. (company number 00341605) being incorporated on 20 June that year.

1,121: During the evening of 29 September 1938 the Hull trawler St. Sebastian (H470) ran aground on the north-east coast of Bear Island in the western reaches of the Barents Sea, with the total loss of the vessel and her 16 crew (though it was reported that a single survivor had been sighted trying to reach the shore by scrambling over the rocks).

1,122: Following the SOS transmitted by the trawler St. Sebastian, sister Hull trawlers Cape Duner (H174) and Davy (H332) steamed to her assistance, along with the Kingston Cairngorm (H175), the Mildenhall (GY124), the Loch Oskaig (H431) and the Norwegian salvage ship Jason. It was crew members aboard the Mildenhall who reported seeing a lone survivor on the rocks.

1,123: St. Sebastian was owned by Messrs. Thomas Hamling & Co Ltd., and skippered by William Weightman (27) of 63 Belvedere Road, First Lane, Hessle. The vessel left Hull on the morning tide of 15 September 1938.

1,124: Following the running aground of the St. Sebastian, a search party comprised of the strongest and fittest men from the crews of Cape Duner, and Davy, with the rocket apparatus of the Bear Island Radio Station, trekked across the island to the site of the wreck but could find no sign of survivors. (Bear Island was uninhabited, save for the crew operating the island's small wireless station.)

1,125: On 13 October 1938 Hull's Priory Cinema was opened at the junction of Spring Bank West and Calvert Lane. The single-screen, 1,284-seat cinema, the facade of which was designed in the Art Deco style, had a 30 feet wide proscenium and a 14 feet deep stage, with dressing rooms. The venue also provided a café, and ample car parking facilities to the rear of the building.

1,126: As well as holding the club record for the most career points (1,842), legendary Hull FC goal kicker Joe

Oliver also holds the club record for the most career goals (687)—scored over his twelve years with the club.

1,127: After her retirement from the film industry, Dorothy Mackaill made her home in Honolulu, in room 253 of the Royal Hawaiian Hotel. She subsequently made several guest appearances in the American police drama, *Hawaii Five-0*.

1,128: Before the Second World War, Joseph Leopold (Sir Leo) Schultz successfully campaigned for the local authority to build bomb shelters across the city; their construction eventually saved thousands of lives. He was appointed OBE in 1946 for his role as Deputy Chairman of Hull's Air Raid Precautions Committee, received his knighthood in 1966 for political and public services in Yorkshire, and was given an honorary LL.D. from Hull University in 1979.

1,129: On 14 January 1939 Hull City recorded their biggest victory when they beat Carlisle United 11-1 at home in the Third Division North.

1,130: On 1 September 1939, at the outbreak of the Second World War, 50,000 people left Hull in one day when a mass evacuation operation was set in motion with the aim of protecting the city's children from possible German bombing raids. The evacuees were transported to what were considered to be safer destinations—Beverley, Market Weighton, Scarborough, Whitby, and various other villages and towns—in trains, buses and steam packets. More than 50 trains departed from Paragon Station in a twelve hour period; and seven steam packets left Corporation Pier carrying in excess of 1,000 children.

1,131: On 2 September 1939, the day before Neville Chamberlain announced that Britain was at war with Germany, Hull City drew 1-1 with Southport in City's last

Third Division North game before the suspension of the Football League for the duration of the Second World War. The previous week, on Saturday 26 August, City had drawn 2-2 away at Lincoln City.

1,132: The official opening date of the New Theatre, Hull (16 October 1939) was the same day that Germany chose to execute its first air raid on the UK. The theatre also shares its 'birthday' with William de la Pole, 1st Duke of Suffolk, and the playwright Oscar Wilde.

1,133: On 18 November 1939 the steam trawler Wigmore (GY469) was lost with all hands after being torpedoed by the German U-boat U22 (commanded by Karl-Heinrich Jenisch) 25 miles north west of Rattray Head, north east Scotland. She was part of a convoy heading for the Icelandic grounds. Built in 1928 by Cook, Welton & Gemmell Ltd. (Hull), for Letten Bros. (Grimsby), her last owners were the Clan Steam Fishing Co. Ltd. (Grimsby). Wigmore was skippered by Walter Bore, with William Lodge (39) formerly of Wassand Street, Hull as his Mate.

1,134: Margot Fonteyn performed at the New Theatre, Hull with the Vic-Wells Ballet (later The Royal Ballet Company) in December 1939 and again a few months later, in February 1940. She returned to the theatre again, in February 1976, with her one-woman show.

1,135: Although Hull suffered ferocious bombing during the Second World War, and the windows of the Hessle Road store of W. Boyes & Co. Ltd. were smashed on several occasions, the staff managed to ensure the store traded continuously throughout the war.

1,136: By 1939 the butchers, cooked meats and baking business of Harry Fletcher (which would eventually become H. Fletcher & Son Ltd.) had expanded into a small chain of three shops: two on Hessle Road (Nos. 302 and 470) and one on Anlaby Road (No. 473).

1,137: During the Second World War, Ralph Thomas served with the 9th Lancers, eventually making the rank of Major and, in 1942, being awarded the Military Cross. He was invalided out of active service in 1944, before becoming an instructor at the Royal Military College.

1,138: The conversion of the Little Theatre and the Assembly Rooms into the New Theatre, Hull was executed to the designs of R. Cromie and W.B. Wheatley.

1,139: During the Second World War, Hull's Priory Cinema, at the junction of Spring Bank West and Calvert Lane, was used as a Civil Defence Centre.

1,140: Hull-born actor Ian Carmichael was the nephew of the three brothers (Robert, James and Herbert) who ran the eminent R.P. Carmichael & Co. Ltd., Jewellers and Silversmiths store in George Street, Hull. His father, Arthur, had chosen to train as an optician and subsequently established a practice in the family store.

1,141: In 1939 the equestrian statue of King Billy was removed from its city centre location in Lowgate and taken for safe-keeping to Houghton Hall, Sancton for the duration of the Second World War. The statue was re-gilded in 1947 after being returned to its original location. Since then it has been re-gilded on two further occasions: once in 1973 and again in 1987.

1,142: On 14 January 1940 the steam trawler Lucida (A175) was lost with all hands after striking an enemy mine. Built in 1914 by the Dundee Shipbuilding Co. Ltd. (Dundee) for the Devon Steam Trawling Co. Ltd. (Fleetwood), her last owners were the Boston Deep Sea Fishing & Ice Co. Ltd. (Fleetwood). She was skippered by Albert Thundercliffe (38) of 18 Swanland Grove, Hull.

1,143: On 3 April 1940 the steam trawler Sansonnet (A862) sank and was lost with all hands after being bombed by enemy aircraft 18 miles east-by-south of Muckle Flugga, Shetland Isles. The Sansonnet was built in 1908 by Alexander Hall & Sons Ltd. (Aberdeen), for the Beacon Steam Fishing Co. Ltd. (Grimsby). She was skippered by William McCallum (53). Hull seamen Albert Hall (Deckhand) and James McGarry (Trimmer) were among the crew.

1,144: On 19 June 1940 the first air raids of the Hull Blitz began. Hull, anonymously described as 'a north-east coast town', was one of the Second World War's most heavily bombed UK cities (some reports say the second most heavily bombed after London) with the loss of 1,200 lives, and 86,715 (95%) of the city's houses being damaged. Around 3,000 people were injured and 152,000 made homeless. The city spent more than 1,000 hours under air raid alert.

1,145: Amy Johnson died tragically on 5 January 1941 when in rough weather the twin-engined Airspeed Oxford aircraft she was flying crashed into the Thames Estuary. Her body was never recovered.

1,146: On 16 February 1941 the steam trawler Thomas Deas (M253) was lost with all hands following an explosion (presumed to be an enemy mine) four miles off Spurn Point. Built as a non-standard 'Castle' class trawler in 1917 by Smith's Dock Co. Ltd. (Middlesbrough) and launched as the James Johnson, the vessel was acquired by the Admiralty and re-registered as the Thomas Deas in December 1919; at the time of her loss she was owned by J. Marr & Son Ltd. (Fleetwood). Skippered by W. Scott, at least six Hull seamen were among the crew, including the vessel's Mate John Raywell (25) of 78 Rosamond Street, Hull.

1,147: On the night of 17/18 March 1941, Hull's National Picture Theatre took a direct hit during an air-raid in which 378 Luftwaffe aircraft bombarded the whole city, resulting in 96 deaths. Fortuitously, none of the theatre's 150 patrons, who were reportedly sheltering in the foyer, were injured. The film being screened on the evening of the air-raid is reputed to have been Chaplin's *The Great Dictator*. The theatre itself was destroyed, with just the badly damaged foyer and the building's facade surviving.

1,148: On 26 April 1941, while heading for the Icelandic grounds, the Hull steam trawler Commander Horton (H233) was lost with all hands after being hit by an enemy U-boat. Built in 1915 by Goole Shipbuilding & Repair Co. Ltd. (Goole), for the Hellyer Steam Fishing Co. Ltd. (Hull), the Commander Horton was skippered by Ernest Lewis (43) of 10 Plaxton Bridge, Woodmansey. Her last owners were the Eastern Steam Fishing Co. Ltd. (Hull). She was torpedoed by the U-boat U552 (commanded by Erich Topp) at around 2am, to the south west of Iceland.

1,149: Although the bar in the New Theatre had been reinforced as a bomb shelter (the theatre's programmes informed its patrons: 'the theatre is a safer place than your own home'), during the Hull Blitz of 7 and 8 May 1941 the building took a direct hit, with two auditorium doors and the front row of the stalls being destroyed, along with all the props and costumes of the visiting Sadler's Wells Opera Company.

1,150: Hull's Riverside Quay suffered serious damage along its whole length during air raids on the city on the night of 7 May 1941. More centrally, the Prudential building in Hull's King Edward Street was destroyed after taking a direct hit from a parachute mine, resulting in the loss of sixteen lives, including four children between the ages of 11 and 15. Only the Prudential tower survived the bombing, but this had to be demolished later for reasons of safety.

1,151: The Ritz Cinema on Holderness Road was yet another casualty of the Hull Blitz, being destroyed in the raids that took place during the night of 8 May 1941.

1,152: On the night of 8/9 May 1941, during an intensive bombing raid of the Hull Blitz—focussed primarily around the centre of Hull and the dock areas—all the trading records of the Asbestos and Rubber Company were destroyed.

1,153: The original Cecil Theatre was all but destroyed during the Hull Blitz of May 1941. It was eventually demolished in 1953.

1,154: Hull's Alexandra Theatre—along with the glass and iron sliding roof of its auditorium, and its distinctive corner tower and revolving searchlight—was destroyed during the Hull Blitz of May 1941.

1,155: The Carlton Picture Theatre, opened in 1928, was a fine example of suburban Art Deco cinema construction. Its Fitton & Haley organ was moved to the original Cecil Theatre, and subsequently became another casualty of the Hull Blitz of May 1941.

1,156: Having survived his wife by seven years (never remarrying) Sir Alfred Gelder—earliest of the architects of Modern Hull—died at his home on South Street, Cottingham on 26 August 1941. His funeral at the Anlaby Road Methodist Church (which he designed) took place on 29 August. His architectural legacies to Hull—including Hull City Hall, Queen's Gardens, and the wider more spacious streets and public places—have become significant landmarks in the general consciousness of the city's population.

1,157: On 27 August 1941 the steam trawler Ladylove (LO167) was lost with all hands after being hit by an enemy U-boat south of Iceland. Built in 1902 by Cook, Welton & Gemmell Ltd. (Hull) for Pickering & Haldane's Steam Trawling Co. Ltd. (Hull), as the Ophir (H725), the Ladylove left Fleetwood heading for the Icelandic grounds, but had become involved in rescuing survivors from the torpedoed Norwegian steamer Inger, and had landed three survivors at Stornoway before proceeding. The Ladylove, skippered by Alfred Crozier Fletcher (60), sailed from Stornoway on 25 August 1941. She was hit on Wednesday 27th by a torpedo from the U-boat U202 (commanded by Hans-Heinz Linder). The Ladylove's last owners were the Hewett Fishing Co. Ltd. (London). At least three Hull seamen were among the crew.

1,158: On 6 September 1941 the steam trawler King Erik (GY474) was lost with all hands after being torpedoed by the German U-boat U141, off Iceland. Built in 1899 by Cochrane & Cooper Ltd. (Selby), King Erik was skippered by Francis Henry Davidson (39); the owners were the Boston Deep Sea Fishing & Ice Co. Ltd. (Fleetwood). At least six Hull seamen were among the crew.

1,159: In November 1941 Winston Churchill visited Hull, attending a luncheon at the Guildhall—given by the Sheriff of Hull Robert Tarran—to commemorate both the 600th anniversary of the commencement (under Henry VI) of the Sheriffdom of Kingston upon Hull—when, in 1439, John Spencer became the first person to be appointed to that office—and the 400th anniversary of the signing of the charter of the Hull Trinity House. With Churchill taking in a walk around the city centre and a tour of the docks, the visit also served to boost morale and give encouragement to the people of Hull, who during the spring and summer of 1941 had experienced some of the country's most severe bombing of the Second World War. A painting by local artist Fred Elwell, which at the time of writing (10 December 2016) is listed in the Hull Museums Collections (Accession No: KINCM: 2005.30) as: 'The Visit of Sir Winston Churchill (The Tarran Luncheon)' commemorates the luncheon; the painting is similarly listed on the artuk.org website. [It is dated 1945 and Churchill did not become 'Sir Winston' until 24 April 1953]. Loncaster and Shields (2014) give the title as: 'The Sheriff's Luncheon - Winston Churchill Visits Hull'.

1,160: In 1941 the factory of J.H. Fenner & Co. Ltd. at Marfleet was destroyed by bombing, and shadow factories in West Yorkshire and Lancashire had to take over the company's production during the war years.

1,161: Geoffrey Dummer was part of the team in the Air Ministry Research Establishment, Malvern, which built the first ever plan position indicator (radar screen).

1,162: During the Second World War, Fenner V-belts formed part of the drives used on the bouncing 'Dambuster' bombs developed by Barnes Wallis and used in *Operation Chastise*, carried out by RAF 617 Squadron in May 1943.

1,163: On 30 August 1943 the Hull steam trawler Strathlyon (H19) was lost with all hands after striking an enemy mine off Iceland. Built in 1928 by Hall, Russell & Co. Ltd. (Aberdeen) for the Aberdeen Steam Trawling & Fishing Co. (Aberdeen), her last owners were Jutland Amalgamated Trawlers Ltd. (Hull). She was skippered by Ernest Hall (59) of 10 Dorset Street, Hull.

1,164: During the 1880s Joseph Rank became a strict Methodist. In 1934 he endowed the Joseph Rank Benevolent Fund with over £300,000 for the relief of poverty in Hull, and to help 'poor persons of good character'; and in 1935 he was given the honorary

Freedom of the City of Hull, the only public honour he ever accepted. He died at his Surrey home, Colley Corner, Reigate Heath, on 13 November 1943.

1,165: On 24 November 1943 the steam trawler Hondo (H565) went missing and was lost with all hands off Barra Head, Outer Hebrides. Built in 1912 by Cochrane & Sons Shipbuilders Ltd. (Selby), for Boston Deep Sea Fishing & Ice (Grimsby), her last owners were Henry L. Taylor & Co. (Grimsby). She was skippered by John Nicholson (43).

1,166: Hull-born Ian Carmichael left the family business for London's Royal Academy of Dramatic Arts (RADA) in order to pursue his ambition to be an actor. He married twice: Jean Pyman McClean (in 1943), with whom he has two daughters; and again in 1992 (after 9 years as a widower) to novelist Kate Fenton.

1,167: On 13 January 1944 the Hull trawler Alonso (H887) was reported missing in the North Sea with the loss of all hands. The cause of her disappearance was unknown, but it was classified as a war loss. Alonso was built for Hellyer by Mackie & Thomson (Govan) and launched in 1906. Although originally owned by Hellyer Steam Fishing Co. Ltd. (Hull), the vessel was sold-on several times before eventually being acquired by Hull Merchants Amalgamated Trawlers Ltd. (Hull) in 1942. She was skippered by George Underhill (68) of Cleethorpes.

1,168: On 23 February 1944 the steam trawler Iranian (GY728) went missing off Hornsea and was lost with all hands (presumed to be as a result of enemy action) after leaving Grimsby on 12 January for the North Sea fishing grounds. Built in 1911 by Cook, Welton & Gemmell Ltd. (Hull), for Thomas Robinson (Grimsby) the vessel was sold to Sir Thomas Robinson & Sons Ltd. (Grimsby) in 1927. Her last owners were the Rossall Steam Fishing Co. (Fleetwood); and she was skippered by R.R.D. Bland.

Local seaman Timothy Oliver (65) of 75 Spring Street, Hull was the vessel's Steward.

1,169: On 20 June 1944 Ralph Thomas married Joyce Evelyn Spanjer (a driver in the Military Transport Corps) at St. John's Wood Synagogue. They had two children: a son (Jeremy, who produced the Oscar winning *The Last Emperor*) and a daughter (Jill Purdom who followed a career in animation).

1,170: Thomas Sheppard, museum curator, autodidact and amateur geologist, retired in 1941. He died at home four years later, on 18 February 1945, and was cremated on 21 February 1945. A green heritage plaque, erected by the Avenues and Pearson Park Residents' Association, marks his former home at 3 Victoria Avenue, Hull. The inscription reads:

THOMAS SHEPPARD curator lived here 1888–1892

1,171: On 17 March 1945, just six weeks before Germany surrendered in Italy, 12 people were killed in the last piloted air-raid of the Second World War to cause civilian casualties, at the hands of a maverick German Heinkel 111 crew who opened fire on people leaving Hull's Savoy Picture Theatre as the bomber flew over Holderness Road.

1,172: Despite the heavy bombing suffered by Hull during the Second World War, and the fact that its offices were in the city centre, the *Hull Daily Mail* continued uninterrupted with not a single edition being missed.

1,173: Malcolm Stanley Healey was born in June 1944. He founded Humber Kitchens in 1976, and subsequently (1981) acquired the *Hygena* brand name, before selling Humber Kitchens to MFI in 1987 making £200m. He then set up Mills Pride kitchen manufacturers in Middlefield, Ohio (USA), which he sold in 1999 for £800m.

1,174: Having in 1942 founded the Synthetic Training Design Group, responsible for the design, manufacture and maintenance of radar training equipment during the Second World War, Geoffrey Dummer was awarded an MBE for this work in 1945.

1,175: Maureen Lipman was born in Hull on 10 May 1946, the daughter of Maurice Julius Lipman (a local tailor who had a shop on Monument Bridge in the city centre) and his wife Zelma (*née* Pearlman), who had married in 1943. She is a former pupil of Newland High School for Girls, and trained at the London Academy of Music and Dramatic Art. Lipman was married to dramatist Jack Rosenthal for thirty years until his death in 2004. She was awarded an honorary D.Litt by the University of Hull in 1994 and was appointed CBE in 1999 for services to comedy and drama.

1,176: On 26 May 1946 legendary Hull guitarist Mick Ronson was born in a nursing home on Beverley Road, to George and Minnie Ronson (*née* Morgan), who married on 26 January 1944, and whose family home was on Hull's Greatfield Estate.

1,177: With the re-commencement of the Football League after the Second World War, Hull City started 1946 with a new Board of Directors, led by local businessman Harold Needler. City fans looked forward to a new era, with a new ground (Boothferry Park) and a new manager in Major Frank Buckley.

1,178: The Hull-based William Jackson Bakery Limited was initially registered at Companies House as Crystal of Hull Limited (incorporated on 20 August 1946), before becoming Goodfellows (15 October 2003), and Jackson's Bakery (10 April 2008)—all familiar names to Hull residents over a certain age.

1,179: On 31 August 1946 Hull City's new ground, Boothferry Park, was opened when City entertained Lincoln City in a 0-0 draw in the Third Division North—City's first game after the suspension of Football League fixtures due to the Second World War. The ground was opened by Hull's then Lord Mayor, Isaac Robinson; and the teams were led onto the pitch by local mounted police officer sergeant J.T. 'Tommy' Brooke, riding his white horse.

1,180: Actor Barrie Rutter was born in a 'two-up, two-down' terraced house in the fishing community area of Hull's Hessle Road on 12 December 1946. His theatrical training included spells at the Royal Scottish Academy of Music and Drama, and the National Youth Theatre.

1,181: In 1946, having being demobilized from the army, Ralph Thomas worked for the Rank Organisation in its trailer production department. He was offered the chance to direct after the head of Gainsborough Pictures, Sydney Box, saw a trailer that Thomas had made for *Miranda* (1948). His first film as Director was *Once upon a Dream* (1949), starring Googie Withers; this was followed by *Helter Skelter* later the same year.

1,182: On 1 January 1947 J.R. Rix & Sons was formed by John Robert Rix—the eldest son of the founder of Robert Rix & Sons—with a working capital of £7,000 and a single motor ship; and on 25 January 1957 J.R. Rix & Sons Limited was registered at Companies House, with the company's shareholders being named as John Robert Rix (ship owner) of 'Cranbrook', Dunswell Road, Cottingham; Robert Kenneth Rix (ship owner) of 'Banchory', 29 Northgate, Cottingham; and John Leslie Rix (ship owner) of 'Cranbrook', Dunswell Road Cottingham. The company's first directors were Robert Kenneth Rix and John Leslie Rix.

1,183: In January 1947, in his continuing efforts for increased component reliability, Geoffrey Dummer (in partnership with Dr A.C. Vivian) produced the first plastic 'potted circuit' to insulate electronic components from shock and moisture.

1,184: On Sunday 6 July 1947, whilst travelling to Hull following a series of dates in Scotland, Laurel and Hardy (whose taxi had broken down) dropped in at the Dixon's Arms public house in Woodmansey, about 7 miles north of Hull. Frederick Porter (the landlord) and his family entertained the duo and their party with 'a nice spread of sandwiches and cake' whilst the vehicle was being attended to. The stars posed for photographs (taken by the landlady Doris Porter) with the family; and later provided the family with complimentary tickets to one of the shows and an invite to visit the pair backstage afterwards.

1,185: Laurel and Hardy played twice at Hull theatres. The first in 1947, as part of their UK tour, when they played Hull New Theatre, twice-nightly for five nights during the week commencing 7 July. During the run they stayed at the Royal Station Hotel, and reputedly went for a drink in the Old English Gentleman pub.

1,186: One of the most iconic album covers ever produced (that of Mike Oldfield's *Tubular Bells*) was created by Hull-born photographer and graphic designer (John) Trevor Key. Born in Hull on 10 July 1947, Key's photographic work features on many of the releases from bands, such as Joy Division (*Love Will Tear Us Apart*), Orchestral Manoeuvres in the Dark (*Tesla Girls*), China Crisis (*No More Blue Horizons*), and around 14 releases from New Order, including 'Blue Monday'. He was also very closely involved in the design of the *Virgin* 'scrawl' brand for Richard Branson. Trevor Key died of a brain tumour, at the age of 48, on 6 December 1995.

1,187: After military service Gerald Thomas worked at Denham film studios where his brother was supervising the making of film trailers for the Rank Organization. While at Denham, he worked as an assistant editor on *The October Man* (1947) and Olivier's *Hamlet* (1948); and then as an associate editor on Carol Reed's *The Third Man* (1949).

1,188: On 3 April 1948 Raich Carter played his debut match for Hull City in a 1-1 draw with York City. Within days of his arrival at the club, manager Frank Buckley had resigned, so Harold Needler installed Carter as the club's player-manager. City finished 5th in the table that season.

1,189: After the Second World War, a 443 yards speedway track was developed at Staithes Lane, Hedon— on the site of the Hedon aerodrome—shortly before the start of the 1948 season. The home team was named the Hull Angels and racing took place on Saturday evenings, in the National League Division Three. Unfortunately, this venture lasted less than two years, and in August 1949 the track—which was serviced by a railway halt on the Hull to Withernsea line—became the first British post-war speedway track to close mid-season. Hull Angels made their final appearance at the Hedon track on 27 August 1949, against Liverpool.

1,190: The heaviest home defeat suffered by a Hull speedway team is 42-66 when Hull Angels lost to Cradley Heath, in the Qualification Competition Round 2 [first leg] of the 1948 National Trophy on 1 May 1948. The heaviest away defeat (again, Hull Angels at the hands of Cradley Heath) was 29-78, in the Qualification Competition Round 2 [second leg] of the 1948 National Trophy on 7 May 1948.

1,191: At the end of the 1948 season Hull Angels finished ninth (of twelve) in speedway's National League Division Three table, with a total of 38 points, Mick

Mitchell being the team's best performing rider with 78 wins from 166 races. The league was won by Exeter on 65 points.

1,192: Work on the reconstruction of the Marfleet factory of J.H. Fenner & Co. Ltd., destroyed by bombing in 1941, began in 1947. The new factory was fully operational before the end of 1948.

1,193: Edward Arthur Milne wrote several specialist books, including *Thermodynamics of the Stars* (1930), *Relativity, Gravitation and World Structure* (1935), and *Kinematic Relativity* (1948); and was the recipient of numerous awards and honours, including being elected to the Royal Society (1926), being awarded the Royal Medal of the Royal Society (1941), being awarded the Gold Medal of the Royal Astronomical Society (1935), and being appointed President of the Royal Astronomical Society (1943–45).

1,194: On 24 January 1949, whilst living at 55 Newland Park, Hull, Dr Eva Crane founded the Bee Research Association (BRA), later the International Bee Research Association (IBRA). This, the marital home of Dr Crane and her Hull-born husband Jim, became the Association's headquarters until the Cranes moved house in 1955. Ten years earlier, Dr Crane had been appointed Secretary to the Research Committee of The British Beekeepers Association (BBKA), whose remit was the organization and coordination of UK research into 'beekeeping and allied subjects'. However, by 1948 it was recognized that the task was beyond the scope and capability of the BBKA. Hence the founding of BRA.

1,195: In 1949 Hull City reached the last eight in the FA Cup for the first time since their 1929–30 season cup run (when they were knocked out by Arsenal in the semi-final). A record attendance of 55,019 saw City, led by Raich

Carter, lose 1-0 to the cup holders Manchester United in the Sixth Round, at Boothferry Park, on the 26 February.

1,196: In early 1949, following the Rank Organisation's closure of the Gainsborough Pictures film studio, Ralph Thomas began work at the Rank Organisation's film studio base at Pinewood, and directed *The Clouded Yellow* (1950), starring Jean Simmons and Trevor Howard for the Betty Box Independent Production company—for Carillon Films.

1,197: The track record for the Staithes Lane home venue of Hull Angels speedway team was 82.4 seconds, set by Billy Bales for visitors Yarmouth, on 14 May 1949.

1,198: In August 1949 Brian Rix married Elspet Gray, an actress with his Viking Theatre Company. They eventually had four children. Their first child, Shelley Elspet, was born with Down's Syndrome, which inspired Rix to become a lifelong activist and campaigner for the public awareness of learning disabilities, and for disability rights generally. Shelley Elspet Rix died in 2005, aged 53.

1,199: Within three years of the club's new regime (led by Harold Needler, with the team now under the player-management of Raich Carter) Hull City topped the Third Division North at the end of the 1948–49 season to gain promotion back into the Second Division, where they remained, with a generally steady decline in success, until the end of the 1955–56 season, when they were relegated, once again, back into the Third Division North.

1,200: The Rix Shipping Company Limited, incorporated on 21 March 1950, changed its name to Bankmile Limited on 5 January 2005, and changed its Registered Office from Witham House, 45 Spyvee Street, Hull to 7 Fore Street, Mousehole, Penzance, Cornwall on 23 July 2009.

1,201: The Holderness Hall Cinema on the corner of Witham and Clarence Street was renamed the Gaumont on

3 July 1950, but closed before the end of the decade on 10 November 1959.

1,202: The Hull-born astrophysicist, mathematician and cosmologist Edward Arthur Milne died of a heart attack at the age of 54 in Dublin on 21 September 1950.

1,203: Following the Creswell Colliery disaster of 26 September 1950, in which 80 lives were lost due to a fire caused by a damaged rubber and canvas conveyor belt becoming trapped in a machine (resulting in an overheated motor), J.H. Fenner & Co. Ltd. became involved in a research programme to develop fire-resistant conveyor belting. The product developed was the solid-woven, PVC impregnated *Fenaplast*, which was first produced in the Marfleet factory in 1952 and was subsequently used in the mining industry worldwide.

1,204: After closing as the Gaumont on 10 November 1959, the Holderness Hall Cinema re-opened as a live music venue (the Majestic Ballroom), eventually closing on 7 March 1965, following which it was converted into a bingo hall. After a period as a furniture warehouse, it was finally demolished in early 2004.

1,205: Hull-born Johnny Whiteley signed for Hull FC in December 1950 at the age of 20 for a fee of £100, playing his debut in Hull's 19-10 victory over York on 23 December; he became the club captain in 1957, a role he kept until he retired from playing in 1965. He holds the club record for number of appearances (417) and was never dropped from the side; he retired from the game in 1972 and was honoured with an MBE in 2015 for his services to rugby league and the community.

1,206: Gerald Thomas's first role as Film Editor was on John Paddy Carstairs' *Tony Draws a Horse* (1950); he subsequently edited several films directed by his brother

Ralph, including *Appointment with Venus* (1951), [renamed *Island Rescue* for its release in the USA], *A Day to Remember* (1953), and *Doctor in the House* (1954).

1,207: In 1950 Ralph Thomas began his association with film producer Betty E. Box, a working relationship that lasted for a quarter of a century and produced thirty films including the first of the very successful *Doctor...* series: *Doctor in the House*.

1,208: Hull-born explorer and merchant adventurer John Boyes died in Nairobi on 19 July 1951. He was buried at Nairobi's Forest Road Cemetery on 20 July 1951.

1,209: In 1951 a railway shuttle from Paragon Station to the Boothferry Park Halt began, providing a match-day service that enabled both home and away supporters to travel by train directly from Hull city centre to the ground. The service was first used on 6 January when 595 fans travelled on six trains to watch City beat Everton 2-0 in the Third Round of the FA Cup. That year, City went on to reach the Fifth Round, before being defeated 3-0 by Bristol Rovers.

1,210: As an infant Mick Ronson exhibited a keen interest in music, becoming excitedly animated whenever music was played in the house, but his first musical instrument was the family's second-hand accordion. When Mick was five years old his mother Minnie bought a piano for £73; but when she tried to arrange piano lessons for her son, she was told he was too young (Mick was memorising tunes instead of learning to read the music).

1,211: In 1951 Smith & Nephew acquired the research company Herts Pharmaceuticals Ltd. (formerly Beiersdorf UK Ltd., the UK subsidiary of Beiersdorf Ltd.) the company credited with developing PAS—the first oral treatment for tuberculosis—in 1944. Beiersdorf Ltd., a German company based in Hamburg, was founded in 1882 and developed the *Nivea Creme* skin-care brand introduced in 1911. In 1952 Smith & Nephew Research was formed from Herts Pharmaceuticals.

1,212: In 1951 the New Theatre, Hull was acquired by Whitehall Theatres Ltd., with the existing management remaining intact. The theatre was bought by Hull City Council (with the help of Alderman Frederick Holmes and Councillor Lionel Rosen) in 1961.

1,213: The National Census of 1951 reported the population of the county borough of Hull as 299,105.

1,214: Emily (Madame) Clapham died on 10 January 1952 at her home Southwood, South Street, Cottingham. She was buried in Cottingham Cemetery.

1,215: Geoffrey Dummer's idea for an integrated circuit was first presented publicly in a paper delivered at the US Symposium on Quality in Electronics Components, in Washington DC on 7 May 1952. American investors were eventually persuaded to take the financial risk, leaving the UK lagging years behind in the semi-conductor industry.

1,216: On 4 October 1952, at approximately 7:40 am, the Hull steam trawler Norman (H289) was lost with nineteen of her twenty crew when in thick fog she struck an uncharted rock and foundered off Cape Farewell, Greenland. The only survivor was deckie learner Norman Spencer (19). Built in 1943 by Cook, Welton & Gemmell Ltd. (Hull), she was skippered by Jack Dukes (39) of 36 Subway Street, Hull; the owners were the Northern Fishing Company (Hull) Ltd.

1,217: When the Hull trawler Norman (H289) was lost in 1952, it was the first year that British trawlers had fished the grounds south of Cape Farewell, and so the available charts were incomplete and, therefore, unreliable. The Norman sailed from Hull on 17 September, the skipper having been briefed by a representative of the Hull Steam Trawlers' Mutual Insurance & Protection Company, Ltd. (the vessel's insurers), who highlighted the need for caution due to the incomplete charts and pointed out the known hazards around the coastline. The owners received a circular from the insurers on 30 September containing new relevant information regarding navigation hazards in the area where the Norman was fishing, but Mark Hellyer neglected to forward this information to Jack Dukes, the skipper of the vessel.

1,218: Following the death of his brother in 1952, J. Arthur Rank focussed his energies back on the family milling business, but endowed his interests in film companies on the Rank Foundation charity, which distributed around £100m during his lifetime. He retired as Chairman of the Rank Organisation in 1962. He refused a peerage from Clement Attlee, but was created Baron Rank, of Sutton Scotney, in 1957.

1,219: When Mick Ronson eventually began piano lessons it was with Trevor Bolder's grandmother, a connection his fellow Spiders from Mars member was unaware of until recording David Bowie's *The Rise and Fall of Ziggy Stardust and the Spiders from Mars* album (1971–72).

1,220: In 1953 Laurel and Hardy appeared in Hull for a second time, when they brought their 'New Comedy' *Birds of a Feather* to the Palace Theatre of Varieties, Anlaby Road, twice-nightly for five nights during the week commencing 7 December 1953.

1,221: Whilst in Hull with their *Birds of a Feather* in 1953, Laurel and Hardy were invited to cut the ribbon at the official opening ceremony of Paragon Jewellers, in Toll Gavel, Beverley. At noon on Friday 11 December Oliver Hardy made a theatrical attempt to cut the ribbon with a two-inch pair of scissors, before Stan Laurel stepped forward with a pair of garden shears to complete the job.

1,222: During each of their appearances in Hull (1947 and 1953) Laurel and Hardy were invited by the Society of Cinema Managers in Hull to be guests at luncheons held in honour of the comedy pair: the first took place on the first floor at the Royal Station Hotel on Wednesday 9 July 1947; the second in the Georgian Room at the White House Hotel, Paragon Street on Wednesday 9 December 1953.

1,223: In 1953 Basil Reckitt (the great-grandson of Isaac Reckitt) arranged for the Reckitt family charitable trusts to finance essential repair work to the Maud Foster windmill, built in 1819 for Thomas and Isaac Reckitt.

1,224: Gerald Thomas was Film Editor for Ken Annakin on Disney's *The Sword and the Rose* (1953), starring Glynis Johns, Richard Todd and James Robertson Justice.

1,225: In 1953, when they were both twenty years old, Hull-born literary innovators Jean and George Hartley founded the literary magazine *Listen*, publishing work by poets such as John Heath Stubbs, Henry Treece, Anthony Thwaite, Donald Davie, Al Alvarez, Kingsley Amis, and Philip Larkin, from their home at 253 Hull Road, Hessle. When the Hartleys started out in publishing with *Listen*, George Hartley was still on the dole.

1,226: In 1953 George William Gray received his PhD from the University of London for his thesis entitled 'Mesomorphism of Aromatic Carboxylic Acids' his first book on the subject, *Molecular Structure and the Properties of Liquid Crystals*, was published in 1962.

1,227: On 29 January 1954 J.H. Fenner & Co. Ltd. changed its name to J.H. Fenner & Co. (Holdings) Ltd.

1,228: On 8 May 1954 Paul Jackson—who established the New Adelphi Club, De Grey Street, Hull as one of the most significant Independent Music venues in the UK, if not the world—was born at the Townsend Maternity Hospital, Cottingham Road, Hull. He grew up in the villages of Swanland (where he attended the local primary school), North Ferriby, and Cottingham (where he attended Cottingham High School).

1,229: Following a campaign led by its first Principal, Arthur Morgan, University College Hull was granted a Royal Charter in 1954 establishing it as an independent university, with the power to grant degrees and honorary degrees, and to call itself a university rather than a university college. The announcement that University of Hull had been granted its Royal Charter was made on 15 May 1954.

1,230: On 17 May 1954 Arthur Lucan—the comic actor who found fame as Old Mother Riley—died after collapsing in the wings at Hull's Tivoli Theatre. Lucan was born on 16 September 1885 at Sibsey, Lincolnshire. He was the third of seven children born to Tom Towle and his wife Lucy Ann (*née* Mawer). Originally named Arthur Towle, he adopted the surname Lucan in 1913 whilst working in Dublin, where he met his future wife the sixteen-year-old Kitty McShane. He was buried in Hull's Eastern Cemetery on Friday 21 May, following a requiem mass at St. Patrick's Church, Spring Street.

1,231: At the end of what turned out to be their final UK tour, from October 1953 to May 1954, Laurel and Hardy returned to Hull on 30 May to sail on 2 June (on the Danish cargo ship M.S. Manchurian) back to the United States, hoping to arrive in Los Angeles on 27 June.

1,232: In 1954 H. Fletcher & Son opened its branch at 288–290 Holderness Road, and also opened its meat processing plant and bakery at 44 Southcoates Lane, East Hull (employing at this time about 50 people). The Southcoates Lane address was also used as the company's Registered Office, until 14 August 2001 when the Registered Office was changed to 44 Saturday Market, Beverley.

1,233: The 1954 film *Doctor in the House* was the first in which Ralph Thomas directed Dirk Bogarde, who went on to star for Thomas in several other films, including *Doctor at Sea* (1955), *Doctor at Large* (1957), *Doctor in Distress* (1963), and *The High Bright Sun* (1965).

1,234: Hull's David Whitfield was the first British male singer to receive a Gold Disc for record sales with his recording of 'Cara Mia' (issued in 1954), which went on to sell 2.5m copies.

1,235: An economic survey in 1954 suggested that for every fisherman working at sea there were another three people working ashore in jobs associated with the fishing industry, which amounted to 50,000 shore workers—approximately 20% of Hull's entire population at that time.

1,236: On 26 January 1955, after responding to a distress call from the Kingston Garnet (H106), Hull trawlers Lorella (H455) and Roderigo (H135) became so laden with ice and snow that the water they each took on, in the freezing and treacherous hurricane conditions of the Greenland Sea, 90 miles north-east of Iceland's North Cape, caused both vessels to heel over, capsize and sink, with the loss of forty lives. The Kingston Garnet, whose distress call was sent out on 23 January because her propeller had become fouled by wire, had managed to free herself and head for safety the day before the Lorella and Roderigo arrived at the scene.

1,237: In 1955 Jean and George Hartley set up a small publishing concern, The Marvell Press, and published their first book: Philip Larkin's breakthrough collection *The Less Deceived* (invoiced on 24 November 1955), which made Larkin's international reputation as a poet of significance, and marked The Marvell Press as publishers to be reckoned with. The same year, on 21 March , Philip Larkin took up the position of Librarian at the University of Hull.

1,238: Singer and entertainer Joseph Patrick (Joe) Longthorne MBE was born on 31 May 1955 in the heart of the working class, fishing community area of Hull's Hessle Road, where he attended Villa Place Primary School before going on to Sydney Smith High School. After achieving regional success in 1969 with appearances on Yorkshire Television's *Junior Showtime*, he first came to national attention following an appearance on London Weekend Television's *Search For A Star* in 1981.

1,239: On Monday 28 November 1955 the new Cecil Theatre opened on the south/east corner of the junction of Anlaby Road and Ferensway. With a seating capacity of 2,052, and boasting the largest CinemaScope screen in the country at 57 feet wide, the new Cecil also had a 100-seat restaurant and bar. The first film screened was *The Seven Year Itch* starring Marilyn Munroe.

1,240: The new Cecil cinema (now Mecca Bingo) was the first cinema to be built on a new site anywhere in Britain after the Second World War.

1,241: The Hull Brewery Company Limited was the first company to supply Marks & Spencer with canned beer.

1,242: Geoffrey Dummer—who has been called 'The Prophet of the Integrated Circuit'—sought investment from within the UK for the development of integrated circuitry, but was met only by indifference (from both the Ministry of Defence and commercial companies) through lack of vision about the possible applications of the technology. He died in Malvern on 9 September 2002.

1,243: At the end of the 1955–56 season Hull FC finished fourth in the league table (with 51 points), behind Warrington (55), Halifax (58), and St. Helens (54). In the play-off semi-final Hull beat Warrington 17-0, before going on to beat Halifax 10-9 in the final on 12 May at Maine Road, Manchester to take the Championship title for the fourth time in the club's history.

1,244: At the end of the 1955–56 season Hull City came bottom of the league and were relegated yet again to Division Three North. However, their stay in the lower division was relatively short; they were promoted to the Second Division as runners up (to Plymouth Argyle) three years later, at the end of the 1958–59 season.

1,245: In October 1956 Philip Larkin moved into 32 Pearson Park (in the Avenues area of west Hull) where he lived until 1974.

1,246: On 12 November 1956 the Berkeley Cinema was opened on Greenwich Avenue in the heart of Hull's Bilton Grange Estate. Built for Hull Picture Playhouses Ltd., the single-screen, 1,200-seat Berkeley was equipped with a 38 feet 6 inch wide CinemaScope screen and a Western Electric (WE) sound system. It closed on 30 September 1967 and, rather predictably, was converted into a bingo hall, which by July 2005 had also closed. Subsequently a tower block called Berkeley House was built on the site.

1,247: In 1956 H. Fletcher & Son Ltd. opened its flagship city centre branch at 41–45 King Edward Street,

Hull—one of the most prominent retailing sites in the city—with the gregarious and astute Mr Raymond Witty as manager.

1,248: On 13 November 1956, following the opening of their city-centre branch, the first money taken over the counter at H. Fletcher & Son Ltd.—a gold sovereign tendered as payment for a cake—was preserved by the company in a glass display globe.

1,249: The ceremonial mace of the University of Hull was commissioned by Hull City Council in 1956 to acknowledge the institution's new status as a university.

1,250: Gerald Thomas made his directorial début with *Circus Friends* (1956), written by Peter Rogers. This was followed by *The Vicious Circle* (1957), written by Francis Durbridge, starring John Mills and Wilfrid Hyde-White; and *Time Lock* (1957), with a screenplay by Peter Rogers, from a play by Arthur Hailey.

1,251: In 1957 Hull's Patricia Bredin (born on 14 February 1935 in Swansea) was the first ever UK representative in the Eurovision Song Contest, finishing in seventh position among the ten entrants.

1,252: Patricia Bredin's Eurovision Song Contest performance of the song 'All' in 1957 was the first ever performance in the competition of a song in English and at 112 seconds was (until 2015) the shortest performance in the history of the competition. Although the Eurovision Song Contest began in 1956, the UK did not submit an entry until 1957.

1,253: The legendary pioneer of popular music Buddy Holly performed with his band The Crickets (2 shows, compered by Des O'Connor) at Hull's Regal Cinema on Wednesday 19 March 1958, less than a year before his death at the tragically young age of 22 in February 1959.

1,254: On 22 April 1957 Hull FC beat Halifax 35-12 at The Boulevard to win the European Club Championship in an early, short-lived version of that competition. A week earlier the Black and Whites had drawn 19-19 with French side Racing Club Albi (also played at The Boulevard), setting themselves up for the match against Halifax, which doubled as a regular English League match. The Halifax result put Hull FC top of the four-team European Club Championship table, to win the title. The three other cubs involved in the competition were Halifax, RC Albi (the 1956 French Rugby League Champions), and AS Carcasonne (the 1956 French Rugby League runners-up).

1,255: At the end of the 1956–57 season Hull FC finished second in the Championship league table with 60 points, six points behind Oldham. The Black and Whites beat Barrow to reach the Championship play-off final, but were beaten 15-14 by Oldham on 18 May 1957, at the Provident Stadium, Bradford to become Rugby League runners-up for the first time.

1,256: On 15 August 1957 Gerald Thomas married Barbara Tarry (a fashion buyer) at Caxton Hall register office, Chelsea. They subsequently had three daughters.

1,257: In 1957 the Palace Theatre underwent alterations, with many of the interior fittings being removed to create more space for tables and chairs, and it became known as The Continental Palace (or simply 'The Palace').

1,258: At eight years, between 1957–65, Johnny Whiteley is Hull FC's longest serving club captain, though due to injury he missed the whole of the 1962–63 season, being deputised on the field by Bill Drake. Arthur Keegan comes a close second with six years (1965–71); with Roy Francis at 5 years (1950–55); and Billy Batten (1915–19) and David Topliss (1981–85) at 4 years.

1,259: At the end of the 1957–58 season Hull FC finished fourth in the Championship table with 56 points, behind Oldham (67), St Helens (64), and Workington (58). In the play-off semi-final they beat Oldham 20-8, before going on to beat Workington Town 20-3 on 17 May in the final, at the Provident Stadium, Bradford, to take the Championship title for the fifth time in the club's history.

1,260: In 1958 Gerald Thomas directed *Chain of Events*; and collaborated for the first time with Norman Hudis, on *The Duke Wore Jeans*, written (including songs) by Lionel Bart and starring Tommy Steele; with incidental music by Bruce Montgomery, who would later compose the scores for six of the *Carry On...* films, including (also in 1958) *Carry On Sergeant*.

1,261: The orchestra pit at the Hull New Theatre can accommodate 60 performers; the theatre has a total of 16 dressing rooms: thirteen at basement level and three upstairs.

1,262: Local sweets manufacturer Needlers Ltd. became a public limited company in 1958, with the Needler family retaining a controlling interest; the company was acquired by Hillsdown Holdings for £3.4m in 1985, but was later sold to NORA SA, Norway's largest food group. In January 1996 Needlers was acquired by the Bluebird Confectionery Group, and was renamed Needler Bluebird Confectionery Group in 2000. The company was sold once again in January 2002, to Ashbury.

1,263: With UK cinema attendance falling in the 1950s by around 50%, from a peak of over 1.6 billion in the late 1940s, the single-screen Eureka Picture Palace at 562 Hessle Road closed in February 1959 and was converted into a bingo hall.

1,264: In February 1959 Hull's Priory Cinema closed and was subsequently converted into a supermarket, which was for a period operated by the Kwik Save Supermarket chain. The Kwik Save supermarket closed in 2007.

1,265: At the end of the 1958–59 season Hull FC reached the final of the Challenge Cup (their first ever final appearance at Wembley Stadium), where they were defeated 30-13 by Wigan in front of 79,811 spectators. The nineteen-year-old Arthur Keegan, in his first season as a professional, scored 4 penalty goals and converted Hull's only try, scored by Tommy Finn in the seventy-second minute.

1,266: Following their promotion to the Second Division at the end of the 1958–59 season, Hull City were relegated to the Third Division again after just one season, their shortest stay in the Second Division.

1,267: Hull's Regis Cinema at the Gipsyville end of Hessle Road was closed on 24 October 1959, and though the venue was left standing for a few more years it has since been demolished.

1,268: Hull's Rex Cinema on Endyke Lane was closed on 24 October 1959, and though the venue was still standing in 1965 it has since been demolished.

1,269: Between 1959–61 a remodelling of Queen's Gardens was undertaken, with Frederick Gibberd (the designer of Liverpool's Metropolitan Cathedral) acting as Consultant for the project.

1,270: In 1959 the Regal Cinema was renamed the ABC following a temporary closure to install a new projection room at the rear of the circle.

1,271: In 1959 a £4.75m improvements scheme at Hull's King George Dock was authorised by the British Transport

Commission. The proposals included: £2m for work on the north side to remove the original diagonal berths and convert the berths into linear berths on a straight wharf; and 'removing the redundant coal loading plant'. Further plans for improvement included the construction of two single-storey transit sheds covering 150,000 square feet; and modernisations such as replacing original timber quay structures with more modern concrete structures. £150,000 of the budget was allocated to modernising the existing fleet of mobile cranes, fork-lift trucks etc. to maximise the efficiency of goods handling within the transit sheds.

1,272: A new 1,065ft concrete construction of Hull's Riverside Quay was built in the 1950s and officially opened in 1959.

1,273: The first Humber Bridge Act was passed in 1959, establishing the Humber Bridge Board whose role was to manage and raise funds to build the bridge, and buy the land required for the approach roads.

1,274: On Monday 11 January 1960 Cliff Richard began a one week 'featured guest attraction' in the *Babes in the Wood* pantomime at the ABC Regal, though he did not play a role in the pantomime.

1,275: At the end of the 1959–60 season Hull FC finished third in the league table with 57 points, behind St. Helens (69), and Wakefield Trinity (64); they were defeated 24-4 by Wakefield in the Championship semi-final play-off. In this season, they also reached the final of the Challenge Cup, for a second, successive year, where they were defeated 38-5 by Wakefield Trinity, in front of 79,773 spectators. Stan Cowan scored Hull's only try, with Sam Evans providing the goal. The final result (38–5) was a new record Rugby League Challenge Cup score, eclipsing Hull's 30–13 defeat at the hands of Wigan the previous year.

1,276: On 10 July 1960 the Savoy Picture Theatre on Hull's Holderness Road closed. It was replaced by a shop in 1961.

1,277: On 1 September 1960 Horatio Nelson Smith died at his house, Greenacre, at Ringmer (near Lewes), Sussex.

1,278: In October 1960 the Monica Picture House on Hull's Newland Avenue was closed. The venue has been home to the Piper Club since 1965. The Piper Club, which covers approximately 7,000 sq. feet, was bought in May 2015 by Tradepark Ltd. after being put on the market by its then owners the Stonegate Pub Company. Following a three-month renovation the Piper held its official re-opening event on Friday 24 July 2015.

1,279: In 1960 Sir Leonard Hutton—the renowned ex-England cricketer, who holds the record for the highest Test match score by an English batsman—joined J.H. Fenner & Co. Ltd. to work primarily in a public relations capacity, but by 1973 he had been appointed a director of Fenner International Ltd., and eventually worked for the company for 23 years, longer than he had played first class cricket (22 years).

1,280: Mick Ronson attended Maybury Junior School, where he learned to play the violin, which he gave up after about three years because 'people used to make fun of you if you carried a violin case.. I used to pay people to carry my violin because I was afraid to [carry it] myself'.

1,281: Ralph Thomas thrived on the challenges presented by the sheer variety of films offered to him: Comedy (*Doctor in the House*), Political (*No Love for Johnnie*), War (*Conspiracy of Hearts*), Crime (*Deadlier than the Male*), Action (*Nobody Runs Forever*); achieving success, both critically and at the box office, across a wide range of genres.

1,282: With 1958's *Carry On Sergeant* Gerald Thomas and Peter Rogers had stumbled upon a format that would inevitably lead to a commercially successful series, and five more *Carry On...* films (scripted by Norman Hudis) followed in the next five years: *Carry On Nurse*, *Carry On Teacher*, *Carry On Constable*, *Carry On Regardless*, and *Carry On Cruising*.

1,283: Hull-born actor Ian Carmichael was perhaps best known to 1960s TV audiences as P.G. Wodehouse's Bertie Wooster, opposite Dennis Price as Jeeves, in several series of *The World of Wooster* (1965–67).

1,284: The debate about whether the name of the Hessle Road store W. Boyes & Co. Ltd. should be pronounced 'boyz' (bɔɪz), 'boy-yez' (bɔɪ'es) or 'boy-zez' (bɔɪ'ses) is a long-standing one, with most people from the Hessle Road area favouring 'boy-zez' (bɔɪ'ses). Perhaps a useful exercise in support of this pronunciation might be to imagine the store being named W. Jones & Co. Ltd.: customers surely then would speak of buying something from, or visiting, 'joan-zez' (dʒəʊn'ses).

1,285: In 1960 David Fletcher, grandson of the founder, joined H. Fletcher & Son Ltd. He became Chairman in 1993, by which time he had doubled the size of the business from 5 to 11 shops.

1,286: In 1959 Peppino Santangelo retired from the New Theatre, Hull. He was succeeded by William Sharpe who, in response to falling audience numbers, presided over the experimental introduction in 1961 of bingo sessions at the venue.

1,287: While the experimental bingo sessions introduced at the New Theatre, Hull were clearly popular with the public, the move proved to be the impetus for the Hull City Council to arrange an emergency meeting to discuss the possibility of the Council purchasing the venue in order to secure its future as a theatre. The City Council bought the theatre and the Kingston upon Hull New Theatre Company was formed to run the venue. The Kingston upon Hull New Theatre Company was incorporated on 8 January 1964.

1,288: Rock'n'Roll pioneer Gene Vincent appeared twice at Hull's Majestic Ballroom on Holderness Road. Both shows were put on by promoter Don Arden: the first, with support act Sounds Incorporated, on 1 May 1961; with Vincent's second and final appearance on 22 November, topping the bill; with support acts Johnny Kidd & The Pirates, Johnny Duncan & The Bluegrass Boys, Jess Conrad, and Sounds Incorporated.

1,289: On 18 October 1961 the Hull steam trawler Arctic Viking (H452), battling a heavy storm off Flamborough on her way home from the Norwegian fishing grounds with 1,400 kits, was inundated with water on her port side deck before capsizing, turning right over and eventually floating bottom upwards. Some of the crew scrambled into a collapsible liferaft, while others had to take their chances in the raging North Sea. Fortunately a Polish motor trawler, Derkacz, had seen the distress flares sent out by the Arctic Viking, and responded immediately.

1,290: The skipper of the Derkacz decided he couldn't risk heading for port until the weather had significantly calmed. Consequently, it was two days before the rescued crewmen of the Arctic Viking arrived back at Hull and before the families of the Hull trawlermen discovered which of their men had survived—and which hadn't. The five crew members lost were Edward Kent (38) of 51 Hessle Road; Arthur Waddy (47) of 35 Harrow Street; Dennis Lound (29) of 8 Endsleigh Villas, Wellsted Street; John Robinson (22) of 22 Foston Grove, Preston Road; and David Craft (34) of 254 Wansbeck Road, Longhill Estate.

1,291: Ryszard Sleska, skipper of the Derkacz, spent four hours in heavy seas rescuing the crewmen from the Arctic Viking's liferaft. When the Derkacz eventually delivered the rescued crew home, the crew and skipper of the Polish trawler were given a civic reception at Hull's Guildhall in recognition of their heroic act in saving the surviving Hull trawlermen.

1,292: On 9 December 1961 an eighteen-year-old Clive Sullivan marked his debut on the wing for Hull FC with the first three of his record 250 tries for the club, in an emphatic victory over Bramley. It was a game that also saw fellow winger South African Wilf Rosenberg's debut for the club. Rosenberg scored two tries in Hull's 39-9 victory at The Boulevard.

1,293: The National Census of 1961 reported the population of the city & county borough of Hull as 303,261.

1,294: On 13 May 1962 Jerry Lee Lewis appeared at the Cecil Cinema on Anlaby Road. He would have been twenty-six years old.

1,295: On 13 September 1962 Chubby Checker, best known for his world-wide chart hits 'The Twist' and 'Let's Twist Again', appeared at Hull's ABC Theatre. He would have been just twenty years old.

1,296: On 15 October 1962, compered by local comedian Norman Collier, the Everly Brothers appeared at Hull's ABC Theatre. The supporting acts included Frank Ifield, and the Vernons Girls.

1,297: On 10 November 1962, ending a trophy drought of 33 years (since winning the Yorkshire Cup for the second time in November 1929) Hull Kingston Rovers beat Huddersfield 13-10 at Headingley to win the first Eastern Division Championship.

1,298: In 1962 Smith & Nephew Associated Companies bought 2 Temple Place—the former Astor Estate Office building overlooking the Thames near Victoria Embankment—as its Group Headquarters.

1,299: The Beatles performed in Hull on four occasions: twice at the Majestic Ballroom (20/10/62 and 13/02/63) and twice at the ABC Cinema (24/11/63 and 16/10/64).

1,300: In 1963 a new six-pylon 250-lamp floodlight system was installed at Boothferry Park, replacing the previous inadequate 96-lamp, two-gantry system. Four of the six pylons of the new £50,000 system were used for the first time on 7 October 1964 during a match against Barnsley. City won 7-0, with Chris Chilton scoring four of the goals, and Ray Henderson scoring the other three.

1,301: On 15 October 1963, third on the bill after Johny Kidd and The Pirates, and Heinz, the Rolling Stones appeared at the City Hall, Hull. Tickets for the 'Main Floor' were priced at seven shillings and sixpence.

1,302: In 1963, at the funeral of President John F. Kennedy, two tunes featured that were written by Hull's John Bacchus Dykes: 'Holy, Holy, Holy' was played by the marching Marine Band in the funeral procession, between Constitution Avenue and the White House; and The Naval Academy Catholic Choir sang 'Eternal Father, strong to save' at the north portico of the White House upon the arrival of the cortège.

1,303: 'Eternal Father, strong to save' has been played at the funerals of at least four other serving or former US presidents: Franklin D. Roosevelt (it was FDR's favourite hymn), Richard Nixon, Gerald Ford, and Ronald Regan.

1,304: In 1963 Hull City Chairman Harold Needler gave the club £200,000 worth of shares when he floated his company Hoveringham Gravel on the stock market. He also offered City's manager Cliff Britton a ten year contract, heralding the halcyon days of Henderson, Wagstaff, Chilton, Houghton and Butler. City topped the Third Division at the close of the 1965–66 season, with 109 goals and 69 points (four points clear of runners-up Millwall) thereby gaining promotion to the Second Division.

1,305: In 1963 Johnny Whiteley became player/coach for Hull FC, eventually taking over full-time as the club's coach when Roy Francis retired in 1965.

1,306: In 1963, as part of Smith & Nephew's modernization programme, the company installed (at its Birmingham base) a Lyons Electronic Office (LEO) computer to automate the textile production processes in its mills.

1,307: The LEO range of computers, developed by the famous J. Lyons & Co. catering and baking firm, was the first computer used for commercial business applications. The earlier (LEO II) model had been delivered to a number of firms, including W.D. & H.O. Wills (Bristol); the Ford Motor Co. (both Aveley and Dagenham); and the Ministry of Pensions (Newcastle).The model installed by Smith & Nephew was the LEO III (Serial No. 11), and it remained at the company's Birmingham base until 1970.

1,308: On 28 February 1964, Philip Larkin's heavily Hull-inspired *The Whitsun Weddings* was published by Faber and Faber (London); the following year he was awarded the Queen's Gold Medal for Poetry.

1,309: On 5 May 1964, fourth on the bill after Dave Clark Five, The Hollies, and Mark Wynter, the Kinks appeared at Hull's ABC Theatre. They returned to the venue later that year, on 2 November, this time third on the bill after Gerry and The Pacemakers, and Gene Pitney. Also on the same bill was Marianne Faithful.

1,310: At the end of the 1963–64 season Hull Kingston Rovers made their first ever visit to Wembley Stadium, where they were beaten 13-5 by Widnes in the Rugby League Challenge Cup final on Saturday 9 May 1964, in front of 84,488 spectators.

1,311: At the end of the 1963–64 season, the second season of the Rugby League consisting of two divisions, Hull FC finished bottom of the Championship league table (on 8 points) and were relegated into the Second Division.

1,312: Before he found fame with David Bowie, Mick Ronson played in several local bands, including the Mariners, with whom he supported the Rolling Stones at Bridlington Spa on 11 July 1964; he also played lead guitar with the Crestas, and the Rats.

1,313: In June 1964 Robert Boyes, (manager of the Hessle Road store of W. Boyes & Co. Ltd. since it opened in 1920) died. His replacement at Hessle Road was Gerrit van der Heijden, who later assumed over-all responsibility for all the company's Hull stores.

1,314: On 21 September 1964, in a concert promoted by Robert Stigwood, the Rolling Stones, made their second appearance in Hull, topping the bill at Hull's ABC Theatre, supported by: Inez and Charlie Foxx, Mike Berry & The Innocents, Simon Scott & The Le Roys, and The Mojos.

1,315: On 29 November 1964 the Mayfair Cinema closed before being converted into the Mayfair Casino Bingo Club, an independent establishment that was subsequently taken over by Mecca Bingo Clubs (following the Gaming Act of 1968, Mecca re-branded all their casinos as Mecca Social and Bingo Clubs). Grand Met paid £33m to take over Mecca in 1970, and in 1990 the Rank Group bought Mecca for £512m.

1,316: In 1964 a £50,000 gymnasium training facility was opened behind the South Stand at Boothferry Park; and throughout the 70s, 80s and 90s numerous reconfigurations and refurbishments were carried out at the stadium itself, including the demolition of the North Stand to make way for a supermarket, and alterations (designed to comply with the 1990 Taylor Report) that saw the ground's capacity eventually reduced to 15,160.

1,317: Between 1958–92 Gerald Thomas directed 31 *Carry On...* films, helping to make their starring actors: Kenneth Williams, Sid James, Charles Hawtrey, Joan Sims, Kenneth Connor, Hattie Jacques, etc. household names.

1,318: In 1964 the entrance to the Victoria Dock from the river Hull was closed and remodelled.

1,319: On 18 January 1965 Chuck Berry, in arrangement with promoter Robert Stigwood, appeared at the ABC Theatre. Berry topped the bill, with Long John Baldry & The Hoochie Coochie Men, Graham Bond Organization and the Moody Blues also included in the line-up.

1,320: On 1 March 1965 Roy Orbison topped the bill at Hull's ABC Theatre. Supporting were the Rocking Berries, Marianne Faithful, and Cliff Bennett and the Rebel Rousers.

1,321: On 14 May 1965, topping the bill, Shirley Bassey appeared at Hull's ABC Theatre. She was supported by Cyril Stapleton & His Showband.

1,322: In the 1964–65 season the two divisions of the Rugby League merged back into one division. At the end of the season Hull KR finished in eighth position with 44 points; Hull FC finished thirteenth, with 38 points.

1,323: In the 1964-65 season, when he signed for Hull City from Mansfield Town, Ken Wagstaff was the Third Division's leading goalscorer, with a total of 35 goals.

1,324: During the summer of 1965, aged 19, Mick Ronson was living at 74 De La Pole Avenue (just 20 houses away from where poet Stevie Smith was born).

1,325: The Palace Theatre of Varieties on Anlaby Road closed down in July 1965, finally being demolished in 1966. The site subsequently remained unoccupied for 20 years before a tower-block of flats was constructed there.

1,326: The Who first played Hull on 6 December 1965, at Hull University. The band's original line-up returned a further four times: 16 June 1966 (Hull University); 3 May 1968 (Hull University); 15 February 1970 (City Hall); 29 October 1971 (ABC cinema).

1,327: W. Boyes & Co. Ltd. opened its Holderness Road store on the site of the former Savoy Cinema on 10 December 1965, the lease of the property having been taken over by Boyes from the supermarket chain Fine Fare. The opening ceremony was carried out by the two longest serving staff members of the Hessle Road store, Mrs A. Casterton and Mr A. Dove.

1,328: The innovative and influential traditional English folk group The Watersons originated from Hull, with the three original band members Mike, Norma and Elaine (Lal) Waterson all having been born here. Martin Carthy and Norma Waterson once lived at 34 De La Pole Avenue—the early childhood home of Stevie Smith.

1,329: The Sir Leo Schultz High School on Hull's Orchard Park estate, one of the first purpose-built comprehensive schools in the country, was named in honour of Joseph Leopold (Sir Leo) Schultz. The school, which cost £798,256 to build, opened in 1965 and finally closed in 1986.

1,330: With the increased continental port traffic of the 1960s, new kinds of vessels were built to cater for the shift in usage, trade and cargoes, allowing traffic to drive on and off the ships. This new service became known as Ro-Ro (roll-on, roll-off). In 1965 North Sea Ferries introduced a Ro-Ro service between Hull and Rotterdam Europort and, later, Hull and Zeebrugge. These services were bought by P&O (originally Peninsular and Oriental Steam Navigation Company) in 1996 and renamed P&O North Sea Ferries.

1,331: In 1966 Hull City reached the Sixth Round (Quarter-Finals) of the FA Cup, where they played Chelsea. They drew 2-2 away at Stamford Bridge on 26 March before losing the replay 3-1 on 31 March at Boothferry Park in front of over 45,000 spectators.

1,332: Hull Kingston Rovers favourite Roger Millward joined the club as a player on 8 August 1966 from Castleford, for a fee of £6,000, making his Rovers debut the following week on 15 August, away at Hunslet. He became club captain in 1969, aged 21; and the club's coach in 1977 (following the death of Harry Poole), a position he held until 1991.

1,333: On Sunday 11 September 1966 the rock supergroup Cream, featuring Ginger Baker, Jack Bruce and Eric Clapton played at Hull's Skyline Ballroom. (Four days later, Cream played at the Gaumont Cinema Hanley, Staffordshire, where Jimi Hendrix joined them on stage for one song.) The official Jack Bruce website confirms the gig at the Skyline Ballroom in September; but the Eric Clapton information website whereseric.com have Cream playing at the Manor Lounge, Stockport on that date, but playing the Skyline on 7 December.

1,334: On 9 March 1967 Jimi Hendrix made his only appearance in Hull, with the Jimi Hendrix Experience at the Skyline Ballroom (later Romeo & Juliet's), in Jameson Street. Support bands were The Family, The Strollers, local cover-band The Small Four, and, from

Scarborough, Robert Palmer's first band The Mandrakes. Tickets were priced at twelve shillings and sixpence. There is some suggestion that the Jimi Hendrix Experience played Hull's Wellington Club on 6 October 1967, but I have found no evidence to support this. In fact, on that date the Jimi Hendrix Experience were being recorded at the Playhouse Theatre, London for the *Top Gear* radio programme, where they recorded six songs that would later appear on *The Jimi Hendrix Experience: BBC Sessions* album of 1998.

1,335: Having suffered from pleurisy following the Titanic disaster, Joseph Boxhall's health grew progressively worse with age. The last of the Titanic's surviving deck officers, Boxhall died on 25 April 1967 aged 83. Following his cremation his ashes were scattered at the position he had calculated the Titanic had sunk—just 15 miles away from where the wreck was eventually found in September 1985. In 2006 a green heritage plaque, erected by the Avenues and Pearson Park Residents' Association, was unveiled at 27 Westbourne Avenue by the Lord Mayor of Hull, Councillor Trevor Larsen, to mark Boxhall's former home. The inscription reads:

> JOSEPH GROVES BOXHALL (1884–1967) Fourth Officer of RMS Titanic and survivor of the disaster lived here

1,336: The Carlton Picture Theatre at 474 Anlaby Road closed in April 1967 and subsequently, somewhat predictably, was converted into a bingo hall, becoming part of Rank Group PLC's Mecca Bingo leisure company until 2008.

1,337: At the end of the 1966–67 season Hull KR finished 2nd in the league with 54 points, behind Leeds on 58 points; but on Saturday 15 October 1966 they beat Featherstone Rovers 25-12, in front of 13,241 spectators at Headingley, to take the Yorkshire Cup for a third time.

1,338: On 9 June 1967 Pink Floyd played at the Hull College of Art, the first of four gigs played by the band in Hull. The band's other appearances in Hull were: 28 September 1967 (Skyline Ballroom); 11 March 1969 (Lawns Centre, Cottingham): 17 January 1970 (Lawns Centre, Cottingham).

1,339: Besides the four gigs played in Hull by Pink Floyd, the band had two further scheduled gigs cancelled: 10 August 1967 (Skyline Ballroom); 7 February 1969 (University of Hull).

1,340: The current Hull Royal Infirmary, constructed to a design by Yorke, Rosenburg & Mardall (and built on the site of the old Western General Hospital, which was demolished in 1963) was opened by Queen Elizabeth II on 16 June 1967. The old Hull Royal Infirmary building at Prospect Street was demolished in 1972, with the Prospect Shopping Centre being built on the site.

1,341: In 1967, five years before the release of David Bowie's *The Rise and Fall of Ziggy Stardust and the Spiders From Mars*, Mick Ronson and his fellow band members in The Rats recorded a track at Fairview Studios (Willerby) titled 'The Rise and Fall of Bernie Gripplestone', a title coined by drummer John Cambridge.

1,342: In order to reach the levels of sustain he wanted from his guitar Mick Ronson had his volume settings so high that when he was recording with The Rats at Fairview Studios (Willerby) in 1967, the studio owner/engineer, Keith Herd, had to record Mick's guitar with blankets covering his amplifier to avoid distortion through the microphone.

1,343: In 1967 the Asbestos and Rubber Company began its expansion beyond the Hull area when it acquired

Budgen and Hare in Teesside, suppliers of safety clothing and equipment, and industrial products.

1,344: Local Art Historian and former Hull University Medical Officer Robert Raines—in his *Marcellus Laroon* (1967) from the Studies in British Art series published by the Paul Mellon Foundation—states: 'The argument for a visit to this country by Rembrandt are based on a statement by Vertue and the existence of some drawings by Rembrandt of English scenes.' After examining the transcript of Vertue's relevant notebook, and careful consideration of the 'four drawings by Rembrandt of scenes in England', none of which are Yorkshire scenes, Raines concludes: '.. however much as a true Yorkshireman I should like to think of Rembrandt in my native town of Hull, I do not believe any of the insubstantial evidence for a visit is acceptable'. (see fact 108 and fact 1,939)

1,345: On the morning of 10 January 1968 the Hull trawler St. Romanus (H223) and her crew of 20, sailed from St. Andrew's Dock, bound for the Norwegian fishing grounds. By 19:30 the vessel reported that she was 120 miles NNE of the river Humber. This was the last time there was any communication with the vessel, apart from the dubious report from the First Mate of the Icelandic trawler Vikingur III of a Mayday call, supposedly heard at 16:30 on 11 January. Skippered by James Wheeldon (26) of 50 Ulverston Road, Hessle, the St. Romanus was built in 1950 by Cook, Welton & Gemmell Ltd. (Beverley); she was owned by Messrs. Thomas Hamling & Co Ltd. (Hull).

1,346: In the early afternoon of 10 January 1968 the Hull trawler Kingston Peridot (H591) and her crew of 20, sailed from port, bound for the Icelandic fishing grounds. On 26 January, fishing off the north coast of Iceland, she told the skipper of the Kingston Sardius (H588) in a radio communication, that she had become iced up and intended heading east to escape the severe weather conditions; but she was never heard of again. The Kingston Peridot was lost with all hands 'somewhere to the northwestward of Tjornesgrunn'. Skippered by Raymond Wilson (33) of 57 St.Nicholas Avenue, Hessle, the vessel was built in 1948 by Cook, Welton & Gemmell Ltd. (Beverley), and was owned by Hull Northern Fishing Co. Ltd. (Hellyer Bros. Ltd.) (Hull).

1,347: In the early hours of 13 January 1968 a fully inflated life-raft from the St. Romanus was picked up by a Danish vessel, but this was not reported until the vessel returned to the Danish port of Esbjerg on 20 January. A lifebuoy from the St. Romanus was found on a beach near Hirtshals, Denmark, on 21 January.

1,348: On the morning of 20 January 1968 the Hull trawler Ross Cleveland (H61) and her crew of 20, sailed from St. Andrew's Dock, bound for the Icelandic fishing grounds. On 26 January the vessel went into Isafjord to land the cook, William Howbrigg, who had become ill. The vessel then continued to the Kogurgrunn fishing ground. On 4 February, seeking shelter in Isafjardhardjup from the extreme blizzards and gale-force winds, the vessel heeled over to her port side, capsized and sank. Skippered by Philip Gay (41) of 117 Colville Avenue, Anlaby Common, the Ross Cleveland was built in 1949 by John Lewis & Sons Ltd. (Aberdeen); she was owned by Ross Trawlers Ltd.—Hudson Brothers Trawlers (Hull).

1,349: On 4 February 1968, when the Hull Trawler Ross Cleveland heeled over before capsizing and sinking, the vessel's Mate, Harry Eddom, was able to free the life-raft; he and two fellow crew members (Bosun, Walter Hewitt and Sparehand, Barry Rogers) managed to scramble into it, but neither Hewitt nor Rogers survived. Harry Eddom was the sole survivor of the 20 man crew.

1,350: Following the foundering of the Ross Cleveland, Harry Eddom somehow made his way to land in the vessel's life-raft. He sheltered by a disused farmhouse and was found the following morning by a local shepherd boy who helped him to the family home, where he was given dry clothes and hot drinks. The bodies of the two other crew members were later found; though one was wearing a life-jacket, the cause of death in both cases was drowning. In 1990 a blue heritage plaque was erected at St. Barnabas Court, at the junction of Hessle Road and the Boulevard, Hull to mark the achievements of Lillian Bilocca ('Big Lil') in leading the 'headscarf revolutionaries' in their campaign for improved safety for their seafaring menfolk. The inscription reads:

> In recognition of the contribution to the fishing industry
> by the women of Hessle Road, led by Lillian Bilocca,
> who successfully campaigned for better safety measures
> following the loss of three Hull trawlers in 1968

1,351: On 15 April 1968 Hull FC winger Clive Sullivan set the club record for most tries in a match when he made seven touchdowns in Hull's 57-6 victory over Doncaster, away at Tattersfield.

1,352: At the end of the 1967–68 season Hull KR finished third in the league with 49 points, behind Leeds (56 points) and Wakefield Trinity (49); but they beat Hull FC 8-7 at Headingley on 14 October 1967 to take the Yorkshire Cup for a fourth time.

1,353: In 1968 the third generation of the Martin family took the helm at the Asbestos and Rubber Company when Thomas Martin and his younger brother Stephen became joint managing directors of the forerunner to the leading safety company, ARCO.

1,354: The Hull City player with the record for the most League appearances is Andy Davidson, who played a total of 520 League games for the club during the period 1952–68 (he made a further 59 appearances in Cup matches).

1,355: In 1968 Smith & Nephew, weakened by a stagnant share price, successfully fought off a takeover bid by multinational conglomerate Unilever.

1,356: John Bacchus Dykes' 'Eternal Father, strong to save' has brought comfort and hope to many seafaring communities, not least that of the Hessle Road district of his birthplace; where, during times of doubt, fear and anguish, schoolchildren regularly sang the hymn in their morning assemblies; an act of faith equal to any of those enumerated by local historian Alec Gill in his *Superstitions: Folk Magic in Hull's Fishing Community* (1993).

1,357: In 1968 Jean Hartley left the family home (with her two young daughters, Laurien and Alison)—ending her association with The Marvell Press—and moved into an attic flat at 14 Victoria Avenue, Hull. She enrolled on a BA degree course, with a 'glowing reference' from Philip Larkin, who had also set up a £25 book account for her at Brown's University of Hull bookshop. Around the same time, she also helped her friend Ted Tarling to set up his poetry magazine *Wave*. Following her BA degree she took an MA in Victorian Studies at Hull.

1,358: The New Theatre, Hull, was refurbished in 1968, with £30,000 being spent on improvements to the auditorium (re-seating and the enlargement of the orchestra pit, deepening the stage etc.), along with the instalment of new dressing rooms, toilets and showers; and a new lighting board, making it one of the leading theatrical venues in the country.

1,359: In 1968 work began on the construction of a 28 acres extension to King George Dock. Built on reclaimed mudflats situated south-east of the main dock, Queen Elizabeth Dock cost £6.75m to complete.

1,360: Railway Dock was closed to shipping in 1968.

1,361: Junction Dock, which had been operational for 139 years, was also closed to shipping in 1968.

1,362: Following the death of her aunt, Margaret Spear in 1968, Hull-born poet Stevie Smith lived alone at 1 Avondale Road, Palmers Green, London until her final illness. In 1970 she became ill with a brain tumour, which eventually took her life on 7 March 1971. She died at Ashburton Cottage Hospital, Devon, her funeral taking place on 12 March in Holy Trinity Church, Buckfastleigh, Devon. She was cremated in Torquay. Her final collection, *Scorpion and other Poems*, was published posthumously by Longmans in 1972.

1,363: Philip Larkin turned down an OBE in 1968. Andrew Motion writes in his biography of the poet that the rejection was made on the grounds that Larkin felt he 'deserved something better'.

1,364: In January 1969, as part of a nationwide initiative to provide access to the best independent films and world cinema, Hull Screen was launched at Hull's Central Library as a joint venture between the British Film Institute and Hull City Council. With a seating capacity of 247 and a stage 8.2 metres wide and 5.2 metres deep (the theatre's other facilities included two dressing rooms), the single-screen theatre was one of the earliest regional film theatres in the United Kingdom. The first film screened was a 1967 Swedish sex comedy titled *Puss & Kram* (Hugs and Kisses) with a running time of 1h 34m, written and directed by Jonas Cornell.

1,365: An extension arm to the south east of the former Joint Dock, sharing the same lock, was officially opened on 4 August 1969 by Queen Elizabeth II (accompanied by the Duke of Edinburgh and H.R.H. Princess Anne) as the Queen Elizabeth Dock.

1,366: On 20 September 1969 Hull FC won the Yorkshire Cup for the second time when they beat Featherstone Rovers 12-9 at Headingley, Leeds.

1,367: Philip Larkin was very encouraging towards Hull poet Douglas Dunn whilst Dunn was writing *Terry Street* (1969), his first collection of poems; he suggested to Dunn the title of the collection; and arranged the poems in the order in which they appear in the volume.

1,368: At the age of 23, after being recommended by local bass player Rick Kemp, Mick Ronson played on Michael Chapman's 1969 breakthrough album *Fully Qualified Survivor*.

1,369: In the 1960s, George Gray was unable to secure funding for his research from the former Science and Engineering Research Council (SERC), but eventually secured funding from the Medical Research Council and Reckitt & Colman. Later, whilst still Senior Lecturer in Organic Chemistry at Hull, he submitted a further proposal for funding from SERC. However, SERC once again rejected his proposal; and on this occasion they advised him to 'employ the services of a competent organic chemist'.

1,370: Mick Ronson first featured on a David Bowie recording when he provided some uncredited handclaps and 'a little bit of guitar' on 'Wide Eyed Boy from Freecloud' in 1968. The track was released on the 1969 *David Bowie* album (re-released in 1972 as *Space Oddity* to capitalize on the success of the single of that name).

1,371: Hull's Victoria Dock closed on 1 February 1970 and was subsequently infilled.

1,372: After attending a David Bowie gig at the Marquee (London) on 3 February 1970, Hull guitarist Mick Ronson joined Bowie's band Hype. Two days later Mick performed with Bowie on John Peel's *Sunday Show*, recorded at the BBC's Paris Studio and broadcast on 8 February.

1,373: Having been treated for cancer during the 1960s Ethel Leginska died in Los Angeles on 26 February 1970 after suffering a stroke as a result of heart disease.

1,374: Hull-born Ethel Leginska—a pioneer for women in music—founded the Boston Women's Symphony Orchestra, and the National Women's Symphony Orchestra (New York); she was the first woman to conduct at Carnegie Hall; and the first woman conductor of the Berlin Philharmonic, the London Symphony, the New York Symphony, and the Paris Conservatoire Orchestras; and she was the first woman to conduct her own opera at a major opera house.

1,375: On Wednesday 5 August 1970, at Boothferry Park, Hull City became the first team ever to be knocked out of a competition in a penalty shoot-out in England. The FA had just agreed to allow the penalty shoot-out procedure to decide the result in cases where matches were drawn. City were playing Manchester United in the semi-final of the newly inaugurated Watney Mann Invitation Cup. City and United were level at 1-1 after extra time, so the penalty shoot-out was invoked. George Best converted United's first penalty and City ultimately lost the tie 4-3 on penalties. City keeper Ian McKechnie was the first goalkeeper ever to save a penalty in a penalty shoot-out; Denis Law, whose shot McKechnie saved, was the first person to miss; and McKechnie was the first goalkeeper to take a penalty in a shoot-out in England.

1,376: On Friday 23 October 1970 there was a major explosion in the subway tunnel connecting Bankside to

Hull's St. Andrew's Dock when a British Road Transport lorry carrying liquid gas struck the roof of the tunnel. The escaped gas vaporized and ignited. Two people were killed and 17 others needed hospital treatment for serious burns.

1,377: When Mick Ronson travelled to London in early 1970 to team up with David Bowie for the first time, he was accompanied by his pregnant girlfriend Denise Irvin, who returned to Hull within the week and subsequently (14 October 1971) gave birth to their son Nicholas.

1,378: When producer Tony Visconti and David Bowie met Mick Ronson for the first time, they were amazed at how he instinctively knew what to play, without being taught the songs: Visconti is reported as saying he: 'watched our hands on the guitar and bass necks and he just knew what to play'.

1,379: In 1970, through his connection with producer Gus Dudgeon, Mick Ronson played guitar on the first studio version of the Elton John song 'Madman Across the Water', recorded during the sessions for Elton's *Tumbleweed Connection* album. The track was re-recorded with a different line-up for inclusion on the *Madman Across the Water* album of 1971.

1,380: Former Widnes and Hull FC full-back/centre Colin Hutton was the Hull KR coach from 1957–70, guiding the club through one of its most successful periods. Hutton was succeeded in 1970 by Johnny Whiteley.

1,381: Roy Francis, Hull FC coach between 1949–63, is thought to have been Britain's first black coach of a professional sports team; and in the early 1970s Hull FC winger Clive Sullivan became the first black captain of any national British sporting team when he captained the Great Britain national rugby team, the Great Britain Lions.

1,382: In 1970 Cliff Britton became General Manager at Hull City, and was instrumental in the choice of Terry Neill as his successor as manager. Neill became player-manager in June 1970, at the age of 28. He retired from playing in 1973, and left City a year later to be replaced as manager by John Kaye in September 1974.

1,383: The nucleus of what would become the Hull Truck Theatre Company's Spring Street home had originally been a Methodist Hall—first used as a theatre (the Humberside Theatre) in 1970 and closed in 1982. Hull Truck took over the premises and renamed it the Hull Truck Theatre in 1983.

1,384: In 1970 a group of Gastown developers commissioned Vern Simpson to create a statue of 'Gassy Jack'. After being relocated several times it now stands on the site where Deighton built his Globe saloon in 1867. In 1986 the statue was dedicated to the city of Vancouver by the current owner of the site, and a new plaque was installed on the base of the statue identifying 'Gassy Jack' as the 'Founding Father of Gastown' and pointing out that: 'John Deighton was born in Hull, England'.

1,385: Between 1961–71, while living and working in Hull, Philip Larkin contributed regular monthly jazz reviews to the *Daily Telegraph*. These reviews were brought together and published as a collection in *All What Jazz: a record diary 1961–1968* in 1970. Larkin's reputation as a jazz aficionado meant he was known to many musicians and music lovers more for his reviews than for his poetry.

1,386: Hull-born actor Ian Carmichael was a lifelong cricket lover, and a member of the MCC; he was also Chairman of the Lords' Taverners cricketers' charity in 1970.

1,387: The idea of bringing speedway to The Boulevard had first been mooted at the end of Hull Angels' 1949 season, and then again in 1966. The necessary permissions were eventually granted in 1971. The first race at The Boulevard took place on 7 April that year with a challenge match against Sunderland Stars, from which Hull Vikings emerged comfortable winners at 47-25. During the match Sunderland's Russ Dent created the first track speed record of 76.4 seconds.

1,388: Hull Vikings speedway team's first league match took place at The Boulevard on 28 April 1971, when they beat Workington 43–33.

1,389: At the end of the 1971–72 season Hull KR finished 14th in the league with 36 points; but they beat Castleford 11-7 at Headingley on 28 August 1971 to win the Yorkshire Cup for a fifth time.

1,390: The container terminal at Hull's Queen Elizabeth Dock was opened on 4 October 1971.

1,391: The Hull City player with the record for the most League goals for the club is Sproatley born-and-raised Chris Chilton who during his time with the Tigers (1960–71) scored 193. He scored a further 29 goals in Cup and other competitions. Running a close second, is his striking partner and fellow Tigers legend Ken Wagstaff, with 173 League goals (+ 24). Chilton and Wagstaff were each with Hull City for 11 seasons: Chilton from 1960; Wagstaff from 1964.

1,392: After finding it impossible to secure employment, Mike Bradwell founded Hull Truck as a touring company, based in a truck, in 1971. Its first production (opening on 10 March 1972), *The Children of the Lost Planet*, was staged at the Gulbenkian Studio Theatre following three months of rehearsals in a damp rented house in Coltman

Street. Two further shows followed before the end of 1972: a children's show titled *The Land of Woo* (staged in a nun's garage at an orphanage) and a second adult production: *The Last Of The Great Love Goddesses*, which toured further afield around Humberside.

1,393: In 1971 the 100-seater restaurant and bar of the new Cecil Theatre was converted into a second screening room (Cecil 2) with a seating capacity of 137.

1,394: The National Census of 1971 reported the population of the county borough of Hull as 285,970.

1,395: Paul McCartney included Hull University in his impromptu university tour of 1972. The news that McCartney and his band Wings were about to give a concert in the West Refectory room circulated quickly and 800 people each paid 50 pence to attend.

1,396: J. Arthur Rank, industrialist and founder of the Rank Organisation, died on 29 March 1972, at the Royal Hampshire County Hospital, Winchester after suffering a ruptured abdominal aneurysm. He was buried at Sutton Scotney.

1,397: Following their move to the purpose-built Anchor Brewery in Sylvester Street in 1868 the Hull Brewery Co. Ltd. expanded by acquiring a series of small breweries, bottlers and wine merchants— including the Hull-based breweries of Smithsons, John Hunt, and John Tate—until (with almost 250 tied premises) it was acquired in March 1972, at a value of approximately £12m, by Northern Dairies; with the name being changed to North Country Breweries in 1974. In May 1985 North Country Breweries was acquired by Mansfield Brewery PLC for £42m.

1,398: During August 1972 Mick Ronson co-produced (with David Bowie) Lou Reed's breakthrough album *Transformer*. Ronson's influence (he played guitar, piano, recorder and sang backing vocals) was pivotal to the album's reception and success, with major contributions from Ronson to the song arrangements, particularly on 'Walk on the Wild Side', 'Perfect Day', and 'Satellite of Love'.

1,399: In 1972 members of The East Riding Quality Bacon Producers Group held discussions on the feasibility of producing their own pig feed. On 29 September 1972 a company named Dungeons Farms Limited was registered. at Companies House. This 'off-the-shelf' company's name was changed to Cranswick Mill Limited—founded in 1974 by (among others) farmers Jim Bloom and Mike Field— and filed its first accounts for the period ending 31 March 1975. It would later become Cranswick PLC.

1,400: In October 1972 the Albert Dock (along with the William Wright Dock) was closed to commercial shipping and adapted for use as a fish dock. The fish docks at St. Andrew's closed to shipping on 3 November 1975, when the Hull fishing fleet relocated to the two newly adapted docks.

1,401: Having teamed up with David Bowie in 1970, Hull guitarist Mick Ronson was a key element in Bowie's artistic and commercial success, creating several classic and memorable guitar parts and solos ('Width of a Circle', 'Moonage Daydream', 'Song for Bob Dylan', 'Ziggy Stardust'), as well as being pivotal in scoring the musical arrangements on hit albums such as *The Man Who Sold the World*, *Hunky Dory* (including the string arrangement for 'Life on Mars'), and *The Rise and Fall of Ziggy Stardust and the Spiders From Mars*.

1,402: David Doyle-Davidson became Hull FC coach in 1972, being replaced by Clive Sullivan in 1973, only to resume the role in 1974, remaining until 1977. He was succeeded by Arthur Bunting in 1978.

1,403: In 1972 Gerald Thomas directed *Bless This House*, the film version of the popular TV series which starred Sid James, with other original cast members Diana Coupland and Sally Geeson. Terry Scott, June Whitfield and Robin Askwith also starred. The screenplay was by Dave Freeman, who between 1971–76 had written 15 episodes of the TV series.

1,404: In 1972 Anthony Minghella came to the University of Hull to begin a degree course; he graduated in 1975 with a First Class Honours Degree in English Drama. He immediately embarked on a PhD at Hull, and became a lecturer in the Drama department, leaving in 1981 to work for the BBC writing radio plays and screenplays; one of his early jobs was as a script editor for *Grange Hill*. He returned to Hull in 1997 to receive an Honorary Degree and to give some drama master-classes. A green heritage plaque, erected at 168 Park Avenue by the Avenues and Pearson Park Residents' Association, identifies the house where Minghella lived whilst in Hull. The inscription reads:

> ANTHONY MINGHELLA Playwright and Film Director lived here 1976–1981

1,405: In 1972 the main auditorium of the Cecil Theatre was divided into two smaller screening rooms (Cecil 1 and Cecil 3) each with a seating capacity of 307. At the same time the Mecca Bingo Club was opened in the area where the stalls had previously been.

1,406: On 23 January 1973 two Ro-Ro (roll-on, roll-off) terminals were opened at Hull's King George Dock.

1,407: On 23 March 1973 the first edition of *The Oxford Book of Twentieth-Century English Verse*, chosen by Philip Larkin, was published by Oxford's Clarendon Press. The following year, on 3 June 1974, Larkin's final poetry collection *High Windows* was published by Faber and Faber (London), securing his position as one of the finest poets in English literary history.

1,408: At the end of the 1972–73 season Hull FC finished twenty-fifth (sixth from bottom) in the league table, with just 22 points, consigning themselves to the Second Division in the following season, when the Championship was once again split into two divisions for the start of the 1973–74 season.

1,409: On 12 November 1973 the New Theatre, Hull was designated a Grade II Listed Building (English Heritage Building ID: 387638) under the Planning (Listed Buildings and Conservation Areas) Act 1990.

1,410: On 12 November 1973 the Tower Cinema on Anlaby Road was designated a Grade II Listed Building (English Heritage Building ID: 387447) under the Planning (Listed Buildings and Conservation Areas) Act 1990.

1,411: W. Boyes & Co. Ltd. opened its store at the Bransholme Centre on 30 November 1973. The shopping centre had been officially opened by TV personality Hughie Green, but the Boyes store was opened by the cutting of tape by Molly van der Heijden, the wife of the General Manager of the Hull store.

1,412: The foundations of the ground-floor W. Boyes & Co. Ltd. store in the Bransholme Centre were strengthened to allow the possibility of adding a first-floor selling area at a future date.

1,413: In 1973 Hull Truck's third adult production *The Weekend After Next* was performed at Glasgow's Close Theatre and The Royal Court Theatre; and the company's first adult-only show, *The Mackintosh Cabaret*, was banned in Hull because of its explicit content.

1,414: In 1973 the auditorium of the former Priory Cinema was destroyed by fire and a purpose-built supermarket structure was built where the auditorium had stood, though the existing facade remained. Since its construction in 1938, the building has been used as a cinema, Civil Defence Centre, supermarket, indoor market, furniture store, and carpet warehouse.

1,415: On 22 January 1974 the Hull trawler FV Gaul (H243) sailed from port, heading for the Norwegian fishing grounds in the Barents Sea. On 8 February weather conditions became severe, and on 10 February she failed to report in as scheduled. Despite an extensive search operation, no trace of the vessel was found. It was assumed the Gaul sank in the severe storm conditions some time between 8–9 February, with the loss of all 36 crew. Skippered by Peter Nellist (43) of 2 Mead Walk, Anlaby Park, Hull, the Gaul (formerly named Ranger Castor) was built in 1972 by Brook Marine (Lowestoft); she was owned by British United Trawlers (Hull) Ltd., who had bought the vessel in October 1973 from Ranger Fishing Co. Ltd. (North Shields).

1,416: On the vessel's outward bound trip to the Barents Sea, the Mate of the Hull trawler FV Gaul (H243), George Petty, became ill and was put ashore at Lødingen, Norway on 26 January. He was replaced two days later when Maurice Spurgeon joined the ship at Tromsö; the Gaul reached the fishing grounds on 29 January.

1,417: On 7 February 1974 the Hull trawler FV Gaul (H243) reported her position on the 1030 skippers' schedule, and was known to be fishing on the North Cape Bank in the Barents Sea; later that day, on the 2330 skippers' schedule, she reported further updates. The final report from the vessel was posted on the 1030 skippers' schedule of the 8 February. The last sighting was made by the Mate of the freezer trawler Swanella on the same morning; and the very last time anything was heard from the Gaul was in two private telegrams sent by radio at 1106 and 1109, also on the morning of 8 February.

1,418: Following David Bowie's announcement on 3 July 1973 that he was retiring his Ziggy Stardust persona from live performance, Mick Ronson released two solo albums: *Slaughter on Tenth Avenue* was released in February 1974 and reached No. 9 in the UK album charts; *Play Don't Worry* was released in January 1975, reaching No. 29 in the UK album charts.

1,419: On 9 May 1974, to finance the company's feed mill project, Cranswick Mill Ltd. issued a further 96,148 shares, bringing the total number of shares in issue to 96,150. Directors who held shares in the company were: James C. W. Bloom: 4,800; Michael Field: 6,300; H. Fraser: 4,800; and Richard Marginson (Chairman): 7,200.

1,420: In May 1974 one of the Gaul's lifebuoys was picked up by the Norwegian whaler Rover approximately 75 miles south east of where the wreck of the vessel was eventually found.

1,421: The search for the missing Hull trawler FV Gaul (H243) involved twenty-three trawlers; various British naval vessels, including HMS Hermes and HMS Mohawk; several Norwegian Royal Navy vessels, including KNM Stavanger and KNM Trondheim; and Nimrod, Orion and Sea King aircraft. The search continued from the morning of 11 February until 15 February, and covered an area of 177,000 square miles.

1,422: The statue of Amy Johnson carved from Portland Stone by local sculptor Harry Ibbetson, and sited in Prospect Street outside the Prospect Centre, was unveiled by airwoman Sheila Scott on 18 June 1974.

1,423: On 27 June 1974 Philip Larkin moved out of 32 Pearson Park and into 105 Newland Park where he would remain until his death in 1985. A commemorative blue plaque was unveiled at his former Newland Park home to mark the last house in which he lived. The plaque, made by local potter Peter Colbridge, was funded and erected by The Philip Larkin Society. The inscription reads:

> Poet & writer PHILIP LARKIN (1922–1985) lived here 1974–1985

1,424: In September 1974 Bobby Collins replaced John Kaye as manager of Hull City, but during his tenure City managed just four wins from nineteen games. Collins was replaced by caretaker manager Wilf McGuinness in February 1978, until Ken Houghton took over three months later, in April 1978.

1,425: In the autumn of 1974, a Formal Investigation was convened into the disappearance of the Hull trawler FV Gaul (H243). The investigation was held in the City Hall, Hull and lasted 14 days. It considered evidence from 60 witnesses, and concluded that the Gaul must have been 'overwhelmed by a succession of heavy seas'. Despite this conclusion, more sinister causes were suspected for the disappearance; and the relatives of the lost trawlermen continued to campaign for an underwater search to recover evidence that might provide indisputable proof about the fate of the vessel and its crew.

1,426: Because of the rumours circulating in Hull at the time (that the Gaul had been seized by the Soviet Union and may be captive in a Russian port) the speculation that the vessel had been involved in intelligence gathering had been seriously considered by the 1974 Formal Investigation into her loss; but the idea was dismissed as impossible due to the prevailing weather conditions at the time of her disappearance. This conclusion did nothing to dispel the rumours of a conspiracy theory. In fact, on three separate occasions the Formal Investigation's Chief Inspector had asked the representatives of the Gaul Families Association for any evidence that would support such a theory, but none had been provided.

1,427: In 1974 Hull Truck was commissioned by the BBC to produce a play for BBC's *Second City First* season. The Hull Truck contribution *The Writing on the Wall*, produced by Tara Prem and directed by Mike Bradwell, was screened on BBC 2 at 21:35 on Saturday 1 November 1975.

1,428: In 1974 William Sharpe retired from managing the New Theatre, Hull. He was succeeded by David Sandford, who developed the 'receiving theatre' side of the business, encouraging regular visits by touring theatre companies.

1,429: In 1974 the William Jackson Food Group created frozen Yorkshire puddings for the Butlins holiday camp group. This resulted in the launch of retail-sector frozen Yorkshire puddings in 1985 under the *Tryton Foods* brand, before the *Aunt Bessie's* brand was introduced in 1995.

1,430: In 1974 Hull Truck Theatre Company's improvised play *The Knowledge* was staged at the Forum Theatre Manchester (where it was billed as a 'hippy whodunnit'). The audience figures shrunk from 50 to 22 and the Theatre's management cancelled the show. However, *The Knowledge* toured nationally, including a run at London's Bush Theatre where all of Hull Truck's productions up to 1983 would eventually be staged.

1,431: By 1975 Cranswick Mill Ltd. was a members-only milling company, with 23 pig producer members, four of whom were directors of the company. In the financial year ended 31 March 1975 the company made a loss of £5,847 (on a turnover of £301,885), incurred as a consequence of 'heavy administrative costs during the construction of [its] feed milling and mixing unit'.

1,432: In the 1970s, in recognition of Dorothy Mackaill's devotion to Hawaii, Honolulu declared 'Dorothy's Day' and serenaded and praised the retired actress at her hotel.

1,433: At the end of the 1974–75 season Hull KR finished 2nd in the Second Division Championship league table with 41 points, behind Huddersfield on 42 points, and were promoted back into the First Division; they also beat Wakefield Trinity 16-13 at Headingley on 26 October 1974 to win the Yorkshire Cup for a sixth time.

1,434: Mick Ronson was invited to play with Bob Dylan on his 1975–76 Rolling Thunder Review tour. Other musicians included Joan Baez, Roger McGuinn, T-Bone Burnett and Steven Soles. The 57-date tour (30 in Canada and the northeastern seaboard of the US; 27 in the American South and south-west) extended over the autumn of 1975 through to the spring of 1976.

1,435: In 1975 Barry Nettleton joined the Hull Truck Theatre Company as its Administrator.

1,436: By 1975 Hull's Queen Elizabeth and King George docks had a total of six Ro-Ro terminals between them.

1,437: The Prospect Centre shopping centre opened its doors to the public for the first time in 1975.

1,438: In the financial year ended 31 March 1976, its second year of trading, Cranswick Mill Ltd. made a trading profit of £21,943 (on a turnover of £521,143); and in the financial year ended 31 March 1977 trading profit had risen to £108,642 (on a turnover of £1,633,374).

1,439: At the end of the 1973–74 season Hull FC finished

6th in the Second Division, with 32 points; at the end of the 1974–75 season they finished 8th, with 25 points; and at the end of the 1975–76 season they finished 5th, with 39 points, and were also runners-up in the Players No. 6 Trophy, when they lost to Widnes 19-13, at Headingley, Leeds on 24 January.

1,440: In 1976 the Hull Truck Theatre Company received its first substantial grant from the Arts Council of Great Britain. In later years it received regular annual funding of around £540,000. However, since moving to the £14.5m purpose-built premises in Ferensway the company has struggled financially. Arts Council England (ACE) awarded grant funds of £1m in 2011 and 2012, due to the company being at 'immediate and serious financial risk'; they provided another £300,000 in 2014, along with £100,000 from Hull City Council; and ACE once again bailed out the company in 2015 with a £250,000 emergency grant. In total, Hull Truck has benefited from Arts Council bail-outs of well over £1.5m since 2011.

1,441: In 1976 the main auditorium of the ABC cinema was converted into five smaller screening rooms of varying seating capacities, from 96 up to 569.

1,442: Brian Rix was appointed CBE in the 1977 Silver Jubilee Birthday Honours, for 'services to the handicapped'; and was knighted in June 1986, for services to charity. On 27 January 1992 he was created a life peer, becoming 'Baron Rix of Whitehall, in the City of Westminster and of Hornsea in Yorkshire'. He was awarded honorary degrees by at least ten universities, including the University of Hull, which awarded him an honorary MA in 1981.

1,443: At the end of the 1976–77 season Hull FC finished top of the Second Division, with 45 points, ensuring themselves Championship league rugby—along with Dewsbury (40 points), Bramley (38), and New Hunslet (37)—for the 1977–78 season.

1,444: On 9 November 1977 the whole of the share capital of the unlimited company H. Fletcher & Son was acquired by H. Fletcher & Son Limited (formerly Brobeder Limited, initially registered at Companies House as an 'off-the-shelf' company on 18 October 1976).

1,445: Philip Larkin's last great poem 'Aubade' was first published in *The Times Literary Supplement* of 23 December 1977.

1,446: In 1977 Mick Ronson married Suzi Fussey—the former hairstylist of David Bowie and the Spiders from Mars. Their daughter Lisa was born that year.

1,447: In 1977 H. Fletcher & Son Ltd. opened its branch at Unit 37, Bransholme Centre (North Point Shopping Centre).

1,448: Following the 1935 transformation (into a cinema venue) of Hull's Grand Opera House on George Street, the venue was operated by Associated Hull Cinemas Ltd. and continued as a popular cinema for many years. However, with the general decrease in cinema-going of the 1970s the venue closed in 1977, thereafter only occasionally being used for special screenings and concerts.

1,449: At the end of the 1977–78 season Hull FC were relegated back into the Second Division—after finishing fourth from bottom of the league with 23 points—along with the three other newly promoted teams: New Hunslet (22 points), Bramley (14), and Dewsbury (6). The following season (1978–79) they were promoted back up to the Championship league after a remarkable season in which they won every match, finishing top of the league with 52 points. This achievement remains unequalled.

1,450: At the end of the 1977–78 season, Hull Kingston Rovers finished fourth in the Championship league with 35 points, behind Widnes (50 points), Bradford Northern (44), and St. Helens (45); but they won the BBC 2 Floodlit Trophy when they beat St. Helens 26-11 in the final at Craven Park on 13 December 1977, in front of a crowd of 10,099.

1,451: At the end of the 1977–78 season Hull City (with 28 points, and winning just 8 of their 42 games) came bottom of the Second Division and were relegated to the Third Division. They were relegated to the Fourth Division three years later, at the end of the 1980–81 season, after finishing bottom of the Third Division.

1,452: By the time of its closure Hull's Regent Cinema on Anlaby Road had become an 'X'-rated cinema venue.

1,453: Following its closure on 16 September 1978 the Tower Cinema on Anlaby Road was put up for auction with G.H. Evison & Sons, of Beverley on 21 November 1978. At the public auction, which took place at the venue, bidding began at £10,000, but with an unresponsive (or uninterested) public, the property was withdrawn when it was realized the auction would not achieve more than £21,000.

1,454: Hull's Heron Foods Ltd. was established by Malcolm and Sheila Heuck (*née* Grindell), as Grindells Butchers Limited (with premises at 119 Greenwood Avenue), a family owned business that was incorporated as a private limited company (No. 1392197) on 3 October 1978. The first Heron branded store opened at 179 Holderness Road, Hull in 1979.

1,455: In December 1978 Arthur Bunting joined Hull FC (from Hull Kingston Rovers) to become the club's team manager, heralding the start of one of the most successful periods in the club's history (including the 1978–79 season's record-breaking clean sweep of 26 wins from 26 games, securing the club promotion from the Second Division). Bunting was Hull FC team manager until 1985.

1,456: The fathers of both Malcolm Heuck and Sheila Grindell (the founders in 1978 of what would become Heron Frozen Foods Ltd.) were 'journeyman butchers' by trade.

1,457: In 1978 Cranswick Mill Ltd. started a livestock trading business which would become the second largest in the UK; and in 1979 it started a Grain Trading division.

1,458: The Hull Kingston Rovers club record for the most international appearances is held by Roger Millward, who made 45 appearances for Great Britain, plus 2 as a substitute (including several as team captain), in the period 1966–78.

1,459: In 1978 H. Fletcher & Son Ltd. opened its second flagship branch, at 44 Saturday Market, Beverley.

1,460: In the 1970s Hull Truck produced plays by such playwrights as Ken Campbell and Flann O'Brien; with actors such as David Threlfall and Jim Broadbent among the company of their productions.

1,461: The biggest home victory for a Hull Speedway team was 81-25, won by Hull Vikings on 1 June 1979 against Sheffield Tigers in the British League Knock Out Cup. The biggest away victory was also won by Hull Vikings, when they beat Wolverhampton Wolves 52-26 in the British League on 5 October 1979.

1,462: In 1979, during Hull City Transport's 80th anniversary celebrations in which they painted two buses in the livery of their original trams, W. Boyes & Co. Ltd.

bought all the advertising space (inside and out) on one of the buses for the whole year. On 5 July 1979, the bus was given to the company by the Lord Mayor of Hull.

1,463: George Gray, along with his research collaborators, won the Queen's Award to Industry for Technological Achievement in 1979 and the Rank Prize for Optoelectronics in 1980. He was elected a Fellow of the Royal Society in 1983, a Fellow of the Royal Society of Edinburgh in 1989, and was appointed CBE in 1991.

1,464: In the 1978–79 season Geoff 'Sammy' Lloyd set the Hull FC club records for scoring the most goals (170), and the most points (369) in a season.

1,465: Ralph Thomas's willingness to take on almost anything he was offered inevitably led to a decline in the quality of his output. From the mid 1960s the films he directed, with the occasional exception, received fewer and fewer plaudits. His final film was *A Nightingale Sang in Berkeley Square* (1979), a crime comedy with a cast that included David Niven and Elke Sommer. In the 1980s he worked occasionally in TV.

1,466: In 1979 Hull's Regent Cinema on Anlaby Road was sold to local ex-boxer Wally Mays, who registered a change of use for the venue, restyling it as the Arena Roller Disco.

1,467: Hull Vikings' most successful campaign in the British League was in 1979 when they finished runners-up with 50 points (behind Coventry on 52 point); a season in which they won all 17 of their home matches, and Ivan Mauger recorded 100 wins from 148 races.

1,468: On 2 September 1979 Hull Vikings' star rider Ivan Mauger won his record-breaking sixth World Championship title at Katowice, Poland.

1,469: In 1979 Hull was twinned with Freetown, Sierra Leone. The twinning, established at the instigation of the former Sierra Leone High Commissioner Dr S.T. Matturi (a graduate of the University of Hull) was established to:

> promote friendship and understanding between the two cities

> strengthen commercial, educational and cultural links between the two cities

> stimulate and foster mutual exchanges at all levels between the people of the two cities

1,470: The official twinning of Hull with Sierra Leone took place when a civic delegation from Hull visited Freetown in October 1980; and in September 1981—with the support of the City Council—The Freetown Society of Kingston upon Hull was established.

1,471: Hull's Dorchester Cinema (previously the Grand Opera House) on George Street was finally shut down in 1979. It was eventually demolished in 1987.

1,472: After suffering a brain haemorrhage, whilst touring Australia for the 13th time, Hull singer and entertainer David Whitfield died in a Sydney hospital on 15 January 1980, the evening before he was due to fly home.

1,473: The Hull Tidal Surge Barrier, at the confluence of the rivers Hull and Humber, was inaugurated in April 1980. The 212 tonne, 30 metre-wide barrier is the second biggest flood barrier in the country after the Thames barrier.

1,474: The Hull Tidal Surge Barrier, supported by two 40 feet towers and protecting over 17,000 properties, was built on the site of the old South Bridge (opened in 1865).

1,475: The Hull Tidal Surge Barrier, designed to provide a 1 in 200 year flood defence, is closed about 12 times a year to protect Hull from flooding as a result of high tidal surges.

1,476: In May 1980 the North Humberside Hospice Project was registered as a charity, laying the foundation for the creation of the Dove House Hospice project.

1,477: The track record for the home venue (The Boulevard) of Hull Vikings speedway team was 68.6 seconds, set by the Vikings' Dennis Sigalos on 23 July 1980.

1,478: At the end of the 1979–80 season Hull FC finished third in the league, with 39 points, behind Bradford Northern (46), and Widnes (45); and on 3 May 1980 they met Hull Kingston Rovers in the Rugby League Challenge Cup final in front of a 95,000 crowd at Wembley.

1,479: At the end of the 1979–80 season Hull KR finished 7th in the Championship league table with 33 points. However, they progressed to the final of the Challenge Cup, where they met Hull FC in the first ever Hull rugby Challenge Cup final derby. Hull KR's Steve Hubbard was the Championship's joint top try scorer (30) in this season—along with Salford's Keith Fielding—and also scored the second most goals (138), behind Steve Quinn of Featherstone Rovers (163).

1,480: The meeting between Hull FC and Hull KR in the Challenge Cup final at Wembley on 3 May 1980 was the only Hull Challenge Cup final derby to-date. Hull KR emerged as victors, beating Hull FC 10-5, and in doing so took revenge for their earlier 13-3 defeat at the hands of the Black and Whites at The Boulevard on 18 December 1979 in the final of the last ever BBC 2 Floodlit Trophy.

1,481: On 11 September 1980 Irish rock band U2 played their only ever gig in Hull, at Hull's Wellington Club on the fifth date of their *Boy* tour. The band had started the tour at Coventry's General Wolfe; then played two venues in London (the Lyceum Ballroom and the Marquee Club); and had played Bristol's Berkeley on the Tuesday, before coming to Hull on the Thursday. From Hull, they moved on to Scarborough's Taboo Club the following night. N.B. Although all the U2 resources that I've consulted on the Internet (and a *Hull Daily Mail* website posting of 12/02/16) confirm this appearance, a good friend who is a great U2 fan, believes the gig was cancelled.

1,482: In 1980 Heron Frozen Foods Ltd. opened their Gillett Street cold store; their Neptune Street cold store followed in 1983.

1,483: The Hull Kingston Rovers record for the most career tries is held by Roger Millward who scored 207 tries in the period 1966–80.

1,484: During the 1980s Hull City had six managers, including Colin Appleton (twice) and Eddie Gray; with Brian Horton (taking on the role of player-manager) occupying the position longer than any of the others— from 12 June 1984 until April 1988—and steering City into the Second Division in 1985. Following a 4-1 defeat at the hands of Swindon Town on 12 April 1988, City Chairman Don Robinson sacked Brian Horton

1,485: During the 1980s a performance of a musical comedy version of *A Christmas Carol* at the Hull New Theatre was finished outside in Kingston Square, after the theatre's fire alarm went off.

1,486: In the 1980s Hull's Cecil Theatre was acquired by Cannon Cinemas, who ultimately decided to dispense with the three cinemas. The cinemas closed on 26 March 1992. The Cecil continues to operate as a bingo club.

1,487: Although Philip Larkin was a staunch conservative with a reputation for holding strong right-wing views, he was a very strong supporter of John Saville, the Senior Lecturer in Economic History at Hull University who created an archive of Labour and Socialist history, which Larkin referred to as Saville's 'subversive archive'. On one occasion when Saville was ill, Larkin went round to his house to see how he was getting on.

1,488: At an Extraordinary General Meeting on 20 February 1981 it was decided to change the name of the Asbestos and Rubber Company Limited to ARCO Limited.

1,489: On 2 May 1981 Hull KR made their third Challenge Cup final appearance at Wembley, where they lost 19-8 to Widnes in front of a crowd of 92,496. Chris Burton scored Rovers' only try, with Steve Hubbard scoring their 3 goals.

1,490: At the end of the 1980–81 season Hull KR finished third in the Championship league table with 38 points, behind Bradford Northern (41 points), and Warrington (39); but they beat Hull FC 11-7 at Headingley on 16 May to win the Slalom Premiership for the first time.

1,491: When Hull FC and Hull Kingston Rovers met in the Premiership Trophy final at Headingley, Leeds, on 16 May 1981, it was the first of three consecutive Premier Trophy final defeats for the Black and Whites. Widnes provided the opposition in the following two finals (both played at Headingley, Leeds), with Hull FC losing 23-8 on 15 May 1982; and 22-10 on 14 May 1983. Hull FC were Premiership Trophy runners-up for a fourth time when the were beaten 18-10 (once again by Widnes) at Old Trafford, Manchester, on 14 May 1989.

1,492: The Humber Bridge was officially opened by Her Majesty Queen Elizabeth II on 17 July 1981 (though it opened to traffic on 24 June). The ferry service between

Hull's Corporation Pier and New Holland Pier ended on 24 June 1981, when the Humber Bridge opened to traffic.

1,493: Just before the ferry service between Hull and New Holland ended in 1981, adult passenger fares were 76p for a 'Single' crossing and £1.52 for an 'Ordinary Return'. One-week, one-month, three-month and annual season tickets were also available.

1,494: Just before the ferry service between Hull and New Holland ended, the 'Single' vehicle fares ranged between £1.52 for a motorcycle without a sidecar, to £8.35 for a commercial vehicle not over 2 tons unladen weight ('loaded or empty'). Vehicles over 2 tons unladen weight were not accepted. The vehicle fares did not include the driver's fare.

1,495: The Humber Bridge was the longest single-span suspension bridge in the world for 17 years, until Japan's Akashi Kaikyō Bridge opened on 5 April 1998. It is currently (2016) the world's 5th-longest single-span bridge, and the 8th-longest suspension bridge.

1,496: The Humber Bridge stretches 2,220m—the main span is 1,410m, with the span on the north bank being 280m and the span on the south bank 530m—and rises to a height of 155.5m.

1,497: The Humber Bridge was developed out of a design for the Severn Bridge near Bristol. Its design lifespan is 120 years.

1,498: The total weight of the concrete used in the building of the Humber Bridge was 480,000 tonnes. The weight of the steel used was 27,500 tonnes. The clearance height above high water is 30m.

1,499: Both the north- and the south-bound 2-lane carriageways of the Humber Bridge are 7.3m wide, with a lower level 3m wide footpath on each side. The total deck-width of the bridge is 28.5m.

1,500: Hull Vikings held their final league speedway meeting at The Boulevard on 30 September 1981, when they beat Birmingham 42-36.

1,501: On 7 October 1981 the final speedway meeting was run at The Boulevard when Hull Vikings beat Halifax 46-32 to win the Yorkshire Cup, although—since nobody knew the whereabouts of the trophy—no presentation was made. Following the end of the 1981 season Hull FC terminated the licence allowing Hull Vikings to hold speedway meetings at the ground, and speedway meetings at The Boulevard came to an end.

1,502: At an EGM held on 18 November 1981 a Special Resolution was passed sanctioning a change of name for Grindells Butchers Limited; and on 11 December 1981 the company formally became Heron Frozen Foods Limited.

1,503: In 1981, when local businessman and former boxer (retired through serious injury) Wally Mays bought the Tower Cinema on Anlaby Road, he put his son Robert in charge of the renovation programme. A group of young unemployed unpaid volunteers were taken on to carry out the work of renovating the building.

1,504: The National Census of 1981 reported the population of the local authority district of Hull as 266,751.

1,505: On 23 January 1982 Hull FC recorded their only John Player Trophy success when they beat Hull Kingston Rovers 12-4 in front of 25,425 spectators in the final at Headingley, Leeds. The Black and Whites' Ron Wileman scored the only try of the game, with FC prop Trevor Skerrett winning the Man-of-the-Match award.

1,506: On 25 February 1982, with Chairman Christopher Needler having been advised not to continue funding the club, and with increasing and recurring financial difficulties, Hull City's always precarious situation culminated in them becoming the first English football club to be placed into receivership. The dismissal of manager Mike Smith was the first step on the road to recovery.

1,507: When Hull City became the first professional football club in Britain to call in the receivers, the club was £700,000 in debt and losing £9,000 a week.

1,508: The Hull City player with the record for scoring in the most consecutive games for the club is Les Mutrie, who scored a total of 14 goals in 9 consecutive games between 13 February and 20 March 1982.

1,509: Hull's Karen Inman MBE (*née* Briggs), born on Holderness Road on 11 April 1963 and educated at Bransholme High School, became world Judo champion four times between 1982 and 1989.

1,510: At the end of the 1981–82 season Hull FC finished 2nd in the league with 47 points, behind Leigh (49); and on 1 May 1982 they met Widnes in the Rugby League Challenge Cup final in front of 92,147 spectators at Wembley. The game ended in a 14-14 draw, necessitating a replay (for the first time since 1954) at Elland Road, Leeds on Wednesday 19 May. Hull overwhelmed Widnes 18-9 in the replay, scoring four tries: Topliss (2), Kemble, and Crooks (who also scored three goals). Wright scored one try for Widnes, with Burke scoring their three goals.

1,511: The medals won by Clive Sullivan in Hull KR's 10-5 victory over Hull FC in the 1980 Challenge Cup final, and playing for Hull FC in the 1982 final replay against

Widnes at Elland Road, make him the only player to win a Challenge Cup winners' medal as a player with both Hull clubs.

1,512: In May 1982, when Hull City were in the Fourth Division, Don Robinson (then Chairman of Scarborough FC) became City's majority shareholder and took over as Chairman of the club, bringing with him Scarborough manager Colin Appleton as City's new manager. At the end of the 1982–83 season, after two seasons in the bottom division, the Tigers finished 2nd in the table and were promoted back to Division Three.

1,513: On 30 September 1982 Hull's Alexandra Dock was closed to commercial shipping. (see fact 1,629)

1,514: In 1982 Hull Truck and the company's founder, Mike Bradwell, parted company when Bradwell left to become a freelance director: he was succeeded by Pam Brighton. In the same year, on 11 November, Hull Truck premièred Peter Sheridan's first play *Diary of a Hunger Striker* at the Round House, London; and the company took the play to the British Festival of Theatre in New York, but the production was vetoed.

1,515: In 1982 Mick Ronson worked with John Mellencamp on his *American Fool* album, playing guitar, but contributing in even more significant ways. Mellencamp attributes the final arrangement of the album's hit single 'Jack & Diane' to Ronson after Mellencamp had 'thrown it on the junk heap'. At Ronson's suggestion, baby rattles were added as percussion; and the 'let it rock, let it roll' refrain, sung in the style of a choir, was also Ronson's idea. As Mellencamp admits: 'that is the part everybody remembers on the song'. Both the single and the album reached No. 1 in the US Billboard chart.

1,516: 1980s chart duo Everything But the Girl (Tracey Thorn and Ben Watt) took their name from the sales slogan of the Beverley Road furniture shop, Turners. The slogan appeared on the company's shop-front signage at 34–38 Beverley Road. Thorn and Watt were both studying at the University of Hull in 1982, and before they teamed up had each signed as a solo artist with the independent label Cherry Red Records.

1,517: Between the time of its opening in 1970 and the theatre closing down in 1982, the Humberside Theatre at Spring Street staged productions from various other companies as well as their own, including several plays written by Alan Plater.

1,518: Following its acquisition by local businessman and former boxer Wally Mays, the Tower Cinema was restored and reconfigured as a Rock Music and boxing venue, with the Hull Film Society occasionally presenting film screenings on an irregular, ad hoc basis.

1,519: Following a name change from the Humberside Theatre in 1981, the Spring Street Theatre closed in 1982 and remained empty until the Hull Truck Theatre Company acquired the premises in 1983.

1,520: On 4 April 1983 the Hull Truck Theatre Company launched its opening season at the Spring Street Theatre with the première of Nigel Williams' *The Adventure of Jasper Ridley*. Also in 1983, Pam Brighton resigned and John Godber was appointed as the theatre's Artistic Director.

1,521: Hull-born singer and entertainer Joe Longthorne was named the Variety Club of Great Britain's 'Most Promising Artiste' in 1983, and given their 'Lifetime Achievement Award' in May 2007.

1,522: In May 1983 Hull Marina was opened on the site

of the former Humber Dock; and was extended into the former Railway Dock in 1984.

1,523: At the end of the 1982–83 season Hull FC finished top of the league, taking the Championship title, with 47 points—4 points ahead of local rivals Hull Kingston Rovers. On 2 October 1982 Hull FC also won the Yorkshire Cup at Headingley, Leeds (beating Bradford Northern 18-7); they also reached the finals of the Challenge Cup (losing 14-12 at Wembley to Featherstone Rovers) and the Premiership Trophy (losing 22-10 to Wigan).

1,524: The early 1980s change of use at the Tower Cinema on Anlaby Road to a Rock Music venue was less than successful, and on 23 November 1983 the venue was once again put up for sale; but with no buyers coming forward the owners decided to try another change of format, so it was changed into a nightclub and fun-pub venue, with daytime keep-fit and dance classes also being introduced.

1,525: On Friday 12 August 1983 Hull writer and comedian Lucy Ann Beaumont was born, 6lb 2oz (six weeks prematurely), at the Royal Cornwall Hospital at Treliske, Truro while her mother was on holiday with Lucy's grandparents. She was brought up in Hull and Hessle, with her maternal grandparents playing a very influential role in her life. She is the only child of Nick and Gill Beaumont (*née* Adams). [Incdentally, the youngest daughter of former Prime Minister David Cameron, Florence Rose Endellion, was also born prematurely (three weeks) at Treliske Hospital—on 24 August 2010, while the Camerons were on holiday in Cornwall (St. Endellion is a small village in north Cornwall, about 5 miles from where the Camerons were staying at Daymer Bay.)]

1,526: Hull band Red Guitars achieved both local celebrity status and national attention in 1983 when their single 'Good Technology' was picked up and championed by the BBC's John Peel. Always keen to demonstrate they were 'Fiercely independent and suspicious of record companies' it was decided to release the single on the band's own Self Drive label. Regular Radio 1 airplay followed, along with appearances on *The Whistle Test* and Channel 4's *The Tube*, resulting in the single selling 60,000 copies and topping the Independent Music chart.

1,527: On 2 December 1983 Channel 4's *The Tube* broadcast a 'Hull Bands Special' featuring Red Guitars, Indians in Moscow, and International Rescue. The programme's presenter Jools Holland was shown ambling around the WCs beneath the statue of King Billy in Lowgate, punning on the word 'willy'.

1,528: Additional facilities at Hull Truck's Spring Street Theatre venue included storage space for touring equipment; and office space and dressing rooms, which utilized former studio space. Even though the theatre was intimate and welcoming, there was very little space for expansion. The Spring Street Theatre was finally demolished in November 2011.

1,529: The original seating capacity at Hull Truck's Spring Street Theatre was 200, but this was later increased to 282. The ground-floor auditorium consisted of single-tier seating that faced the stage on three sides.

1,530: At the end of the 1983–84 season Hull KR finished top of the Championship league table with 46 points, ahead of Hull FC on 45 points. They also won the Slalom Premiership for the second time when they beat Castleford 18-10 at Headingley, becoming the first team to win the Championship/ Premiership double.

1,531: After given up his job as a shipping clerk with local industrial transmission belting manufacturer J.H.

Fenner Ltd., Paul Jackson became the owner of the New Adelphi Club on 1 October 1984, having bought the freehold to the club for £57,000. To facilitate his purchase of the club he re-mortgaged a small house in Cottingham, but was still left with a shortfall of £45,000, which the Whitbread Brewery agreed to lend him.

1,532: The car park at the New Adelphi Club, De Grey Street, Hull occupies the site of the three previously neighbouring properties: Nos. 83, 85 and 87, which were destroyed by German bombs, probably one of the High Explosive bombs that fell on De Grey Street on 15 July 1941. [It is usually stated that the destruction of the neighbouring properties took place in 1940, but the Hull & East Riding at War website—which chronicles the bombing of the area—records no bombing of De Grey Street in 1940].

1,533: Paul Jackson has been quoted as saying that the Housemartins were the third band ever to play at the venue following his acquisition of the club in October 1984. The first two bands to play at the venue were called Vagrant and Cold Dance.

1,534: The New Adelphi Club has hosted some of the UK's most successful and influential indie bands, including Pulp, Oasis, Happy Mondays, Radiohead, The Stone Roses, and PJ Harvey. Besides bringing these bands to Hull for the city's music lovers to enjoy, the club has also (for over thirty years) provided a credible venue for generations of Hull's original-music creators (and other performance artists) to meet, and to showcase (and build an audience for) their work.

1,535: On 15 October 1983 Hull FC beat Castleford 13-2 at Elland Road, Leeds to win the Yorkshire Cup for a fourth time; and (as previously mentioned) at the end of the 1983–84 season, finished second in the Championship league with 45 points, just one point behind local rivals Hull Kingston Rovers on 46 points.

1,536: On 27 October 1984 a local derby decided the winners of the Yorkshire Cup, with Hull FC and Hull Kingston Rovers battling it out at Boothferry Park in front of 25,237 spectators. Hull FC took the honours, beating Rovers 29-12, and winning the Yorkshire Cup for the fifth time, and for a third successive year.

1,537: In December 1984 Philip Larkin was offered the chance to succeed Sir John Betjeman as Poet Laureate but declined, being unwilling to accept the high public profile and associated media attention of the position; but also (as he had expressed in a letter in August that year) because he felt that although it was acceptable for a Poet Laureate to lose inspiration and therefore cease to write poetry, he didn't feel it was appropriate for someone who had lost 'the compulsion to write poems' to be appointed to the position from the outset.

1,538: Following the success of their debut release 'Good Technology', Hull band Red Guitars issued two follow-up singles. 'Fact' and 'Steeltown' were released in 1984, reaching number 7 and number 2 in the Independent Music chart respectively. The band also released two LPs: *Slow to Fade* (1984) on their own Self Drive label; and *Tales of the Expected* (1986) on nascent serial entrepreneur Richard Branson's Virgin Records. Virgin stable-mates with releases the same year included Human League, Japan, Culture Club, Simple Minds, Marc Almond, and P.I.L.

1,539: Roland Gift was born on 25 May 1961 in Birmingham's Sparkhill district, and went on to become the lead singer with 80s chart band Fine Young Cannibals. Although born in Birmingham, Gift moved to Hull aged 11 and attended Hull's Kelvin Hall School. He became a member of local ska band Akrylykz, who toured with The Beat. Following the dissolution of The Beat in 1983, Andy Cox (guitar) and David Steele (bass) formed Fine Young Cannibals in 1984, and asked Gift to join as lead vocalist. Their first single, 'Johnny Come Home' (1985) reached number 8 in the UK charts. Roland's mother, Pauline, ran several vintage-clothes and bric-a-brac shops, including Pauline's Gift Shop on Princes Avenue.

1,540: In 1984, having narrowly missed delivering a back-to-back promotion for Hull City, Colin Appleton left the club to become manager of Swansea City. Don Robinson then, surprisingly, brought in Brian Horton from Luton to become City's player-manager. Horton steered City into the Second Division at the end of the 1984–85 season.

1,541: In 1984, in its first year of operation, audience figures at Hull Truck's Spring Street Theatre reached 30,000; and John Godber wrote *Up 'n' Under*, which premièred at the Assembly Rooms, Edinburgh Festival Fringe. The play won the Laurence Olivier Comedy of the Year Award after just six West End performances.

1,542: In 1984 Hull's Eureka Picture Palace at 562 Hessle Road was re-fashioned as a live-concert venue. The change of use was not a long-term success and in 1989 the venue was sold with a view to redevelopment, which never took place. Sadly the venue remained unoccupied and stood empty and deteriorating for decades, finally becoming derelict.

1,543: In the 1980s Cargill UK Ltd.—the owners of the grain silo at Hull's King George Dock—allowed Bob Geldof's *Band Aid* project to use the facility as a distribution point for its shipments of grain for famine relief in Ethiopia.

1,544: In 1984 Anglia Oils (later, AarhusKarlshamn UK Ltd., or simply AAK), established at King George Dock in 1982 as a wholly owned subsidiary of Danish company Aarhus Olie, opened an automated vegetable oil refinery at the dock. In 2013 AAK began a two-year, £10m investment programme for its Hull refinery.

1,545: On 26 January 1985 Hull Kingston Rovers and Hull FC battled it out in the final of the John Player Special Trophy in front of 25,326 spectators at Boothferry Park. Hull KR took the honours, beating the Black and Whites 12-0.

1,546: In 1985 Hull Truck's audience figures increased by 33% to 40,000, and the company undertook its first Community Theatre tour of Humberside, with John Godber's *Happy Jack*, which was inspired by the 60 year marriage of the playwright's grandparents. On 26 March *Up 'n' Under* opened in London's West End. Also in 1985, for the second year in succession, Hull Truck received a nomination for the Laurence Olivier Comedy of the Year Award (for *Bouncers*).

1,547: In 1985 Cranswick Mill Ltd. was floated on the Unlisted Securities Market (USM) as Cranswick Mill Group PLC, and made record profits of £840,000 in the financial year ended 31 March 1986 (its first year as a USM listed company) against a forecasted £825,00 at the time of floatation.

1,548: At the end of the 1984–85 season Hull FC finished sixth in the league with 35 points, 13 points behind top of the league local rivals Hull Kingston Rovers; and on 4 May 1985 they played Wigan in the Challenge Cup final at Wembley Stadium, in front of 97,801 spectators, but lost 28-24, becoming Challenge Cup runners-up for the tenth time in their history.

1,549: At the end of the 1984–85 season Hull KR finished top of the Championship league table with 48 points, ahead of St. Helens on 45 points, winning the Championship for a second successive year. As well as winning the John Player Special Trophy (see fact 1,545), they reached the final of the Slalom Premiership Trophy for a second successive year, but were defeated 36-16 by St. Helens, at Elland Road, Leeds.

1,550: On 15 June 1985 it was announced in the Queen's Birthday Honours that Philip Larkin had been appointed CBE, for Services to Poetry.

1,551: On Thursday 20 June 1985 Hull band the Housemartins signed their record contract with the London-based record label Go! Discs on stage at Hull's legendary New Adelphi Club during a performance of their cover of the Lloyd Charmers song 'I'll be Your Shelter'.

1,552: Originally constructed of wood, the 'Threepenny' stand at Hull FC's Boulevard Stadium was so named because that was the price of admission to the stand when it first opened. The stand was the preferred location of many Hull FC fans for watching the games, and was where the club's anthem 'Old Faithful' would invariably begin, before resounding around the whole stadium. The stand was closed for safety reasons in July 1985, and was eventually replaced by a new, safer structure; a plaque to the city's lost trawlermen taking pride of place on the new structure, reading:

This Stand is dedicated to Trawlermen Past and Present

1,553: Brewing finally ceased at the former Hull Brewery Company Limited brewery in Sylvester Street on 15 August 1985; and in 1989 local firm R.E. Hatfield Contractors Ltd. bought the Sylvester Street premises for commercial redevelopment, naming the development 'The Maltings'.

1,554: In November 1985 part of the A63 approach road (between the Humber Bridge and the city centre) was renamed Clive Sullivan Way in honour of one of the city's favourite adopted sons, who during his career played rugby league for both Hull FC and Hull Kingston Rovers.

1,555: Since the time of his father's death at the age of 63 (on 26 March 1948) the great English poet Philip Larkin was convinced that he would also die at that age. Until his own death in 1985, Larkin worked for 30 years as Librarian at Hull University. He died of cancer at 1:24 a.m. on Monday 2 December 1985, at Hull's Nuffield Hospital. He was 63 years old.

1,556: Jon Culshaw, the impressionist who would voice (among others) John Major in ITV's *Spitting Image* series, was a presenter on Hull-based commercial radio station VikingFM during the 1980s.

1,557: The William Jackson Food Group produces more than 20m of its *Aunt Bessie's* branded Yorkshire puddings each week at its Freightliner Road factory in Hull.

1,558: The Hull Kingston Rovers record for the most individual tries scored in a single season is held by Gary Prohm, who scored 45 tries in the 1984–85 season.

1,559: The Hull New Theatre has two licensed bars: the stalls bar (accessible from the staircase from the foyer) and the circle bar on the upper floor.

1,560: The Hull New Theatre has a seating capacity of 1,159. There are 680 seats in the stalls, 185 seats in the dress circle, 282 seats in the upper circle, and 6 seats in each of the two boxes either side of the stage.

1,561: In 1985, following another major refurbishment, the New Theatre, Hull was renamed Hull New Theatre. The name change was marked by a Royal Gala (attended by Princess Anne) featuring Opera North and the English Philharmonic Orchestra.

1,562: In 1985 Hull's St. Andrew's Dock was filled in and the site used for redevelopment into the St Andrews Quay out-of-town retail park.

1,563: In 1985 Christian McDonald Langton, then a student at the University of Hull, was awarded a PhD for his groundbreaking work in developing a system that used broadband ultrasound attenuation (ultrasound) for the early detection of osteoporosis. This work led to the subsequent development and utilization—throughout the world—of bone-density scanners to detect osteoporosis.

1,564: On 29 September 1986 the format of the *Hull Daily Mail* changed from broadsheet to tabloid; and, having acquired land at the junction of Beverley Road and Spring Bank in 1977, the paper moved production to its newly constructed premises at Blundell's Corner in October 1989.

1,565: On 22 April 1986 the Memorandum of Association of Heron Frozen Foods Limited was altered by Special Resolution, and the Share Capital of the company was increased to £100,000 divided into 100,000 shares of £1 each, from the previous £10,000 divided into 10,000 shares of £1.

1,566: At the end of the 1985–86 season Hull KR finished 7th in the Championship league table with 33 points, and they reached their fourth Wembley Challenge Cup final where they were defeated 15-14 by Castleford in front of a crowd of 82,134 on 3 May 1986.

1,567: On 26 July 1986 Hull athlete Dave Smith won gold in the hammer throw at the Commonwealth Games in Edinburgh. His throw of 74.06m was more than 3.5m further than that of the silver medal winner, Northern Ireland's Martin Girvan, who managed a throw of 70.48m.

1,568: In 1986 Hull Truck produced *Blood, Sweat and Tears* inspired by the achievements of local judo world champion Karen Briggs, and BBC 2 broadcast a TV version, with the original cast, in its *Screenplay* series. In the same year, London Weekend Television's *The South Bank Show* dedicated a complete programme to the story of Hull Truck Theatre; and Hull Truck's 50 seat studio theatre at Spring Street opened in November of 1986.

1,569: Hull FC have finished as runners-up in the Yorkshire Cup on 12 occasions, losing in 1912 (23 November, Batley, 17-3, Headingley); 1914 (28 November, Huddersfield, 31-0, Headingley); 1920 (27 November, Hull Kingston Rovers, 2-0, Headingley); 1927 (26 November, Dewsbury, 8-2, Headingley); 1938 (22 October, Huddersfield, 18-10, Odsal); 1946 (2 November, Wakefield Trinity, 10-0, Headingley); 1953 (31 October, Bradford Northern, 7-2, Headingley); 1954 (23 October, Halifax, 22-14, Headingley); 1955 (2 November, Halifax, 7-0 [replay, after 10-10 draw at Headingley], Odsal); 1959 (31 October, Featherstone Rovers, 15-14, Headingley); 1967 (14 October, Hull Kingston Rovers, 8-7, Headingley); 1986 (11 October, Castleford, 31-24, Headingley).

1,570: On 2 December 1986 Heron Frozen Foods Limited changed the company's registered office, relocating to Walcott Street from Gillett Street.

1,571: Don Suddaby, a research chemist at Croda International, Hull who distilled and purified erucic acid into Lorenzo's Oil to help stabilize the condition of adrenoleukodystrophy (ALD) sufferer Lorenzo Odone, was born on 17 September 1922 in the Sculcoates district of

Hull. He agreed to become involved in the research project in early 1986, produced the first litre of Lorenzo's oil within six months, and Croda shipped it to the Odone family in December 1986. The oil was immediately introduced into Lorenzo Odone's diet, resulting in the dramatic halting of the progression of the disease. Don Suddaby, who portrayed himself in *Lorenzo's Oil*, the Hollywood film based on the Odone's campaign to find a cure for their son, died on 1 August 1993 in Withernsea.

1,572: Several scenes from the 1986 film *Clockwise*, featuring John Cleese and Alison Steadman, were filmed in Hull. The locations include: Paragon Railway Station, the BP petrol station at 390 Cottingham Road (where the McDonald's burger restaurant now stands), West Ella Way (Kirk Ella), and 26 Ganstead Lane.

1,573: The global fast-food chain McDonald's opened its first Hull restaurant in Jameson Street in 1986.

1,574: In 1986 Russell Hills took over the role of Theatre Director at the Hull New Theatre.

1,575: In 1986 a blue heritage plaque was erected on 6 High Street, Hull to mark the site of the original Hull Dock Company offices. The inscription reads:

> Built 1820 for Hull Dock Company next to the lockpit to Queen's Dock, the OLD DOCK OFFICES became inadequate for the expanding port and in 1871 the new offices opened at the western end of the dock

1,576: In 1987 a blue heritage plaque was erected on the east elevation of the Hull Marina Office building at Warehouse 13, Railway Street, on the side of Hull Marina, to mark the opening of the Hull Marina Development Complex by Queen Elizabeth II. The inscription reads:

> The Hull Marina Development Complex was opened by HER MAJESTY THE QUEEN on 17th July 1987

1,577: Luke Campbell, Hull's 2012 Olympic gold-medal-winning southpaw bantamweight boxing champion, was born on 27 September 1987. As an amateur, Campbell boxed out of St. Paul's Boxing Academy, North Church Side, in the Old Town area of the city.

1,578: In 1987 Smith & Nephew PLC made a profit of £109.6m, breaking through the £100m barrier for the first time.

1,579: In 1987 Hull Truck received £2,000 sponsorship from Mansfield Breweries. This figure was matched by the government's Business Sponsorship Incentive Scheme. Also in 1987, plans were approved for a new 400-seat Hull Truck theatre in the city centre.

1,580: Hull-born singer and entertainer Joe Longthorne was told in 1987 that he had blood cancer (which he overcame); he was diagnosed with (and beat) leukaemia in 2006; and he was diagnosed with throat cancer in 2014.

1,581: In 1988 Thomas Gordon Martin, the son of Tom Martin, and one of the fourth generation of the Martin family to run the company, joined ARCO. He was appointed as a director on 1 May 1994.

1,582: By 1988 Heron Frozen Foods had expanded to include 15 stores, and had acquired its first 18 ton liveried HGV. The company achieved its first weekly turnover of £100,000 in July 1989.

1,583: On 14 September 1988 Olympic Gold figure skating champion John Curry OBE opened the Humberside Ice Arena (now the Hull Arena). Curry became Britain's first ever figure skating gold medalist in February 1976 when he won Britain's first winter games medal in 12 years. The arena's foundation stone was laid by HM Queen Elizabeth II on 17 July 1987.

1,584: Having served as Secretary General at Mencap from 1980, Brian Rix became the learning disability charity's Chairman in 1988, before becoming its President in 1998—a position he occupied until his death in 2016.

1,585: In 1988 a blue heritage plaque was erected on the side of the Marina, near the junction of Castle Street and Humber Dock Street, to mark the opening of the Humber Dock Promenade. The inscription reads:

> Humber Dock Promenade This promenade was opened on 26th April 1988 by Councillor Miss V.A. Mitchell Lord Mayor of Kingston upon Hull & Admiral of the Humber

1,586: In 1988 a blue heritage plaque was erected near the old steam packet wharf on the pier, on the west elevation of the west- and south-most building (Mariner View) of Minerva Terrace, to commemorate the heroic actions of Grace Darling in helping to rescue the survivors from the PS Forfarshire, which had sailed from Hull. The inscription reads:

> This plaque commemorates the fateful voyage of the paddle steamer Forfarshire from Hull to Dundee on 5th September 1838. P. S. FORFARSHIRE AND GRACE DARLING 1838 Grace Darling saved many lives by her heroic efforts when the ship foundered on the Farne Islands

1,587: In 1988 the Hull Truck Theatre Company took 5 productions to the Edinburgh Festival: John Godber's *September in the Rain*, *Bouncers* and *Salt of the Earth*; John Burrows' *Viva Espana!*; and Frederick Harrison's *A Hard Day's Night*.

1,588: In 1988 the redevelopment of the former Victoria Dock site began with a £63m plan to build a housing estate featuring a mini marina and a promenade.

1,589: Emerging from the demise of Red Guitars came the wittily-named The Planet Wilson, with former Red Guitars musicians Hallam Lewis (guitar/vocals) and Lou Howard (bass) forming the nucleus of the band. The band released three singles and two albums: *In The Best of All Possible Worlds* (1988) with Virgin, and *Not Drowning But Waving* (1989) with Records of Achievement.

1,590: At the end of the 1988–89 season Hull KR finished bottom of the Championship league table with just 13 points, and were relegated to the Second Division. However, the following season (1989–90) they finished top of the Second Division with 50 points, ahead of Rochdale Hornets (48 points), and Oldham (also 48) and were promoted back up to the Championship league.

1,591: In 1989 the ABC cinema on Ferensway was renamed the Cannon and eventually closed its doors to the public for the final time on 29 June that year.

1,592: In 1989 more than 250,000 people went to see the Hull Truck Theatre Company on tour; the company took 7 productions to the Edinburgh Festival: John Godber's *Bouncers*, *Teechers* and *Northern Lights*; Jane Thornton's *Catwalk*; David Llewellyn's *Playing Away*; Brian Patten's *Gargling with Jelly*; and Shakespeare's *Twelfth Night*. John Godber's adaptation of *A Christmas Carol* was the 1989 Christmas production at the Spring Street theatre.

1,593: In 1989 Ronnie Hilton married a second time (his first wife, Joan, having died in 1985). The same year, he was awarded a British Academy of Song Composers and Authors gold medal for services to popular music.

1,594: In 1989 ex-trawlerman John Crimlis and local historian Alec Gill founded the St. Andrew's Fish Dock Heritage Group (STAND). Among other activities, STAND organizes and sponsors an annual winter Memorial to Lost

Trawlermen Service. Volunteers from the group also manage (in partnership with the City Council) the maritime visitor attraction the Arctic Corsair (the last surviving sidewinder trawler), now berthed on the river Hull.

1,595: By the end of the 1980s Smith & Nephew were one of the biggest companies in the global health-care sector, with a wide range of trusted and respected household brands stabled within their product range.

1,596: In 1989 Hull New Theatre issued a special enamel lapel pin-badge to commemorate its 50th anniversary.

1,597: At an Extraordinary General Meeting of J.H. Fenner & Co. Ltd., held on 5 January 1990, a resolution was 'duly passed' that the company name be changed to Fenner PLC.

1,598: On 5 April 1990 Hull's Odeon Cinema opened at Kingston Street in the city's Kingston Retail Park. Operated by Odeon UCI Cinemas Group—whose parent company is Terra Firma Capital Partners Ltd., a UK-based private equity firm—the Odeon was initially an eight-screen multiplex cinema, with two more auditoria having been added in July 1995. The ten auditoria are equipped with Audio Engineering Society standard Digital Sound; with 2 wheelchair spaces provided at the rear of each auditorium. The seating capacity of the auditoria ranges from 90 to 460, providing a total of 1,882 seats.

1,599: On 12 August 1990 Hull-born actress Dorothy Mackaill died, aged 87, of liver failure. Plans were made for her friend Harry Robello to scatter her ashes off Waikiki Beach, where she had sunbathed almost every day until her health failed.

1,600: In August 1990 many of the buildings on Hull's Alexandra Dock were listed as being of architectural and historic interest by the Department of the Environment.

1,601: On 19 August 1990 Hull Kingston Rovers achieved their highest score, when they beat Nottingham City 100-6 in the preliminary round of the Yorkshire Cup at Bentley Road Stadium, Tattersfield, Doncaster in front of a crowd of 1,010. Greg Austin scored 6 tries for KR, with Anthony Sullivan scoring 5; Colin Armstrong scored 14 goals. Rovers were eventually knocked out in the semi-final on 12 September, when they lost 29-6 to Castleford at Wheldon Road, Castleford, in front of 7,940 spectators.

1,602: On Sunday 7 October 1990 fire ravaged the Royal Hotel (formerly the Royal Station Hotel) in Hull city centre. Ultimately the facade was saved, but the interior needed rebuilding before the hotel could re-open, which it did in 1992.

1,603: On 16 November 1990 the UCI cinema opened at Hull's St Andrews Quay. Owned by United Cinemas International (UCI), this 8-screen multiplex venue, with auditorium seating capacities ranging from 134 to 292, was closed on 1 July 2004. Towards the end of 2004 the Odeon & UCI Cinemas Group was formed when the European arm of UCI and competitors Odeon Cinemas were merged after both were bought by Terra Firma Capital Partners Ltd. Subsequently, the majority of the UCI-branded cinemas were re-branded under the Odeon name. As Hull already had an Odeon cinema (opened earlier that year) at the Kingston Retail Park, this UCI cinema on St Andrews Quay was never re-opened. The venue was demolished in 2005, to be replaced by a branch of the Dixon Carphone-owned Currys (electrical retailers).

1,604: On Sunday 16 December 1990, at the British Comedy Awards held at the London Palladium, Hull-born film director Gerald Thomas, along with the rest of the

Carry On team, received the 'Lifetime Achievement for Film' award, which was presented by Sir John Mills.

1,605: In December 1990 the area surrounding the lockpit of Hull's St. Andrew's Dock was designated a Conservation Area.

1,606: During the 1980s and 90s Cranswick PLC made a series of strategic acquisitions, including Rawson Pork Cuts (1988), Yorkshire Country Pork (1991), FT Sutton & Son (Rossendale) Ltd. (1992), and Mr Lazenby's specialist sausage manufacturing (1998); a joint venture with Simply Sausages, London (1995) resulted in the Sainsbury 'Taste the Difference' range, leading the way for other retailers to produce 'Gourmet Style' equivalents in the sausage line.

1,607: In 1990, while producing the Swedish female duo EC2, Mick Ronson developed a relationship with the duo's Carola Westerlund, with whom he later had a son, Kym (Joakim Ronson Westerlund), his third and youngest child.

1,608: The Hull Kingston Rovers record for the most individual points scored in a single season is held by Mike Fletcher, who scored 450 points in the 1989–90 season.

1,609: The Hull Kingston Rovers record for the most individual goals scored in a single season is held by Mike Fletcher, who scored 199 goals in the 1989–90 season.

1,610: The company established in Hull by the US-based National Radiator Company, on what in 1907 would be named National Avenue, went through many expansions, enlargements, renames, mergers and takeovers: Ideal Standard (1953), Metal Box (1976), Caradon Heating (1989); eventually becoming Caradon Ideal in 1993, and manufacturing boilers under the *Ideal* brand.

1,611: In 1990 the Hull Truck Theatre Company toured nationally with *Romeo and Juliet*. Featuring Roland Gift, the former lead vocalist with international chart-topping band Fine Young Cannibals, the production was also staged at the State University of New York at Stony Brook.

1,612: In 1990 the interior of the former Gaiety Theatre/ Playgoers Theatre was stripped away, and while the B.S. Jacobs facade of the building was renovated and restored, the venue was converted into an extension of the Market Hall. The external walls of the original auditorium remain.

1,613: In 1990 a blue heritage plaque was erected at the corner of Machell Street and Catherine Street, Hull to mark the site of the city's first public utility. The inscription reads:

> This building operated from 1876 as the HYDRAULIC POWER STATION serving the Old Town and other areas. The first hydraulic system laid by Act of Parliament in England, it was also the first public utility in Hull

1,614: In 1990 a blue heritage plaque was erected at Hall Street, to mark the location of the station of the city's former Volunteer Fire Brigade. The inscription reads:

> This building was erected as a station for the VOLUNTEER FIRE BRIGADE formed in 1887 to assist the regular brigade. The carved firemen's heads are said to be of Captains of the time. The volunteers disbanded in 1891

1,615: In 1990 a blue heritage plaque was erected on Warehouse No. 6 at the corner of Princes Dock Street and Castle Street to mark the location of Myton Gate—one of the four main entrances through the old town walls. The inscription reads:

> One of the four main entrances through the town walls MYTON GATE built in the 14th century stood close to here until demolition in the late 18th century

1,616: In 1990 a blue heritage plaque was erected on the dock-side at Humber Dock Street to mark the location of Hessle Gate—one of the four main entrances through the old town walls. The inscription reads:

> One of the four main entrances through the town walls, HESSLE GATE stood here, spanning a fresh water moat. It was stopped up against threatened invasion from the Scots in 1640, not reopened until 1761 and demolished c1800

1,617: On 15 March 1991 the Princes Quay shopping centre opened its doors to the public for the first time.

1,618: In the financial year ended 31 March 1991 Cranswick PLC, for the fist time, made profits before tax of more than £1m, recording a figure of almost £1.4m on a turnover of £75m. The figure exceeded £2m for the first time just two year later when profit on ordinary activities before tax reached £2.2m (on a turnover of £107.2m).

1,619: At the end of the 1990–91 season Hull City were relegated to the Third Division, where they remained the following year, although the division was re-designated 'Division Two' when the Premier League was founded in 1992. They remained in Division Two until the end of the 1995–96 season, when, with 31 points, they were placed bottom of the league and were relegated to Division Three.

1,620: At the end of the 1990–91 season Hull FC finished third in the league with 34 points, behind Wigan (42), and Widnes (40); but they beat Widnes 14-4 on Sunday 12 May 1991, at Old Trafford, Manchester, to win their only Rugby League Premiership title to date.

1,621: In May 1991, after an exploratory operation to investigate persistent back pains and weariness, Mick Ronson was diagnosed with cancer of the liver.

1,622: On 13 June 1991 David and Andrew Heuck, two of Malcolm and Sheila Heuck's three sons, were appointed directors of Heron Frozen Foods Ltd. David, the middle of three brothers, was born on 3 March 1961; Andrew, the youngest, was born on 7 December 1962.

1,623: In October 1991 Dove House Hospice (formally opened on 24 June 1992 by HRH Diana, Princess of Wales) accepted patients to its bedded units for the first time.

1,624: The heaviest defeat recorded by Hull Kingston Rovers was when they lost 76-8 to Halifax on 20 October 1991. This points difference of 68 equalled the 68-0 defeat, again by Halifax, on 3 April 1956.

1,625: In November 1991 sales of ambient grocery products (non-chilled/frozen) at Heron Frozen Foods stores reached £100,000/week; while in 1992, in Hornsea, the company opened its 30th store, helping the company to service a total of 100,000 customers a week.

1,626: At an Extraordinary General Meeting held on 2 December 1991 it was agreed that the name of Cranswick Mill Group PLC be changed to Cranswick PLC.

1,627: In 1991 H. Fletcher & Son Ltd. opened its Hessle branch at 5 Prestongate.

1,628: The Hull Kingston Rovers record for the most appearances for the club is held by Mike Smith, who in the period 1975–91 made 481 appearances. He made a further 8 appearances as substitute.

1,629: In 1991, in response to the ever increasing commercial traffic at the port, the British Ports Authority re-opened Hull's Alexandra Dock. (see fact 1,513)

1,630: The National Census of 1991 reported the population of the local authority district of Hull as 254,109.

1,631: On 27 January 1992 Take That appeared at both Malet Lambert School and Kingston High School before performing at the LAs nightclub in Ferensway that night.

1,632: On 20 April 1992 Mick Ronson played one of the biggest gigs of his career when he joined David Bowie and Ian Hunter (backed by the remaining members of Queen, with backing vocals by Def Leppard's Joe Elliot and Phil Collen) for a performance of 'All the Young Dudes' at Wembley in the Freddie Mercury Tribute Concert.

1,633: In 1992 the Hull Truck Theatre Company celebrated its 21st anniversary: the company took *Up 'n' Under* to the United States; and on 23 April it premièred John Godber's *April in Paris* at the Spring Street Theatre; and later that year, on 8 September, it premièred Godber's *The Office Party* at the Nottingham Playhouse, before taking it on a sell-out tour of the UK.

1,634: On Sunday 31 May 1992 Radiohead played in Hull for the first time, at the New Adelphi Club. The band (originally called On A Friday) had signed a six-album deal with EMI in November 1991 and, at the record label's suggestion, had changed their name. The name Radiohead was taken from the Talking Heads song 'Radio Head' on that band's 1986 album *True Stories*. Radiohead were scheduled to return to the Adelphi on 5 November the same year, before supporting Hull's Kingmaker at the city's Tower Ballroom on 29 November. They played the New Adelphi (and Hull) for the final time on Thursday 25 February 1993.
N.B. The publication *One Man & his Bog* (2004), which chronicles the history of the Adelphi, records just two visits to the venue by Radiohead (31 May 1992 and 25 February 1993); while a number of Radiohead fan websites, including greenplastic.com, additionally record the above mentioned gig on 5 November 1992 (as does

Susanna O'Neill in her *The Hull Book of Days*). I have taken the official Adelphi history to be correct, but think it reasonable to assume that the band were at some point scheduled to play at the venue on that date—which incidentally would have been Radiohead guitarist Jonny Greenwood's 21st birthday.

1,635: On 27 July 1992 new Articles of Association were adopted by ARCO Limited when the authorised share capital was set at £80,000 divided into 80,000 ordinary shares of £1 each.

1,636: In his final year Mick Ronson recorded a series of songs for the album *Heaven and Hull*, posthumously released in 1994. The album included guest vocal appearances by The Pretenders' Chrissie Hynde ('Trouble with Me'), David Bowie ('Like a Rolling Stone'), John Mellencamp ('Life's a River') and Def Leppard's Joe Elliot ('Don't Look Down'), as well as the live performance of 'All the Young Dudes' recorded at the Freddie Mercury Tribute Concert at Wembley in 1992.

1,637: The Hull City player with the record for being the club's youngest player in a League match is Matthew Edeson, who played for the Tigers in a 3-3 draw away against Fulham on 10 October 1992, aged 16 years and 62 days.

1,638: In 1992 Mick Ronson took on the role of producer for the final time, performing the honours on *Your Arsenal*, the fourth solo album by Morrisey. Though he doesn't receive a playing credit in the album notes, Ronson's musical influence is obvious and was a major contributing factor to the album's success, with *Q* magazine listing it among the top fifty recordings of 1992.

1,639: After a break of around twenty years, Mick Ronson appeared on a David Bowie record for a final time when he accepted an invitation to play lead guitar on Bowie's cover of Cream's 'I Feel Free', on *Black Tie White Noise* (1993).

1,640: In 1992 Hull-born actor Barrie Rutter founded the innovative Northern Broadsides theatre company, based in the Dean Clough Mill, Halifax. He was appointed OBE (presented by the Princess Royal, Princess Anne) in the 2015 New Year Honours, for services to drama.

1,641: In February 1993 Heron Frozen Foods recorded a turnover of over £300,000 a week for the first time. A new milestone was reached three years later when, in April 1996, turnover grew to £500,000 a week.

1,642: On 29 April 1993, aged 47, legendary Hull guitarist Mick Ronson died of liver cancer, at his home in Hasker Street, London, the house lent to him by his (and David Bowie's) former manager Tony Defries.

1,643: On 6 May 1993 a Memorial Service for Mick Ronson was held in London, at the Church of Jesus Christ of the Latter-day Saints. The following day he was buried in the family plot, alongside his father, in Hull's Eastern Cemetery.

1,644: In the Autumn of 1993 Hull Truck's Spring Street Theatre was closed for refurbishment, re-opening in April 1994 with the capacity increased from 200 to 292.

1,645: On Saturday 15 May 1993 'Better the Devil You Know' (written by Hull actor/singer-songwriter Dean Collinson) was runner-up in the Eurovision Song Contest, held at the Green Glens Arena in Millstreet, Ireland. The song was performed by the UK representative Sonia.

1,646: On 9 November 1993 Gerald Thomas died of coronary thrombosis at his home in Buckinghamshire.

1,647: By the end of 1993, with the addition of branches at Driffield, Stockton-on-Tees, Newton Aycliffe and Beverley, W. Boyes & Co. Ltd. had taken the total number of stores in the chain above twenty for the first time, with a total of twenty-two branches across Yorkshire, Lincolnshire and the North East.

1,648: In 1993 a £12m terminal for large Ro-Ro vessels (originally named River Terminal 1, but later renamed the Rotterdam Terminal) was opened on the banks of the Humber south of Hull's King George Dock.

1,649: Founded in 1993, the Hull Jazz Festival 'brings the best in world jazz to Hull' with their jazz festivals in July and November. Hull Jazz Festival also presents world jazz on the Yellow Bus Stage at the Hull Freedom Festival in September.

1,650: On 21 January 1994 the North Bridge Dry Dock (on the south side of Charlotte Street) which is approximately 150 feet long with an entrance of less than 40 feet wide, was given Grade II Listed Building status.

1,651: On 29 April 1994, exactly one year after his death, a tribute concert for Mick Ronson was held at the Hammersmith Odeon. With the aim of including Ronson in the evenings proceedings, video footage, some rarely seen before, was screened throughout the concert. The evening was compered by former *Old Grey Whistle Test* presenter Bob Harris; performers included The Rats, Dana Gillespie (with Rolf Harris on wobble board), Glen Matlock and The Mavericks, Big Audio Dynamite, Gary Brooker, Captain Sensible, The Spiders from Mars, Bill Nelson, Steve Harley, Queen's Roger Taylor, and Ian Hunter,—but not David Bowie.

1,652: There are three blue heritage plaques marking the old Town Walls, the most northerly of which (erected in

1994, and accessible from the north end of Princes Dock Street) is on the rear (south facing) elevation of 2 Alfred Gelder Street (at the time of writing, H. Samuel, jewellers); the other two plaques (erected in 1990) are located, within walking distance of the first: in Humber Dock Street (south of the A63) on the side of the Humber Dock Marina. They bear a uniform inscription:

> The brindled paving indicates the position of the TOWN WALLS constructed of brick in the 14th century and repeatedly strengthened against threatened invasions. In ruins by the late 18th century they were demolished to permit construction of the docks

1,653: In March 1995 Heron Frozen Foods acquired its first 3 stores in the North East of England from Quayside Frozen Foods, and on 6 April 1998 it acquired the trade and assets of Snow City, a chain of 11 frozen food stores in the North West, for £1,225,253. (Records at Companies House for Snow City Foods Ltd. show the company was incorporated on 18 July 1997, but has been dormant since that date.)

1,654: On 5 April 1995 speedway resumed in Hull when Hull Vikings moved to a new track at the New Craven Park Stadium, the home of Hull KR rugby club; and subsequently enjoyed spells in both the Elite League and the Premier League, with their most successful period culminating in the Premier League Championship in the 2004 season, when they came top of the league with 58 points, 9 points ahead of their nearest rivals Workington Comets. The 2004 season also saw Hull Vikings winning the Premier League Knock-Out Cup and the Craven Shield, an achievement that prompted *Hull Daily Mail* reporter Richard Tingle to assert that Hull Vikings were 'the most successful sporting team to come out of the city'.

1,655: On 9 April 1995 the Hull Truck Theatre Company staged the world première of John Godber's *Lucky Sods*, at the Spring Street Theatre, Hull.

1,656: In 1995, ten years after the poet's death, the Philip Larkin Society was founded as a national and international focus for those interested in Larkin and his writings and to: 'promote awareness of the life and work of Philip Larkin (1922–1985) and his literary contemporaries; to bring together all those who admire Larkin's work as poet, novelist, jazz critic and librarian; and to bring about publications on all things Larkinesque'.

1,657: Long after she ended her association with The Marvell Press, Jean Hartley remained a close friend of Philip Larkin, until his death in 1985. She was also an active supporter of Hull's artistic community and a keen promoter of the city's cultural heritage. She was instrumental in helping to establish The Philip Larkin Society in 1995, and was the first editor of the Society's newsletter *About Larkin*.

1,658: In 1994/95 the exterior of the Hull New Theatre was restored, and access was improved with the provision of a lift from street level to the foyer and from the foyer to the lounge bar.

1,659: In the 1990s it was proposed that a riverside container terminal, QUAY 2000 (later called QUAY 2005), be developed at the West Wharf location adjacent to Hull's Alexandra Dock. Following a Public Enquiry which refused permission for the scheme to go ahead, the Department of Transport over-ruled that decision, and the scheme was eventually approved in December 2005, with the *Associated British Ports (Hull) Harbour Revision Order 2006* sanctioning the commencement of the work in that year. QUAY 2005 was later subsumed into the plans to develop a wind turbine manufacturing facility at Hull.

1,660: At the end of the 1993–94 season Hull KR finished second from bottom of the Championship league table with just 18 points (Leigh finished bottom on 5 points), and were relegated to the Second Division. Two seasons later (1995–96) KR finished top of the Second Division with 36 points, ahead of Leigh Centurions (32 points), and were promoted back up to the Championship league.

1,661: The Hull City player with the record for scoring the most goals in a single game is Duane Derby, who scored six goals in the Tigers' 8-4 victory over Whitby Town in the FA Cup First Round replay at Boothferry Park in front of 2,900 spectators on 26 November 1996.

1,662: In 1996 the Hull Truck Theatre Company celebrated its 25th anniversary, but funding problems forced the theatre to close for three months. However, following the intervention of Hull-based safety equipment supplier ARCO with major sponsorship, the theatre opened again in November with John Godber's *Gym and Tonic* which had been premièred the previous month, on 4 October, at the Derby Playhouse in a co-production with Hull Truck.

1,663: In 1996, the inaugural season of the Super League (and the transformation of rugby league with the introduction of a summer season) Hull FC fell victim to a club re-brand when they were renamed Hull Sharks. Despite initial success in winning the Division One championship in 1997 (and promotion to the Super League) under manager Phil Sigsworth, Hull Sharks fell into deep financial difficulties and went out of business. Hull FC was saved only by a merger with Gateshead Thunder, in which the newly merged club retained the Hull name, and played its home games at The Boulevard.

1,664: On 6 June 1997, the eldest of Malcolm and Sheila Heuck's three sons, Michael Heuck, born on 21

September 1958, was the last of the three Heuck brothers to be appointed as a director of Heron Frozen Foods, joining his parents and his brothers David and Andrew.

1,665: In the summer of 1997 former tennis player David Lloyd bought Hull City along with the Hull Sharks Rugby League club, only to sell 65% of his shares in City to Stephen Hinchcliffe and Nick Buchanan the following year.

1,666: On Sunday 10 August 1997, as a tribute to the Hull guitarist, producer and arranger who was so influential in the success of David Bowie (as lead guitarist and arranger for Bowie's band the Spiders from Mars), the Mick Ronson Memorial Covered Stage was opened and dedicated in Queen's Gardens. The idea for the stage came from Pete Allen, Assistant Director of Hull Leisure Services, who had known Ronson when he worked for the Council's Parks Department.

1,667: Following the Dedication of the Mick Ronson Memorial Covered Stage on Sunday 10 August 1997, brief speeches were made by Maggie and Minnie Ronson before an inaugural concert with performances by a mix of 'local' and 'name' bands, including Yellow Monkey (who arranged and hosted the first tribute concert to Ronson, in Japan), Glen Matlock, The Grip, and Eddie and the Hot Rods.

1,668: A plaque adjacent to the Mick Ronson Memorial Stage in Queen's Gardens provides a hint to visitors that the gardens are situated on the site of the former Queen's Dock: 'Robinson Crusoe, most famous character in fiction, sailed from here September 1st 1651', and bears a quotation from Defoe's 1719 novel: 'Had I the sense to return to Hull, I had been happy'.

1,669: In August 1997 the wreck of the Hull trawler Gaul (H243) was finally discovered 70 miles north of

Norway's North Cape, by an expedition funded by Anglia Television and the Norwegian television company NRK. Following the discovery of the wreck, the Deputy Prime Minister, John Prescott (MP for Hull East), directed the Department of Transport's Marine Accident Investigation Branch (MAIB) to conduct an underwater survey of the wreck site and report its findings. An underwater survey of the wreck was carried out by MAIB in August 1998. Accompanying the expedition were three representatives from the Gaul Families Association, and a team from BBC North. The results of the survey were broadcast on 6 November 1997 in *Secrets of the Gaul*, a Channel 4 Dispatches programme.

1,670: In 1997 filming began on an adaptation of John Godber's *Up'n'Under*, starring Neil Morrisey and Samantha Janus. Also in 1997, on 24 November, John Godber's *It Started with a Kiss* premièred at the Spring Street Theatre.

1,671: In 1997 the northern dry dock at the north-east arm of King George Dock was converted into a covered terminal (the Hull Steel Terminal), primarily for the purpose of handling cargo for British Steel.

1,672: In 1997 a blue heritage plaque was erected on the exterior of the Royal Mail Sorting Office at St. Peter Street to mark the site of Hull's 16th and 17th century town defences. The inscription reads:

> This building lays over part of the town's 16th & 17th century defences, designed respectively by John Rogers (a military engineer to King Henry VIII) & Martin Beckman (a military engineer to King Charles II)

1,673: In 1997 a blue heritage plaque was erected at 163 Coltman Street to mark the location of the house in which Hull artist Henry Redmore lived. The inscription reads:

> Marine artist HENRY REDMORE (1820–1887) lived
> here from 1870 until his death in 1887

1,674: In 1997 a blue heritage plaque was erected at 37 Washington Street to mark the birthplace of Hull author Hubert Nicholson. The inscription reads:

> Poet, author and journalist, HUBERT NICHOLSON (1908–1996) was born here 23rd January 1908

1,675: In 1997 a blue heritage plaque was erected in Humber Street to mark the location of the postern Watergate. The inscription reads:

> The southern arm of the 14th century town wall included at this point a postern called THE WATERGATE. This led to the South End, a landing on the Humber foreshore which was also used as a town tip & battery

1,676: Thursday 22 January 1998 saw the première of the film version of John Godber's *Up'n'Under*; and the following Monday, 26 January, his play *Hooray for Hollywood* premièred at the Spring Street Theatre. Also in 1998, Godber's *Bouncers* was ranked as one of the greatest plays of the century in the National Theatre's NT2000 poll.

1,677: On 17 March 1998 Smith & Nephew unveiled a new purpose-built wound management factory in Hull. The official opening, performed by Deputy Prime Minister and MP for Hull East, the Rt Hon John Prescott, marked the completion of the first phase of the company's £41.3m 'Project Neptune' programme to redevelop the company's manufacturing site in the city.

1,678: On Friday 10 April 1998 Hull FC played their first ever home game in the Super League when they beat London Broncos 6-4 in front of 6,386 spectators at The Boulevard. The Black and Whites' first Super League game was played away to Sheffield Eagles at the Don Valley

Stadium on the previous Sunday, where a crowd of 5,200 saw them get off to a promising start with a 34-24 win.

1,679: The 1998 Marine Accident Investigation Branch report on the underwater survey of the wreck of the Gaul recommended that, based on the new and significant evidence found, the Secretary of State for the Environment, Transport and the Regions should re-open the Formal Investigation into the circumstances in which the vessel sank in February 1974.

1,680: During the MAIB underwater survey of the Hull trawler Gaul (H243) in 1998, a miniature camera was used to search for evidence of human remains in the sunken vessel's cabins, but none was found. The report concluded that the Gaul was 'lost due to downflooding through open weathertight doors and hatches on her trawl deck after being 'knocked-down' by several very large breaking waves'. A finding, it points out, 'very similar to the conclusion reached by the FI [Formal Investigation] in 1974'.

1,681: In 1998 Hull's Mayfair Bingo Club closed and the venue was converted into a public house (first the Hogshead and then Hollywood & Vine), which closed in 2011; the building remained vacant until being sold in December 2013 for £225,000 to a brother and sister team of developers (Beverley Willson and Richard Hart) who received planning permission to convert the building into a mix of 30 one- and two-bedroom apartments. Phase one of the development, supervised by David Piercy of Hull-based architects Piercy Design, was completed by February 2015.

1,682: In 1998 a blue heritage plaque was erected at Park Street, Hull to mark the centenary of Hull College. The inscription reads:

A century of learning HULL COLLEGE Park Street

Centre has provided further education for the people of
Hull since 1898

1,683: In 1998 a blue heritage plaque was erected on the
north side of Holderness Road, Hull (between Jalland
Street and Village Road) to mark the site of the house in
which Andrew Marvell lived while his father was Master
of the Charterhouse. The inscription reads:

> Here, from 1624 until 1640 while his father was Master
> of the Charterhouse, lived ANDREW MARVELL
> 1621–1678 Poet, public servant and Member of
> Parliament for Kingston upon Hull

1,684: The Hull Kingston Rovers record for the most
career points is held by Mike Fletcher who scored 2,760
points in the period 1987–98.

1,685: The Hull Kingston Rovers record for the most
career goals is held by Mike Fletcher, who scored 1,268
goals in the period 1987–98.

1,686: On 22 June 1999 Heron Frozen Foods acquired
17 First Freeze stores for £2.1m from the receiver of
Dawn til Dusk PLC. The acquisition took Heron's total
number of stores to 102. First Freeze was formerly part
of Milbank Foods Ltd., a subsidiary of Dawn til Dusk (a
chain of convenience stores founded in 1986).

1,687: In 1999 Hull City Council sold 50.1% of its shares
in Kingston Communications when the municipally owned
telephone company was floated on the Stock Market.

1,688: Kingston Communications was listed on the UK
Stock Market for the first time on 12 July 1999.

1,689: Subsequent to the release of *Heaven and Hull* in
1994, three further posthumous Mick Ronson albums were
released: *Just Like This* (1999), recorded between 1976 and
1977 as Ronson's follow up to *Play Don't Worry*; *Showtime*

(1999), an album consisting of two live gigs recorded in 1976 and 1989; and *Indian Summer* (2001), a soundtrack album for a film that was never produced.

1,690: In 1999 a blue heritage plaque was erected at the Charterhouse to mark its foundation by Sir Michael de la Pole; along with identifying the location where John Rochester and James Walworth were detained prior to being taken to York and hung by chains from that city's battlements. The inscription reads:

> Here, from its foundation by Sir Michael de la Pole in 1378, until 1539, stood the priory of Saint Michael, called THE CHARTERHOUSE the Carthusians John Rochester and James Walworth were detained here before their execution in 1537

(350 years later, in 1888, Rochester and Walworth were both beatified by Pope Leo XIII)

21st century

1,691: In 2000 Joanne Carolyn Richardson (*née* Martin), the elder daughter of Stephen and Carolyn Martin, joined the family business ARCO as Financial Controller. She was appointed Financial Director on 1 March 2001.

1,692: UGC opened its 9-screen 2,019-seater multiplex cinema at Gibraltar Road, Kingswood Retail Park, Hull, on 5 May 2000. The complex was taken over by Cineworld in December 2004, and renamed Cineworld in November 2005. Its nine screening auditoria vary in seating capacity from 98 up to 498. It boasts the largest 3D capable screen in the city in its 498 seater auditorium.

1,693: In June 2000 it was announced that Hull-born actor Barrie Rutter had been awarded the first-prize of £100,00 in the Creative Britons 2000 awards for his work as a theatre pioneer. The prize was presented by Keith

Bedell-Pearce—on behalf of the prize sponsors the Prudential—and Chris Smith, Secretary of State for Culture, Media and Sport.

1,694: In October 2000, a year after the club faced its most severe financial crisis and almost went bankrupt, it was announced that Hull City Council would buy The Boulevard stadium from Hull FC for £750,000, helping to secure the club's Super League status and its existence.

1,695: John Godber's 40th play *On a Night Like This* premièred at the Spring Street Theatre on 7 December 2000.

1,696: Cranswick PLC's programme of expansion through acquisition continued into the new millennium, with the purchase of Continental Fine Foods (2000), Pethick & Co. (Hull) Ltd. (2001), North Wales Foods Ltd., and Lite Bite (2002), The Sandwich Factory (2003); and, at over £80m, the company's largest acquisition to date, Perkins Chilled Food (2005).

1,697: ARCO, the Hull-based safety equipment supplier, continued its long-term investment in Hull when it opened its National Distribution Centre (NDC) at Henry Boot Way, Priory Park East in mid 2000, its distinctive exterior design becoming a landmark for users of Clive Sullivan Way. The innovative, externally supported construction eliminates the need for internal columns, allowing maximum utilisation of the internal space. The NDC operates 24hrs a day, five days a week and has 40,000 stock locations, with 17,000 products in stock.

1,698: In 2000 Heron Frozen Foods Ltd. acquired its first 44 ton articulated HGV; at this point the company served around 500,000 customers a week; by 2006 the company's turnover had reached £2m a week.

1,699: In 2000 Paul Bull of Brian Bull & Associates,

mosaic specialists based in Chipping Sodbury, was approached by Hull-based mosaic and tiling specialist Toffolo & Son with a view to his remaking the two illegally removed domes on the Tower Cinema on Anlaby Road. The remit would be to re-create, as closely as possible, the original domes, but using modern materials. (Bull eventually used Italian glass mosaic and gold mosaic from the Italian company Orsoni.)

1,700: In 2000 the Finland Terminal (with more than 70,000m² of covered storage primarily for the handling of paper products from Finland) opened at Hull's King George Dock. The terminal also includes saw-mill and timber treatment facilities.

1,701: On Monday 6 March 2000, BBC News announced that Hull's Kingston Communications were to join the FTSE 100 Index the following morning, after the company's shares peaked at £15.92. This short-lived FTSE 100 Index listing was a result of the Royal Bank of Scotland's takeover of NatWest and the deleting of NatWest shares, leaving a space in the top 100 Index. The sixfold increase in the Kingston Communications share price left Hull City Council—who had held on to 45% of the shares—with a £2bn windfall.

1,702: In 2000 a blue heritage plaque was erected at 365 Holderness Road, Hull to mark the house where Alfred Gelder, its designer, lived. The inscription reads:

> A Hull architect and city improver who was mayor of Hull for five years ALFRED GELDER designed this house and lived here from 1888 to 1903

1,703: In 2000 a blue heritage plaque was erected at 371 Holderness Road, Hull to mark the birthplace of J. Arthur Rank. The inscription reads:

> A Hull industrialist who became Britain's chief maker

and distributor of motion pictures, J ARTHUR RANK
was born here on 22 December 1888

1,704: In 2000 a blue heritage plaque was erected at the
Land of Green Ginger to mark the street's association with
Winifred Holtby, who titled a novel after it. The inscription
reads:

> One of the oddest street names in the country, LAND
> OF GREEN GINGER was the title of a Winifred
> Holtby novel. The name's origin remains a mystery

1,705: In 2000 a blue heritage plaque was erected at
High Street to mark the location of Pease's Bank, the first
bank to be founded in Yorkshire. The inscription reads:

> On this site, in 1754, was founded PEASE'S BANK,
> the first bank to be founded in Yorkshire It later became
> part of Barclays Bank PLC

1,706: In 2000 a blue heritage plaque was erected at No.
5 Scale Lane to mark the location of Hull's oldest
domestic building and the city's only substantial
surviving timber-framed building. The inscription reads:

> Dating back to the 15th century, 5 SCALE LANE is
> Hull's oldest domestic building

1,707: In February 2001 the 'Principal Business' of H.
Fletcher & Son Ltd. was recorded at Companies House as
the 'Manufacture of bread, fresh pastry & cakes'; 'Retail
of fruit and vegetables'; and 'Retail bread, cakes,
confectionery'.

1,708: In February 2001 Hull City went into
Administration, with the High Court appointing Kroll
Buchler Phillips as joint Administrators of Hull City AFC.
Just a few hours after the announcement, Nick Buchanan
resigned as City's Chairman. The club's debts were
believed to total £1m.

1,709: When David Lloyd sold Hull City to Stephen Hinchcliffe and Nick Buchanan in 1998, he held on to the ownership of Boothferry Park, part of which had been earmarked for redevelopment into a supermarket. City's new owners, now tenants of David Lloyd, failed to pay their rent on time and in February 2001, when City were also facing a winding-up order over an unpaid £500,000 VAT bill, Lloyd the landlord locked the club out of the ground.

1,710: Having initially had a stroke in 1976 Ronnie Hilton, died on 21 February 2001 at Hailsham, East Sussex, after suffering another. He was 75 years old.

1,711: On Thursday 8 March 2001, a meeting of Hull City's creditors took place in which they and the club's shareholders agreed to a deal that would save the club. The following Monday, 12 March, the club's new owners were revealed to be former Leeds United Commercial Director Adam Pearson and Leeds-based Internet entrepreneur Peter Wilkinson, who had bought the club from the Administrator for £360,000.

1,712: On 17 March 2001 Ralph Thomas died from coronary artery disease and cancer of the colon, at 8A Wellington Place, Westminster. He was survived by his wife Joy; and children, Jeremy Thomas and Jill Purdum.

1,713: In 2001, with no family succession to take over the running of the business, H. Fletcher & Son Ltd. was offered for sale, with the business being bought in March that year by 27-year-old Beverley-based businessman Mark Paul Campey, who operated it as a private limited company by the name of Fletcher's Fine Foods Limited. Chairman of H. Fletcher & Son Ltd., David Fletcher, was quoted in the *Yorkshire Post* of 19 March 2001: 'my preferred aim was to achieve a sale which would ensure continuity, protect the employment of the staff and see our business grow' and expressed his delight at selling the business to someone 'who will secure the future of...the workforce in the long term'. Prior to the sale the company's turnover was around £90,000 per week and it had approximately 150 people on the payroll.

1,714: On 16 May 2001 Hull MP and Deputy Prime Minister John Prescott punched protester Craig Evans, after Evans threw an egg at him in Rhyll, north Wales.

1,715: On 1 May 2001 the official opening took place of the Rotterdam Terminal, built on the site of River Terminal 1 (south of King George Dock, on the banks of the Humber) as part of an agreement between Associated British Ports (ABP) and P&O North Sea Ferries. The terminal was officially opened by Mrs Darral Fell (wife of ABP's Port Director Mike Fell).

1,716: During the financial period ending 29 December 2001 the number of people employed by Heron Frozen Foods Ltd. exceeded 1,000 for the first time when the average number of employees, including executive directors reached 1,062: 1,031 in sales and distribution, and a further 31 in administration.

1,717: In 2001 leading Hull-based safety equipment supplier ARCO merged its internal and external Safety and Maintenance sales teams in its branches, and launched its *Big Red Book* which integrated its three previous catalogues into a single volume, enabling customers to buy from one catalogue, while being serviced by a single account manager and an integrated Branch Service Team.

1,718: The player with the record for the most appearances for their national team while registered as a Hull City player is Theodore Whitmore, who played 28 times for his national team of Jamaica between 2000–01.

1,719: With the arrival of Adam Pearson, and the bitter taste of David Lloyd fading, the end of the 2000–01 season saw Hull City finish 6th in the table, qualifying for the Third Division play-offs; and although they beat Leyton Orient 1-0 in the home leg of the play-off semi-final, they went down 2-0 away, thereby losing 2-1 on aggregate and consigning themselves to what would turn out to be another three seasons in the Third Division.

1,720: In 2001, when a production of *Sunset Boulevard* was staged at the Hull New Theatre, a special larger entrance had to be created backstage to allow a staircase used in the show to be brought into the theatre.

1,721: In 2001 the Hull Truck Theatre Company celebrated its 30th anniversary with a total sell-out for the world première of John Godber's *Our House* at the Spring Street Theatre.

1,722: Grossing at 59,925 tonnes each; and capable of carrying 1,360 passengers in 546 cabins, the two cruise ferries operated by P&O North Sea Ferries on their Hull-Rotterdam route are Pride of Rotterdam and Pride of Hull. The service is used by around 1m passengers a year.

1,723: Hull's Rotterdam Terminal was built, at a cost of £14.3m, to accommodate the world's largest cruise ferries operated by P&O North Sea Ferries between Hull and Rotterdam, one of which (Pride of Rotterdam) completed her maiden voyage at the official opening.

1,724: In 2001 a blue heritage plaque was erected at Wilmington Bridge, off Wincolmlee, Hull to mark its being built in 1907 for NER, and the fact that it replaced an earlier bridge built for the York & Midland Railway. The inscription reads:

> Built for the North Eastern Railway and opened on 10 May 1907, THE WILMINGTON BRIDGE replaced a

single track bridge built in 1853 for the York & Midland Railway

1,725: In 2001 a blue heritage plaque was erected in Salthouse Lane to mark the location of the building that was once the Hull branch of the Bank of England. The inscription reads:

> Built circa 1784, and known as 50 Salthouse Lane, this building was from 1828 a branch of the BANK OF ENGLAND. From 1860 it was used as a sailors' home and is now known as 105 Alfred Gelder Street

1,726: In 2001 a blue heritage plaque was erected at The Mission in Posterngate to mark the location of the old Seamen's Mission. The inscription reads:

> Built in 1866 at the expense of Charles H. Wilson M.P. THE SEAMEN'S MISSION was extended in 1926/7 to form the Mariners' Church of the Good Shepherd

1,727: In 2001 a blue heritage plaque was erected in Whitefriargate to mark the location of the old Neptune Inn. The inscription reads:

> Built in 1797 as the town's premier hotel, THE NEPTUNE INN was Hull's Custom House for nearly 100 years

1,728: The National Census of 2001 reported the population of the unitary authority of Hull as 243,594.

1,729: The Deep, promoted as the world's first submarium, opened its doors to visitors for the first time on Saturday 23 March 2002, after being officially opened by Prince Andrew, the Duke of York the previous day. It is located at Sammy's Point, formerly the site of the shipyard of Martin Samuelson & Co.—the head of that company, Martin Samuelson, was Lord Mayor of Hull in 1858. Designed by Sir Terry Farrell, and partially funded by the Millennium Commission, the Deep (which cost £45.5m to build) has become a key visitor attraction.

1,730: In March 2002 Gareth Tudor Price was appointed Associate Director of the Hull Truck Theatre Company.

1,731: In April 2002, with Hull City failing to build on the promising finish to the previous season, and with their form steadily deteriorating, former Liverpool player and Danish international Jan Molby was recruited to take over from Brian Little as City's manager. Molby's tenure spanned just seven months before his departure and the arrival, in October 2002, of former England Under-21 coach, Peter Taylor.

1,732: On 20 September 2002 Hull FC played their last ever Super League game at The Boulevard when they lost 32-18 to Bradford in front of 8,630 spectators. A week later, on the 27 September, the final match of the club's 2002 Super League campaign (which saw the Black and Whites finish fifth in the league table with 32 points) took place at Headingley, where they lost 36-22 to Leeds.

1,733: On 22 October 2002 Hull FC, captained by hooker Lee Jackson, played their last ever game at The Boulevard when they entertained New Zealand, losing 28-11, in front of an emotional capacity crowd of 12,092. Hull FC winger Paul Parker scored the club's last ever try at The Boulevard, the Black and Whites' hallowed stadium, just a few seconds before the end of the game.

1,734: Before the last ever Hull FC match at The Boulevard, the club's elder statesman Johnny Whiteley led out two teams of veterans for the pre-match curtain-raiser; and schoolchildren, circled around the pitch, released a spectacular dispersal of black and white balloons into the night sky above the stadium.

1,735: Hull City played their final senior team match at Boothferry Park (against Darlington) on 14 December 2002. Peter Taylor's team lost 1-0—in front of a near-capacity crowd—to a 45th minute goal by Darlington defender Simon Betts.

1,736: Within months of Peter Taylor taking over as manager of Hull City in October 2002, the club moved to its new £43.5m new home, the Kingston Communications Stadium, located close to the site of the club's original Anlaby Road football ground. City baptised the venue with a match against Sunderland on 18 December 2002 where over 22,000 spectators saw Steve Melton score the only goal for City to win the Raich Carter Memorial Trophy.

1,737: In 2002 Wright & Wright Architects LLP of London were appointed as the architects for the new Hull Truck Theatre premises, to be constructed on Ferensway. The building, which opened on 23 April 2009, has subsequently won numerous awards, including Best UK Public Building: Brick Awards 2009; RIBA Award 2010; Building of the year: RIBA White Rose Award 2009; and the Civic Trust Special Award for Inclusive Design 2010.

1,738: On 12 November 2002 the *Yorkshire Post* ran a story reporting that the Hull-based business formerly known as H. Fletcher & Son Ltd.—Fletcher's Fine Foods Limited—had been placed into voluntary liquidation, with the loss of more than 160 jobs, 20 months after being sold to Beverley-based businessman Mark Campey. By February 2002 the 'Principal Business' of H. Fletcher & Son Ltd., as recorded at Companies House, was 'Letting of own Property' and 'Rent other Machinery & Equipment', suggesting that while the everyday business of H. Fletcher & Son Ltd. had been sold to Mr Campey (who then operated it as Fletcher's Fine Foods Limited until it was placed into voluntary liquidation), the premises, equipment and machinery had not.

1,739: In 2002, as part of Hull Time Based Arts' Rivercommissions series, Huddersfield-born artist Stefan

Gec created a bronze sculpture (mounted on a steel pillar on the river Hull) of the busts of two Inuit teenage lovers, Memiadluk (17) and Uckaluk (15), brought to Hull from Greenland in 1847 by the captain of the whaler Truelove, John Parker. (Parker had performed a marriage service for the couple on board the Truelove the night before they set sail for England.) The Truelove, one of Hull's most celebrated whalers and one of the last operating out of the port, made 58 voyages to Greenland and the Davis Straits between 1784 and 1852. In the spring of 1849, in the early stages of Memiadluk and Uckaluk's return voyage, Uckaluk died following an outbreak of measles aboard the ship.

1,740: BBC Radio Humberside's *Raw Talent* programme, launched in 2002, bears the signal distinction of being a trailblazer for the BBC's *Introducing* brand, which requires users of its 'Uploader' tool to allow the BBC to use their material for 'the full period of copyright' and (under the Terms of what the BBC calls *creations*) 'we won't pay you for it'—effectively ghettoizing, on a national scale, the vast majority of local songwriters, musicians and bands; creating a kind of musical apartheid between up and coming musicians and their more established counterparts. BBC *Introducing* was launched nationally in 2007 to produce 'local' programmes (supposedly supporting local, 'unsigned, undiscovered and under the radar musicians') some five years after the inauguration of BBC Radio Humberside's *Raw Talent* (produced by Katie Noone, and presented by Alan Raw), whose aim, ostensibly, was to support 'local' music.

1,741: On 2 February 2003 the founders of Heron Frozen Foods, Malcolm and Sheila Heuck, both retired and resigned as directors of the company.

1,742: Following the resignation (at retirement) on 2 February 2003 of Malcolm and Sheila Heuck, Heron

Frozen Foods was acquired, on 4 February, by Byrstar Limited (No. 4514523), an off-the-shelf company incorporated on 19 August 2002 and later that month acquired by the three Heuck brothers.

1,743: On 8 January 2003, prior to its acquisition of Heron Frozen Foods Ltd., the Registered Office of Byrstar Limited was changed to Walcott Street, Hessle Road, Hull; the company acquired the share capital of Heron Frozen Foods Limited on 4 February 2003, before its name was changed to Heron Food Group Limited on 17 February 2003, resulting in Heron Frozen Food Limited becoming a subsidiary of Heron Food Group Limited (owned by Michael, Andrew and David Heuck).

1,744: In February 2003 the Tower on Anlaby Road was bought by Northern European Leisure (Yorkshire) Ltd., who subsequently removed the two severely deteriorated decorative, mosaic-covered domes on top of the corner towers of the building's facade. The following month Hull City Council granted retrospective Listed Building Consent for the company to remove and replace the domes with similar ones.

1,745: On Sunday 2 March 2003 Hull FC recorded their highest ever score when they beat Sheffield Eagles 88-0 at the KC Stadium in front of 11,729 spectators. In the same match Matt Crowther scored 14 goals, equalling the club record for most goals in a match. Also on 14 goals in one match are Jimmy Kennedy (7 April 1921, at The Boulevard against Rochdale Hornets), and Sammy Lloyd (10 September 1978, at The Boulevard against Oldham).

1,746: In 2003 ARCO appointed cousins Jo Richardson (the daughter of Stephen Martin) and Thomas Martin (the son of Tom Martin) as joint Managing Directors, the fourth generation of the Martin family to run the company.

1,747: Hull-born actor Ian Carmichael was appointed OBE for services to Drama in the Queen's Birthday Honours list 2003.

1,748: In 2003 the St. Andrews Dock Heritage Park Action Group (STAND) launched their Memorial Fund to raise the money necessary to create a long-term memorial to the lost trawlermen of Hull. By 2009 the Memorial Fund had accrued £100,000.

1,749: In 2003 Hull Truck Theatre Company won an Arts and Business regional award for partnership excellence for its partnerships with Smith & Nephew, and the Children's University.

1,750: Following their purchase of Hull's Tower cinema on Anlaby Road in 2003, Northern European Leisure (Yorkshire) Ltd. relaunched the venue as the Emporium nightclub.

1,751: In 2003 a blue heritage plaque was erected at 15/17 Linnaeus Street, Hull, to mark the site of the former Hull Hebrew School. The inscription reads:

> Purchased by the Western Hebrew Congregation in 1901, the Hull Hebrew School used 15/17 Linnaeus Street as a girls' school (1902–45) and a boys' Hebrew evening class (1902–94)

1,752: In 2003 a blue heritage plaque was erected at the Bransholme Library in the North Point Shopping Centre, Bransholme to mark the existence of a Royal Air Force Station in the area from 1939 to 1961. The plaque exists because of the drive, dedication and enthusiasm of local historian Len Bacon, who served in Sutton during the war. Funds for the purchase and placement of the plaque came from sales of Mr Bacon's book *Hull's Own Air Force Station* (2002). The inscription reads:

> In 1939 the RAF 17 Balloon Centre was established in

this area. In 1942 it was renamed as RAF STATION SUTTON ON HULL. From 1943–59 it was home to the RAF School of Firefighting and Rescue. Closed in 1961

1,753: In 2003 a blue heritage plaque was erected at Linnaeus Street, Hull to mark the site of the former Western Synagogue. The inscription reads:

> Built in 1902 to a design by Benjamin Septimus Jacobs the building at the rear was the Western Synagogue used by the Hull Hebrew community until its closure in 1994

1,754: In 2003 a blue heritage plaque was erected at 32–33 Posterngate to mark the location of Harry Lazarus' Hotel. The inscription reads:

> Known as Harry Lazarus' Hotel during the 1870s and 1880s 32–33 POSTERNGATE was used to feed European transmigrants en route to America and Canada

1,755: In January 2004 the neglected former ABC Cinema (formerly the Regal), at 132 Ferensway, was demolished.

1,756: After site preparation and flood defence work in the summer of 2003, the construction began in early 2004 of a four-storey prestigious office building (named One Humber Quays in 2006) at the Island Wharf site. A second building, Two Humber Quays, was completed in November 2007.

1,757: In the financial year ending April 2004 the Hull Truck Theatre Company saw unprecedented attendance figures, with around 60,000 seeing its productions at the Spring Street Theatre.

1,758: At the end of the 2003–4 season Hull City finished second in the Third Division, winning promotion into League One (the third tier of the English football league system after the Premier League and the Football

League Championship). The following season (2004–05) City were runners-up to Luton in League One, thereby securing a back-to-back promotion (for the first time in the club's history) into the Football League Championship.

1,759: The Hull steam trawler Viola (H868) is currently situated in the harbour at Grytviken, a former South Atlantic whaling station on the island of South Georgia. Local historian Robb Robinson was one of the founder members of the Friends of Viola/Dias, a group campaigning to have the vessel recovered and returned to Hull.

1,760: The inaugural meeting of the Friends of Viola/Dias was held in July 2004, where it was agreed that the costs of recovering and restoring the vessel should be investigated, with a view to finding a permanent home for her in Hull.

1,761: The quickest goal scored by Hull City after kick-off was recorded at the KC Stadium on 6 November 2004 when Nick Barmby scored after just 8 seconds in the home game against Walsall. The Tigers went on to win 3-1 in front of 16,010 spectators.

1,762: The stated guiding policy of the Hull New Theatre is to maintain the tradition (introduced by its inspirational founder Peppino Santangelo) of 'playing for the people'; which in practical terms means that the best theatrical productions and performers from around the world continue to entertain the people of what Santangelo called 'this great city and county of Kingston Upon Hull'.

1,763: In 2005 John Godber celebrated his 21st anniversary as Artistic Director of the Hull Truck Theatre Company and his 50th play, *Wrestling Mad*, premièred at the Spring Street Theatre on 7 July that year.

1,764: On 17 July 2005—in front of 9,400 spectators at Bloomfield Road, Blackpool—Hull KR beat Castleford Tigers 18-16 to win the National Rail Rugby League Cup.

1,765: On 27 August 2005 in front of 74,213 spectators, Hull FC beat Leeds 25-24 at the Millennium Stadium, Cardiff, to win the Challenge Cup for the third time.

1,766: In 2005, in the face of overwhelming financial problems, Hull Vikings were unable to complete the season when a home match against Glasgow on 14 September had to be abandoned because of a shortage of electricity, and speedway in Hull came to an abrupt end.

1,767: On 30 November 2005 revised plans were approved for the development of the site of the Albert Hall music hall in Midland Street—along with the adjoining former New York Hotel and former Salvation Army Citadel sites—and for the construction of a 6-storey hotel incorporating 116 bedrooms, conference rooms, lounge, restaurant, bar, and a 48-space basement car park.

1,768: In 2005 a blue heritage plaque was erected at Victoria Dock to mark the site of the east-most point of the old Citadel. The inscription reads:

> This 17th century 'watchtower' marks the east point of HULL CITADEL. Built 1681–90, the citadel was a massive triangular fort incorporating earlier defences alongside the river Hull. It was levelled in 1863–4

1,769: In 2005 Hull Trains named their first British Rail Class 222 (Unit 101) 'Pioneer' high-speed train 'Professor George Gray', with Professor Gray unveiling the plaque dedicating the train in recognition of his achievements. Gray was also honoured by the British Liquid Crystal Society when the Society created its George W Gray Medal, awarded for contributions to liquid crystal research and technology.

1,770: In January 2006 the former Regent Cinema on Anlaby Road was re-named G.W. Horner's, after previously being converted into a public house called the Prince Regent. George W. Horner & Co. Ltd. (Est 1914) were a famous sweet manufacturing company with a large factory in Chester-le-Street, where the first G.W. Horners public house was opened. The company also opened a depot in Hull in the 1920s, along with depots in Glasgow, Dundee, Stockton and Berwick; and branch factories in East Ham, London and Edinburgh.

1,771: On 13 June 2006 Hull City manager Peter Taylor left the club to take over as manager of Crystal Palace. Taylor's replacement was former Colchester United manager Phil Parkinson, whose tenure saw City drop to one place above bottom of the Championship League. Parkinson was sacked on 4 December 2006, with his assistant Phil Brown taking over as caretaker manager until more permanent arrangements could be confirmed.

1,772: On 11 October 2006 Hull FC faced St. Helens in the Grand Final of the Super League. The Black and Whites (with 40 points) had finished second in the Super League table, behind St. Helens who topped the table with 48 points. In the final, St. Helens took the honours, beating Hull 26-4 in front of a crowd of 72,582, at Old Trafford, Manchester.

1,773: At the end of the 2006 season, Hull Kingston Rovers finished top of the National League One table with 32 points (ahead of Widnes Vikings on 28 points). They beat Widnes Vikings 29-16 in the National League Grand Final on 26 October 2006 and were crowned National League Champions, winning promotion into the Super League for the first time.

1,774: In October 2006—at the Spring Street Theatre— the Hull Truck Theatre Company presented Gareth Tudor

Prices's adaptation of *Macbeth*, the company's first production to be staged 'in the round'.

1,775: The Hull Truck Theatre Company's online ticketing service was launched in November 2006.

1,776: The world première of John Godber's *Christmas Crackers* took place at Hull's Spring Street Theatre on 7 December 2006.

1,777: In December 2006 Hull Screen at the Central Library ceased operation, in anticipation of a re-configuration of the Central Library as a whole; and the space it occupied was reclaimed and reintegrated into the new library facilities.

1,778: Heron Frozen Foods recorded its first annual turnover of over £100m in the financial year ending 30 December 2006, when its turnover reached £101,423,677, with the company making a gross profit of £13,125,806.

1,779: In 2006 Tom Martin stepped down as Chairman of ARCO after 24 years in the post, a period during which the company's turnover increased from £21m to £200m, and the branch network increased from 11 to 25. Mr Martin, aged 69, continued as a Non-Executive Director, and agreed to accept the honorary title of President of ARCO.

1,780: In 2006 building work began on the new Hull Truck Theatre in Ferensway. The venue, built at a cost of £15.5m by the Quarmby Construction Company, was completed in 2009. The construction was funded by Arts Council England, Kingston Upon Hull City Council, and the European Regional Development Fund.

1,781: The main public bar of Horner's (the former Kinemacolour Palace/Regent Cinema) on Anlaby Road occupies the old cinema foyer, the auditorium having been demolished during an earlier redevelopment.

1,782: Following the closure of Hull Screen at the Central Library in 2006, the action group Friends of Hull Screen was formed, with the group's first public meeting being held at the Savile Lecture Theatre in the University of Lincoln building on Hull's George Street, the venue where Hull Screen temporarily re-established itself.

1,783: In 2006 a blue heritage plaque was erected at 30 Church Street, Sutton to mark the location of 'Elmtrees', a home for refugee children during the Spanish Civil War. The inscription reads:

> During the Spanish Civil War of 1936–1939, this building 30 CHURCH STREET (formerly Elmtrees) was home to forty refugee children from the Basque region of northern Spain who were cared for by local volunteers

1,784: In 2006 a blue heritage plaque was erected on the lower leg of the west tower of Hull's Tidal Surge Barrier to offer information about the river's source and the possible origins of its name. The inscription reads:

> The river Hull rises on the Wolds near Elmswell and flows southwards to enter the Humber. The name Hull may originate from old Scandinavian for 'Deep One' or Celtic for 'Muddy One'

1,785: On 2 January 2007, at the funeral of former US President Gerald Ford, in Washington, Hull-born John Bacchus Dykes' 'Eternal Father, strong to save' was sung by the Armed Forces Chorus with the United States Marine Orchestra. At other services, with music selected by President and Mrs Ford, two other Dykes tunes were played: 'Holy, Holy, Holy' and 'Nearer, my God, to Thee'.

1,786: On 2 January 2007 Hull's former National Picture Theatre, England's only surviving ruin of a Blitzed civilian building, was designated a Grade II Listed Building (List entry number: 1391850) under the Planning (Listed Buildings and Conservation Areas) Act 1990.

1,787: In January 2007 Hull City confirmed caretaker manager Phil Brown as their new full-time manager. Following the departure of Phil Parkinson, in December 2006, Brown had steered City out of the relegation zone, bringing Dean Windass back to the club (on loan from Bradford City) within weeks of taking over as manager.

1,788: The Rank company, founded by Hull-born Joseph Rank in 1875, acquired Hovis-McDougall in 1962, subsequently becoming Rank Hovis McDougall Limited, which itself was acquired by Premier Foods (for £1.2bn) in March 2007.

1,789: In the devastating Hull floods of 2007, during a run of *Starlight Express*, the basement level dressing rooms at the Hull New Theatre were flooded causing four performances of the show to be cancelled to give time for the replacement of the specialist roller skates required by the performers.

1,790: On 24 July 2007 Northern European Leisure (Yorkshire) Ltd., owner of the Tower, was prosecuted by Hull City Council for failing to comply with a Listed Building Enforcement Notice (served in October 2006) to replace the two decorative domes which it had removed from the building in 2003. The company was fined £2,000 and ordered to pay £500 costs by Hull Magistrates' Court.

1,791: Following shareholder approval, Kingston Communications changed its name to KCOM GROUP PLC in August 2007, though the company retained the Kingston Communications brand for use with the group's business activities in the Hull and Yorkshire area.

1,792: On 2 September 2007 the KC Stadium recorded its highest attendance for a rugby match, for the local derby between Hull FC and Hull Kingston Rovers. A crowd of 23,004 saw Rovers beat FC 42-6 in the Super League.

1,793: On 9 November 2007 the 7-screen Reel Cinema opened in the recently built St. Stephen's shopping centre (opened 20 September 2007) at Ferensway, Hull. Each of the 7 screening rooms is equipped with dolby digital surround sound, and 'modern seating' for watching 'the latest releases in absolute comfort'. Formerly part of the Curzon Leisure Group Ltd. (Est 1999) the Loughborough-based, family-owned, independent cinema company was rebranded as Reel Cinemas in 2005. The company runs a chain of 15 cinema venues, the Hull venue being the second most northerly after York.

1,794: On 21 December 2007 the Vue Hull cinema opened on the top floor of the Princes Quay shopping centre. This 10-screen 1,694-seat venue, with auditorium seating capacities ranging from 110 to 245, was one of the first fully digital cinemas in Europe. Boasting two 3D screens (screens 1 and 10), and 'Sony 4K digital camera experience', with 'four times the megapixels of 2K and HD', the venue also provided Dolby 'Profound Sound' and 4 wheelchair bays at the front in all its auditoria with over 175 seating capacity; and two front wheelchair bays provided in its auditoria having fewer than 175 seats; with all screens being fully digital and fitted with Dolby Digital 6.1 Surround Sound.

1,795: Following the relocation of Hull FC to the new Kingston Communications Stadium in 2002 there were talks of the demolition of The Boulevard, but it re-opened as a greyhound racing venue in 2007. This venture was short-lived, lasting only until the stadium finally closed. The Boulevard was eventually demolished in 2010.

1,796: In 2007 a blue heritage plaque was erected on the inside of the north wall of Paragon Interchange, to mark the site of the former timber railway offices. The inscription reads:

> Two storey timber railway offices, built in 1904, stood against the red brick area of this wall and were dismantled in 2006 to accommodate the Paragon Interchange, opened in 2007

1,797: On Sunday 27 January 2008 the St. Andrews Dock Heritage Park Action Group (STAND) held its annual memorial service at St Andrews Quay for the city's lost trawlermen. The following week a city-wide minute's silence (organized by STAND) was observed to commemorate the 40th anniversary of the Triple Trawler Tragedy in which the Hull trawlers St. Romanus (H223), Kingston Peridot (H591) and Ross Cleveland (H61) were all lost over a period of 25 days in 1968.

1,798: On 27 February 2008 Joanna Carolyn Richardson (*née* Martin), joint Managing Director of ARCO (and, with her cousin Tom, the fourth-generation of the Martin family to run the company) died after a 'prolonged and dignified battle with cancer'.

1,799: Following the death of Joanna Richardson on 27 February 2008, Nick Hildyard was appointed joint Managing Director of ARCO; when he retired in 2012, he was replaced by the company's sales and marketing director Neil Jowsey.

1,800: On 18 March 2008, having undergone surgery the previous week to remove cancer of the tonsils and neck, University of Hull alumnus Anthony Minghella died of a haemorrhage in Charing Cross Hospital, Hammersmith.

1,801: On 1 May 2008 PD Ports (formerly Powell Duffryn), who began operating in Hull in 1990, entered into a new 8-year agreement—in respect of its ongoing operation of the Hull Container Terminal—with Associated

British Ports, committing to invest £4m within 12 months. In 2005 PD Ports handled around 125,000 twenty-foot equivalent units of cargo, increasing to around 150,000 units by April 2008.

1,802: On 24 May 2008 Hull City played Bristol City in the Football League Championship play-off final, at Wembley Stadium. In the 38th minute, the Tigers' local hero (and Man of the Match) Dean Windass scored the only goal, thereby ensuring promotion to the Premier League and top-tier football for the first time in the club's history.

1,803: On 30 August 2008 Hull FC were runners-up in the Challenge Cup for the eleventh time in the club's history when they were beaten 28-16 by St. Helens in front of 82,821 spectators, at Wembley Stadium.

1,804: Hull Freedom Festival is an annual, free, three-day live arts and music festival that celebrates freedom in all its forms. The lasting legacy of Hull's 2007 bicentenary celebrations of the Abolition of the Slave Trade Act—which heralded the abolition of the slave trade across the British Empire—and inspired by the work of Hull's anti-slavery campaigner William Wilberforce, the Freedom Festival's inaugural event took place on Saturday 30 August 2008.

1,805: In November 2008 Hull City Council announced a five-year deal that would see Hull Screen being transferred to a new home at one of the screening rooms of the Reel cinema in the newly built St. Stephen's shopping centre. The last film screened at the old George Street venue was *Cinema Paradiso*.

1,806: As a result of an adjudication by the Premier League's Dubious Goals Committee in December 2008, the Hull City player with the record for being the club's oldest goalscorer in a League game is Dean Windass, who was 39 years and 235 days old when he scored an 89th minute equalizer in the Tigers' 2-2 draw against Portsmouth, at Fratton Park, on 22 November 2008. The decision also makes Windass the second oldest goalscorer (after Teddy Sheringham) in the history of the Premier League.

1,807: Hull's East Park underwent a £10m refurbishment programme, completed in 2008, in which many features, including the maze, ornamental gardens, and the Grade II listed Wicksteed splash boat, were restored. Part of the cost of the refurbishments was met by a Heritage Lottery Fund grant of £6.4m.

1,808: In 2008 the University of Hull named a converted former TV studio (at the back of the Gulbenkian Theatre) after Anthony Minghella. The studio was opened by playwright Alan Plater CBE, a visiting Professor at the University's drama department, on 7 November. Plater also unveiled a photographic tribute to (and of) Minghella.

1,809: In 2008, 50,000 tickets were sold in one day for the Hull Truck Theatre Company's production of *Bouncers*, their final production at the Spring Street Theatre. The production, which opened on 15 January 2009, generated £127,000 through ticket sales, breaking all previous box-office records. The play's final performance at the Spring Street Theatre was on 14 February 2009.

1,810: On 21 April 2009 Hull-based William Jackson Bakery Ltd., which exports its products to over 22 countries, was awarded The Queen's Award for Enterprise: International Trade (Export) (2009) 'for bakery products'.

1,811: When the area in which Hull Truck's Spring Street Theatre venue was located was due to be cleared for redevelopment, the decision was made to move to a new £14.5m purpose-built theatre, part of the new St. Stephen's shopping centre development in the more central Ferensway. The new venue opened on 23 April 2009, with the first production in the new premises, the première of *Funny Turns* by John Godber, beginning on 25 April.

1,812: By April 2009 the Tower Cinema on Anlaby Road had re-opened as a night club, and the two illegally removed domes (2003) had been replaced with inferior moulded versions.

1,813: At the end of the 2009 season Hull KR achieved their highest ever position in the Super League when they finished fourth with 35 points, behind Leeds Rhinos (42 points), St. Helens (38), and Huddersfield Giants (36).

1,814: In 2009, before she started making a name for herself on the comedy circuit, Hull writer and comedian Lucy Beaumont featured in the music video for a song titled 'Fallow Field' by Hull band The Notebook. The video was uploaded to YouTube on 7 June 2009.

1,815: On 3 September 2009 Hull Screen hosted a VIP Champagne reception to mark the occasion of its relocation to the Reel Cinema in the St. Stephen's shopping centre. The occasion was celebrated with the screening of Pedro Almodóvar's most recent offering *Broken Embraces*.

1,816: In September 2009 Heron Frozen Foods Ltd. relocated to its purpose built National Distribution Centre adjacent to the A63, at Jackson Way, Melton, East Yorkshire.

1,817: On 29 October 2009, following a disappointing start to the 2009–10 season, along with speculation surrounding Hull City's finances—with accounts being filed five months late and figures showing concern about the club's 'ability to continue as a going concern'—Paul Duffen stepped down as the club's Chairman, with Adam Pearson being confirmed as the new Executive Chairman on 2 November.

1,818: On 29 September 2009 Heron Frozen Foods Ltd. acquired 53 Cool Trader stores from Iceland Foods Ltd.

1,819: On 1 December 2009 the St. Andrews Dock Heritage Park Action Group (STAND), after weeks of infighting, ousted its long-standing (15 years) Chairman, Adam Fowler, during a general meeting attended by 60 members of the group, replacing him with retired schoolmaster Charles Pinder. STAND's legal adviser, Ken Platten, a solicitor and lecturer in Law at Hull University, resigned in protest at the treatment received by, and the 'aggression' shown towards, Adam Fowler.

1,820: The main auditorium of the Hull Truck Theatre in Ferensway has a maximum capacity of 429, while its Studio Theatre has a capacity of 144. Notwithstanding the additional 147 seats, the distance from the stage to the back row of the main auditorium in the new building is less than 6 feet greater than that of the old Spring Street Theatre.

1,821: In 2009 Paul Bull, a mosaic artist based in Chipping Sodbury, was finally given the go-ahead to proceed with the construction of replacements for the two illegally removed domes of the Tower Cinema on Anlaby Road. The work took six weeks just to set out on paper, with the domes eventually taking 943 hours to complete (Paul Bull worked alone). Bull commented : '...the total number of tesseray was around 129,000 all stuck down one at a time'. Toffolo & Son fixed the mosaic to the domes.

1,822: In 2009 the facilities of the 10,000m² covered steel terminal located at the north east arm of King George Dock were extended to accommodate cargoes of Dry Bulk commodities, forest products and paper. Consequently the terminal was renamed the Hull All-Weather Terminal.

1,823: The Boulevard stadium, home of Hull FC rugby club for well over a century, closed in 2009.

1,824: Hull-born actor Ian Gillett Carmichael, once described by P.G. Wodehouse as the definitive Bertie Wooster, died of natural causes at his family home in Grosmont, North Yorkshire on 5 February 2010. He was 89 years old.

1,825: On 12 February 2010, two-and-a-half years after the closure of the Kwik Save supermarket on the site of the former Priory Cinema, the building was re-opened as the Just Save indoor market which included a butcher, a fruit and vegetable store, a café and a mini supermarket. The 20,119 sq. feet indoor market was 'unveiled' by Boothferry Ward councillor Patricia Ellis.

1,826: In March 2010, with Hull City's form deteriorating once again, and the team sinking into the relegation zone of the Premier League, manager Phil Brown's services were dispensed with before Ian Dowie was appointed temporary Football Management Consultant on 17 March. City's 0-0 draw against Liverpool at the KC Stadium on 9 May confirmed their relegation back into the Championship League after two seasons in the top tier.

1,827: On 29 June 2010 former Leicester City manager Nigel Pearson was appointed manager of Hull City, replacing Ian Dowie, whose short tenure had coincided with City's relegation from the Premier League.

1,828: On the morning of Saturday 25 September 2010 Hull FC fans were given the opportunity to claim a piece of their club's heritage when 400 seats from the old Threepenny Stand were offered free of charge on a 'first-come, first-served' basis. The give-away was organized by FC Voices, a voluntary group which represents Hull FC fans. The group had secured an arrangement with Hull City Council by which the seats from the former stand were made available for fans to keep as mementos. All 400 seats were snapped up within twenty minutes.

1,829: On 3 October 2010 Paul Bull's newly created tessellated domes for the Tower Cinema on Anlaby Road were installed in their rightful place on top of the corner towers of the theatre, replacing the illegally removed (2003) original domes.

1,830: The Martin Jennings statue of Philip Larkin at Paragon Interchange was unveiled on 2 December 2010—during the Larkin25 year of commemorative activities—by David Gemmell the Lord Mayor of Hull.

1,831: On 3 December 2010 plans were unveiled to attract major wind turbine manufacturers to Hull. The £100m Green Port Hull initiative to redevelop the city's Alexandra Dock was the result of a partnership between Associated British Ports, Hull City Council, the East Riding of Yorkshire Council and the University of Hull.

1,832: Work to demolish the grain silo at Hull's King George Dock began in December 2010.

1,833: It had originally been intended that the recording of The Who's Hull City Hall concert of 15 February 1970 would be the band's 'live' album release later that year, but it was initially thought that John Entwistle's bass had not been recorded; so, despite preferring the Hull performance, the band decided to release the Leeds recording instead as

Live at Leeds. It was subsequently discovered that only the first few songs of the Hull performance were missing the bass; so to rescue the recording, the bass track from the previous evening's performance at Leeds was spliced into the Hull City Hall recording—only where it was required. The Who's Hull City Hall performance was included as part of the *Live at Leeds* Super Deluxe Edition CD release for the first time in 2010.

1,834: Besides the Grade II listed North Bridge Dry Dock, a second of the city's historic dry docks remains: No.1 Dry Dock, just south of the former basin to Queen's Dock.

1,835: The port of Hull has the UK's first fully enclosed cargo-handling facility, enabling protected handling for the full range of weather sensitive cargoes.

1,836: By 2010, in addition to its All-Weather Terminal, the port of Hull was providing further steel and metal cargo handling facilities at a number of other terminals, operated by Ahlmark Shipping UK Ltd. and NW Trading Ltd. in King George Dock; Rix Shipping Co. Ltd. in Alexandra Dock; and Harding Cargo Handling Ltd. in Albert & William Wright Docks.

1,837: The efficient handling of liquid bulk cargoes has become an increasingly significant service at the port of Hull, with a wide range of edible oils, petroleum-based products and chemicals moving through the port. Facilities are available for bulk liquids to be easily transferred to road or marine tankers.

1,838: The storage facilities at the port of Hull for general cargo incorporate over 40 transit sheds covering 230,000m², and 65 ha. of open storage.

1,839: Finnlines Ferries operates a regular service from the port of Hull to Helsinki, Hamina and Rauma in Finland.

1,840: The port of Hull provides the only passenger service available from the Humber estuary.

1,841: P&O operates daily Hull-Rotterdam/Europort (Terminal 1) and Hull-Zeebrugge/Bruges (Terminal 2) ferry crossings for freight, vehicles, and passengers from Hull's King George Dock.

1,842: In 2010 there were eleven Ro-Ro berths in the enclosed docks at Hull: one at Alexandra Dock, and ten at King George and Queen Elizabeth Docks. A further port of Hull Ro-Ro berth was available on the Humber, outside the enclosed dock system.

1,843: Associated British Ports (ABP) operate the 24,000m² high-specification Hull Cold Store at Hull's King George Dock, with a 10,000-pallet capacity, and the capability to freeze products down to -25°C. It also has European Food Safety Inspection Service (EFSIS) cold store quality accreditation and United States Department of Agriculture (USDA) approval.

1,844: With an annual throughput of approximately 260,000 twenty-foot equivalent units (TEU), the Hull Container Terminal at Queen Elizabeth Dock is the port of Hull's main dock for handling container traffic. Providing 300 metres of quay for its three main container operators: Samskip, EuroAfrica Shipping Lines, and Finnlines. With the facility to allow three vessels to be berthed simultaneously, the Container Terminal storage facilities can accommodate all types of container from hazardous materials to refrigerated goods.

1,845: The main reasons Hull's Alexandra Dock was selected as the most suitable location for the development of a wind turbine manufacturing plant are: it already had existing planning permission for development; the suitability of its existing infrastructure; and its proximity to the three main proposed offshore wind development zones in the UK, each comprised of thousands of wind turbines.

1,846: One of the biggest productions at the Hull New Theatre was *Chitty Chitty Bang Bang*, in June 2010, which during the show required 30 backstage staff— including dressers, hair and make-up, fly men, sound and light engineers, stage movers etc.

1,847: On 20 January 2011 Siemens announced that they had signed a memorandum of understanding in connection with Associated British Ports' proposed Green Port Hull development at Hull's Alexandra Dock, stating that Siemens and ABP had agreed to work together to develop plans for the construction at the port of Britain's first offshore wind turbine manufacturing plant.

1,848: In 2011 Hull-based ARCO, the UK's leading supplier of workplace safety equipment, produced a 'Calender Girls'-style calendar to raise funds for the Jo Martin Cancer Care Trust, set up following the death of the company's joint MD Joanna Richardson who died of breast cancer in 2008. Around 60 female employees from across the country volunteered to 'reveal all' for the calendar.

1,849: In February 2011 Gareth Tudor Price, Artistic Director of the Hull Truck Theatre Company, was made redundant. The company's Chief Executive, Andrew Smaje, had controversially decided to dispense altogether with the role of Artistic Director. In support of Tudor Price, playwright John Godber ended his long association with Hull Truck in December 2010, commenting: 'In support of his position I have voted with my feet and left Hull Truck after 26 years'.

1,850: In its first year of trading (year ended 31 March 2011) City Health Care Partnership Community Interest Company—incorporated on 8 June 2007 by its sole director at the time, Leeds-based entrepreneur Andrew Lawrence Burnell, to 'carry on its activities for the benefit of the community, or a section of the community'—recorded net cash from operating activities of £6,688,056, with a profit before tax of £491,229.

1,851: In its first year of trading City Health Care Partnership CIC posted Administration staff expenses of £105, Operation staff expenses of £1,348, and 'Directors' remuneration and other benefits' of £393,077, with emoluments for the highest paid director recorded at £115,799. Also included in the company's Financial Statement for that period was the note: 'Other reserves of £1,466,471 are non-distributable and represent the net current assets transferred from NHS Hull on 1 June 2010'.

1,852: In April 2011 an exhibition titled *Within These Walls* was opened at Hull Prison detailing the chequered history of the Hedon Road prison. The exhibition was the idea of prison officer Rob Nicholson following his discovery in 2000 of a book about the prison. However, it took ten years for the Prison Service authorities to give their approval for the exhibition to go ahead.

1,853: On 9 May 2011 a statue of Sir Leo Schultz was unveiled in a niche to the west elevation of Hull's Guildhall. In a Planning & Listed Building Consent Application compiled by NPS-Humber Ltd. in August 2009 for the installation of the statue, Sir Leo Schultz is attributed with coining the sentiment: 'Some may think Hull is at the end of the line—but I know and tell you that the line starts from Hull'.

1,854: In June 2011 queues formed outside Hull's Ferens Art Gallery for the opening of an exhibition of David

Hockney's *Bigger Trees*. Attended by the artist in person, the exhibition (which ran until 18 September) drew over 2,000 visitors in its first weekend alone. The exhibition was eventually seen by over 63,000 people.

1,855: Jean Hartley (*née* Holland), publisher, artist, editor and writer, died on 18 July 2011. A memorial celebration of Jean's life took place on 14 August 2011 at The Royal Station Hotel, Hull, where guest speakers included Jean's granddaughter, Sarah Hartley, and Jean's friends, Barrie Rutter, Anthony Thwaite, Daphne Glazer, Pam Flynn, David Keating, Elaine Sommerville, Marita Staite, and Graham Chesters. The Philip Larkin Society's journal *About Larkin* of October 2011 carried a report on the memorial celebration, including a centre-spread of photographs of Jean at various times in her life.

1,856: In November 2011 former Tigers and England player Nick Barmby was appointed caretaker manager of Hull City when Nigel Pearson left to return to his old job at Leicester City. With the team performing well in the first few months of Barmby's tenure, he was given the full-time job; but a relatively disappointing 8th position saw Barmby being sacked shortly after the close of the 2011–12 season.

1,857: Towards the end of the summer of 2011, a £10m refurbishment of the Hull Tidal Surge Barrier was completed, its first overhaul since it was opened in 1980. The majority of the work was scheduled so that it could be carried out over 40 consecutive days in 2009 and a similar period in 2010 when the likelihood of a tidal surge was low. The contractors had assembled the mechanical equipment (used to raise or lower the barrier) in the factory prior to the commencement of the refurbishment. The final schedule of work involved the replacement of window frames and their glazed panels.

1,858: Before it was demolished in 2011 the grain silo at Hull's King George Dock, when working at full capacity, was capable of processing grain from 320 lorries, or 8,000 tonnes, per day.

1,859: A 2011 Environmental Impact Report for the Green Port Hull development stated that the project would require the infill of parts of Alexandra Dock to create additional port operational land to accommodate the shipping of wind turbine components, along with the reclamation of land from the river Humber for use as a facility for the import and export of wind turbines and their components. The infill material required for the above projects was estimated at 780,000m³ and 360,000m³ respectively.

1,860: The National Census of 2011 reported the population of the unitary authority of Hull as 256,406.

1,861: Between 2002–14 over 1m people went to see the annual pantomime at the Hull New Theatre. The theatre's 75th anniversary souvenir brochure named the 2011/12 production of *Cinderella* starring the Chuckle Brothers as the theatre's most successful pantomime up to that point.

1,862: The pre-publicity for BBC Radio 1's 'take over' of Hull in January 2012 stated that the broadcasts would primarily be centred around the BBC *Introducing* branded programmes and presenters such as Zane Lowe, Huw Stephens, Fearne Cotton etc. Disappointingly, the original BBC Media Centre Press Release, announcing 'a series of huge nights from across the musical spectrum!', listed no 'local' bands amongst the line-up; Leeds-based Pulled Apart By Horses being the nearest to a local band programmed to take part.

1,863: During the January 2012 Radio 1 'take over' of Hull, just one local artist, Endoflevelbaddie, was eventually scheduled to play live—on the Zane Lowe show broadcast from the New Adelphi Club on the evening of Thursday 26 January. [Local BBC *Introducing* presenter Alan Raw became the drummer with Endoflevelbaddie in 2013.]

1,864: During the January 2012 Radio 1 'take over' of Hull, one additional local band (Late Night Fiction) was slotted in for the live broadcast from the New Adelphi Club, as support for Leeds-based Pulled Apart By Horses. The line-up for the series of broadcasts from across Hull included 8 artists from London, plus artists from Bristol, Glasgow, France, and Perth (Australia), most of whom had been championed by the national Radio 1 *Introducing* programmes for some time. In the event, the recorded music of another local band (Mr Beasley) was also played during the live broadcast from the New Adelphi Club on the 26 January.

1,865: On the BBC Radio 1 Fearne Cotton show of Wednesday 25 January 2012, the day before the start of BBC Radio 1's 'take over' of Hull, the guitarist (mistakenly introduced as the singer) of local band The Hubbards was interviewed over the phone by the presenter, who played just one of the band's tracks. Cotton talked at length about the good work of the BBC *Introducing* brand, both locally and nationally, but spoke very little about local musicians and bands. She mentioned the name of the local BBC *Introducing* presenter, Alan Raw, more times than she mentioned The Hubbards, the band whose member she was interviewing.

1,866: In November 2004 former Hull FC player and coach Johnny Whiteley was added to the Rugby Football League Roll of Honour; and he was awarded an honorary degree (Doctor of Science, *honoris causa*) from the University of Hull in a ceremony that took place on 27 January 2012.

1,867: On 2 June 2012 the Grade II listed Wicksteed splash boat at East Park re-opened, following a two-year £35,000 restoration programme, after being damaged in an accident.

1,868: On 8 June 2012 former Manchester United centre-back, and Sunderland manager, Steve Bruce was confirmed as Hull City's new manager. Bruce led City back into the Premier League in his first season as manager when City secured automatic promotion by drawing 2-2 with league winners Cardiff City on 4 May 2013, the final day of the season.

1,869: On 16 June 2012 it was announced that Hull-born singer and entertainer Joe Longthorne had been appointed MBE, for his charity work.

1,870: On 17 June 2012 comedian Michael McIntyre brought his show to the Hull New Theatre. Tickets had sold out within a couple of hours, making it the theatre's fastest selling show in recent years.

1,871: Hull fundraiser Jean Bishop (aka The Bee Lady) has been shaking a collection box on behalf of Age UK, Hull since 1999, three years after the death of her husband. On 18 June 2012, on day 31 of the Summer Olympics torch relay, Jean, at the age of 90, became one of the oldest 2012 Olympic torch-bearers. At that point Jean had raised around £87,000 of her £100,000 target.

1,872: On Friday 13 July 2012 a lease was signed between Hull City Council and Threadneedle Investments, the then owners of St Andrews Quay, securing the site for the St. Andrews Dock Heritage Park Action Group (STAND)'s Lost Trawlermen's Memorial. Threadneedle Investments subsequently sold St Andrews Quay to Orchard Street Investment Management for £95.55m.

1,873: On Saturday 11 August 2012 Hull boxer Luke Campbell won an Olympic Gold medal in London.

1,874: On Monday 13 August 2012, in honour of Luke Campbell's Olympic Gold Medal win, the Royal Mail issued a special commemorative stamp. The stamp was the twenty-eighth Gold Medal stamp to be issued by Royal Mail and was available at three Hull Post Office branches and a total of 500 branches across the UK on 13 August and another 4,700 branches within the following week.

1,875: On Friday 24 August 2012 Luke Campbell, and Olympic hammer throw finalist Alex Smith cut the ribbon to officially open the Tokyo nightclub at the former Tower Picture Palace on Anlaby Road.

1,876: On Saturday 25 August 2012 dance and club artist Example officially launched the Tokyo nightclub in the former Tower Picture Palace on Anlaby Road. The refurbishments by Tokyo Industries included an 8 feet high sound system and twin level sky-deck, and an outside bar.

1,877: Graham Ibbeson's statue of David Whitfield, sited in Kingston Square opposite the entrance to Hull's New Theatre, was unveiled by the singer's widow, Sheila Whitfield, on 31 August 2012.

1,878: The Humber Street Sesh is an annual one-day free music and arts festival scheduled in August. The festival, which first took place in 2012, is an extension of The Sesh original-music night, which Mark Page founded in 2001 at the Linnet and Lark pub on Princes Avenue. Its stated aims are: To promote and celebrate the excellence and diversity of Hull's Creative Community; to assist in the regeneration and development of the urban cultural quarter based around Humber Street and its surrounding area; and to inspire future generations to engage and embrace music and the arts, leaving a lasting legacy within the city.

1,879: In August 2012 BBC News announced that the St. Andrews Dock Heritage Park Action Group (STAND) would run a competition for the design of a permanent memorial to the lost trawlermen of Hull, and that STAND 'hoped' the memorial would be unveiled in April 2014. STAND Chairman, Charles Pinder was quoted as saying: 'The memorial will be designed to ensure that this becomes a special place to preserve the memories of thousands of men who lost their lives fishing on Hull's trawlers'.

1,880: In September 2012 Hull Trinity House Academy relocated to the Derek Crothall Building, on George Street (almost opposite its junction with Wilberforce Drive), facilitating an increase in the numbers of pupils the school can accommodate, from 300 to 600.

1,881: In 2012 Hull's Ferens Art Gallery hosted the *Ten Drawings* exhibition of work by Leonardo da Vinci. Running from 10 November through to 20 January 2013, the exhibition attracted approximately 53,000 visitors and featured (suspended from the balcony of the gallery's Centre Court) a sculpture of Leonardo's Flying Machine. The sculpture—on display from Monday 15 October—was made, from recycled material, by artists Michael and Helen Scrimshaw of The Ropewalk Arts Centre in Barton, North Lincolnshire.

1,882: In October 2012 it was announced that, due to the planning process and uncertainty about the government's renewable energy policy, the signing of the deal to build the £210m Siemens wind turbine factory at Green Port Hull had been delayed until 2013.

1,883: On 12 November 2012 Hull writer and comedian Lucy Beaumont won BBC Radio 2's New Comedy Award, at Blackpool's Grand Theatre. Broadcast live on BBC Radio 2, the event's other five finalists were Matt Rees,

Matt Winning, Sunil Patel, Pete Otway and Tommy Rowson. Each of the finalists performed a seven minute set, before the listening public voted via the BBC website or by SMS (text). The winning prize included £1,000 and a commission with BBC Radio Comedy.

1,884: In November 2012 with an air of some mystery, two years after taking up his role as Chief Executive, Andrew Smaje parted company with the Hull Truck Theatre Company leaving no-one in obvious control.

1,885: By December 2012 all but one of the firms previously based at Hull's Alexandra Dock site had completed their relocation in preparation for the Green Port Hull redevelopment. The exception was the ship repair firm MMX, which operates from a dry dock unaffected by the new Siemens development.

1,886: In 2012 the former home of Christopher Pickering, one of Hull's best known benefactors, was sold in a sealed-bid auction for £105,000 to Simon Kelsey and his partner Catherine Robinson. The property, at 114 Coltman Street, built in 1854 by Benjamin Musgrave, was occupied by Christopher Pickering between 1874–90. The couple (who were married mid-project, in August 2013) struck a deal with Hull City Council which meant that ownership of the property would not be transferred to them until the restoration had been completed and approved by the Council.

1,887: In James Hale's 2012 BBC 4 film *David Bowie and the Story of Ziggy Stardust* (narrated by Jarvis Cocker) Steve Harley, in relation to Mick Ronson, commented: "He was one of the great rock musicians, in history—ever: as an arranger, a piano player as well; it must have been like having Stravinsky in your band". In the same film Elton John paid a similar tribute: "For me he was the best guitarist around in those days; I mean he was *THE* guitarist to have. And he contributed so much, 'cause he looked great, too".

1,888: In 2012 the Health Profile for Kingston upon Hull, produced by the Department of Health, concluded that the health of people in the city was 'generally worse than the England average' with 'higher than average' deprivation, and 'about 16,700 children [living] in poverty'. It also highlighted the fact that 'Life expectancy for both men and women is lower than the England average'. Although many figures in relation to key health concerns had shown an improvement in the preceding ten years, the health of people in Hull continued, in general, to be worse than the England average, with the key priorities being identified as smoking, obesity and alcohol.

1,889: Before the introduction of computerised ticketing systems, tickets for productions at the Hull New Theatre were written in longhand as they were sold; usherettes placed *Reserved* notices on all the 'sold in advance' seats. Nowadays, seats can be purchased via the Hull City Council website at www/hullcc.gov.uk/hullnewtheatre. In 2012 the theatre joined twitter: @newtheatrehull.

1,890: In 2012 the former Priory Cinema was converted into the Haus&Home furniture store, but in October 2013 a planning application was made to Hull City Council for a change of use of the first floor of the building from ancillary storage into D2 (entertainment and leisure) use. On 11 December 2013 the change of use application was approved. The premises were subsequently occupied by pole4fitness and the Art of Fitness Champions Gym.

1,891: In honour of Luke Campbell's Olympic Gold Medal win, the Royal Mail painted gold a post box near Campbell's Hessle Road home.

1,892: In honour of Luke Campbell's Olympic Gold Medal win Kingston Communications (KC) painted gold the telephone box nearest to the boxing club of which Campbell was a member.

1,893: Hull's Olympic Gold Medal winning bantamweight boxer Luke Campbell was appointed MBE, for services to boxing, in the Queen's New Year Honours list in 2013.

1,894: In March 2013 the St. Andrews Dock Heritage Park Action Group (STAND) launched its design competition for a permanent memorial for the lost trawlermen of Hull; the Hull City Council website issued a Press Release (dated 20 March 2013) announcing that Alan Johnson MP had agreed to join the panel of judges who would select the winning design.

1,895: On 19 April 2013 Hull Truck Theatre founder Mike Bradwell returned to direct the première of Tim Fountain's *Queen of the Nile*, a romantic comedy about two Hull lasses, Debbie and Jan, who travel out to Egypt as sex tourists.

1,896: On Tuesday 23 April 2013 it was reported that Hull's Olympic Gold Medal champion, Luke Campbell had agreed a deal to turn professional with promoter Eddie Hearn's Matchroom Sport.

1,897: On 26 April 2013 a planning application was made to Hull City Council for the demolition of the large single story frontage of the building, and the installation of new shop fronts, windows and rendering of walls to the former Priory Cinema. The work was to include the refurbishment of the frontage of the original cinema building. On 21 June 2013 Hull City Council approved the planning application.

1,898: George Gray retired from the University of Hull in 1990, becoming an Honorary Professor at Hull and a

Visiting Professor at Southampton University before moving to Poole and becoming Advanced Materials Consultant for Merck Ltd. He died on 12 May 2013, just two weeks after the death of his wife Marjorie.

1,899: In May 2013, six months after the departure of Chief Executive Andrew Smaje, the Hull Truck Theatre Company appointed Mark Babych as its new Artistic Director, a role that Smaje had dispensed with upon his appointment in 2010.

1,900: Following his attendance at the funeral service for ex-Spiders from Mars bass player Trevor Bolder in 2013, *Hull Daily Mail* reporter Angus Young called for 'a much more fitting permanent tribute to Hull's most famous rock band somewhere in their home city'. On 8 July 2014 the *Yorkshire Post* reported plans by Hull Council for £12.7m improvements to the city centre, including 'a new central performance stage in Queen's Gardens', but the plans were subsequently shelved until after 2017.

1,901: In July 2013 the three competing designs for a public memorial for the 6,000 Hull trawlermen lost at sea—to be sited at Hull's St Andrews Quay—were announced: 'Dress for the Weather' by FACTORY Architecture with artist Jacqueline Donachie; 'Lost and Found' by Plincke Landscape Ltd.; and 'Fathers, Sons and Mothers' by Colour Urban Design Limited. The three designs for the memorial, which were to be the centrepiece for the annual lost trawlermen's service held by the lock gates at St Andrews Quay, were displayed at Hull's Maritime Museum.

1,902: On Monday 29 July 2013 it was announced that the public memorial to commemorate Hull's 6,000 trawlermen lost at sea, to be sited at St Andrews Quay, would be 'Fathers, Sons and Mothers' by artist Gordon

Young. The centrepiece of a memorial public space designed by Colour Urban Design Limited, the sculpture was a representation of a cone-shaped fishing net.

1,903: On Friday 9 August 2013, Assem Allam, owner of Hull City, announced his plans to change the club's name to Hull Tigers in the belief that it would better enable the club to generate income from sponsorship and thereby make the club self-financing. However, on 9 April 2014 the Football Association Council announced their decision to reject the club's application for a name change.

1,904: Hull's Olympic Gold Medal champion Luke Campbell fought professionally for the first time on 13 July 2013. The fight, which took place in the open-air at Hull's Craven Park—in front of around 7,000 spectators—saw Campbell knock down his opponent Andy Harris twice before the referee stopped the contest after just 88 seconds.

1,905: On 24 August 2013 Hull FC made it a 'round dozen' times as runners-up in the Challenge Cup when they were beaten 16-0 by Wigan Warriors in front of 78,137 spectators at Wembley Stadium.

1,906: On Monday 9 September 2013 the Boulevard Academy opened its doors to pupils for the first time, welcoming year 7 pupils to the state-of-the-art academy built (in just 37 weeks) on the site of the former Boulevard rugby league stadium.

1,907: On 12 September 2013 over 300 photographs from the archive of the *Hull Daily Mail* were exhibited as The People's Gallery. The exhibition (in the former Peacocks store at 4-5 Whitefriargate), a joint enterprise involving *The Hull Daily Mail*, InterTech Media and Hull Civic Society, was the city's biggest ever free photographic exhibition.

1,908: On Thursday 19 September 2013 Hull FC recorded their heaviest defeat when they lost 18-76 away to Huddersfield Giants in the Super League preliminary semi-final play-off at the John Smith's Stadium, in front of 5,547 spectators.

1,909: On 8 October 2013 Hull fundraiser Jean Bishop (aka The Bee Lady) was presented with the Pride of Britain Fundraiser of the Year award by the stars of the celebrity dance TV show *Strictly Come Dancing*. At the ceremony, a celebrity audience helped Jean to surpass her £100,000 target by topping up the £91,500 she'd already raised with an additional £9,000—the largest donation (£2,500) coming from business woman celebrity Hilary Devey.

1,910: On 15 October 2013, outside the Carr Lane headquarters of KC, Hull fundraiser Jean Bishop unveiled a phone box that had been painted black and yellow in honour of her Pride of Britain Fundraiser of the Year award, which she had picked up the previous week.

1,911: On 20 November 2013 it was announced that Hull would be the UK City of Culture for 2017. The announcement was made in London by the UK Secretary of Culture, Media and Sport, Maria Miller.

1,912: On 5 December 2013 Hull suffered from the effects of a North Sea tidal surge, the level of which had not been seen in over 60 years. The surge, which coincided with high spring tides, resulted in record water levels along the east coast and in the region's tidal rivers. Over 400 properties in Hull and those parts of the East Riding adjacent to the north bank of the Humber were flooded.

1,913: During the tidal surge of 5 December 2013 Hull's Tidal Surge Barrier was within 40cm of being overtopped. Flood defences in Victoria Dock Village and St Andrews Quay were also under threat with water levels approaching their design limits, only narrowly avoiding being overwhelmed.

1,914: The peak level recorded at the Hull Tidal Surge Barrier during the North Sea tidal surge of 5 December 2013 was 5.8m AOD (above ordnance datum—i.e. above sea level). With the lowest levels of defence adjacent to the Albert Dock (at Riverside Quay) being just 5.04m AOD, the dock soon filled, and the water overflowed moving towards the city centre. Consequently, 115 businesses and 149 homes fell victim to flood damage during the surge, with flood water also affecting the English Street area and reaching Anlaby Road (to the north), St Andrews Quay Retail Park (to the west), and Victoria Dock Village (to the east).

1,915: Heron Frozen Foods recorded its first annual turnover of over £200m in the financial year ending 28 December 2013, when it recorded a turnover of £249,688,954 (up from £195m the previous year), making a gross profit of £27,754,620.

1,916: On 28 December 2013 Hull City recorded their biggest home victory in the Premier League when they beat Fulham 6-0, in front of 23,925 spectators at the KC Stadium.

1,917: In 2013 a blue heritage plaque was erected at 64–68 Anlaby Road, on the front (south facing) wall of the Tigers Lair—the former Emigrant Waiting Room. The inscription reads:

> Built in 1871 by the North Eastern Railway Company, the former Emigrant Waiting Room was used by Scandinavian & Jewish transmigrants en route to North America before the First World War

1,918: In 2013 plans proposed by Watergate Developments Ltd. (an associate company of Hull-based

Wykeland Group) to convert Hull's Central Dry Dock into an open-air amphitheatre entertainment venue were approved by Hull City Council. The Central Dry Dock, built for Gleadow's Shipyard in 1843 on the site of the old South End Battery of six guns that protected the old harbour, had been out of use since 1992. A start on the preparatory work to clear the dock of silt began in mid 2012.

1,919: In 2013, at Hull's King George Dock, construction began on a 1m tonne per year capacity, sea-to-rail biomass facility. The facility, with a 164 feet silo, was constructed by Hull's Spencer Group, and was built specifically to supply the recently converted (carbon-dense coal, to wood pellet biomass) Drax power station. The facility was officially opened in December 2014 by the Lord Mayor of Hull, Councillor Mary Glew.

1,920: The research carried out at Hull University by George Gray and his team enabled the development of a multi-billion pound LCD industry with an estimated 750 million associated products selling for a value in excess of £56 billion during 2013 alone.

1,921: On 8 February 2014 a memorial service took place at St Andrews Quay to mark the 40th anniversary of the sinking of the Hull trawler FV Gaul (H243) and the loss of her 36-man crew. Hundreds of people attended the service, which was organized by the RAOB (Hull Province) and held at the Bullnose at St Andrews Quay to commemorate those lost in the Barents Sea off the coast of Norway in 1974.

1,922: On 22 February 2014 Hull City recorded their biggest away victory in the Premier League when they beat Cardiff City 4-0, in front of a crowd of 26,167 at the Cardiff City Stadium.

1,923: On 25 March 2014 Siemens confirmed its intention and commitment to invest £160m in Green Port Hull at the city's Alexandra Dock and in a new blade factory in Paull, East Yorkshire. Associated British Ports also confirmed its agreement to invest £150m in the development. A Siemens spokesperson indicated that 550 jobs would be created at the Paull blade factory, and a further 450 at Green Port Hull.

1,924: On 23 April 2014 'Slipstream', a sculpture by London-born, twice Turner Prize nominee Richard Turner, was unveiled at Heathrow Airport. The 77 Tonne work of art—supported by four structural columns and suspended 18 metres above the ground in the Covered Court of Heathrow's new £2.5bn Terminal 2—comprised 23 separate sections, and was engineered and fabricated by Hull-based Commercial Systems International, off Marfleet Avenue.

1,925: An estimated 20 million people a year passing through Heathrow Airport will see Richard Turner's 'Slipstreem' sculpture. The artwork is reported to be 'Europe's largest privately funded sculpture' ; and at 70 metres is the 'longest piece of permanent art in Europe'. The sculpture was transported to Heathrow—in branded 'City of Culture' lorries—from the Marfleet Avenue works of Commercial Systems International Ltd.

1,926: In April 2014 the *Hull Daily Mail* reported that a 'confidential report' from 2010 revealed that Hull City Council were subsidizing, in the sum of £16.93, the cost of each ticket sold at the alternative film theatre Hull Screen.

1,927: On 3 May 2014 Hull City qualified for competitive European Football for the first time in the club's history. Everton's defeat at home against Manchester City secured Arsenal's place in the Championship League, resulting in the Tigers taking a place in Europe whether or not they beat Arsenal in the FA Cup final on 17 May.

1,928: Steve Bruce delivered again in 2013–14, his second season in charge, when Hull City reached the Final of the FA Cup for the first time in the club's history. In a cup run that saw City dispose of Middlesbrough, Sunderland and Sheffield United, they faced Arsenal in the Final at Wembley Stadium on 17 May 2014. City scored first after four minutes, through James Chester, and increased their lead after eight minutes with a goal from Curtis Davies; but goals from Arsenal's Santi Cazorla and Laurent Koscielny, forced the match into extra time. Aaron Ramsey decided it for Arsenal, four minutes into the second period of extra time.

1,929: Hull City Council withdrew funding for the Hull Screen cinema in its budget of May 2014, and Hull Screen has not screened any films since its contract expired in July 2014. With the disappearance of the city's only independent cinema, all hope of sustaining an 'art house' independent cinema in Hull has turned to Hull Independent Cinema Project (HICP): founded in 2012, formally constituted as a charity in April 2014, and becoming a Registered Charity on 14 September 2015. Since the loss of Hull Screen, HICP has presented screenings at various venues across the city, including Artlink (Princes Avenue) and Kardomah94 in the city centre.

1,930: On 4 June 2014 it was recommended that plans be approved to demolish the former Trinity House School and to create a short-stay car park and event space on the site. The space, named Zebedee's Yard (Zebedee Scaping was the school's Headmaster from 1854–1909) was opened in September 2015.

1,931: On 25 June 2014 a green Avenues and Pearson Park Residents' Association heritage plaque was erected at

82 Victoria Avenue, Hull, to mark the former home of Jean Hartley. The inscription reads:

> JEAN HARTLEY writer and publisher of Philip Larkin lived here from 1971 to 2011

1,932: Hull City's first competitive European match was in the Third Qualifying Round of the UEFA Europa League, away to FK AS Trenčín, of Slovakia, on 31 July 2014. The away leg at the Štadión na Sihoti finished 0-0; but a week later, on 7 August, City won the home leg 2-1 with goals from Ahmed Elmohamady and Sony Aluko taking them through to the play-off round of the competition.

1,933: In July 2014, following the separation of the artist (Gordon Young) and architects (Urban Colour Design) of the chosen design for the Lost Trawlermen's Memorial, Andrew Fenton, the owner of Hull design company InterTech, offered his company's design—which featured the profile of a stern trawler—free of charge to the St. Andrews Dock Heritage Park Action Group.

1,934: In August 2014 Hull City received a club record transfer fee when they sold Republic of Ireland international striker Shane Long to Southampton for a reputed £12.5m. Long had been with the Tigers for just seven months, having signed for the club in January 2014 from West Brom in a deal thought to be worth £7m. He had scored 4 times in 15 appearances for the Tigers.

1,935: On Thursday 23 August 2014 Hull City faced their second EUFA Europa League opponents, K.S.C. Lokeren Oost-Vlaanderen, in the play-off round of the competition. City lost 1-0 at the Daknamstadion in Lokeren, Belgium. They managed to win the home tie 2-1 on 28 August, but went out of the competition on the away-goal ruling.

1,936: One of Cuthbert Brodrick's last remaining buildings in Hull—Wellington House, at the corner of

Wellington Street and Queen Street—was demolished in August 2014.

1,937: In September 2014, as part of the planned new open-air amphitheatre development, Hull-based PBS Construction began work on a £350,000 contract to build a 650 tonne concrete and steel defence wall at the southern end of Hull's Central Dry Dock isolating it (and the Humber Street area generally) from the Humber. The work was expected to be completed by March 2015.

1,938: In September 2014, just before the transfer deadline, Hull City paid the club record transfer fee to sign Uruguayan striker Abel Hernández (24) from Palermo for £10m in a three year deal with an option for the club to extend the contract by a further 12 months.

1,939: In October 2014 the *Hull Daily Mail*, along with several national newspapers, ran a story about the imminent auction of Rembrandt's *Portrait of a Man with Arms Akimbo*, completed in 1658, suggesting it might have been painted whilst the artist was reputedly living in Hull. The *HDM* of 4 October quoted historian Simon Schama, the author of *Rembrandt's Eyes* (1999): 'The only definite documentary evidence we have was that he was seen in Hull in the early 1660s at a time when there are no records of him being in Amsterdam'. Further speculation appeared in *The Independent* of Friday 10 October, when it was reported that Rembrandt had been 'fleeing from a messy love life and bankruptcy' when he arrived 'in the Humber port in 1661, staying for a year'. (see fact 108 and fact 1,344)

1,940: Following the severe flooding caused by the North Sea tidal surge of 5 December 2013, work began on 12 November 2014 to strengthen the Albert Dock flood defences. The £6.6m project involved the Environment Agency constructing a 950m long, 1m high wall between Albert Dock and the Trans Pennine Trail, with a further 600m of defences being constructed elsewhere around the Port, as well as the sealing up of the disused and dilapidated Dunston Culvert.

1,941: On 21 November 2014 ARCO acquired the entire share capital of Total Access (UK) Limited for £10m; and on 10 July 2015 the company bought the entire share capital of Confined Space Training Services Limited for a 'potential total consideration of £1.9m'.

1,942: In November 2014 it was announced that the £100m contract for the civil engineering work at Green Port Hull had been awarded to a joint venture between national construction, asset management and project investment firm GRAHAM, and civil engineering and building contractors Lagan Construction Group.

1,943: In the company's Financial Statements for the period ending 27 December 2014, Heron Frozen Foods Ltd. recorded a turnover of £255m (up from £250m the previous year), with a gross profit of £27,635,291 and an operating profit of £2,254,956.

1,944: As a child, award winning actress Sheridan Smith—who in 2014 won both critical and public acclaim for her portrayal of Cilla Black in the TV drama *Cilla*—trained at the city's Northern Academy of Performing Arts, and once appeared at the Hull New Theatre in a production of *Annie*.

1,945: In an average year more than 170,000 people will see the productions at the Hull New Theatre.

1,946: The Hull New Theatre has an average of 14 front-of-house staff, 10 bar staff, 10 technical staff, and 2 Box Office staff on duty at each performance. The theatre sells more than 70,000 ice-creams each year.

1,947: In 2014 Hull City Council agreed to pay Reel

Cinemas £120,000 to release itself from a contractual obligation to fund the salary and pensions of three employees transferred to the cinema group from the council-funded Hull Screen in 2009, when Hull Screen was relocated within the Reel Cinema at the St. Stephen's shopping centre. The agreement had committed the council to paying £18,000 a year until 2024 for staff it no longer employed.

1,948: The automated technology used at the biomass silo at Hull's King George Dock can load, in just 35 minutes, 1,600 tonnes of material into 25 rail wagons as they pass through the tunnel at the base of the silo.

1,949: The biomass facility silo at Hull's King George Dock can store up to 1,800 tonnes of wood pellets and is filled by 60 truckloads of biomass over a three-hour period, twice a day, loading at the rate of 600 tonnes an hour.

1,950: Following the ignoring of a repair notice issued in December 2013 to Mr Saleem Hakim, owner of the former National Picture Theatre, Hull City Council decided (on 20 January 2015) to try to use a Compulsory Purchase Order to force Mr Hakim to sell them the site with the aim of transferring ownership to The National Civilian World War Two Trust, for development into a visitor attraction commemorating the Hull Blitz.

1,951: On 22 January 2015 Secretary of State for Energy, Ed Davey, led a 'ground-breaking' ceremony marking the commencement of construction of Siemens' offshore wind turbine manufacturing and assembly facilities at Green Port Hull.

1,952: In March 2015 the *Hull Daily Mail* reported Hull City Councillors 'have already voted ten to four in favour' of a design featuring a bell attached to a wooden pole for the STAND memorial to lost trawlermen; but former trawlermen and the wider fishing community raised objections to the design, complaining that the abstract design bore no relevance to either the trawlermen or the fishing industry. Subsequently, local sculptor Peter Naylor offered his more figurative design as an alternative.

1,953: On 17 March 2015 a ceremony was held at the site of the former Savoy Picture Theatre to mark the 70th anniversary of the death of 12 patrons of the cinema when they were fired upon by the machine guns of a German Heinkel 111 bomber towards the end of the Second World War. The management of the current business occupier of the site, W.M. Boyes & Co. Ltd., had previously installed a commemorative plaque on an exterior wall of their store.

1,954: In the financial year ended 31 March 2015 Cranswick PLC recorded a turnover in excess of £1bn for the first time (£1,003m); with a 'Profit before Tax' figure of £52,836,000, and the company employing more than 8,000 people across the Group.

1,955: In the financial year ending 25 April 2015 the *Aunt Bessie's* brand (owned by the Hull-based William Jackson Food Group), with more than 370 employees, had an annual turnover of over £70m, generating an operating profit of £8.5m.

1,956: The Hull City player with the record for being the club's oldest player in a League match is Steve Harper, who at 40 years and 60 days old, played in a 0-0 draw at home against Manchester United on 24 May 2015.

1,957: At the end of the 2014–15 season, following a brief, two-year spell in the Premier League, Hull City were relegated back to the Championship League when they drew 0-0 with Manchester United at the KC Stadium on 24 May, finishing third from bottom of the table after winning just eight of their thirty-eight games, and accumulating only 35 points. Elsewhere, Newcastle United beat West Ham 2-0, thereby securing (at the Tigers' expense) their own Premier League status for the 2015–16 season.

1,958: In its 'Consolidated Financial Statements' for the year ended 31 March 2015 City Health Care Partnership CIC (CHCP) listed the following companies as Group 'Subsidiaries', with CHCP holding 100% of the share capital of each: City Health Pharmacy Limited (nature of business: retail and dispensing pharmacist), Brocklehurst Chemist Limited (nature of business: retail and dispensing pharmacist), City Ventures Limited (nature of business: property rental), Tangerine Discretionary PCC Limited (nature of business: contingency and risk management), City Health Care Partnership Foundation (nature of business: incorporated charity limited by guarantee).

1,959: In its 'Consolidated Financial Statements' for the year ended 31 March 2015 City Health Care Partnership CIC (CHCP) listed the following companies as Associated companies, with CHCP holding 25% of the share capital of each: Albion Health Alliance Limited (nature of business: community and social care), Albion Care Alliance CIC (nature of business: community and social care).

1,960: In its 'Consolidated Financial Statement of Profit or Loss' for the year ended 31 March 2015 City Health Care Partnership Community Interest Company (incorporated on 8 June 2007 by its sole director at the time, Leeds-based entrepreneur Andrew Lawrence Burnell, to 'carry on its activities for the benefit of the community, or a section of the community') posted a profit of £1,497,251 on revenue of £70,350,792.

1,961: Following the issue of a Section 215 Notice by Hull City Council, the demolition began on Monday 1

June 2015 of the facade of the Albert Hall music hall in Midland Street. The building had been empty for more than 20 years. A survey carried out after a fire at the derelict former New York Hotel (the backs of the properties were next to each other) found the building to be in a potentially dangerous condition.

1,962: On 6 June 2015, 8 plaques and memorial benches commemorating the city's fishing heritage were unveiled at the Hessle Road end of the Boulevard. The benches commemorate the four women who came to be known as the 'Headscarf Revolutionaries': Lillian Bilocca, Yvonne Blenkinsop, Mary Denness and Christine Jensen MBE. The skippers of the ships lost in the Triple Trawler Tragedy of 1968 also had benches dedicated to their memory, along with the skipper of the Hull trawler FV Gaul (H243) and her 36-man crew, lost in February 1974.

1,963: On 19 June 2015 plans were announced to 'kick-start' the redevelopment of the city's former St. Andrew's Dock. The ambitious plans, which would see the site's owner John Levison team up with Andrew Fenton (owner of local commercial design company InterTech) included the possibility of clearing the silted-up dock and refilling it with water; but perhaps most significant was the stated 'first step' of the plan: to create a 'new historical feature reflecting the city's fishing heritage', called The Last Trip. The announcement pointed out that the proposals by STAND for a permanent Lost Trawlermen's Memorial on the nearby St Andrews Quay had stalled. Andrew Fenton commented: "STAND has their own memorial and good luck to them but this would be a completely separate project".

1,964: In January 2015, Hull's former National Picture Theatre was put up for auction by its owner Mr Saleem Hakim; but failed to sell, with bidding falling £3,000 short of the £60,000 reserve price. The theatre failed to sell at auction a second time on 26 June 2015, when bidding fell £1,500 short of the £40,000 reserve.

1,965: At the AGM of the St. Andrews Dock Heritage Park Action Group on 27 June 2015, members of the group voted-in a new committee, with STAND's former treasurer Ron Wilkinson being elected as acting Chairman replacing the outgoing Chair, Charles Pinder. Mr Wilkinson had resigned as the group's treasurer in July 2014, and had recently been extremely critical of the Silent Bell centrepiece for the proposed Lost Trawlermen's Memorial. This was the latest in a protracted series of incidents that raised questions about the competence of STAND, and their ability to deliver any kind of memorial to the city's 6,000 lost trawlermen. By 30 June Mr Wilkinson's position had been ratified and Anita Waddy had resumed the role of Secretary, a position she had resigned in March 2015.

1,966: As of 30 June 2015 Hull-based ARCO, the UK's leading safety company, had 45 branches, with a total operating profit after tax of £13.4m, on sales of £283,171m.

1,967: In July 2015 VolkerFitzpatrick were appointed as the contractor for Siemens' 431,000 sq. feet offshore wind turbine blade manufacturing facility at Green Port Hull, leading to the creation of around 200 construction jobs.

1,968: In March 2015 an independent panel, appointed by the Court of Arbitration for Sport, ruled that the Football Association Council's process by which the proposed name change from Hull City AFC to Hull Tigers was blocked had been 'flawed', and therefore the decision could not stand. However, in July 2015, following a meeting at St. George's Park, 69.9% of votes cast at an FA council meeting to consider the proposal rejected the club's application for a name change.

1,969: As of 19 August 2015, Heron Food Group Limited, the parent company of Heron Frozen Foods Limited, was owned equally by David, Andrew, and Michael Heuck (the sons of the company's founders, Malcolm and Sheila Heuck), each with a holding of 300,200 Ordinary Shares.

1,970: In 2015 Hull KR reached the final of the Rugby League Challenge Cup, where they were defeated 50-0 by Leeds Rhinos at Wembley Stadium on 29 August, in front of a crowd of 80,140. This was Rovers' fifth Wembley Challenge Cup final, and their first for almost 30 years.

1,971: In August 2015 InterTech, the company behind The Last Trip memorial to the city's fishing heritage, announced details of how people could sponsor one of the 90 chrome mini ship bows (resembling the bow of a trawler) cut into the design. People were invited to sponsor a full bow for £500, or half a bow for £250. Sponsors could have their bow engraved with wording of their own choosing. Also offered for sale were the 240 ship rivets used to hold the sculpture together. Those buying a rivet would have their names recorded on a separate plaque at the site. The Hull Bullnose Heritage Group was given responsibility of fundraising for the scheme.

1,972: In August 2015 Siemens awarded a construction contract at Green Port Hull—to build a 132,000 sq. feet service and logistics centre to act as a national wind power maintenance hub, and to store parts and equipment—to Scunthorpe firm Clugston.

1,973: On Saturday 19 September 2015, as part of Hull FC's 150th anniversary celebrations, a memorial was unveiled by the city's Lord Mayor, councillor Anita Harrison, in the grounds of the Boulevard Academy, marking the site of the former Boulevard rugby league stadium, the home of Hull FC for 107 years. The inscription of the memorial reads:

> This memorial marks the site of the famous Boulevard
> Stadium, home of Hull Rugby League Football Club from
> 1895 to 2002. Provided by Kingston Upon Hull City
> Council and by the supporters of the club, it also
> commemorates the last resting place of the many fans of
> Hull FC whose ashes were scattered at the ground
> throughout the years

The first verse of the Hull FC anthem 'Old Faithful' is
reproduced beneath the club's 150-year anniversary
badge.

1,974: A 'road rage' incident that took place on Hull's
Bransholme estate on 21 September 2015 became a viral
Internet sensation when the victim of the incident, Hull
motorcyclist Steve Middleton, uploaded to YouTube video
footage of the incident the following day. The perpetrator of
the 'road rage', Citroën driver and Grandfather-of-five,
Ronnie Pickering, was shown shouting abuse at Mr
Middleton, repeatedly asking "Do you know who I am?", and
shouting his own name "Ronnie Pickering". Within 48 hrs
the video had been watched by almost 2m people and had
made Mr Pickering's name known internationally, with
countless spoof versions of the video being produced by
YouTubers across the world. The incident was reported on
all the main TV news programmes, including BBC 2's
Newsnight.

1,975: On 16 October 2015 the University of Hull
officially opened the E.A. Milne Centre for Astrophysics,
a 'cutting-edge' research centre named in honour of the
Hull-born astrophysicist, mathematician and cosmologist
Edward Arthur Milne. The opening of the Centre, whose
Director is Professor Brad Gibson, saw around a dozen
members of the global astrophysics community gather at
the university for the ceremony. Around 70 guests,
including Milne's daughter Meg Weston Smith, along with

other family members, attended the launch of the Centre at the Art Gallery of the University of Hull's Brynmor Jones Library. Other invited guests included the Deputy Lord Major of Hull, Hull East MP Karl Turner, representatives from the Royal Navy, and the President of the Royal Astronomical Society.

1,976: On 28 November 2015 InterTech, the company behind The Last Trip memorial to the city's fishing heritage, announced that the sculpture, designed by InterTech owner Andrew Fenton, was under construction at steel fabricators W. Campbell and Son in Harpings Road, west Hull. The Last Trip was expected to be completed before Christmas. All the components of the sculpture were being made by Hull companies.

1,977: On Tuesday 1 December 2015, representatives from the Environment Agency, Hull City Council, Associated British Ports, and the Humberside Local Enterprise Partnership marked the completion of the £6.6m strengthening of the Albert Dock flood defences with an official visit to inspect the completed project.

1,978: On 2 December 2015 the *Hull Daily Mail* reported that two of the city's best known maritime heritage icons had been offered for sale as scrap to Eddie Franklin of Waterloo Antiques Reclaimed, in Great Union Street. The anchor and propeller, which had both been outside the city's Maritime Museum for decades, were offered to Mr Franklin by contractors working for Hull City Council on the ongoing facelift of the city centre in preparation (ironically) for Hull's term as the 2017 UK City of Culture. A spokeswoman for Hull City Council was reported as putting the incident down to 'miscommunication'.

1,979: Following a petition and a public campaign opposing Hull City Council plans to cover up the ruins of the city's historic defences at Beverley Gate, the public of Hull were asked to register their views in a survey during December 2015 about the future of the site. The two proposals under consideration were on display until 12 December. The proposals were: to replace the existing railings with a glass enclosure; or cover the entire site and create a public space. Of those taking part 90% expressed a preference for the first option, with just 480 of the 3,889 respondents voting to cover the site to create a new public space. Only 27 people expressed no preference.

1,980: On 12 December 2015 Hull's 2012 Olympic bantamweight Gold medallist, Luke Campbell, suffered his first defeat as a professional boxer, loosing on points to France's Yvan Mendy at the O2 Arena in London. After being knocked down by a short left hook in the 5th round, Campbell lost his 13th professional fight (the first time he'd boxed 12 rounds) by a split decision, the judges awarding Mendy the fringe WBC International Lightweight title: 115-112, 115-113, 113-115. Campbell had won all his previous 12 professional fights, 10 of which were knockouts.

1,981: On 20 December 2015, at the premises of InterTech at Priory Park in west Hull, over 300 people attended the unveiling of The Last Trip, a memorial to the city's fishing heritage; the overarching plan being to eventually move the memorial to a permanent site at the former St. Andrew's Fish Dock, subject to planning permission being granted. After 15 years of waiting the fishing community of the city has its first Lost Trawlermen's Memorial—every aspect of which (design, funding, construction, siting) is ingrained with Hull-ness.

1,982: As of December 2015 the wholly owned subsidiaries of J.R. Rix & Sons Limited included: Rix Petroleum (Hull) Limited, Rix Petroleum (Scotland)

Limited, along with several other regional Rix Petroleum (*) Limited companies selling petroleum products; Rix Transport Limited (Shipping Agency); a number of Rix Shipping and ship owning companies, including The Lerrix Tankship Limited and The Lizrix Tankship Limited companies; Jordan & Company (Hull) Limited (motor vehicle sales); and Victory Leisure Homes Limited (caravan production).

1,983: In 2015 extra security was installed to monitor the Wicksteed splash boat at Hull's East Park after it suffered £4,000 worth of damage due to vandalism. In April the same year, the attraction had to be closed after a pair of coots were found to be nesting there. It received a further 'makeover' in April 2016, when maintenance to gearing, rails, electrics and anti-slip decking was carried out.

1,984: Although Thomas James Smith started the company, it was the entrepreneurial acumen and vision of his nephew Horatio Nelson Smith that set Smith & Nephew on the road to becoming one of the most successful pharmaceutical companies in the world, today employing approximately 15,000 people around the world and achieving global sales of $4.6 billion in 2015.

1,985: As of 2015 the total water acreage of the port of Hull was approximately 3,000 acres, with around 10m tonnes of cargo being handled each year.

1,986: The anticipated lifespan of Green Port Hull is approximately 30 years, after which time the site should be able to revert to its prior general port use without any demolition or deconstruction of the adapted infrastructure.

1,987: On 11 January 2016, following the resignation of Catherine McKinnell (MP for Newcastle upon Tyne), Hull East MP Karl Turner was appointed Shadow Attorney General in Jeremy Corbyn's Shadow Cabinet.

1,988: During the 2015–16 season, Hull City's 6-0 victory over Charlton Athletic on 16 January 2016 was the Championship's joint-highest home win of the season, sharing the achievement with Bristol City, who beat Bolton Wanderers by the same score on 16 March 2016.

1,989: In 1964, with just 4 stores, takings at W. Boyes & Co. Ltd. reached the £1m milestone; by 1968, with 6 stores, takings reached £2m; and by 1970, with 7 stores, takings had reached £3m (the 1970 figure includes £1m taken at just the Hessle Road and Holderness Road Hull stores). By 1995, with 22 stores, Group turnover for W. Boyes & Co Ltd. was £34m. At the close of the financial period ending 30 January 2016, with a portfolio of 55 stores, Group turnover had reached £75.2m.

1,990: In January 2016 Hull was named one of the *Rough Guide*'s '10 cities to visit in 2016'. Coming in at No. 8, ahead of Vancouver [co-incidentally, founded by John 'Gassy Jack' Deighton, a former Hull seaman], and Agra, India; Hull was listed alongside Reykjavik, Mexico City, Seoul, Nashville and Amsterdam.

1,991: In 2015 Heron Frozen Foods Ltd. opened its new store on Endyke Lane, Hull; and in April 2016 the company opened its largest store to date (7,000 sq. feet), in the former Priory Cinema, at the junction of Spring Bank West and Calvert Lane, and Willerby Road, Hull.

1,992: The Healey brothers, Eddie and Malcolm, both left school at 16—with no formal qualifications—to work in their father Stanley's Hull-based painting and decorating business, which eventually (run by their older brother John) became Status Discount DIY, with over 40 stores across the country. For a long time the brothers were listed as the wealthiest businessmen in Yorkshire. However—with a current combined fortune reduced by £70m to an estimated £1.43bn—in the *Sunday Times* Rich

List published in April 2016 they were ousted from that position by the family of American-born Duty Free Shopping entrepreneur Robert Miller—owners of the Gunnerside Estate in Swaledale, one of the largest sporting country estates in Britain—with an estimated fortune of £1.58bn.

1,993: On Monday 2 May 2016, surrounded by his family, Hull Kingston Rovers legend Roger Millward (aged 68) lost his long battle with cancer. He passed away in the High Dependency Unit at Leeds General Infirmary after suffering a haemorrhage on the side of his face on Saturday 30 April.

1,994: At the end of the 2015–16 season, Hull City AFC finished fourth in the Football League Championship with 83 points, behind Burnley (93 points), Middlesbrough (89), and Brighton & Hove Albion (89); which secured the club's qualification for the Championship play-offs along with Brighton & Hove Albion, Derby County, and Sheffield Wednesday (who finished 6th on 74 points).

1,995: On 15 May 2016, in the first leg of the Football League Championship play-off semi-final, Hull City AFC beat Derby 3-0 away at the iPro Stadium, before losing the second leg 2-0 at the KC Stadium on the 17 May; but their 3-2 aggregate win was enough to see them into the play-off final against Sheffield Wednesday on 28 May at Wembley Stadium.

1,996: On Saturday 28 May 2016 Hull City AFC won promotion back to the Premier League (after being relegated to the Football League Championship just 12 months earlier) when they beat Sheffield Wednesday 1-0 at Wembley Stadium in the Football League Championship play-off final in front of 70,189 spectators, the lowest ever attendance for a Championship play-off final at the new Wembley Stadium. The winning goal was scored by Hull City midfielder Mohamed Diame, who struck what manager Steve Bruce described as 'a wonder goal' from 20 yards into the top corner of the net to secure Premiership football in 2016–17 for the Tigers.

1,997: In the EU Referendum held throughout the UK on 23 June 2016, Hull voted overwhelmingly in favour of leaving the EU, with just 32.4% of those who turned out casting their vote in favour of remaining. The total vote for Leave (76,646) was more than double that for Remain (36,709). The turnout was a fairly respectable 62.9%, with 113,439 votes cast from an electorate of 180,230.

1,998: On 26 June 2016 Hull East MP Karl Turner resigned as Labour's Shadow Attorney General. His was the 10th resignation in a single day from Jeremy Corbyn's Shadow Cabinet following the EU Referendum of 23 June, the subsequent political uncertainty, and the sacking of Hilary Benn as Shadow Foreign Secretary. The reason for Mr Turner's resignation (dissatisfaction with the direction Jeremy Corbyn was leading the Party) echoed those of his predecessor Catherine McKinnell ('increasingly negative path', 'internal conflict').

1,999: On the morning of Saturday 9 July 2016 the *Sea of Hull*, a site-specific commission by the renowned New York-based visual artist Spencer Tunick, was created in Hull city centre. The series of photographic installations is Tunick's response to Hull's maritime history, and involved more than three thousand local participants covered in body paint the colours of the sea found in paintings owned by the Ferens Art Gallery.

2,000: The original idea for the *Sea of Hull* commission came from Kirsten Simister, curator at the Ferens Art Gallery; along with Andrew Dixon (adviser to Hull 2017 City of Culture team), and Simon Green (Director of Cultural Services for Hull).

2,001: The *Sea of Hull*, the series of photographic installations by New York's Spencer Tunick, is scheduled to be presented at the Ferens Art Gallery during 2017.

2,002: On Friday 22 July 2016 Steve Bruce brought his frustrating tenure as manager of Hull City to an end when he resigned just 21 days ahead of the start of the 2016–17 Premier League season, after four years in charge at the club. A breakdown of Bruce's relationship with Hull City Vice-Chairman Ehab Allam was reported to have contributed to his decision to part company with the club. Later that evening, in a brief meeting with Ehab Allam, Hull City assistant manager Mike Phelan was asked to take temporary charge.

2,003: On Friday 29 July 2016, at Doncaster's Keepmoat Stadium, Hull FC beat Wigan Warriors 12-16 in the semi-final of the 2016 Challenge Cup, in front of 10,448 spectators, to reach the Final of the competition for the sixteenth time in the club's history. Warrington Wolves defeated Wakefield Trinity Wildcats 56-12 in their semi-final at Leigh Sports Village on Saturday 30 July in front of 10,358 spectators.

2,004: Following three years of concerns between 2013 (when Hull was awarded UK City of Culture 2017) and 2016, anger and frustration was vented when the bulk of applications for grants by local artists were rejected in July 2016. Local film-maker Dave Lee was reported on the *Hull Daily Mail* website as saying: 'Businesses are being looked after, sponsors are being looked after but the people who create art day in, day out and have done for years in Hull have been ignored, marginalised and pushed out'.

2,005: During the 2016 preparations for Hull's City of Culture 2017 programme of events, confidence (in the Hull City of Culture 2017 team) among many of the prominent and long-standing leaders of the city's cultural and arts community, had sunk to such a level that local artists were discussing the possibility of organising a rival *Hull Fringe* season of events. Director of Communications for Hull City of Culture 2017, Ben McNight, was reported as saying: 'more than 90 per cent of the funded projects were from organisations based in Hull'; there was no confirmation regarding what percentage of the £500,000 total of available grants had been awarded to 'organisations based in Hull'.

2,006: On Saturday 30 July 2016 the *Hull Daily Mail* posted on its website an article by Allison Coggan reporting on the anger of some of the 'Leading lights in Hull's arts community' at having their funding applications for local community-based projects rejected by the Hull City of Culture 2017 team. Stalwarts of the local arts scene, including film-makers, dramatists, musicians and photographers were claiming that local talent which 'laid the foundation for the city's successful bid for City of Culture' had been overlooked.

2,007: On Saturday 16 August 2016 the *Hull Daily Mail* reported that the 'finishing touches' were being added to a memorial by sculptor Peter Naylor, commemorating Hull's lost trawlermen. The sculpture, consisting of 13 6ft high steel silhouettes of trawlermen, was the winning design in a competition judged by a public vote, organized by the fishing heritage group STAND. The sculpture is to be built by the local, family-run, engineering business W. Campbell & Son Ltd., and will be installed as part of a Memorial Garden to be sited adjacent to the Sailmakers pub at St Andrews Quay. Although the Memorial Garden is not scheduled to be completed until 2018, the sculpture is expected to be in place for the annual Lost Trawlermen's Day service in January 2017.

2,008: Brian (Lord) Rix, the Hull-born actor, activist, disability rights advocate and leading campaigner for people with a learning disability, died on 20 August 2016 after suffering a terminal illness. In the months prior to his death Lord Rix had written to the Speaker of the House of Lords saying he hoped Parliament would soon act to allow people with conditions such as his to be legally helped to end their lives. (In 2006 he'd voted against an Assisted Dying Bill due to his fears that those with learning disabilities might become unwitting victims of the Bill.)

2,009: On Saturday 27 August 2016 Hull FC laid a ghost to rest when they finally won the Challenge Cup at Wembley, beating Warrington Wolves 12-10 in front of 76,235 spectators. After falling behind 10-0, two home-grown talents led the Black and Whites to a spectacular recovery, with full-back Jamie Shaul scoring a crucial late try (converted by Marc Sneyd), and Danny Houghton making the tackle of his life in the last minute of the game to prevent Ben Currie stealing the trophy for Warrington.

2,010: At the end of the 2016 season Hull FC finished top of the Super League table with 34 points, just one point ahead of second placed Warrington Wolves. However, in a season in which Hull FC's Marc Sneyd was the Super League's top points scorer with 203 points— his total of 110 goals saw him ranked as the second highest goal scorer—the Black and Whites eventually finished in third place, after losing 23-6 to Warrington Wolves at the KCOM Stadium on 23 September in front of 17,453 spectators; resulting in Warrington taking the League Leaders' Shield and dashing Hull's hopes of winning the Super League treble of the Challenge Cup, League Leaders' Shield and Super League Grand Final.

2,011: Hull FC featured heavily in the 2016 Super League 'End of Season Awards', with Danny Houghton being named both 'Man of Steel' and 'Hit Man'; Marc Sneyd winning 'Rhino Top Gun'; Lee Radford taking

'Coach of the Year'; and Hull FC being named 'Super League club of the year'.

2,012: On Friday 30 September 2016 Hull-born actress Maureen Lipman unveiled a new statue of her fellow daughter-of-Hull, the pioneering aviator Amy Johnson. The statue, which is one of a pair (the first was sited at Herne Bay, close to where Johnson disappeared during her final flight) was built to commemorate the 75th anniversary of Amy Johnson's death. It is located at the Hawthornes housing development, close to the site of Johnson's childhood home, and was created by artist Stephen Melton. The unveiling marked the end of the Amy Johnson Festival, which ran from 1 July to 6 September 2016.

2,013: On 1 October 2016 Hull KR lost 18-19 to Salford Red Devils in the Super League's Million Pound Game in front of 6,562 spectators at the Lightstream Stadium, ensuring their relegation from the Super League, and consigning them to Championship rugby in 2017. After leading 12-10 at the break, and 18-10 with two minutes of the match remaining, KR allowed Salford to draw level by full time, taking the match into sudden-death golden-point extra time. Salford's Gareth O'Brien decided the game with a drop-goal in the first period of extra time.

2,014: In 2016 ARCO reaffirmed its commitment to Hull when it announced plans for a £25m expansion to its National Distribution Centre (NDC) at Priory Park East. The development, scheduled to begin in 2017, has the potential to create 200 new jobs in the city. If planning permission is given, the new NDC2 is expected to open in 2018, and will offer more than double the area of the original NDC.

2,015: On Thursday 13 October 2016, after twelve weeks of negotiations and uncertainty [it was reported that he had been offered the job of manager on a permanent basis on 15 September] Hull City appointed caretaker manager Mike Phelan as the club's new head coach. Phelan, who had been in temporary charge of the club since the departure of Steve Bruce on 22 July, began his first full-time management job with a heavy defeat when the Tigers lost 6-1 away at Bournemouth on 15 October, leaving the new manager feeling 'very embarrassed'.

2,016: On 29 November 2016 a penalty shoot-out decided the winner of the League Cup quarter-final when Hull City beat Newcastle United 3-1 at the KCOM Stadium in front of 16,243 spectators to qualify for the League Cup semi-final for the first time in the club's history. Following the dismissal of Dieumerci Mbokani—on loan from Dynamo Kiev—in the final minute of the match, the Tigers were forced to play extra time with ten men. Former City striker Mohamed Diame gave Newcastle the lead after eight minutes of extra time before Robert Snodgrass equalized for City shortly after, making it 1-1 at the end of extra time. During the penalty shoot-out Newcastle missed three penalties, with City keeper Eldin Jakupovic saving two, and Huddlestone, Dawson and Snodgrass scoring for the Tigers. The Tigers are due to play Manchester United at Old Trafford in the first leg of the semi-final on Tuesday 10 January 2017, with the second leg scheduled for Thursday 26 January at the KCOM Stadium.

2,017: On 2 December 2016—following a campaign begun by Larkin's former secretary Betty Mackereth in the run up to the 2010 Larkin25 commemorative activities—Philip Larkin was memorialised in Westminster Abbey's Poets' Corner when a ledger stone was unveiled on the 31st anniversary of his death. The stone was carved by Martin Jennings, the sculptor of the Larkin statue at Hull's Paragon Interchange.

BIBLIOGRAPHY:

BIBLIOGRAPHY

Abernethy, John S.: *The Life and Work of James Abernethy FRSE*
 (Brettell & Co, London, 1897)
Allen, Thomas: *A New and Complete History of the County of York*
 (I.T. Hinton, London, 1831)
Baines, Edward: *History, Directory & Gazetteer, of the County of York: With
 Select Lists of the Merchants & Traders of London, and the Principal
 Commercial and Manufacturing Towns of England; and a Variety of Other
 Commercial Information: Also a Copious List of the Seats of the Nobility
 and Gentry of Yorkshire, Volume 2* (Edward Baines, Leeds, 1823)
Baldwin, M.W., 'The Engineering History of Hull's Earliest Docks', in
 Transactions of the Newcomen Society, Vol. 46, Iss. 1 (1973)
Barnard, Robert: *Barley, mash and yeast; a history of the Hull Brewery
 Company 1782–1985* (Hutton Press/Hull College of Further Education,
 1990)
Bethell, Richard, ed.; 'Kingston-Upon-Hull Docks Bill – Minutes of
 Evidence'. Reports of the Committees, House of Commons Papers 9.
Biographical Dictionary of the Society for the Diffusion of Useful Knowledge
 (Longman, Brown, Green, and Longmans, 1842)
Bloomfield, Barry Cambray: *Philip Larkin, A Bibliography: 1933–1994* (The
 British Library, London, 2002)
Bodeen, DeWitt: *Films in Review*, December 1977 (Vol.XXVIII No. 10)
Boyes, John (Bulpett, C. W. L., ed): *A White King in East Africa; the
 remarkable adventures of John Boyes, trader and soldier of fortune, who
 became king of the savage Wa-Kikuyu* (McBride, Nast & company, New
 York, 1912)
Boyes, Stores: *1993: Boyes Branch Out* (Boyes, Scarborough, 1993)
– *Boyes, Stores: The Story of a Family* (Boyes, Scarborough, 1981)
Boyle, J. R.: *Holy Trinity Church Hull: A Guide and Description* (A. Brown
 & Sons Ltd., Hull, 1890)
Browne, Horace B.: *The Story of the East Riding of Yorkshire* (A. Brown &
 Sons Ltd., Hull, 1912)
Carmichael, Ian: *Will the Real Ian Carmichael...* (MacMillan, London, 1979)
Collier, Linda *et. al.*: *A New History of Swanland: the 18th & 19th Century*,
 Collier, Linda; Holmes, John; Dalby, Shirley (Swanland Village History
 Group, 2002)
Cook, John.: *The History of God's House of Hull commonly called The
 Charterhouse* (Peck & Son, Hull, 1882)
Corlass, R.W.: *Sketches of Hull Authors*, Ed. Corlass, C.F. and Andrews,
 William (H. Bolton, Hull, 1879)
Cronin, Michael, and Mayall, David: *Sporting Nationalisms: Identity,
 Ethnicity, Immigration and Assimilation* (Routledge, London, 1998)

Crosse, John: *An account of the rise and progress of the subscription library at Kingston-upon-Hull* (William Rawson, Hull, 1810).

Dolan, Simon: *How to Make Millions without a Degree: and How to get by even if you have one* (Matador, Leicester, 2010)

Downs, Carolyn: 'Mecca and the birth of commercial bingo 1958–70: A case study', in *Business History*, 52:7, 1086–1106, (2010)

Earle, The Rev. A.: *Essays Upon the History of Meaux Abbey...* (Brown & Sons, London, 1906)

Fletcher, Raymond: *Classics: Hull Rugby League Football Club: Fifty of the Finest Matches* (Tempus, Stroud, 2003)

Folkart, Burt A. 'Dorothy Mackaill, 87; Went From Ziegfeld Follies to Film', (*Los Angeles Times*, 15 August 1990)

Fowler, Rev. J.T., ed.; *Life and Letters of Rev. John Bacchus Dykes* (John Murray, London, 1897)

Frost, Charles: *Notices relative to the early history of the town and port of Hull* (J. B. Nichols, London, Hull, 1827)

Gent, Thomas: *Gent's History of Hull* (M.C. Peck and Son, Hull, 1869)

Gillett, Edward and MacMahon, Kenneth A.: *A History of Hull* (Hull University Press, Hull, 1989)

Gill, Alec: *Lost Trawlers of Hull 1865–1987* (Hutton Press, Beverley, 1989)

– *Superstitions: Folk Magic in Hull's Fishing Community* (Hutton Press, Beverley, 1993)

Hartley, Jean: *Philip Larkin, The Marvell Press and me* (Carcanet, Manchester, 1989)

Hawkshaw, John Clarke.: 'The Construction of the Albert Dock at Kingston-upon-Hull', in *Minutes of Proceedings of the Institution of Civil Engineers with other Selected and Abstracted Papers* Vol.XLI, Session 1874–75, Part III (1875).

Home, Gordon: *Yorkshire* (A. & C. Black Ltd., London, 1932)

Hulbert, Roger: *Hull Speedway 1930–81* (Tempus, Stroud, 2004)

Hull FC V New Zealand, Commemorative Programme; (22 October 2002)

Hurst, Alex A.: *Thomas Somerscales, marine artist* (Teredo Books, Brighton, 1988)

Hurtzig, Arthur Cameron: 'The Alexandra Dock, Hull', in *Minutes of Proceedings of the Institute of Civil Engineers*, Session 1887–88, Part II Proceedings (1888)

Inform: the journal of the American Oil Chemists' Society

Lang, John: *Titanic: A Fresh Look at the Evidence by a Former Chief Inspector of Marine Accidents* (Rowman & Littlefield, Lanham, MD; 2012)

Loncaster, Wendy Ann, and Sheilds, Malcolm: *Fred Elwell R.A.– a Life in Art* (Loncaster and Shields, 2014)

Marine Accident Report No. 4/99: 'Report on the Underwater Survey of the Stern Trawler GAUL H. 243', (Department of the Environment, Transport and the Regions, London, 1999)

Markham, John: *Streets of Hull—A History of their Names* (Highgate, Beverley, 1987)

Maw, Willim Henry. 'Hull South Bridge', in *Modern Examples of Road and Railway Bridges: Illustrating the Most Recent Practice of Leading Engineers in Europe and America* (London: Published at the offices of *Engineering*, 1872)

Miller, Charles: *The Lunatic Express* (History Book Club, London, 1971)

Monk, William Henry, ed.: *Hymns Ancient and Modern* (William Clowes and Sons, London, 1889)

Murray, John: *Handbook for Travellers in Yorkshire* (John Murray, London, 1867)

Oldham, James: 'On the Rise, Progress and Present Position of Steam Navigation in Hull', in *Report of the British Association for the Advancement of Science* (British Association for the Advancement of Science, John Murray, London, 1854)

Owst, Kenneth: *Laurel and Hardy in Hull* (Highgate Publications, Beverley, 1990)

Page, W.G.B.: 'Notes on Hull Authors, Booksellers, Printers and Stationers, etc.', in *Book Auction Records, Vol.6 Part 1*; Karslake, Frank (Ed.), (Karslake & Co., London, 1908)

Parsons, Edward: *The Tourist's Companion; Or, The History of the Scenes and Places on the Route by the Railroad and Steam-packet from Leeds and Selby to Hull* (Whittaker & Co., London, 1935)

Partridge, Eric: *A Dictionary of Catch Phrases* (Routledge & Keegan Paul, London, 1977)

Pevsner, Nikolaus: *The Buildings of England: Yorkshire: York and the East Riding* (Penguin Books, Harmondsworth, Middlesex, 1995 [by Nikolaus Pevsner and David Neave])

Raines, Robert: *Marcellus Laroon: Studies in British Art* (Paul Mellon Foundation, Routledge & Keegan Paul, 1967)

Robinson, Barbara: *Hull Daily Mail: A Part of the Community* (Highgate., Beverley, 2009)

Roy, Donald: 'A theatre for all seasons: the Queen's Theatre, Hull, 1846–1869', in *Theatre Notebook*; The Society for Theatre Research (1st October, 2006)

Seaward, M. R. D.: 'The Amazing Mr Sheppard': http://www.hullgeolsoc.co.uk/hg1501.htm

Sheahan, James Joseph: *General and Concise History and Description of the Town and Port of Kingston-upon-Hull* (Simpkin, Marshall & Co, London, 1864)

Sheppard, June: *The Drainage of the Hull Valley* E.Y. Local History Series: No.8. (The East Yorkshire Local History Society, Hull, 1958)

Sheppard, Thomas: *Handbook to Hull & the East Riding of Yorkshire* (A. Brown & Sons Ltd., Hull, 1922)

Some Scarborough Faces (Past and Present): Being a Series of Interviews. Illustrated with Photographs (*Scarborough Gazzette*, Scarborough 1901)

Simpson, John: *Humber Pilots: Important Dates* (John Simpson, 2009)

Skempton, A.W., ed. *et al.*: *A Biographical Dictionary of Civil Engineers in Great Britain and Ireland: 1500–1830* (Thomas Telford Ltd., London, 2002)

Smith, Ian, ed. *et al.*: *One Man & his Bog: 20 Years on the Toilet Tour* (Made in Hull, Hull, 2004)

Smith, James: *Proceedings Relative to the Pearson's Park* (Yorkshire Printing and Publishing Company, Hull, 1860)

Spencer-Silver, Patricia, 'George Myers, 1803–75, Stonemason, Builder, Contractor', in *Construction History, Vol.5* (1989)

Staveley, Gwen: *William Mason: A son of Hull, a fame forgotten* (The Georgian Society for East Yorkshire, 2011)

Staveley, Norman: *Two Centuries of Music in Hull* (Hutton Press, 1999)

Steel, Mr Justice David: *Report of the Re-opened Formal Investigation Into the Loss of the FV Gaul* (The Stationery Office, London, 2004)

Stewart, John: *The Acrobat: Arthur Barnes and the Victorian Circus* (McFarland & Co., 2012)

Symons, John: *Hullinia: or Selections from Local History: including The Siege of Hull, Our Ancient Churchyards, and Past Poets of Hull* (W. Adam, Hull, 1872)

Tomlinson, W. W.: 'Developments at Hull', in *The North Eastern Railway, its Rise and Development* (Longmans, Green & Company, London, 2015)

Timperley, J: 'An Account of the Harbour and Docks at Kingston-Upon-Hull', in *Transactions of the Institute of Civil Engineers* Vol. 1, (John Weale, London,1842)

Turner, J. Horsfall, ed.; *Yorkshire Bibliographer*, Vol. 1 (Horsfall, Bradford, 1888)

Walker, Penelope, ed.; Jones, Richard, ed.; *Eva Crane: Bee Scientist 1912–2007* (International Bee Research Association, 2008)

Weird and Gilly: *The Spider with the Platinum Hair* (Independent Music Press, London, 2003)

Wright, Sir William: 'The Hull Docks', in *Minutes of Proceedings of the Institution of Civil Engineers with other Selected and Abstracted Papers*, Vol.XLI, Session 1874–75-Part III (1875).

Wilkinson, Tate: *The wandering patentee; or, A history of the Yorkshire Theatres ...*, V1-2. (Tate Wilkinson, 1795)

ONLINE RESOURCES:

ONLINE RESOURCES

AarhusKarlshamn UK Ltd: aak-uk.com/about-aak-uk/history
Aberdeen Built Ships: aberdeenships.com/
Aerodrome, The: theaerodrome.com
Aircrew Remembered: aircrewremembered.com
All Music: allmusic.com/
Amber Nectar (non-franchised Hull City website): ambernectar.org
Anlaby Road History: carnegiehull.co.uk/the-anlaby-road
ARCO: arco.co.uk
Associated British Ports: abports.co.uk/
AQA Education: aqa.org.uk/
BBC Sport: bbc.co.uk/sport/
Biographical Dictionary of Sculptors in Britain, 1660–1851:
    liberty.henry-moore.org/henrymoore/
BizDb: bizdb.co.uk/company/reel-cinemas-limited-03561597/
Black History Month: blackhistorymonth.org.uk/
Blue Plaque Places: blueplaqueplaces.co.uk
Bosun's Watch: The Fleetwood Steam and Sailing Trawler:
    fleetwood-trawlers.info/
Boulvard Academy: theboulevardacademy.com/
Brain Damage—Pink Floyd News Resource:
    brain-damage.co.uk
British Civil Wars, Commonwealth & Protectorate 1638–1660:
    bcw-project.org
British Executions: britishexecutions.co.uk/
British Film Locations: british-film-locations.com
British History Online: british-history.ac.uk
    British Library: bl.uk/collection-items/a-playbill-for-the-grand-provin-
    cial-tour-of-messrs-strange--wilsons-great-pictorial-scientific-musical-
    and-illusionary-entertainment
British Listed Buildings: britishlistedbuildings.co.uk/
Bulmer's *History & Directory of East Yorkshire* (1892):
    specialcollections.le.ac.uk/cdm/ref/collection/p16445coll4/id/278593
Burton-Upon-Stather Heritage Group: burtonstatherheritage.org/
Charity Commission: charitycommission.gov.uk
Chester le Street History:
    www2.newsquest.co.uk/the_north_east/history/echomemories/durham/
    306/230806.html
Christie's auctioneers: christies.com/
Chrome Oxide: chromeoxide.com/cream.htm
Chuck Berry—Mr Rock'n'Roll: chuckberry.de/tour1962.htm
Cinema Organ Society: toff.org.uk/console/illuminatedsurro.html

Cinema Treasures: cinematreasures.org/
Clyde Built Ships: clydeships.co.uk/
Companies House Beta: beta.companieshouse.gov.uk/
Company Histories: company-histories.com/
Compton Family Trees: rgcrompton.info/crompton/1811info5b.html
Computer Conservation Society: ourcomputerheritage.org/leo_15.htm
Computer History Museum: computerhistory.org
Concerts & Package Tours 1956–1967: bradfordtimeline.co.uk/music.htm
Cranswick PLC: cranswick.PLC.uk/
Croydon Airport: croydonairport.org.uk/The-Airport/Amy-Johnson
DATAB.US: datab.us/i/Hull%20F.C.
DueDil: duedil.com/
Electoral Commission: electoralcommission.org.uk/
Early Cinema: earlycinema.com/pioneers/lumiere_bio.html
East Riding Museums: museums.eastriding.gov.uk/
Economics Help:
    economicshelp.org/blog/6693/business/cinema-attendance-in-uk/
Encyclopedia Titanica: encyclopedia-titanica.org/
Engineering Timelines:
    engineering-timelines.com/scripts/engineeringItem.asp?id=1043
Extravagant Crowd: Carl Van Vechten's Portraits of Women:
    brbl-archive.library.yale.edu/exhibitions/cvvpw/gallery/bryher.html
Family Maw: family-maw.co.uk/
Far Horizons: hull.ac.uk/mhsc/FarHorizons/farhorizons.htm
Fenner 150 years Serving Industry Worldwide—1861–2011 150 years
    anniversary brochure:
    fennerdunlopeurope.com/ir/fenr/marfleet/pdf/150yr_Anniversary_Broc
    hure.pdf
Fenner Family Tree: fennerfamilytree.me.uk/data_C/4796.htm
Final Seconds before Collision, The'; Trinque, Bruce A.:
    wormstedt.com/titanic/trinque.html
Find a Grave: findagrave.com
First World War on this day:
    firstworldwaronthisday.blogspot.co.uk/2014/09/91-died-on-this-day-
    tue-29091914.html
Fleetwood Online Archive of Trawlers: ibase.lancashire.gov.uk/
FootballSite.co.uk: footballsite.co.uk/Statistics/ClubbyClub/ClubHistories/
    HullCity.htm
FootyMad:hullcitymad.co.uk/feat/edy1/
    19041915_the_formative_years_30224/index.shtml
Friends of West Norwood Cemetery: fownc.org/pdf/newsletter35.pdf
Funding Universe: fundinguniverse.com/company-histories/
Gastown's Gassy Jack: gassyjack.com/
Geograph: geograph.org.uk/photo/617940

Goole ships: gooleships.co.uk/
GOV.UK: gov.uk/
Grace's Guide to British Industrial History: gracesguide.co.uk
Green Port Hull—Environmental Impact Assessment Report:
    webarchive.nationalarchives.gov.uk/20140108121958/
    http://www.marinemanagement.org.uk/licensing/
    public_register/eia/documents/screening_scoping/hull.pdf
Green Plastic Radiohead: greenplastic.com
Grimsby Vessels Lost in the Great War:
    homepage.ntlworld.com/terence.munson/
    webfiles%20folder/gy1421/index.htm
Guardian Online: theguardian.com/uk
Guide to the City's Heritage Plaques: Hull City Council (2006):
    web.archive.org/web/20130419005109/http://www.waterfrontcommuni-
    tiesproject.org/downloads/Hull/BluePlaques.pdf
Hansard: hansard.millbanksystems.com/
Hessle Local History Society:
    sites.google.com/site/hesslelocalhistorysociety
Heritage Group for the Chartered Institution of Building Services
    Engneers: hevac-heritage.org
Heroes of Hull: heroesofhull.co.uk/pages/blitz/Worst_Nights.php/
Heron Foods: heronfoods.com/site/timeline
Historic England: historicengland.org.uk/
History of Parliament—British Political, Social & Local History:
    historyofparliamentonline.org
Hoist magazine: hoistmagazine.com/
Hull & District Local History Research Group:
    sites.google.com/site/hlhrg14/statues-in-hull
Hull and East Riding at War: hullandeastridingatwar.co.uk
Hull Bullnose Heritage Group: hullbullnoseheritagegroup.co.uk/
Hull City AFC: hullcitytigers.com/club/since_1904/
Hull City Council Flood Investigation Report—December 2013
    City Centre Tidal Surge Flood Event:
    hullcc-consult.limehouse.co.uk/ file/3476015
Hull City Kits: hullcitykits.co.uk/category/kits-of-the-1900s/
Hull Daily Mail: hulldailymail.co.uk
Hull FC Official: hullfc.com
Hull History Centre: hullhistorycentre.org.uk
Hull Independent Cinema Project:
    hullindependentcinemaproject.com/2014/08/21/
    nymphomaniac-review/
Hull Museums Collections: hullcc.gov.uk/museumcollections/
Hull Now: hullnow.co.uk/concepts/heritage-dock
Hull Trawler: hulltrawler.net

Hull Truck Theatre: hulltruck.co.uk
Hullwebs: hullwebs.co.uk/
Humber Bridge Board: humberbridge.co.uk/
Humber Packet Boats: humberpacketboats.co.uk
Hurley Coates genealogy pages: jamter.co.uk/fhwebsite
Illustrated Vancouver:
    illustratedvancouver.ca/post/75606174503/gastown-by-mcsweeney
International Safety Management code: ismcode.net:
    ismcode.net/legal_and_technical_reports/
    The_Norman_House_of_Lords_1960.pdf
Internet Archive: archive.org
Internet Movie Database: imdb.com
Jack Bruce: jackbruce.com/
Jackson's Bread: jacksonsbread.co.uk
Jewish Chronicle, The: thejc.com/
Jimi Hendrix: earlyhendrix.com/6743/1967.htm
John Godber: johngodber.co.uk/
Kinematograph Yearbook:
    archive.org/search.php?query=creator%3A%22Kinematograph+Publi-
    cations+Ltd.%22
Kingston upon Hull War Memorial: ww1hull.org.uk/
Lagan Construction Group:
    laganconstructiongroup.com/2014/11/graham-lagan-construction-group-
    joint-venture-named-main-contractor-green-port-hull-build/
Lives Online: livesonline.rcseng.ac.uk
Lloyd, Arthur, 1839–1904, The Music Hall and Theatre History
    site—Dedicated to: arthurlloyd.co.uk/:
London Gazette: thegazette.co.uk/
Lost Trawlermen of the Port of Hull:
    hullhistorycentre.org.uk/discover/pdf/LOST_TRAWLERMEN.pdf
Maggi Ronson: maggironson.com
Marketing the Humber [Bondholders]:
    marketinghumber.com/bondholders
Maritime Memorials: weblog.rmg.co.uk/memorials/
Marmalade Skies: marmalade-skies.co.uk/mar1967.htm
Maud Foster windmill: maudfoster.co.uk/
Mick Ronson Website, The: home.swipnet.se/~w-54404/
Musician Guide: musicianguide.com/
National Portrait Gallery (Australia): portrait.gov.au
New Theatre, Hull 75th anniversary souvenir programme:
    providerfiles2.thedms.co.uk/eandamedia/YS/2173061_1_1.pdf
Northern Broadsides theatre company: northern-broadsides.co.uk
Northern Echo: thenorthernecho.co.uk/history/3603187.
    Humble_miller_s_son_who_gave_away_a_million_to_his_workers/

Northern Rail: northernrail.org/news/613

Odeon & UCI Cinemas Group: odeon.co.uk/

Old Town (southern part)—Conservation Area Character Appraisal: hullcc.gov.uk/pls/portal/docs/PAGE/ HOME/PLANNING/CONSERVA-TION/CONSERVATION%20AREAS/OLD%20TOWN%20(SOUTH)%20CACA_0.PDF

Office for National Statistics: ons.gov.uk/ons/index.html

Oxford Dictionary of National Biography: oxforddnb.com/

Parliamentary Publications: publications.parliament.uk/

Paul Gibson's Hull and East Yorkshire History: paul-gibson.com

Pastscape: pastscape.org.uk/

Philip Larkin Society: philiplarkin.com

PortCitiesSouthampton: plimsoll.org

Port of Hull; Wikipedia: en.wikipedia.org/wiki/Port_of_Hull

Ports and Harbours of the UK: ports.org.uk

Port Technology: porttechnology.org/

Press Release Distribution: prlog.org/

Public Health Observatories: www.apho.org.uk/resource/item.aspx?RID=50342

Reference for Business: referenceforbusiness.com/history2/23/The-Rank-Group-PLC.html

River Humber: riverhumber.com/index12b.htm

Rolling Stones Database: nzentgraf.de/books/zent.htm

Rootschat: rootschat.com/forum/index.php?topic=98229.0

Royal Pharmaceutical Society: rpharms.com

Rugby League official: rugby-league.com/

Rugby League Project: rugbyleagueproject.org/

Rix & Sons Ltd.: rix.co.uk

School of Mathematics and Statistics; University of St Andrews, Scotland,: www-history.mcs.st-and.ac.uk/

Science Museum: sciencemuseum.org.uk/

Scunthorpe Telegraph: scunthorpetelegraph.co.uk

SEH commercial: sehcommercial.co.uk/case-study/tidal-barrier-hull/

Ships Nostalgia: shipsnostalgia.com/ showthread.php?t=7986&page=2

Silicone Cowboy: siliconcowboy.wordpress.com

Smith & Nephew: smith-nephew.com

SPG Note 27 Heritage & Development Management at Garrison Side, Hull: hullcc.gov.uk/pls/portal/docs/PAGE/ HOME/PLANNING/CONSERVATION/SCHEDULED% 20MONU-MENTS/MONUMENT%20AT%20GARRISON% 20SIDE.PDF

Stage Online: thestage.co.uk/

STAND: St.Andrew's Fish Dock Heritage Group: hullfishingheritage.org.uk/

Statto: statto.com/
Stefan Gec: stefangec.com
St.Mary's Lowgate: stmaryslowgate.weebly.com/history.html
Tower Hill—We Will Remember Them:
   benjidog.co.uk/Tower%20Hill/WW1%20
   Sallagh%20to%20San%20Zeferino.html#Salvia
Trinity House Academy: hthacademy.org.uk
Theatres Trust: theatrestrust.org.uk/
Tidal Harbours Commission. *The Humber, its roads, shoals, and
   capabilities*: https://books.google.co.uk/books/about/
   Tidal_Harbours_Commission_The_Humber_its.html?id=8ZVWAAAA-
   cAAJ&redir_esc=y
Troubles Archives: troublesarchive.com/artforms/theatre/piece/
   diary-of-a-hunger-strike
U2.COM: u2.com
U-boat.net: uboat.net/wwi/boats/index.html
University of Hull: www2.hull.ac.uk/
Urban Conservation and Design, St.Andrews Dock, Conservation
   Area Character Statement:
   hullcc.gov.uk/pls/portal/docs/PAGE/HOME/PLANNING/CONSERVA-
   TION/CONSERVATION%20AREAS/ST%20ANDREW'S%20DOCK
   %20CACA.PDF
Viola/Dias: viola-dias.org
Visitor UK: visitoruk.com
Wayback Machine: archive.org/web/
Westminster Abbey: westminster-abbey.org/our-history/people/
   william-mason
Wikipedia: en.wikipedia.org/
WiredGov: wired-gov.net/wg/wg-news-
   1.nsf/0/7E3C772E2646068A802578570034CD15?OpenDocument
Who Concert Guide, The: thewholive.net/
William Jackson Food Group: wjfg.co.uk
World Port Source: worldportsource.com/
Wreck Site: wrecksite.eu
Wright & Wright Architects LLP: wrightandwright.co.uk/
Yorkshire Film Archive: yorkshirefilmarchive.com/
Yorkshire Post: yorkshirepost.co.uk
You Never Told Us: Stories from Brian Cooke's days as a music business
   photographer: younevertoldus.com/?page_id=908

INDEX:

Mitchell, Samuel (skipper) 141
Mitchell, Walter (skipper) 103
Mobbs, Francis (skipper) 185
Molby, Jan 329
Mollison, Jim 201
Monica Picture House 160, 244
Montgomery, Bruce 241
Monument Bridge 224
Moody Blues, The (band) 251
Moore, Richard (skipper) 132
Morgan, Arthur 235
Morley Street 102
Morley, Thomas 172
Morris, Dan 156
Morton, William 136
Morton's Lecture Hall 186
Moss, Mr (alderman) 81
Mothersdill, Thomas (skipper) 176
Motion, Andrew 260
Mountain, Charles 39, 204
Mr Beasley (band) 355
Munzer, Charles (skipper) 130
Murdoch, Dr. Mary Charlotte 87, 117
Museum of Fisheries & Shipping 154, 155
Musgrave, Benjamin 359
Music Hall (Jarratt Street) 60, 76
Mutrie, Les 286
Myers & Wilson, Messrs. 50, 64
Myers, George 36, 41, 44, 45, 46, 55, 56, 57, 63, 65, 66, 67, 69, 76, 91
  death 94
Mylne, Robert 26
Myton 1, 2, 3, 4, 13, 42
Myton Gate 7, 306
Mytongate 26, 138-139

N

National Avenue 147, 305
National Picture Theatre 160, 218, 339-340, 372, 375-376

Natural History Museum 154
Naylor, Peter 373, 386
Needler Hall 202
Needler, Christopher 286
Needler, Frederick 80, 126, 135-136, 202
Needler, Harold 224, 227, 229, 248-249
Needlers Ltd. 80, 126, 135-136, 182, 241
Neill, Terry 264
Nellist, Peter (skipper) 270
Nelson Street 6
Nelson, William (skipper) 103
Neptune Inn 328
Neptune Street 70, 142, 282
Netherton, Thomas 187
Nettleton, Barry 274
New Adelphi Club 235, 291, 295, 309-310, 355
New Amphitheatre (Queen's Theatre) 57-58
New Cleveland Street 131-132
New Hippodrome 141
New Holland 6, 66, 284
New Mechanics' Theatre [*See* Mechanics' Music Hall]
New Palace Theatre of Varieties 124-125, 195
New Theatre, Hull 73, 88, 204, 215, 216, 218, 232, 245, 259, 269, 273, 297 [*See also* Hull New Theatre]
New York Hotel 336, 375
Newcastle, Earl of 17, 18, 19
Newland Avenue 160, 244
Newland High School for Girls 206, 224
Newland Park 153, 228, 272
Newport, Earl of 18
Newstead Street 136, 164
Newton Street 112
Nicholson, Hubert 318
Nicholson, John (skipper) 222